THE WELL-BEING OF CHILDREN IN THE UK

IN THE UK

Third edition

Edited by Jonathan Bradshaw

First published in Great Britain in 2011 by

The Policy Press
University of Bristol
Fourth Floor
Beacon House
Queen's Road
Bristol BS8 1QU, UK
t: +44 (0)117 331 4054
f: +44 (0)117 331 4093
tpp-info@bristol.ac.uk
www.policypress.co.uk

North American office:
The Policy Press
c/o International Specialized Books Services
920 NE 58th Avenue, Suite 300
Portland, OR 97213-3786, USA
t: +1 503 287 3093
f: +1 503 280 8832
info@isbs.com

British Library Cataloguing in Publication Data
A catalogue record for this book is available from the British Library.

Library of Congress Cataloging-in-Publication Data
A catalog record for this book has been requested.

ISBN 978 1 84742 836 3 (paperback)
ISBN 978 1 84742 837 0 (hardcover)

Cover design by The Policy Press
Front cover: photograph kindly supplied by www.alamy.com
Printed and bound in Great Britain by Hobbs, Southampton

Contents

List of figures and tables

Figures

—

Tables

—

List of abbreviations

ALSPAC	Avon Longitudinal Study of Parents and Children
B-SEM	Bristol Social Exclusion Matrix
BHPS	British Household Panel Survey
BYPS	British Youth Panel Survey
CARD	Child abuse-related deaths
CCFR	Centre for Child and Family Research
CEOP	Child Exploitation and Online Protection
ChiMat	Child and Maternal Health Observatory
CYPU	Children and Young People's Unit
DCSF	Department for Children, Schools and Families
DfES	Department for Education and Skills
DfT	Department for Transport
DH	Department of Health
DMD	Drug Misuse Declared (Survey)
DWP	Department for Work and Pensions
EAAD	European Alliance Against Depression
ECHP	European Community Household Panel (Survey)
EHRC	Equality and Human Rights Commission
EPPE	Effective Provision of Pre-school Education (Project)
EPPSE	Effective Pre-school, Primary and Secondary Education (Project)
ESRC	Economic and Social Research Council
ETHOS	European Typology of Homelessness and Housing Exclusion
EU	European Union
EYFS	Early Years Foundation Stage (framework)
FACS	Families and Children Study
FES	Family Expenditure Survey
FRS	Family Resources Survey
FSM	Free school meals
FSP	Foundation Stage Profile
GDP	Gross domestic product
GHQ	General Health Questionnaire
GHS	General Household Survey
HBAI	Households Below Average Income
HBSC	Health Behaviour of School-aged Children (Survey)
HHSRS	Housing Health and Safety Rating System
HMRC	Her Majesty's Revenue and Customs
HSE	Health Survey for England
IDACI	Income Deprivation Affecting Children Index
IDF	International Diabetes Federation
ISAAC	International Study of Asthma and Allergies in Childhood
ISC	Independent Schools Council

KS	Key Stage
LEA	Local Education Authority
LFS	Labour Force Survey
LGBT	Lesbian, gay, bisexual and transgender
LIS	Luxembourg Income Study
LSOA	Lower layer super output area
MCS	Millennium Cohort Survey
NATSAL	National Survey of Sexual Attitudes and Lifestyles
NEET	Not in education, employment or training
NICHD	National Institute of Child Health and Human Development
NNI	Neighbourhood Nurseries Initiative
NSPCC	National Society for the Prevention of Cruelty to Children
NVQ	National Vocational Qualification
OCJS	Offending Crime and Justice Survey
OECD	Organisation for Economic Co-operation and Development
Ofsted	Office for Standards in Education, Children's Services and Skills
ONS	Office for National Statistics
PEEP	Peers Early Education Partnership
PISA	Programme for International Student Assessment
PPP	Purchasing Power Parity
PSA	Public Service Agreement
PSSRU	Personal Social Services Research Unit
SCIE	Social Care Institute for Excellence
SDQ	Strength and Difficulties Questionnaire
SEN	Special educational needs
SILC	Statistics on Income and Living Conditions
SNS	Social networking site
SPC	Social Protection Committee
SDDU	Smoking, Drinking and Drug Use (Survey)
TCRU	Thomas Coram Research Unit
UASC	Unaccompanied asylum-seeking children
UKCCIS	UK Council for Child Internet Safety
UKCGO	UK Children Go Online
UN	United Nations
UNCRC	United Nations Convention on the Rights of the Child
UNICEF	United Nations Children's Fund
WDI	World Development Indicators
WHO	World Health Organization
YIPPEE	Young people from a public care background, pathways to education in Europe

Notes on contributors

Karen Bloor is Senior Research Fellow in the Department of Health Sciences at the University of York. Her research focuses on the economics of health policy. As part of a broader research portfolio she is involved in various projects relating to child health, including a cohort study of children 'Born in Bradford'. She also constructed the health domain of the Local Index of Child Well-being.

Jonathan Bradshaw CBE, FBA, is Professor of Social Policy at the University of York. In recent years his research has focused on international comparisons of child poverty, child benefit packages and child well-being. He has also written about family policy. He is a member of the Board of the International Society for Child Indicators (ISCI) and of the Foundation for International Studies in Social Security (FISS). For more information, see www-users.york.ac.uk/~jrb1/

Sharon Grace is Teaching Fellow in the Department of Social Policy and Social Work at the University of York. Her career as a criminologist began at the Home Office Research and Planning Unit in 1989 where she spent 10 years conducting and managing research on domestic and sexual violence, policing, probation and administration of justice (including a secondment to the Crown Prosecution Service). For the last six years she has taught undergraduates in Applied Social Science, specialising in administration of justice, illicit drug use and victimisation.

Carol-Ann Hooper is Senior Lecturer in Social Policy at the University of York. Her research and teaching focus on the overlapping fields of child abuse, child protection and family support, and gender and crime. She is the author of *Mothers surviving child sexual abuse* (Routledge, 1992), co-editor with Una McCluskey of *Psychodynamic perspectives on abuse* (Jessica Kingsley Publishers, 2000), and co-editor with Brid Featherstone, Jonathan Scourfield and Julie Taylor of *Gender and child welfare in society* (Wiley-Blackwell, 2010).

Antonia Keung is Research Fellow in the Department of Social Policy and Social Work at the University of York. Her research focuses on the well-being of children and young people. She has investigated issues such as the impact of life events on children's subjective well-being, and the links between educational outcomes and experience in teenage years. Recent projects have included 'Estimating the life-time cost of 16- to 18-year-olds not in education, employment or training' for the Audit Commission and 'Social exclusion of young people aged 16-24' for the Cabinet Office. She is currently working with The Children's Society on a project investigating the well-being of children in England.

Lisa O'Malley is Lecturer in the Department of Social Policy and Social Work, University of York. Her research interests focus on the links between crime, risk and place. She also teaches undergraduate students, specialising in criminal justice, policing and punishment.

Deborah Quilgars is Senior Research Fellow at the Centre for Housing Policy, University of York. She has 20 years' experience in homelessness policy research. She undertook the last major review of youth homelessness in the UK and has conducted a number of evaluations of services for homeless people and other excluded groups including teenage parents. Deborah jointly represents the UK in the European Observatory on Homelessness under the auspices of the Fédération Européenne d'Associations Nationales Travaillant avec les Sans-Abri (FEANTSA). For more information, see www.york.ac.uk/inst/chp/Staff/quilgars.htm

Gwyther Rees is Research Director for The Children's Society and Visiting Associate at the Social Policy Research Unit, University of York. Much of his research has focused on young runaways, and on child protection and safeguarding issues in relation to older young people. In addition, over the last five years he has taken a lead role in developing The Children's Society's ongoing programme of research on children's and young people's subjective well-being, in collaboration with the University of York.

Christine Skinner is Senior Lecturer in Social Policy at the University of York. She has considerable expertise in relation to childcare and early education policy and child support policy. Over the last 12 years she has published in both areas including research projects on how couples and lone parents coordinate work, childcare and education. Most recently she has completed a research evaluation of free early years services for vulnerable two-year-olds for a local authority in England.

Mike Stein is Research Professor in the Social Policy Research Unit at the University of York. During the last 30 years he has been researching the problems and challenges faced by young people leaving care. He is a joint coordinator of the International Research Network on the Transitions to Adulthood for Young People Leaving Public Care (INTRAC). For more details, see www.york.ac.uk/spru

Acknowledgements

This is the fourth book on child well-being that we have produced from the University of York, and each builds on the one that went before. We are therefore grateful for the sponsors of the earlier volumes. The first volume was supported by the Economic and Social Research Council (ESRC) ('Children 5-16: Growing into the 21st century' research programme), and it was published by the Family Policy Studies Centre. The second and third volumes were sponsored and published by Save the Children (UK), and we remember the contribution of their liaison officer, Kath Pinnock.

We are also grateful to our colleagues who worked on earlier volumes but for various reasons did not contribute to this volume. From the last volume they include Dr Bryony Beresford, Bob Coles, Dr Naomi Finch, Dr Ian Gibbs, Emese Mayhew, Professor Joanne Neale, Dr Dominic Richardson, Dr Beverley Searle, Professor Ian Sinclair and Professor Patricia Sloper.

We are grateful for the funding that we have received over the years that has supported the research that has contributed to this book. This includes support from UNICEF (the UK office, the Innocenti Centre and the CEE/CIS Regional Office), The Children's Society, the European Commission, the Joseph Rowntree Foundation, the Social Exclusion Task Force of the Cabinet Office and the Department for Communities and Local Government.

We are very grateful to Lorraine Radford, Head of Research at the NSPCC, for allowing pre-publication access to their new survey report, and for reading and commenting on a first draft of Chapter Ten.

We are grateful for the contribution made towards the expenses of this volume by ChiMat (Child and Maternal Health Observatory), and our liaison officer there, Dr Helen Duncan.

Finally, many thanks to Anne Burton, who prepared the typescript with her usual attention to detail and good spirit.

Jonathan Bradshaw
University of York, January 2011

ONE

Introduction

Jonathan Bradshaw

> The true measure of a nation's standing is how well it attends to its children – their health and safety, their material security, their education and socialization, and their sense of being loved, valued, and included in the families and societies into which they were born. (UNICEF, 2007, p 1)

In the United Kingdom we have no official means of establishing how our children are doing, no 'state of UK children' report. This book is an attempt to fill that gap. It is the fourth in a series of volumes that have been produced out of the University of York stable since Bradshaw (2001). That book emerged from the Economic and Social Research Council (ESRC) 'Children 5-16: Growing into the 21st Century' research programme and was motivated by anxiety about the impact that the doubling of relative child poverty rates might be having on the well-being of children in the UK. It concluded by recommending that the UK should produce a regular review of the well-being of its children, and that perhaps the Office for National Statistics (ONS) should have responsibility for such a review. When this looked unlikely, Save the Children (UK) stepped in and supported the publication of two further volumes – Bradshaw (2002) and Bradshaw and Mayhew (2005).

The latter volume reported the situation of children around 2001/03. Since then, cohorts of children have gone through infancy, primary and secondary schools, and much that might affect children today has changed.

For ten years after the election of the Labour government in 1997, the UK experienced an unprecedented period of economic growth – employment rates reached record levels and unemployment was never so low, until the recession began to bite in 2008. During this period, there were substantial increases in public expenditure on education, health, transport, and cash and tax benefits for families with children. Sure Start was launched in 1998, and nursery education was extended to three- and four-year-olds and there was new investment in pre-school childcare. In schools, the standards agenda sought to improve literacy and numeracy and to improve performance at Key Stages and at GCE level. Efforts were made to increase staying on rates at school and to expand opportunities for tertiary education. During this period the government was pursuing the child poverty strategy announced by the Prime Minister in 1999, which aimed to eradicate child poverty by 2020 and to halve it by 2010.

There were also institutional transformations. By the time the last volume was published in 2005, the Children and Young People's Unit (CYPU) had been established in England and a strategy was published (CYPU, 2001). The CYPU had just been absorbed into the Department for Education and Skills (DfES). Now a Minister for Children has been appointed, and it has become the Department for *Children*, Schools and Families (DCSF), and acquired a new strategy in *The Children's Plan* (DCSF, 2007a). Commissioners for Children were established in all countries of the UK. There was also a transformation of children's services locally, with the establishment (in England) of Children's Trusts and Partnerships.

Efforts to monitor child well-being

Of course there is already a great deal of material available on children's well-being in the UK, and we shall be drawing on it in this volume. However, the objective of this book is to bring the evidence together in one place, in a critical discursive review, which has not been done elsewhere.

From 1999 the Department for Work and Pensions (DWP) published an annual report, *Opportunity for all*, which was originally designed to monitor the poverty strategy, but included a set of indicators on children and young people, and went beyond income poverty to include indicators of health, education, housing and children in care. This publication stopped after 2007, however, and the web page has now been removed to The National Archives![1]

The *Every Child Matters* Outcomes Framework[2] was a very ambitious effort run by the DCSF. Each of its five domains was associated with a set of five or more targets, each with a number of indicators:

- Be healthy
- Stay safe
- Enjoy and achieve
- Make a positive contribution
- Achieve economic well-being

To help populate these indicators, Ofsted launched the TellUs Survey in 2007 from a massive school-based sample of children in Years 6, 8 and 10. The Survey was repeated in 2008 and 2009, but the new Coalition government abandoned the next one due to take place in 2010. The *Every Child Matters* indicators never really became a statistical series used to monitor child well-being over time, and there is some doubt about whether the Outcomes Framework will be sustained under the new government.

In early 2007 DCSF published *Children and young people today* (DCSF, 2007b). This was a review of evidence to support the development of *The Children's Plan* and although it included an annex that provided an assessment of evidence against the *Every Child Matters* Outcomes Framework, it tended to be stronger on the coverage of DCSF responsibilities (especially education) than other elements of child well-being. In 2009 the DCSF also published a progress report on *The Children's Plan* (DCSF, 2009a).

There have been many other reports focusing on children. For example, the ONS has web pages providing a 'Focus on children' and 'Focus on young people'.[3] Under Ken Livingston, the Mayor of London, the *State of London's children* was published, the last report in 2007 (Mayor of London, 2007). However, there is still no study that analyses child well-being critically across the UK, exploring what has been happening to child well-being over time.

Child Wellbeing Research Centre

In 2009 the DCSF let a contract for a new Childhood Wellbeing Research Centre.[4] The aims of the Centre are to establish:

- What constitutes a good childhood and how can we ensure this is available to all children?
- What are the key drivers of well-being and how do they interact?
- What are the costs and benefits of interventions that are designed to improve levels of well-being?
- What are the relationships between well-being and learning outcomes?
- Who does not experience a good childhood and why? How can we identify and safeguard those 'at risk'?
- How do countries vary on what they consider to be a good childhood? What can we learn from international comparisons?

At the time of writing (2010) the Centre has only just begun its work, delayed by the 2010 General Election – and so far only one review has been produced (Statham and Chase, 2010).

What does child well-being mean?

In a recent review, McAuley and Rose (2010) identified four major influences on the concept of child well-being:

- Children's rights as set out in the United Nations (UN) Convention on the Rights of the Child and also in European Convention on Human Rights. Included in the UN Convention is the clause that says that 'the primary consideration in all actions concerning children must be in their best interests *and their views must be taken into account*' (emphasis added).
- The so-called new sociology of childhood, which argues that childhood should be treated as a stage in life with its own value and not just as a passage towards adulthood. Thus the well-*being* of children in childhood should be the main focus of attention, not just how successful adults they became – well-*becoming* – indeed well-becoming could be in conflict with well-being.

- The ecological perspective on child development, which locates the child in the context of the family, friendship networks, school, neighbourhood and the family's place within the community. Well-being is influenced by many dimensions – it is multidimensional. What matters to children is not just how well they do at school, or what their health is like, or how they get on with friends, but all of these things and more.
- The new science of happiness has been mainly applied to adults and has roots in hedonic psychology and self-assessed evaluations of quality of life. Economists such as Layard (2005) have argued that increasing wealth beyond a point does not necessarily result in improved happiness, that happiness or life satisfaction should be the focus of endeavour in our societies, not wealth, and that inequity associated with market competition does not enhance society. More recently in *The spirit level*, Wilkinson and Pickett (2009) have argued that inequality in society is actually harmful. These ideas have spread to children and to an increasing preoccupation with what makes for 'a good childhood' (Layard and Dunn, 2009). On 25 November 2010 the Prime Minister announced that:

> 'From April next year we will start measuring our progress as a country not just by how our economy is growing, but by how our lives are improving; not just by our standard of living, but by our quality of life.'

He has asked the ONS to undertake the monitoring. ONS had already produced a series of background papers, one of which was devoted to children (Thomas, 2009).

This book has been influenced by these developments and also by the so-called child indicators movement. The study of child well-being is not new – Ben-Arieh (2010) finds 'state of the child' reports were being published as early as the 1940s, and the child indicators movement was influenced by the social indicators movement in the 1960s. It was believed that well-measured and consistently collected social indicators could provide a way to social progress. The child indicators movement developed further towards the end of the last century, with UNICEF publishing the first *State of the world's children* in 1979. The movement was advanced in a series of meetings organised by Ben-Arieh under the umbrella of the so-called 'Jerusalem Project', and this eventually developed into the 'Multinational Indicators Project' that sought to develop indicators for monitoring and measuring child well-being. This in turn developed into the International Society for Child Indicators, that publishes a journal, *Child Indicators Research*, and a newsletter, and organises seminars and conferences.[5]

Ben-Arieh (2010) lists eight major developments in the child indicators movement:

- A shift from preoccupation with physical survival and basic needs to development and well-being.
- A shift from negative indicators of problems and failure to positive indicators that hold societies accountable for more than the warehousing of children.

- Incorporating child rights perspectives which focus on the child.
- A shift from well-becoming to well-being.
- A shift from traditional domains such as education and health to new domains such as life skills and civic involvement.
- A shift from an adult to a child perspective – focusing on children's lives.
- A new focus on data at the local level.
- The development of more policy-oriented indicators.

He also discusses a trend towards producing single composite indices, the use of the child as a unit of observation and the emerging importance of subjective measures.

Comparative indices of child well-being

UNICEF was the pioneer of well-being indices. Professor Andrea Cornia, working at the UNICEF Innocenti Centre in Florence, became anxious about what was happening to children in rich countries, and commissioned a series of national case studies, including one for the UK (Bradshaw, 1990, updated by Kumar, 1995). UNICEF eventually published a book on the well-being of children in industrialised countries in 1997 (Cornia and Danziger, 1997). This work led in turn to a series of Innocenti Report Cards comparing aspects of child well-being in OECD countries.

The first overall comparative index of child well-being was, however, a comparison of European Union (EU) countries (Bradshaw et al, 2007a), which showed the UK placed 21 out of 25 EU countries **on overall child well-being**. Bradshaw, Hoelscher and Richardson (2007b) then carried out work for the UNICEF (2007) Innocenti Report Card no 7, which caused a great stir in the UK, because the UK found itself at the bottom of a league table of 21 OECD (Organisation for Economic Co-operation and Development) countries. In 2009 Bradshaw and Richardson updated the EU comparisons for the 29 European countries – the UK came 24th. Then the OECD itself undertook a similar analysis, but cut the domains rather differently and excluded subjective well-being and children's relationships. Although the OECD did not produce a league table, it is easy to estimate one – the UK came 20th out of 30 OECD countries.

None of these indices, using slightly different combinations of variables, gives a very positive comparative picture of the *average* well-being of children in the UK. Innocenti Report Card no 9 (UNICEF, 2010a) is the first to attempt an index of the *dispersion* of child well-being, exploring inequalities in three domains. Out of 24 OECD countries, the UK was:

- 19th on material well-being inequality
- 13th on educational inequality
- 11th on health inequality.

Overall the UK came in the fourth group of countries out of five.

Spending on children

This book is about outcomes, but spending on children is about inputs. Nevertheless, the comparative studies of child well-being have found an association between spending on children and child outcomes. This is illustrated in Figure 1.1, which shows that spending on families with children explains 36% of the variation in overall well-being. The UK is one of the outliers, achieving lower levels of child well-being than the general relationship might suggest that it should do. The spending data excludes health and education expenditure, and there may also be a lag between spending and well-being. Time will tell.

Figure 1.2 shows that spending on families with children in 2005 in the UK was second only to France and Luxembourg. This is an improvement. In 2003, spending in the UK was in the middle of the OECD league table.

Unfortunately UK national accounts do not monitor expenditure on children, although Sefton (2004) demonstrated how it could be done, and we reported the results of his work up to 2001/02 in Bradshaw and Mayhew (2005). Sefton's work has yet to be updated.

Figure 1.1: Spending on families with children in 2005 and overall well-being in the EU

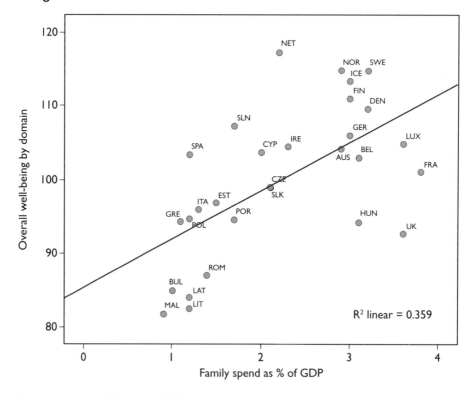

Source: Bradshaw and Richardson (2009)

Figure 1.2: Spending on families with children as % of GDP, 2005

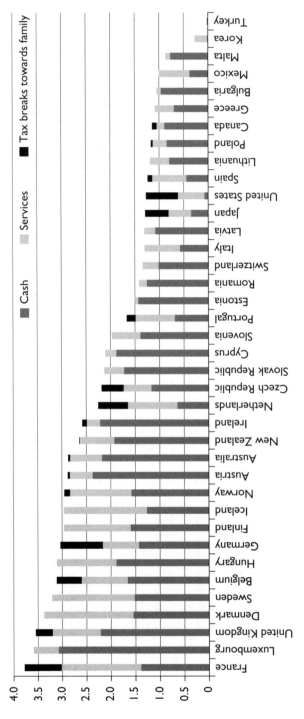

Source: OECD (2009a, PF1.1)

Figure 1.3 shows that expenditure on education and health both show substantial increases since 1999. Education spending is almost all devoted to children and young people. It is much less certain that the huge increase in health expenditure benefited children, although there is evidence from Sefton's analysis (2004) that spending per capita rose for pre-school children and that spending was probably more skewed to deprived areas. However, most of the extra health spending went on improvements to doctors' and nurses' salaries and the NHS has continued to prioritise acute (and adult) medicine.

OECD data on spending on families with children (see Figure 1.4) indicates that since 1990 it has been increasing in most countries, including the UK.

Figure 1.3: Education and health spending as % of GDP

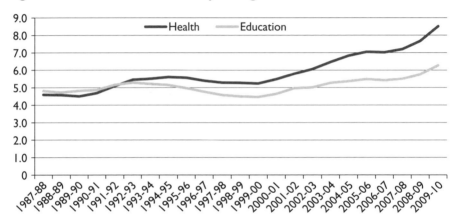

Source: HM Treasury (2010a)

Figure 1.4: Spending per child as a proportion of per capita GDP

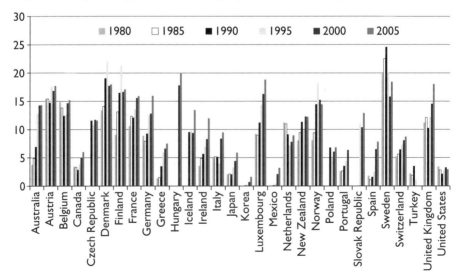

Source: Own analysis of the OECD social expenditure data base

Anxiety has been expressed (Esping-Anderson and Sarasa, 2003) that, with an ageing population in industrialised countries, there may be a tendency for children to lose out in the competition for public resources. Figure 1.5 shows spending per child as a percentage of spending per elderly person. All countries spend more on the elderly than they do on children, although the ratio varies considerably between countries. In the UK, spending per child fell between the 1980s and the 1990s but recovered in the 2000s. In most countries, spending on children has increased as a proportion of spending on the elderly – the exceptions are the Nordic countries, where spending on children as a proportion of the elderly was lower in 2005 than it had been in 1995.

Figure 1.5: Expenditure per child as % of expenditure per elderly person

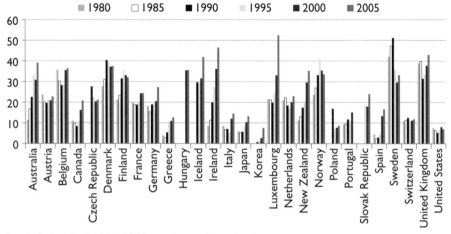

Source: Own analysis of the OECD social expenditure data base

The structure of this book

The first Bradshaw (2001) volume conceptualised well-being into four domains:

- Physical well-being, including mortality and morbidity, accidents, diet, abuse and neglect
- Cognitive well-being – mainly educational attainment
- Behavioural well-being – crime, drugs, alcohol, tobacco
- Emotional well-being – mental illness, happiness and self-esteem

The Bradshaw (2002) edition organised well-being around 23 topics in separate chapters. The Bradshaw and Mayhew (2005) edition considered organising the material around the five *Every Child Matters* outcome domains listed above and the five domains in the multinational indicators set:

- Safety and physical status
- Personal life
- Civic life
- Economic resources and contribution
- Activities

It settled instead for the structure that is more or less repeated in this volume.

Chapter Two starts with what is called the 'demography of childhood' but which is about trends in fertility, about the number and distribution of children, about trends in family formation and dissolution and about the families that children live in – their size and structure, their ethnicity.

The different domains of child well-being are then dealt with in each chapter.

- Childhood poverty and deprivation
- Physical health
- Subjective well-being and mental health
- Education
- Housing and the environment for children
- Children's time and space
- Children and young people in and leaving care
- Child maltreatment
- Children and early years
- Children, crime and illegal drug use

The concluding chapter, Chapter Thirteen, brings together the findings and attempts to develop an index of child well-being for the UK.

In tackling this subject matter chapter by chapter, the book tries to sustain a framework of questions:

- What are the key trends? Are things getting better or worse over time? (with a special effort to assess change over the period of the Labour administration, 1997-2010)
- How do the countries of the UK compare? It is not always possible to do this on a consistent basis – indeed, one of the outcomes of the establishment of the devolved governments and administrations is a decline in the comparability of the data available. But also the institutional framework is different and becoming more so, and it is inevitable that this book tends to fall back on England, where 84% of the UK's children live.
- What are the associates of the outcomes that are being reviewed? How do they vary by age, gender, class, ethnicity, family structure, poverty?
- How do we compare with other industrialised countries? International comparisons are fraught with difficulties but without them we cannot establish how well we are doing for our children. We can say whether things are getting

better or worse, but we cannot say how well or badly we are doing or whether we are doing as well as we could be.

Conclusion

Children are our future. Their well-being matters to us all. As a nation we pay enormous attention to the well-being of our economy, the state of the weather, sporting league tables, the City and the Stock Market. Indicators of these take up pages of the media every day.

We need to make more effort to monitor the well-being of our children and we need to devote more resources to understanding how they are doing and to ensuring that their childhood is as good as it can be. This book is a small contribution to that end.

Notes

[1] http://webarchive.nationalarchives.gov.uk/+/http://www.dwp.gov.uk/publications/policy-publications/opportunity-for-all/

[2] www.education.gov.uk/publications/standard/publicationdetail/page1/DCSF-00331-2008

[3] www.statistics.gov.uk/focuson/children/default.asp and www.statistics.gov.uk/focuson/youngpeople/default.asp

[4] www.cwrc.ac.uk/ – the Childhood Wellbeing Research Centre is an independent research centre with funding from the Department for Education (DfE). It is a partnership between the Thomas Coram Research Unit (TCRU) and other centres at the Institute of Education, the Centre for Child and Family Research (CCFR) at Loughborough University and the Personal Social Services Research Unit (PSSRU) at the University of Kent. Professor Ann Phoenix (TCRU) and Professor Harriet Ward (CCFR) jointly lead it.

[5] www.childindicators.org/

TWO

Demography of childhood

Jonathan Bradshaw

Key statistics

- In 2009 there were 11.5 million children under the age of 16 in the UK.
- The majority of children in 2009 were white – 86%. The largest group of ethnic children were Asian, forming 7% of the child population.
- In 2009 24% of children were living in a lone-parent family and 27% of families with children were lone-parent families.
- The UK has the highest proportion of children living in lone-parent families in the European Union (EU).

Key trends

- The number and proportion of children has been declining, especially in Scotland. Children made up 18.7% of the UK population in 2009.
- Rates of childlessness have increased, from 10% of women born in 1945 not having children to 21% of women born in 1965. Average family size is falling and there are more one-child families.
- Fertility increased after 2003, mainly as a result of migration, but the increase stopped in 2009 and has not reached replacement level.

Key sources

- Office for National Statistics (ONS) and *Population Trends*
- Family Resources Survey (FRS)
- Labour Force Survey (LFS)
- Millennium Cohort Study (MCS)
- European Union Statistics on Income and Living Conditions (EU-SILC)

Introduction

This chapter provides a review of recent developments in the demography of childhood in the UK as well as children's changing social relationships within the family. It describes the demographic characteristics of children – their numbers, gender, age, ethnicity, geographical location and family composition. It presents comparisons of UK children with those of other countries, and reviews evidence of the impact of family structure on child well-being.

Child population

In 2009 there were 11.5 million children under the age of 16 in the UK. Of these, 5.9 million were boys and 5.6 million girls. Table 2.1 shows how the numbers and proportion of children under 16 have changed between 1971 and 2009 in each country of the UK. The number of children under 16 in the UK fell by 2.7 million and the overall proportion of children under 16 in the population fell from 25.5% in 1971 to 18.7% in 2009. The largest reduction in the proportion of children has been in Scotland, and the distribution of children in the UK has shifted towards England, which in 2009 contained 84% of all children in the UK.

Table 2.1: Trends in the child population, 1971-2009

	England	Wales	Scotland	Northern Ireland	UK
1971					
Thousands	11,648	686	1,440	483	14,257
% of children in the population	25.1	25.0	27.5	31.4	25.5
% of children in the UK	81.7	4.8	10.1	3.4	100
1981					
Thousands	10,285	626	1,188	444	12,543
% of children in the population	21.9	22.3	22.9	28.7	22.3
% of children in the UK	82.0	5.0	9.5	3.5	100
1991					
Thousands	9,658	589	1,021	417	11,685
% of children in the population	20.2	20.5	20.1	25.9	20.3
% of children in the UK	82.7	5.0	8.7	3.6	100
2001					
Thousands	9,908	587	970	397	11,863
% of children in the population	20.0	20.2	19.2	23.5	20.1
% of children in the UK	83.5	4.9	8.2	3.3	100
2009					
Thousands	9,704	550	912	382	11,549
% of children in the population	18.7	18.3	17.6	21.3	18.7
% of children in the UK	84.0	4.8	7.9	3.3	100

Source: *Population Trends 141*, Autumn 2010, Table 1.4

Age composition of the child population

Table 2.2 shows how the age composition of children in the UK has changed from 1971 to 2009. The number of preschool-age children has been steadily decreasing since 1971, interrupted by a brief recuperation during the late 1980s and early 1990s. However, in 2003 the number of births began to rise again and

Table 2.2: Trends in the number of children by age, UK (000s)

	1971	1976	1981	1986	1991	1996	2001	2009
Under 1	899	677	730	748	790	719	663	784
1-4	3,654	3,043	2,726	2,886	3,077	3,018	2,819	2,994
5-14	8,916	9,176	8,147	7,143	7,141	7,544	7,624	7,017

Source: Population Trends 141, Autumn 2010, Table 1.4

with it the preschool population. The number of school-age children has declined since 1976 – there were more than two million fewer children aged 5-14 in the UK in 2009 than there had been in 1976.

Figure 2.1 shows the projected numbers of children in different age groups in the UK, based on the latest (ONS, 2009) Government Actuary's Department projections. The projections estimate that the numbers of preschool children will rise until 2012 and then rise again after 2016. The 5-9 age group is already increasing rapidly and will continue to increase until after 2017. The numbers in the other two age groups (10-14 and 15-19) are still falling, with the 10-14 age group beginning to increase after 2014 and the 15-19 age group after 2018.

Figure 2.1: Projected numbers of children in different age groups, UK (000s)

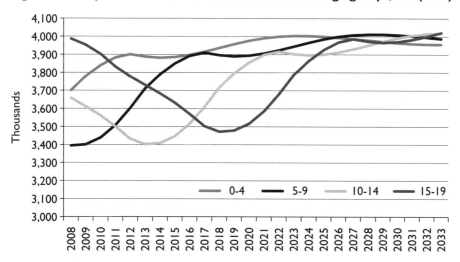

Source: ONS (2009) Government Actuary's Department projections 2008 (www.statistics.gov.uk/downloads/theme_population/NPP2008/NatPopProj2008.pdf)

Fertility

These fluctuations in the number and age composition of children reflect changes in fertility and birth rates. The total period fertility rate is the number of children that would be born to a woman if current patterns of fertility persisted throughout her childbearing life. It has been low and relatively stable in the UK for the last

30 years. Figure 2.2 shows that it reached a postwar high point in 1964 at 2.93 and then declined rapidly to a low point of 1.66 in 1977. Thereafter, it was remarkably stable and below replacement level (2.1) until very recently. In 2003 fertility began to rise again, increasing every year and reaching 1.97 in 2008. In 2009 it was 1.96, which may indicate that the recuperation has run its course. Scotland's fertility rate has been below the England and Wales rate since 1981, and in 2009 was 1.77. The Northern Ireland fertility rate was above the replacement rate until the early 1990s, but fell rapidly, and was 2.04 in 2009.

The fertility rate is influenced by changes in the number of children women will have, the timing of births and migration patterns. The age-specific fertility rates are shown in Figure 2.3, and it can be seen that they have been declining for

Figure 2.2: Trends in fertility rates, England and Wales

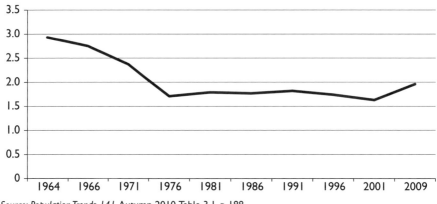

Source: *Population Trends 141*, Autumn 2010, Table 3.1, p 188

Figure 2.3: Age-specific fertility rates – births per 1,000 women in the age group

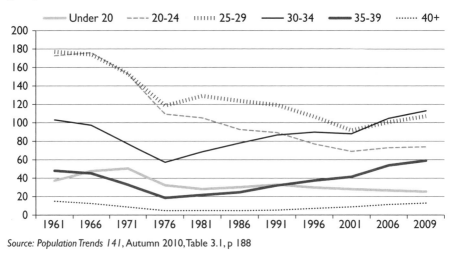

Source: *Population Trends 141*, Autumn 2010, Table 3.1, p 188

younger women (under 30) and increasing for older women (over 30). However, one of the main reasons for the increase in fertility has been a recovery of the age-specific fertility of women aged 25-29 as well as a rise in the 30-34 rate. Tromans et al (2009) explored the reasons for the increase in births between 2001 and 2007, and concluded that two thirds of the increase could be attributed to the increase in the number of births to foreign-born women in the UK who have higher fertility rates.

Average family size

Table 2.3 shows that the rates of childlessness among women increased dramatically towards the end of the 20th century. Only 10% of the 1945 cohort of women was childless as opposed to 21% of those born in 1965. While some women are voluntarily childless, others may be unable to have children as a result of fertility problems. The postponement of motherhood to later in life can lead to difficulties in conceiving. The increased rate of childlessness has been reinforced by decreases in the number of children mothers will have, especially those having three or more children, which was 33% in the 1945 cohort and 28% in the 1965 cohort. As a result, the average completed family size is getting smaller.

Table 2.3: Number of children and average completed family size by women's year of birth, England and Wales

	Actual completed family size					Predicted family size when completed				
	1945	1950	1955	1960	1965	1970	1975	1980	1985	1990
Childless	10	14	16	20	21	20	21	22	22	22
1 child	14	13	13	12	13	14	15	15	15	15
2 children	43	44	41	38	38	40	39	40	40	40
3 children	21	19	19	20	18	17	16	16	16	16
4+ children	12	10	10	10	10	9	8	8	7	7
Average family size	2.19	2.07	2.02	1.98	1.91	1.87	1.80	1.78	1.76	1.75

Source: ONS Birth statistics 2008, Series FM1, No 37 (www.statistics.gov.uk/downloads/theme_population/FM1-37/FM1_37_2008.pdf); ONS (2009)

Ethnicity

The vast majority of children living in the UK are of white ethnic origin. Table 2.4 shows the distribution of ethnicities in 2008/09. The best source of this data would be the Population Census, but the 2001 Census is now too out of date for estimates of ethnicity, especially because of the very substantial inward migration over the last 10 years. The analysis used here is based on a large sample survey, the Family Resources Survey (FRS). In 2008/09, 86% of UK children were

Table 2.4: Ethnicity of children in the UK, 2008/09

Ethnic group	%
White	86
Mixed	1
Asian or Asian British	7
Indian	2
Pakistani and Bangladeshi	4
Black and Black British	4
Black Caribbean	1
Black non-Caribbean	2
Chinese or other ethnic group	2
All 12.8 million children	100

Source: DWP (2010, Table 4.3)

white. The largest ethnic group were Asian (7%) and within them Pakistanis and Bangladeshis. Black children only accounted for 4% of all children.

Marriage, cohabitation and lone parenthood

One of the main precursors of late childbearing is the postponement of marriage. The mean age of first marriage for women rose from 23.1 years in 1981 to 29.9 years in 2008 (in England and Wales). The majority of births (59.2% in 2009) still occur within marriage, so the postponement of marriage leads to later fertility.

However, marriage rates have continued to fall. In England and Wales, the first marriage rate of men in 2008 was 20.5 per 1,000 single adults as compared to 74.8 per 1,000 in 1961. The first marriage rate of women was 24.3 per 1,000 single adults compared to 83.0 per 1,000 in 1961. Figure 2.4 gives the proportion of live births to unmarried mothers for all ages and women under 20. The percentage of births outside marriage increased from 8.4% in 1971 to 46.2% in 2009. In 2009, 94.6% of live births to women under 20 were outside marriage. Having births inside marriage is most likely in the 30–34 age group, but 29.1% of births to this age group were outside marriage.

The marriage rate in itself reveals increasingly little about household composition because of the substantial increases in the levels of cohabitation. While in the 1970s over 50% of unmarried mothers were lone parents, today this is by no means the case. Now most births outside marriage are registered by both parents living at the same address (65.7% in 2009), and only 13.4% of births to unmarried mothers are sole registrations by the mother. The trends are shown in Figure 2.5.

The Millennium Cohort Study (MCS) (Kiernan and Smith, 2003) provides us with the most recent data on the relationship between partnership status, age of the mother and births. Table 2.5 shows that the proportion of births to married parents increases with the age of the mother, and the proportion with cohabitating or lone mothers decreases with the mother's age.

Figure 2.4: Live birth rates outside marriage, England and Wales

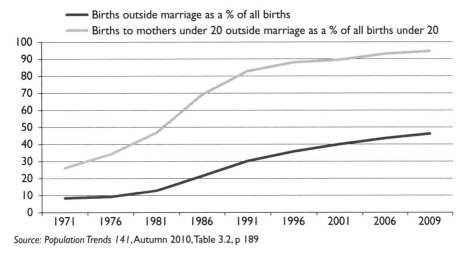

Source: Population Trends 141, Autumn 2010, Table 3.2, p 189

Figure 2.5: Registration of live births outside marriage, England and Wales

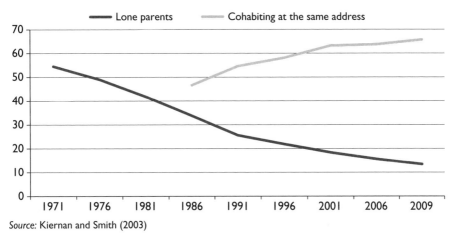

Source: Kiernan and Smith (2003)

Table 2.5: Mothers' age and partnership at the birth of the child, UK (MCS 2000/01)

	14-19	20-29	30-39	40+	All
Married natural parents	9.4	53.5	75.5	72.5	59.2
Cohabiting parents	43.5	30.5	17.7	19.5	26.1
Lone mother	47.1	16.0	6.8	8.0	14.7
Total	100	100	100	100	100
Sample size	1,579	8,667	7,861	39	18,146

Source: Kiernan and Smith (2003)

Divorce and remarriage

In 2008, the divorce rate in England and Wales was 11.2 per 1,000 marriages, slightly lower than the rate in the 1990s. However, with fewer parents marrying, divorce statistics do not provide a helpful picture of what is happening to children. The breakdowns of parental relationships are not recorded in official statistics, and there is also a dearth of data on repartnering. We know that the remarriage rate (per 1,000 divorced people aged 16 and over in England and Wales) was 34.1 for men and 24.3 for women in 2008, and that it has declined even more rapidly than the marriage rate – they are less than one fifth of their levels in the 1970s. But there is a gap in the official statistics of repartnering after parental breakdown. Wilson and Stuchbury (2010) used the longitudinal census data to explore what happened to partnerships between 1991 and 2001. They found that 82% of marriages were still intact and only 61% of cohabitations. They found that being older, male, better qualified and not unemployed increased the odds of partnerships surviving. Having a dependent child also increased the odds by 7%, all other things being equal.

In the absence of better indicators, two types of data have become very important – data on lone parents and that on step parents.

Lone parents

A more reliable indication of what is happening to the families that children live in is the composition of families with children. Perhaps the best indication of all is trends in lone-parent families. Table 2.6 provides one picture of this. It shows that the proportion of (single-unit) households with children as a proportion of all households has been falling, but the proportion of lone-parent families has increased from 13% in 1961 to 27% in 2009. This is a cross-sectional picture. It has been estimated that between a third and half of children will experience the breakdown of their parents' relationships.

Table 2.7 gives a slightly different picture. Here children are the unit of analysis, with 24.3% living in lone-parent families and 12.9% in cohabiting families in

Table 2.6: Trends in the composition of families (single household units) with children, Britain

	1961	1971	1981	1991	2001	2009
Couple +1 or 2 dependent children	55	52	51	48	49	49
Couple +3 or more dependent children	15	18	12	12	10	8
Couple non-dependent children only	18	16	16	19	15	16
Lone parent dependent children	4	6	10	14	18	19
Lone parent non-dependent children	9	8	10	7	8	8
Families with children as % of all households	55	50	49	42	39	37

Source: Calculated from ONS (2010d, Table 2.2)

Table 2.7: Dependent children by type of families, UK (LFS)

	1997	2001	2005	2009
Married couple	72.2	68.2	65.2	62.9
Cohabiting couple	7.5	9.8	11.4	12.9
Female lone parent	18.8	20.5	21.2	22.0
Male lone parent	1.5	1.5	2.3	2.3

Source: Calculated from ONS (2010d, Table 2.5)

2009. Lone-parent families are predominantly headed by women, and in 2009 just over 10% were headed by a man. Male lone parents tend to be older, with older children, and they include more widowers.

Wilson (2010) found that 3.3 million dependent children were living in households with a non-resident birth parent in 2008 using an Opinions survey (ONS) and 3.8 million using the LFS; the LFS also suggests that the percentage of children living with one non-widowed birth parent increased from 27% to 30% between 1999 and 2009. In 2009, 76% of these children were living with a lone parent, 12% in a cohabiting couple and 12% in a (re)married couple. Of these children, only 43% ever stay overnight with their non-resident parent, 18% stay at least once a week and 10% at least once a fortnight.

Figure 2.6 compares the proportion of children living in lone-parent families in the EU using SILC (Statistics on Income and Living Conditions) data. It is actually quite difficult to indentify lone-parent families in EU-SILC. This is mainly because in some countries many lone parents are hidden in multi-unit households and not classified as lone parents, but Bradshaw and Chzhen (2010)

Figure 2.6: Percentage of children living in lone-parent families in the EU, 2008

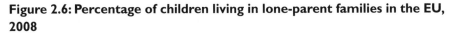

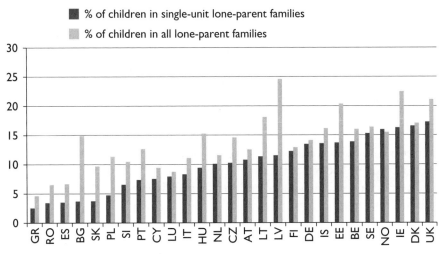

Source: Own analysis of EU-SILC 2008

have manipulated the data using the links in the household grid between adults and children. Both definitions are shown in Figure 2.6. The problem with the revised estimate is that parents with one partner working abroad are classified as lone parents and it is arguable whether this is socially equivalent for a child. However, the main point from Figure 2.6 is that the UK has one of the highest if not *the* highest prevalence of children in lone-parent families in the EU.

Step parents

Changes in the timing and manner of family formation, and increased rates of family dissolution and reformation have increased the complexity of family forms. A complex web of new kin is a result of consecutive separations and repartnering. Children can become part of a large network of relationships, including natural parents, grandparents and siblings, but now more often step parents and other step relationships, half siblings and visiting children from a parent's previous relationships. These patterns of relationships are extremely difficult to summarise and official statistics have yet to get to grips with the issues. The latest estimates for 2007 suggest that 86% of stepfamilies with dependent children have children from the woman's previous marriage/cohabitation, 10% from the man's previous marriage/cohabitation and 4% from both partners' previous marriage/cohabitation. There will be a great deal more complexity than this suggests, with children increasingly splitting their time between their resident and non-resident parent, and indeed it is becoming increasingly difficult to establish who is the main carer.

For aggregate families, the separation of parents is often only one major event in a life already full of fluctuation and change (Wade and Smart, 2002). Repartnering often results in the improvement of household finances, but may create new sources of tension between children and their step parents. Many children find it difficult to take discipline from a step parent, and feel insecure about their position in the family with regard to their step and/or half siblings (Dunn and Deater-Deckard, 2001). Becoming part of a stepfamily seems to be helpful for younger children but harder for older children to adapt to (Hawthorne et al, 2003). Older children have a higher risk of adverse outcomes, especially in areas of educational achievement, family relationships, sexual activity, early partnership formation and young parenthood (Rodgers and Pryor, 1998). In their review, Rodgers and Pryor (1998) concluded that for the child, parental separation resulted in short-term unhappiness, low self-esteem, behavioural difficulties, problems with friendships and loss of contact with extended family. They also found that these effects could be mitigated by communication and contact between parents, and that distress faded over time. Mooney et al (2009) also found a small but significant difference in outcomes for children who experience parental divorce or separation, compared to those children who grow up with both parents. Many of these differences are primarily evident during the initial crisis of separation and diminish over time.

It is also important to remember that the source of most of these findings is long-term follow-up of the 1958 and 1970 birth cohorts. Parental separation was much less common then, at least for the children of the 1958 cohort. Although analysts make brave attempts to control for the effects of other variables, including poverty, which is more or less inevitably associated with lone parenthood in the UK, the data is not very good. Most important of all, this research can never tell us whether it is the separation that is the cause of these outcomes or the parental conflict that preceded the separation.

These points should be borne in mind when claims are made that the children of lone parents do worse in various ways. When UNICEF published Innocenti Report Card no 7, which showed the UK at the bottom of the league table of child well-being, the popular press claimed that it was as a result of family breakdown. When the analysis was updated for EU countries, Bradshaw and Richardson (2009) looked at the relationship between the proportion of children living in 'broken' families – lone-parent and step parent families – and overall well-being. The results are presented in Figure 2.7. There is no relationship between family structure and child well-being at an international level. Indeed, the Nordic countries have high proportions of children in 'broken families' and very high levels of child well-being. This suggests that what matters is how society

Figure 2.7: The relationship between overall well-being and the proportion of children living in lone- and step parent families, EU

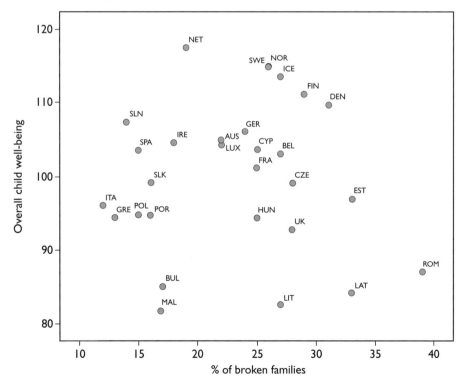

Source: Bradshaw and Richardson (2009)

responds to new family forms and in particular whether it protects lone parents and children from poverty. As we shall see in the next chapter, the UK does not do well in that regard.

There is also some comfort from The Children's Society survey of child well-being in England (Rees et al, 2010a). Children living with both parents in the same household had higher well-being than those living with lone parents, but not higher than those living with step parents. The difference remained significant after controlling for age, gender, employment and ethnicity. But the difference was very small – family structure only explained about 2% of the variation in overall subjective well-being and when the *quality* of family relationships ("My family gets along well together") and changes in family structure in the last year were taken into account, the influence of family structure was even more limited. By far the most important determinant of subjective well-being is the quality of family relationships.

Only children

The reduction in the number of siblings, and especially the growth in the population of only children, raises the question of whether 'only childhood' effects children's social development. The positive aspects of growing up in a small family are associated with reduced risks of experiencing poverty, greater physical space and increased parental attention devoted to the only child, although there are some possible drawbacks. Siblings can play a critical role in child socialisation (Parke and Buriel, 1998). Research shows that children with siblings have better conflict resolution skills (Patterson, 1986) and form closer friendships with peers (Stocker and Dunn, 1990) than only children. Children with siblings can learn through observing parent–sibling interactions and are exposed to experiences that provide the opportunity to learn to deal with differential treatment, rivalry and jealousy (Dunn et al, 1994). Also inter-sibling interactions provide important practice for similar exchanges with peers and help children gain practice with affective perspective taking and consideration of others' feelings (Youngblade and Dunn, 1995). Having a sibling can also be a source of support in periods of stress (such as parental divorce) (Caya and Liem, 1998). The social benefits of being a sibling have a bigger role in childhood than in adulthood. Self-report studies of adults have not found differences between adults with or without siblings in terms of social skills and social competence (Riggio, 1999).

Conclusion

Delayed fertility, falling birth rates and the relative instability of new family forms is giving rise to very different experiences of childhood both within and between peer groups. Children of the 21st century have a higher probability of experiencing parental separation, lone parenting, step families, visiting families, half siblings and being an only child than children of any previous period of time. In 2008/09 28%

of children lived in a household without other siblings. One in four experienced parental separation, one in ten lived in stepfamilies and more than one in four in a lone-parent family. Family disruption and its correlates are associated with increased risk of poverty, academic under-achievement, behavioural problems, early partnership formation and early parenthood. Recent demographic changes challenge the well-being of children in the UK, and the outcomes depend on children's and their family's ability to develop strategies that help successfully to adapt to changing circumstances.

THREE

Child poverty and deprivation

Jonathan Bradshaw

Key statistics

- In 2008/09 22% of children were living in poverty in the UK.
- In 2007, the UK had the fifth highest child poverty rate in the European Union (EU).
- The UK has the highest proportion of children living in workless families in the EU.
- In the countries of the UK, Wales has the highest child poverty rate after housing costs. Among the regions, Inner London has by far the highest child poverty rate both before and after housing costs.
- Child poverty is very spatially concentrated.

Key trends

- The child poverty rate began to fall after 1998/99 but stopped falling in 2004/05. The government failed to meet the 2004/05 target to reduce child poverty by a quarter and will miss the 2010/11 target to reduce child poverty by a half.
- There has been no reduction in the percentage of children living in households with low income and deprivation since the income and deprivation series began in 2004/05.
- The UK was one of only seven countries in the OECD (Organisation for Economic Co-operation and Development) with a reduction in child poverty between the mid-1990s and the mid-2000s.
- There has been a welcome reduction in persistent child poverty.

Key sources

- Households Below Average Income (HBAI)
- Family and Child Survey (FACS)
- British Household Panel Survey (BHPS)
- European Union Statistics on Income and Living Conditions (EU-SILC)
- Millennium Cohort Study (MCS)

Introduction

This book is about all children, not just poor children. However, the well-being of children is affected if they are poor, and, as we shall see, most domains of child well-being are affected by poverty or its proxies. Poor children are deprived of material assets, they experience higher mortality and morbidity, their activities and opportunities are constrained, they are more likely to suffer mental ill health and they are more likely to live in poor housing and poor neighbourhoods. Poverty in childhood has very strong associations with poor well-becoming. Child poverty is thus a very powerful indicator of the well-being of children.

In fact, one of the best measures of the success of governments is the extent to which children are protected from poverty. Children have a moral and legal right not to be poor, and it is socially unjust if they are brought up in poverty. The social and economic success of a country is undermined by children brought up in poverty and there is evidence that in the long term child poverty costs a great deal in national resources. Blanden et al (2010) estimate that the cost of growing up poor amounts to at least 1% of the gross domestic product (GDP).

In 1999 former Prime Minister Tony Blair made the historic commitment to eradicate child poverty in the next 20 years and, as a result, child poverty has since been at the heart of the domestic agenda in the UK. In this chapter we examine the progress that has been made towards this objective.

Child poverty

Figure 3.1 shows that at the start of the 1980s the UK had a child poverty rate (using the conventional threshold of 60% of median income before housing costs) of only 13%. That rate more than doubled while Margaret Thatcher was in power during the 1980s, continued to rise more slowly in the 1990s, began to decline after 1998/99 but the decline more or less came to a halt after 2004-05.

Following the Prime Minister's announcement that poverty would be eradicated in 20 years, the government set targets to reduce child poverty by 25% in five years by 2004-05 and by 50% by 2010-11. They also established a set of child poverty indicators:

- *Relative poverty:* percentage of children falling below 60% of contemporary median income before and after housing costs (DWP, 2010, Table 4.1tr).
- *'Absolute' poverty:* percentage of children falling below 60% of 1998-99 median income held constant in real terms (DWP, 2010, Table 4.2tr).
- *Deprivation:* percentage of children falling below 70% of contemporary median income and a score of 25 or more on prevalence weighted material deprivation index (DWP, 2010, Table 4.5tr).
- *Persistent poverty:* percentage of children living below 60% of contemporary median income in three out of the last four years before and after housing costs (DWP, 2010, Table 7.1).

Table 3.1 summarises changes in the child poverty rate since the aspiration to eradicate child poverty was announced. With the exception of the deprivation measure (only introduced in 2004-05), child poverty has fallen on all the measures.

—

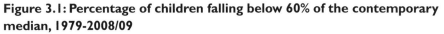

Figure 3.1: Percentage of children falling below 60% of the contemporary median, 1979-2008/09

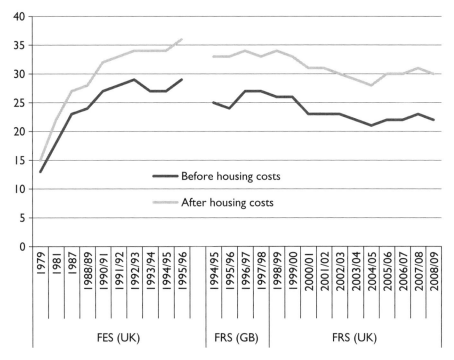

Notes: FES = Family Expenditure Survey; FRS = Family Resources Survey.
Source: DWP (2010, Table 4.1tr)

However, the government missed the target to reduce child poverty by a quarter by 2004-05 (the percentage of children falling below 60% of contemporary median income both before and after housing costs), and it is now more or less inevitable that the 2010 target to reduce child poverty by a half, using the same indicators, will be missed.

The child poverty statistics are based on analysis of the Family Resources Survey (FRS) and are inevitably out of date, but child poverty needs to fall by 1.1 million between 2008-09 and 2010-11 to meet the 2010 target of halving child poverty. Poor children may have benefited from the falling level of inflation in 2009-10, which meant that benefits and tax credits grew in real terms. The bringing forward of the April 2010 uprating of benefits and tax credits might also have helped, but this is likely to have been offset by growing unemployment in 2009-10 and increasing inflation in 2010. The Institute for Fiscal Studies (Brewer et al, 2009) predicted a fall in the number of children in poverty by a further 600,000 by 2010-11 given announced policies, but Joyce et al (2010) for the Institute now believe this prediction is too optimistic. Even if it was achieved, the number of children in poverty in 2010-11 would still exceed the target by 600,000.

Table 3.1: Trends in child poverty rates, % of children in the UK

	<60% contemporary median income		<60% 1998/99 median income		% with low income and material deprivation		<60% contemporary median income in at least three out of the last four years	
	Before housing costs	After housing costs	Before housing costs	After housing costs			Before housing costs	After housing costs
1998/99	26	34	26	34		1995-98	17	23
1999/00	26	33	23	31		1996-99	17	23
2000/01	23	31	19	27		1997-2000	17	22
2001/02	23	31	15	23		1998-2001	17	21
2002/03	23	30	14	21		1999-2002	16	20
2003/04	22	29	14	20		2000-03	14	17
2004/05	21	28	13	18	17	2001-04	12	15
2005/06	22	30	13	19	16	2002-05	11	16
2006/07	22	30	13	19	16	2003-06	10	14
2007/08	23	31	13	19	17	2004-07	10	15
2008/09	22	30	12	19	17			
% reduction	−15	−12	−54	−44	0		−52	−61

When the original child poverty strategy to eradicate child poverty by 2020 was announced by Tony Blair in 1999, the Department for Work and Pensions (DWP) set up a process to monitor progress. This was a set of statistics called *Opportunity for all* (DWP 2007), published annually after 1999. This series covered not only income poverty but also examined children living in workless households, health, education and housing. In all, there were 24 indicators covering children and young people. Unfortunately, the series was abandoned after 2007. By then the indicators had all become Public Service Agreement (PSA) targets and many were incorporated into the UK National Action Plan for Social Inclusion that the UK has to produce every two years for the EU (DWP, 2008). This is unfortunate, because in the UK national report, the indicators covering children are muddled with those for other groups and there is no time series, just an indication of the direction of the trend. However, many of the indicators are used in the chapters in this book. Meanwhile, of the 24 indicators covering children and young people by 2007, 14 had moved in the right direction from a baseline (usually 1997), three had stayed broadly constant, for three there was not enough consistent data and four indicators had moved in the wrong direction. The latter were:

• Education gap: a narrowing of the gap between the educational attainment and participation of looked-after children and their peers (see Chapter Six).

- Infant mortality: a reduction in the gap in mortality for children under one between routine and manual groups and the population as a whole (England and Wales) (see Chapter Four).
- Obesity: a reduction in the proportion of children aged 2-10 who are obese (England) (see Chapter Four).
- Child homelessness: a reduction in the number of families with children in temporary accommodation (England) (see Chapter Seven).

Country, regional and area variations in child poverty

The child poverty rates for the countries and regions of the UK are presented in Table 3.2. Scotland has a lower child poverty rate than the other countries in the UK; Wales and Northern Ireland have the highest rates before housing costs. After housing costs, Northern Ireland has a lower child poverty rate than England. In the English regions, the West Midlands and Inner London have the highest child poverty rates before and after housing costs.

Thanks to the work by the Social Deprivation Research Unit at the University of Oxford on the Index of Deprivation[1] there is now a very useful indicator of child poverty at small area level in England. From administrative statistics, they have derived an index of material well-being known as the Income Deprivation Affecting Children Index (IDACI). The index shows, by area, the proportion of children under 15 receiving the following means-tested benefits:

Table 3.2: Child poverty rates (<60% contemporary median) by country and region (three-year average, 2005-06 to 2008-09)

	Before housing costs	After housing costs
England	12	31
North East	13	34
North West	13	33
Yorkshire and the Humber	12	31
East Midlands	13	30
West Midlands	15	36
East of England	9	26
London	13	39
Inner	15	44
Outer	11	37
South East	8	26
South West	10	26
Scotland	11	25
Wales	13	32
Northern Ireland	13	26

Source: DWP (2010, Table 4.6)

- Children aged 0–15 in households claiming Income Support.
- Children aged 0–15 in households claiming income-based Jobseeker's Allowance.
- Children aged 0–15 in households claiming Pension Credit (Guarantee).
- Children aged 0–15 in households claiming Working Tax Credit in receipt of Child Tax Credit whose equivalised income (excluding housing benefits) is below 60% of the median before housing costs.
- Children aged 0–15 in households claiming Child Tax Credit (but not eligible for Income Support, income-based Jobseeker's Allowance, Pension Credit or Working Tax Credit) whose equivalised income (excluding housing benefits) is below 60% of the median before housing costs.

The IDACI is an improvement on previous DWP area-based benefit data because it includes HMRC (Her Majesty's Revenue & Customs) data on children in poor working families – families receiving Child Tax Credit with incomes less than 60% of the median.

Table 3.3 lists the 20 local authority districts in England with the highest and 20 with the lowest child poverty rates (IDACI scores). The district with the highest

Table 3.3: Child poverty rates by local authority districts in England, IDACI 2005

District	Child poverty rate %	District	Child poverty rate %
Tower Hamlets	66.5	Vale of White Horse	8.7
Hackney	52.7	Tandridge	8.7
Islington	52.2	Craven	8.6
Newham	51.5	Winchester	8.5
Haringey	50.1	Surrey Heath	8.5
Manchester	48.1	East Hertfordshire	8.4
Lambeth	43.2	Rushcliffe	8.2
Southwark	42.4	South Cambridgeshire	8.1
Nottingham	41.3	Mole Valley	8.0
Liverpool	41.2	West Oxfordshire	8.0
Camden	40.8	Waverley	7.9
Barking and Dagenham	40.7	Blaby	7.8
Greenwich	39.6	Uttlesford	7.7
Brent	39.6	Harborough	7.3
Birmingham	39.3	Wokingham	6.8
Waltham Forest	39.1	Ribble Valley	6.6
Leicester	38.7	Rutland	6.5
Hammersmith and Fulham	38.4	Hart	6.3
Westminster	37.9	Isles of Scilly	6.2
Lewisham	37.3	South Northamptonshire	6.0

Source: Own analysis of www.communities.gov.uk/documents/communities/ xls/576508.xls

child poverty rate by some margin is Tower Hamlets, with 66.5% of its children in poverty, and the district with the lowest is South Northamptonshire, with only 6% of its children in poverty.

The child poverty data is also available at lower layer super output areas (LSOAs).[2] Table 3.4 illustrates that certain of these areas have very high percentages of children in poverty – in one in Westminster nearly all the children (99.6%) are living in this situation. In contrast, another LSOA in Westminster has less than 1% of children in poverty.

It is possible to use this data to plot the degree of spatial concentration of child poverty. In Figure 3.2 the cumulative percentage of poor children is plotted against the cumulative percentage of LSOAs, and it can be seen that spatially, child poverty is heavily concentrated, with 80% of LSOAs containing only 36% of poor children and 10% of LSOAs containing over half of all poor children. However, there are some poor children in every LSOA and there are some affluent districts with LSOAs with child poverty. For example, even in wealthy South Northamptonshire there is an LSOA in which 19% of children are poor.

The IDACI spatial child poverty data can also be used to explore the correlates of child poverty. For a project linked to the Index of Deprivation 2007, Bradshaw et al (2009) developed an index of child well-being at small area level (local

Table 3.4: Child poverty rates by LSOA

Highest 20 child poverty rate LSOAs			Lowest 20 child poverty rate LSOAs		
District	LSOA	Child poverty rate %	District	LSOA	Child poverty rate %
Westminster	E01004722	99.6	Newcastle upon Tyne	E01016607	0.9
Manchester	E01005204	99.0	Leeds	E01018700	0.9
Manchester	E01005108	99.0	Ellesmere Port & Neston	E01008423	0.9
Westminster	E01004671	98.9	Westminster	E01011706	0.9
Manchester	E01005209	98.7	Wycombe	E01018530	0.9
Leicester	E01013755	98.6	Vale of White Horse	E01004692	0.9
Leicester	E01013754	98.6	North Hertfordshire	E01017875	0.9
Salford	E01005655	98.4	Salford	E01028747	0.9
Tower Hamlets	E01004252	98.2	St Albans	E01023614	0.8
Manchester	E01005067	98.2	Halton	E01005695	0.8
Birmingham	E01009488	97.8	St Albans	E01023700	0.8
Rochdale	E01005482	97.5	City of London	E01012375	0.8
Wolverhampton	E01010485	97.4	Rushcliffe	E01023675	0.8
Tower Hamlets	E01004215	97.2	Elmbridge	E01000002	0.8
Tower Hamlets	E01004214	97.0	Westminster	E01028388	0.8
Liverpool	E01006516	96.2	Warrington	E01030305	0.7
Newcastle upon Tyne	E01008380	95.8	Westminster	E01004689	0.7
Enfield	E01001424	94.7	Forest Heath	E01012447	0.7
Liverpool	E01006679	94.4	Forest Heath	E01004690	0.6

Source: Own analysis of www.communities.gov.uk/documents/communities/xls/576508.xls

Figure 3.2: Concentration of child poverty in LSOAs in England, 2005

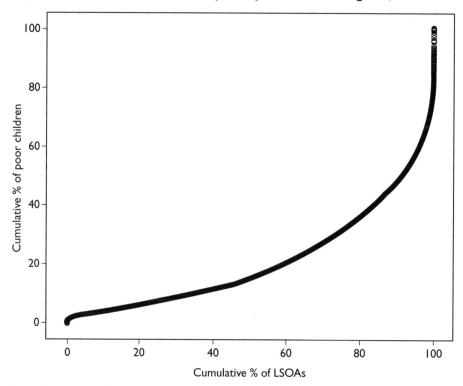

Source: Own analysis of www.communities.gov.uk/documents/communities/xls/576508.xls

authority district and LSOAs). The index was created from mainly administrative data covering six domains: material (the IDACI index), health, education, crime, housing and environment.

Table 3.5 shows the strength of the association between child poverty and the other domains at LSOA level. The strongest association between income poverty is with education (attainment and participation), but all the domains are associated with poverty, thus small areas with high poverty rates also have the worst housing conditions, the poorest child health and the highest crime rates. The lowest correlation, as one would expect, is with the environment, which was made up of two sub-domains, quality and access. Rural environments are better in terms of quality – air quality, green space, woodland, richness of bird species and lower numbers of road traffic accidents – but they do much less well in terms of access to facilities and services.

Table 3.5: Spatial association between poverty and other domains of well-being at LSOA level

Domains	Correlation coefficient
Education	0.80
Housing	0.63
Health	0.56
Crime	0.55
Environment	0.07

Notes: Spearman rank correlations; all coefficients are statistically significant at the <0.01 level.

Source: Bradshaw et al (2009, Table 4)

Characteristics of children in poverty

Table 3.6 provides a summary of the characteristics of children in poverty in the UK – both the composition and the rate. The data is based on the low income and material deprivation measure – on the grounds of greater reliability. However, the percentages are similar to the less than 60% of the median.

- Forty-seven per cent of poor children live with lone parents, and 33% of children living with lone parents are poor, but only 7% of children of lone parents are poor if the lone parents work full time.
- In couple families, children are very unlikely to be poor if both parents are in full-time employment – only 2%. If neither parent is employed, 57% of children are poor.
- Fifty-two per cent of all poor children are living in workless households.
- The risk of poverty is higher if there are three or more children in the family, but most children in poverty are in small families – 57% contain only one or two children.
- Having a disabled adult or a disabled child in the household increases the risk of poverty, but that risk is mitigated if the child is receiving a disability benefit.
- Seventy-seven per cent of poor children are in White families, but there is a much higher risk of poverty for children in Pakistani and Bangladeshi families and indeed all ethnic groups except Indian and Chinese.
- Sixty per cent of recipients of Jobseeker's Allowance and 57% of recipients of Income Support are poor, but only 48% of poor children are receiving either of these benefits.
- Children are more likely to be poor if the youngest child is under five – 50% of all poor children live in households with a child under five.
- The risk of poverty is much higher among children living in the social rented sector, but 26% of poor children are living in owner-occupied accommodation.
- Eighty per cent of poor children live in households with no savings and households with poor children are much more likely to be in arrears with household bills.

The Millennium Cohort Study (MCS) is another important source of data on child poverty. It is a sample of 19,000 births in 2000-01 and is particularly useful because, apart from its size, it has an enhanced sample of minority ethnic births and births in poor areas Mayhew and Bradshaw (2005), Bradshaw et al 2005, Ward et al (2007) and Bradshaw and Holmes (2010) have undertaken analysis of child poverty in the first three waves. In their analysis of the third wave, when individuals in the cohort were aged five, Bradshaw and Holmes (2010) created an indicator of poverty using an overlaps methodology. They assessed whether the child was:

- income poor using the less than 60% of the median threshold;
- deprived, lacking at least one out of five indicators of material deprivation;
- receiving a means-tested benefit; and/or
- subjectively poor – finding it difficult or very difficult to make ends meet.

Table 3.6: Characteristics of children in poverty (low income and material deprivation before housing costs), UK, 2008/09

	Composition (% of children in poverty living in this type of household)	Rate (% of children living in this type of household who are poor)
Economic status and family type		
Lone parent:	47	33
In full-time work	2	7
In part-time work	7	17
Not working	38	55
Couple with children:	53	12
Self-employed	4	6
Both in full-time work	1	2
One in full-time work, one in part-time work	4	3
One in full-time work, one not working	14	13
One or more in part-time work	12	35
Both not in work	18	57
Economic status of household		
All adults in work	16	5
At least one adult in work, but not all	33	20
Workless households	52	58
Number of children in family		
One child	21	13
Two children	36	14
Three or more children	42	27
Disability and receipt of disability benefits		
No disabled adult, no disabled child	63	14
No disabled adult, one or more disabled child(ren)	9	21
In receipt of disability benefits	2	15
Not in receipt of disability benefits	7	24
One or more disabled adult(s), no disabled child	20	28
In receipt of disability benefits	4	22
Not in receipt of disability benefits	16	30
One or more disabled adult(s), one or more disabled child(ren)	8	34
In receipt of disability benefits	2	23
Not in receipt of disability benefits	6	42
Ethnic group of head (3-year average)		
White	77	15
Mixed	2	23
Asian or Asian British	12	28
Indian	2	12
Pakistani and Bangladeshi	9	39
Black or Black British	7	31
Black Caribbean	2	22
Black non-Caribbean	5	36
Chinese or other ethnic group	2	17

(continued)

Table 3.6: Characteristics of children in poverty (low income and material deprivation before housing costs), UK, 2008/09 (continued)

	Composition (% of children in poverty living in this type of household)	Rate (% of children living in this type of household who are poor)
State support received by family		
Disability Living Allowance	8	22
Jobseeker's Allowance	9	60
Incapacity Benefit	6	36
Child Tax Credit	72	21
Working Tax Credit	23	19
Income Support	39	57
Housing Benefit	52	54
Not in receipt of any state support listed above	9	5
Age of youngest child in family		
0-4	50	19
5-10	28	16
11-15	19	16
16-19	4	10
Tenure		
Owners	26	7
Owned outright	5	8
Buying with mortgage	21	6
Social rented sector tenants	56	45
All rented privately	18	25
Savings and investments		
No savings	80	34
Less than £1,500	17	14
£1,500 but less than £3,000	2	5
£3,000 but less than £8,000	1	2
£8,000 but less than £10,000	0	0
£10,000 but less than £16,000	0	1
£16,000 but less than £20,000	0	0
£20,000 or more	0	0
Household bills in arrears		
No bills in arrears	53	11
One bill in arrears	17	40
Two or more bills in arrears	30	52
All children	100	17

Source: DWP (2010, Tables 4.3-4.6)

They also assessed the 'reliably poor', the percentage poor on three or more of these dimensions. Families are generally more likely to be poor if there is only one parent, a large number of children or there are no earners. Families are significantly less likely to be in any definition of poverty if:

• there are two natural parents who are married;
• the cohort member is of white or Indian ethnicity;
• the family lives in owner-occupied housing;
• there are two earners; or
• the mother has tertiary level education; or
• is over 30 at the cohort child's birth.

Of course, many of these characteristics overlap, and so in Table 3.7 multivariate logistic regression was used to explore the logistic odds of being poor on three or more dimensions, after controlling for the other variables. After controlling for other characteristics, the odds of being poor are higher, if:

• there are two or more children in the household, compared with only one;
• the family has two natural parents where at least one parent is not employed compared to two parents being in employment;
• natural parents are cohabiting rather than married;
• a natural mother is living with a stepfather, compared with married natural parents, particularly if they are not both employed;
• the child is living with a lone mother, compared with natural married parents, whether or not the mother is in employment;
• the mother is aged under 30 compared with 35+ at the birth of the cohort child;
• the mother is of Pakistani, Bangladeshi, Black or black British ethnicity rather than White or Indian ethnicity;
• the mother's educational level is less than lower tertiary (NVQ Level 3 or below) compared with NVQ Level 5;
• the family's situation is not that of owner-occupier.

Child poverty dynamics

It is arguable that a brief experience of living in poverty is less likely to be harmful to children than a long episode. The main source of data on persistent poverty is the British Household Panel Survey (BHPS) and it is inevitably somewhat out of date. It can be seen in Table 3.1 that in 2007, 10% of children before housing costs and 15% after housing costs had been living in poverty in at least three out of the last four years. It also shows that there had been a welcome decline in the prevalence of persistent poverty between 1998-99 and 2007.

Bradshaw and Holmes (2010) traced changes in poverty over the first three waves of the MCS using two dimensions of poverty for which there was consistent data – income poverty and subjective poverty. They found a remarkable consistency

—

Table 3.7: Multivariate logistic regression of the family being poor at MCS 3

	Odds ratios
Number of children in household	
I	1.00
2	1.18*
3	1.58***
4+	1.93***
Combined family status and earners	
Married natural parents – two earners	1.00
Married natural parents – one earner	2.70***
Married natural parents – 0 earner	6.18***
Cohabiting natural parents – two earners	1.38*
Cohabiting natural parents – one earner	3.34***
Cohabiting natural parents – 0 earner	9.66***
Natural mother and stepfather – two earners	2.31***
Natural mother and stepfather – one earner	4.85***
Natural mother and stepfather – 0 earner	7.67***
Lone natural mother – one earner	8.65***
Lone natural mother – 0 earner	25.38***
Mother's age at birth	
35+	1.00
30-34	0.88 NS
25-29	1.03 NS
20-24	1.29**
Under 20	1.14 NS
Ethnicity	
White	1.00
Mixed	1.23 NS
Indian	1.20 NS
Pakistani and Bangladeshi	3.08***
Black or Black British	1.31*
Other ethnic groups	2.60***
Mother's highest qualification	
NVQ Level 5	1.00
NVQ Level 4	1.05 NS
NVQ Level 3	1.83***
NVQ Level 2	1.99***
NVQ Level I	2.24***
No recognised qualifications	2.93***
Housing tenure	
Owner-occupier	1.00
Social housing	3.46***
Private rented/other	2.21**

Note: *p<0.05, **p<0.01, ***p<0.001

over MCS sweeps. Poverty rates went down between MCS sweeps 1 and 2 and up again between sweeps 2 and 3, but the differences were very small and not statistically significant. They concluded that there was likely to be no reduction in poverty for this sample as a whole in the first five years of the children's lives.

However, individual families had quite varied experiences. In terms of persistence, 39% of families experienced income poverty, 57.5% subjective poverty and 27.9% were poor in both respects in at least one of the first three sweeps of the MCS. Only 13.8% were income poor, 15.8% subjectively poor and 4.9% were poor in both respects in all three sweeps. Alongside a 'core' group in persistent poverty, a much wider group reported at least one type of poverty at any of the sweeps – more than half of all families and around twice the proportion of families in income poverty at any one time.

Intergenerational transmission of child poverty

There is really no satisfactory data on intergenerational transmission of child poverty in the UK, although there is evidence from the analysis of cohort studies (Blanden and Machin, 2007), shown in Table 3.8, that the links between the relative incomes of children and their parents appear to have strengthened between those born in 1958 and 1970.

Also, the links between the income of parents and the educational attainment level of their children shown in Table 3.9 may have widened (Blanden and Machin, 2007).

Table 3.8: Links between parents' income group and son's earnings 1958 and 1970

		Parent's income group	
Son's earnings at 33/34 (%)		**Bottom 25%**	**Top 25%**
In bottom 25%	Born 1958	30	18
	Born 1970	37	13
In top 25%	Born 1958	18	35
	Born 1970	13	45

Table 3.9: Links between parents' income and educational attainment

	Parent's income group	
Degree by age 23 (%)	**Bottom 20%**	**Top 20%**
Born 1958	5	20
Born 1970	7	37
Born around 1975	11	40
Born around 1979	10	44

Children's views

The best study of the views of children living in poverty is still by Tess Ridge (2002, and also 2005 and 2009), who interviewed children living in families dependent on Income Support. Among her findings she noted the following striking observations:

—

- the extent to which children seek to protect their parents from their own feelings of deprivation, sometimes including hunger;
- the extent to which they feel unable to invite their friends for meals or to stay;
- the importance of grandparents and other relatives in providing extras that mitigate the deprivation in their lives;
- the costs and inconvenience of public transport, particularly in rural areas, which restricts their lives;
- the value of holiday schemes that give children the chance to get away;
- the sense of shame and embarrassment when they are unable to dress like their peers;
- their experience of schools as exclusionary – their inability to go on trips and outings, to contribute to school funds, to dress well and the frequent identification as 'free dinner' children.

In a national school-based survey in England undertaken for The Children's Society of over 6,000 10- and 12-year-olds, Rees et al (2010a) asked 'How happy are you about the things you have?'. The responses were recorded on an 11-point scale, from very unhappy to very happy. The mean score was 8.1, indicating a negatively skewed distribution (that is, most children are happy), with only 5.7% scoring below the middle of the distribution. The older children were less happy, but there was no variation in levels of happiness with the things they had by gender, ethnicity, religious affiliation or disability. However, there was a fairly strong association between happiness with the things they had and overall well-being – the correlation was 0.52, the third highest after happiness with their families and happiness about the amount of choice they had in life, and more important than, for example, happiness with their appearance, health and friends.

Poverty and social exclusion

Although there has been no Poverty and Social Exclusion Survey since 1999 (one is planned for 2011), the Social Exclusion Task Force of the Cabinet Office launched a project on '*Understanding social exclusion across the life course*', and one of the four life course studies focused on families with children (Oroyemi et al, 2009). This project attempted to operationalise the Bristol Social Exclusion Matrix (B-SEM), and used data from the Families and Children Study (FACS). Eighteen markers of risk were constructed from the data, ranging from income poverty to lack of social contact to overcrowded accommodation. They found that 45% of families with children were exposed to multiple risk markers (that is, two or more markers of risk) in 2006, with only a small proportion (less than 2%) experiencing 10 or more risks. Cluster analysis was used to group families into relatively homogeneous 'clusters'. This produced nine distinct clusters of multiple risk families, including:

- 'severely excluded families' (5%) who had an average of nine risk markers;

- 'materially deprived families with no private transport' (8% of families);
- 'families living in poor housing with debts' (4%).

The most at-risk families were more likely to have lone or younger parents, four or more children, live in rented accommodation and live in the most deprived areas.

Children from the most at-risk families also experienced low levels of well-being, and their risks often reflected those of their parents. For example, children with parents in ill health also had disproportionately high rates of illness and children who lacked the use of internet facilities at home were more likely to come from poorer families and have parents with lower levels of education.

Using the longitudinal element of FACS, which 'follows' the same families over time, they found that more families experienced singular, and multiple, forms of risk over a six-year period than 'point-in-time' estimates would suggest. This would indicate that risk touches more families, and children, than estimates based on yearly data imply. A small proportion of families (between 4% and 7%) were found to experience persistent multiple risk.

Families who experienced persistent multiple risk were more likely to be lone parents, those with four or more children, young mothers, mothers from Black ethnic groups, social tenants and those living in urban areas. Families who were successful in making a transition out of multiple risk had experienced events such as partnering and entering employment. On the other hand, moves into multiple risk, or between risk clusters, were generally associated with becoming unemployed, experiencing family separation, lone-parent status, mothers with low levels of education, younger mothers and social and private tenants.

International comparisons of child poverty

There are three main sources of international comparative data on child poverty: the OECD collects data from national governments approximately every five years and their latest analysis was for circa 2005, published in *Growing unequal?* (OECD, 2008); the Luxembourg Income Study (LIS) collects together national micro-social data and makes them available for analysts and they also publish their own summary statistics in LIS Key Figures (their most recent data is for mid-2000s); and for European countries, the Statistics on Income and Living Conditions (EU-SILC) has replaced the European Community Household Panel Survey (ECHP) and become a major resource, with data published on the Eurostat data base and for secondary analysis.

The most current data available is from EU-SILC 2008 (2007 income data), and most of the analysis in this section is based on EU-SILC 2008. However, because EU-SILC only developed after 2005, we turn first, for an historical picture, to the OECD data in Figure 3.3. Between the mid-1990s and mid-2000s most countries in the OECD experienced an increase in their child poverty rates. The UK was one of only seven countries where child poverty decreased, although this reduction was from a comparatively high level. Figure 3.3 uses the latest available

—

Figure 3.3: Percentage point change in child poverty rate between the mid-1990s and the mid-2000s (% of children living in households with equivalent income less than 50% median)

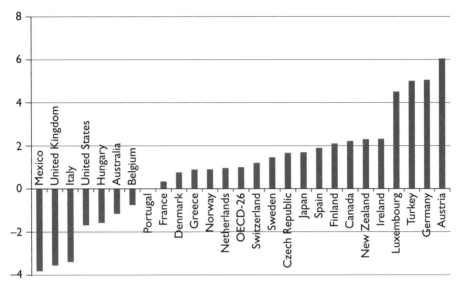

Source: OECD (2009a, CO2.2.B) (www.oecd.org/document/4/0,3343,en_2649_34819_37836996_1_1_1_1,00.html)

Figure 3.4: Poverty rates – countries ranked by child poverty rate (equivalent income less than 60% median), 2008 or 2009

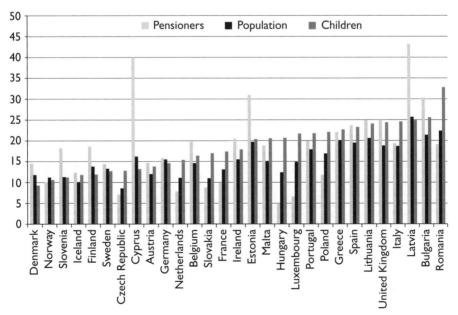

Source: Eurostat Data Explorer accessed 10/11/10 (2009 [2008 incomes] data except 2008 for Bulgaria, Denmark, Ireland, Greece, France, Italy, Cyprus, Poland, UK and Iceland)

EU–SILC data to compare the child poverty rates in the EU countries with the pensioner and population poverty rates. The UK has the fifth from highest child poverty rate out of these 29 European countries. Like all but seven countries, the UK child poverty rate is higher than its population poverty rate. The child poverty rate in the UK is similar to the pensioner poverty rate.

One reason why the UK has a comparatively high child poverty rate is that it has the highest proportion of children living in workless households – 15.5% in 2008 (see Figure 3.5). Of course one reason for this is the comparatively high proportion of lone parents in the UK, as we saw in Chapter Two, and their low work intensity (see below).

It is arguable that of equal importance to the poverty rate is the poverty gap – how far below the poverty threshold poor children are living. Figure 3.6 compares the mean poverty gap for these countries. The UK does rather better in the league table of the gap measure, at 19%. This is considerably better than Bulgaria, where poor children live 41% below their (very low) poverty threshold, but it is not as good as Iceland, where the mean poverty gap is only 12.2% of the poverty threshold.

This analysis is based on the conventional 60% of median income poverty threshold, but leaves much to be desired, especially in comparative analysis.

Figure 3.5: The proportion of children in households with zero work intensity, 2008

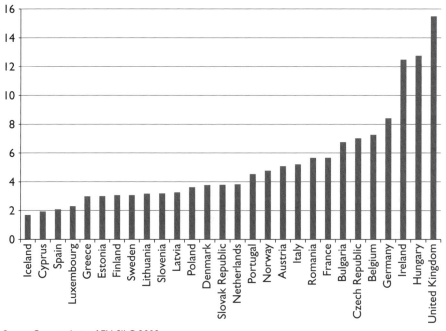

Source: Own analysis of EU-SILC 2008

Figure 3.6: Child poverty gaps (mean % difference between net income and the poverty threshold for those in poverty, equivalent income less than 60% median), 2008 or 2009

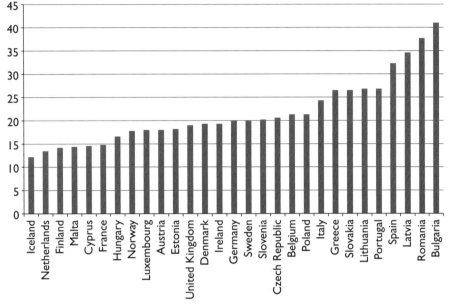

Source: Eurostat Data Explorer accessed 10/11/10 (2009 [2008 incomes] data except 2008 for Bulgaria, Denmark, Ireland, Greece, France, Italy, Cyprus, Poland, UK and Iceland)

- It is hard for non-experts to understand what is meant by 'x% of the population live in households with disposable income less than 60% of the national median equivalised household income'. It does not resonate with persuasive power or credibility.
- Income is only an indirect indicator of living standards.
- It is probably not as good an indicator of command over resources as expenditure, not least because it does not take account of the capacity to borrow, dissavings, gifts and the value of home production.
- The 60% of the median (and any other) income threshold is arbitrary. It is not related to any understanding of need but is merely a line drawn on the income distribution.
- The equivalence scale adopted which is used to adjust income to household need – the modified OECD scale – has no basis in science (and has been abandoned by the OECD who now use the square root of the number of people in the household).

There are limitations of a relative income measure in a comparative context:

- The EU publishes estimates of the monetary value of the poverty threshold in Purchasing Power Parity (PPP) standards. This reveals that we are not comparing like with like when we compare poverty rates between countries using this threshold. So, for example, the relative poverty threshold for a couple with two children in Estonia in 2008 was €9,770 PPP standards per year and in the UK €24,380 per year. The at-risk-of-poverty rate in both countries was 19%. Yet, the poor in Estonia, even taking into account differences in purchasing power, were living at much lower levels.

- In many of the countries, including many using the 60% of the median as their poverty threshold, the cash value of the threshold is very low. The threshold for a couple with two children in 2008 in PPP terms per person per day was €1.71 in Romania and €2.22 in Bulgaria per person per day.

It is for some of these reasons that the European Commission has developed a variety of poverty measures, including:

- at-risk-of-poverty rates at different thresholds (40%, 50%, 60% and 70% of the national median equivalised household income);
- an at-risk-of-poverty gap;
- an at-risk-of-poverty rate 'anchored' at a point in time;
- a persistent at-risk-of-poverty rate;
- a material deprivation indicator. (In 2009, the Social Protection Committee [SPC] adopted a set of indicators and context information on housing and material deprivation.)

More recently, in 2010, the European Council adopted an EU target to lift at least 20 million people out of poverty by 2020. Three poverty thresholds are being prioritised here:

- at-risk-of-poverty – the population living in households with equivalent income less than 60% of the median; or
- material deprivation – the population living in households lacking four or more of nine indicators;[3]
- people living in jobless households – no one working or work intensity of household is below 0.2.

The target is still dominated by the relative income measure in that 80 million people in the EU are living below 60% of median income, whereas only 40 million are living below the other thresholds.

There is a strong case for moderating the relative income measure with two other indicators of poverty – deprivation and subjective poverty. In the richer EU countries there are many households with incomes below 60% of the median that are not lacking any deprivation indicator and say they do not have any difficulty making ends meet. The next section of this chapter employs an 'overlaps' (Bradshaw and Finch, 2003) measure of child poverty to see how the UK compares with the rest of the EU.

—

Figure 3.7 gives the child poverty rate using the three different thresholds:

- percentage of children living in households with income less than 60% of the median;
- percentage of children living in households finding it difficult or very difficult to make ends meet (subjective);
- percentage of children in households lacking three or more deprivation items from a composite index;[4]
- percentage of children living in households poor on *all* of the above indicators.

Comparatively, the UK does rather better on its child poverty rate using the subjective and deprivation measures, and when all three are combined, comes in the middle of the EU league table of child poverty.

Figure 3.7: Overlaps of child poverty by three dimensions, 2008

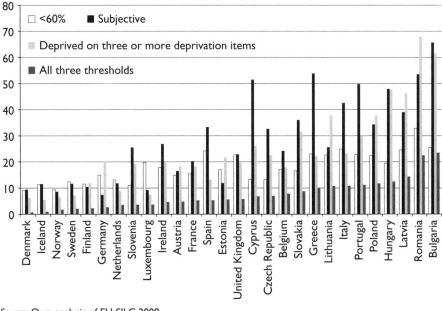

Source: Own analysis of EU-SILC 2008

Figure 3.8 compares the family composition of children living in households that are poor on all three dimensions. It can be see that after Denmark the UK has the highest proportion of lone parents (16.2%). The large proportions of 'other' in some of the poorer EU countries results from the families living in multi-unit households.

Figure 3.9 compares the work intensity of families and poor children and confirms that the UK has a particular problem of worklessness, with the highest proportion of poor children in workless families and many more in part-time

Figure 3.8: Family composition of households poor on three dimensions, 2008

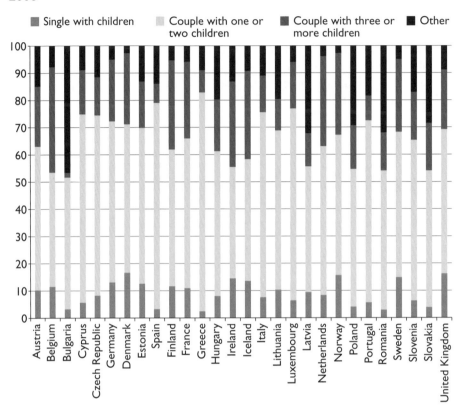

Source: Own analysis of EU-SILC 2008

work. In contrast, the UK has a rather smaller proportion of poor children in families in full-time work than most other countries.

So comparatively, child poverty in the UK is lower than it has been. However, there is still a comparatively high proportion of children living in relative poverty in the UK. This is partly the result of the high proportion of children living in workless households, but also the tax benefit system has been relatively unsuccessful in mitigating the child poverty that is generated by the marketplace. This is illustrated in Figure 3.10, which compares the child poverty rates before and after transfers. Before transfer income is income from the marketplace – mainly earnings. After transfer income is after the impact of taxes and benefits (but not services). It can be seen that the variation in child poverty rates before transfers is much less than after and that, for example, the UK and Austria have very similar child poverty rates before transfers but after transfers Austria has reduced its child poverty rate by 66% whereas the UK has reduced it by only 41%. This is a better rate of poverty reduction than some other countries, but it could still be much more effective. Policy does matter.

Figure 3.9: Work intensity of households with children poor on three dimensions, 2008

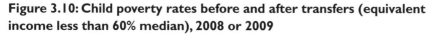

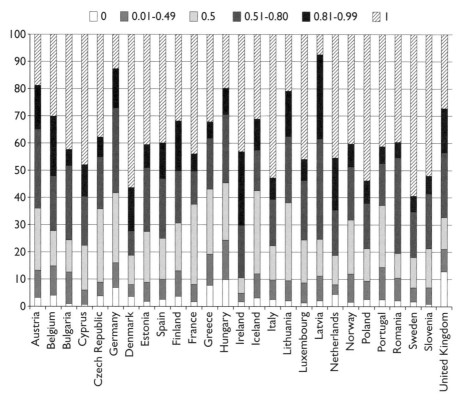

Source: Own analysis of EU-SILC 2008

Figure 3.10: Child poverty rates before and after transfers (equivalent income less than 60% median), 2008 or 2009

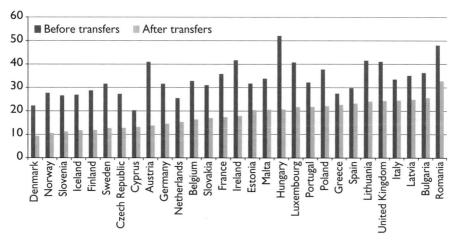

Source: Eurostat Data Explorer accessed 10/11/10 (2009 [2008 incomes] data except 2008 for Bulgaria, Denmark, Ireland, Greece, France, Italy, Cyprus, Poland, UK and Iceland)

Comparisons of material well-being and other domains at an international level

In their comparison of variation in child well-being in the EU, Bradshaw and Richardson (2009) produced an index of material well-being by combining indicators of deprivation, indicators of child income poverty and children living in workless families. The UK came 24 out of 29 European countries in the material well-being domain. Bradshaw and Richardson then explored the association between material well-being and the other domains of well-being. It can be seen in Table 3.11 that there are statistically significant associations with all the domains except relationship (with family and friends), the strongest association being with education.

Bradshaw and Richardson's study combined these domains into an index of overall well-being and then explored the relationship between material well-being and the overall index without including material well-being. Figure 3.11 shows the result – there is a strong association between material well-being and the other domains of well-being formed into a single index – poverty matters. However, the proportion of well-being explained by overall well-being at national level is only 53%, and there are outlier countries where the relationship is less strong. Child poverty does not explain it all. Similar analysis has been produced by the OECD (2009a) and by Bradshaw and Richardson (2008) using data from the UNICEF Innocenti Report Card no 7.

Table 3.11: Correlations between the domains of well-being in the EU

Domain	Correlation coefficient
Education	0.64***
Risk	0.59**
Housing	0.56**
Health	0.52**
Subjective	0.45*
Relationships	0.20

Notes: ***p < 0.001, **p < 0.01, *p < 0.05.

Source: Bradshaw and Richardson (2009, Table 8)

Conclusion

Child poverty has declined since the Labour government came to power in 1997. Nevertheless, it is still double the level it was in 1979, and the government missed its targets to reduce child poverty by a quarter in five years and by a half in 10 years. It is still comparatively high in the UK compared to other countries in the EU. The proportion of children living in workless families is also comparatively high and has not changed much since 1997, despite the fact that until 2009 unemployment was at the lowest level for decades and the employment rates at record levels. But worklessness is only part of the problem. The majority of children in poverty have a parent in employment, wages are too low and the tax and benefit system is not sufficiently effective at reducing child poverty.

One very welcome development is the Child Poverty Act, passed with all party agreement in 2010. It sets new targets for 2020:

―

Figure 3.11: Overall child well-being versus material well-being

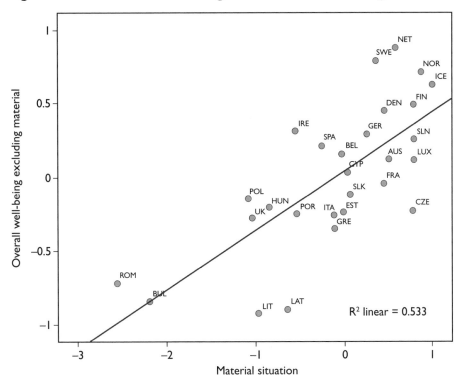

Source: Bradshaw and Richardson 2009

- A rate of relative income child poverty lower than 10% – the latest rate is 21%.
- Less than 5% of children having an income less than 70% median and suffering material deprivation – the latest rate is 10%.
- Less than 5% of children living in households with an income less than 60% of the 2010–11 median income – the current rate is not available but the equivalent latest rate is 12%.
- The persistent poverty target is yet to be specified – the latest actual rate is 10%.

The government is required to publish a strategy to reduce child poverty by March 2011.

However, we are now only tentatively emerging from a recession and facing a massive deficit. The Coalition government published an Emergency Budget in June 2010 and the results of the Comprehensive Spending Review in October 2010. Between them these contain a long list of measures that will affect families with children. It will take some time to make a full assessment of the overall impact of this package and also the impact on poor children of cuts in capital spending, general central and local government services (such as Sure Start), and the loss of 500,000 public sector jobs. Overall, the distributional consequences of the measures are regressive (Browne and Levell, 2010) (although the government seeks to deny this). The Coalition government has claimed that the Spending Review will have no 'measurable' impact on child poverty in the next two years.

The national and international sources available to monitor child poverty have improved since our last volume (Bradshaw and Mayhew, 2005) – both HBAI and EU–SILC are excellent. There is going to be a special extra module in EU–SILC 2009 on child well-being, with extra child deprivation questions. This is a one-off exercise and if these questions prove useful, it is to be hoped that they will be incorporated into subsequent SILCs. A new Poverty and Social Exclusion Survey is being launched in 2011 with many new child socially perceived necessities items, and if these prove useful they could be incorporated into future FRS and FACS. The decision to end the updating of *Opportunity for all* after 2007 is to be regretted, however, and we attempt our own update in the final chapter of this book (see Chapter Thirteen).

Notes

[1] www.communities.gov.uk/documents/communities/xls/576508.xls

[2] LSOAs are 32,482 geographical, spatially contiguous areas with a mean population of 1,500 and minimum of 1,000 that are designed, using the 2001 Census outputs, to be relatively socially homogeneous and constrained to 2003 ward boundaries.

[3] The EU uses the so-called Guio index containing nine items: cannot afford to pay rent or utility bills; keep home adequately warm; pay unexpected expenses; eat meat, fish or equivalent every second day; a week's holiday away from home once a year; a car; washing machine; colour television; telephone.

[4] We have developed a 'composite index'. As well as the nine Guio items, it includes three housing dimensions: leaking roof/damp walls/floors/foundations or rot in the window frames; no bath or shower; no indoor flushing toilet for sole use of the household.

FOUR

Physical health

Jonathan Bradshaw and Karen Bloor

Key statistics

- The UK infant mortality and low birth weight rates remain comparatively high compared with rich countries.
- The child mortality and child accidental death rates are comparatively low.
- Northern Ireland has a higher child mortality rate than the rest of the UK.
- Immunisation rates for infectious diseases are low.
- Breastfeeding rates are low.
- With the exception of physical exercise, most health behaviour is comparatively poor.
- Sexually transmitted diseases have increased rapidly.
- The UK will fail to meet its target on teenage pregnancy.
- Self-assessed health is comparatively poor.

Key trends

- The long-term downward trend in infant and child mortality continues and the infant mortality rate for 2009 was the lowest ever recorded.
- The social class gap in infant mortality has been growing since 1996-98.
- Cancer has overtaken accidents as the main cause of child deaths.
- Immunisation rates have begun to recover, but there have been recent epidemics of measles and mumps.
- Breastfeeding rates have improved.
- The incidence of deaths and serious injuries on the roads has continued to decline.
- Health behaviour has been improving. The exception is early sexual activity, although teenage conceptions have fallen slightly.
- The upwards trend in sexually transmitted diseases may be levelling off.
- There is tentative evidence that obesity rates may be falling.
- Self-assessed health has been improving.

Key sources

- Office for National Statistics (ONS)
- Department of Health (DH)
- Health Survey for England (HSE)

- OECD (Organisation for Economic Co-operation and Development) Health Database
- Health Behaviour of School-aged Children (HBSC) Survey
- Department for Transport (DfT)
- Child and Maternal Health Observatory (ChiMat)

Introduction

This chapter focuses on the physical health of children and their health behaviour, while the following chapter focuses on emotional and mental health. The topics covered include child and infant mortality, birth weight, immunisations, self-reported health, longstanding illnesses and chronic conditions, non–intentional accidents and injuries (also covered with a different perspective in Chapter Ten), HIV/AIDS, sexual health and teenage conceptions. Under health behaviour we cover smoking and alcohol consumption, diet, obesity and physical activity. In the main, the analysis is restricted to children aged 16 or under, although in respect of sexual health, we report data on young people aged 16-19.

Infant and child mortality

Official mortality statistics distinguish between six types of infant mortality:

- perinatal: stillbirths plus neonatal deaths;
- early neonatal deaths: deaths up to six completed days of life;
- late neonatal: deaths at 7–27 completed days of life;
- post-neonatal: deaths at 28 days and over but under one year;
- infant deaths: deaths aged under one year;
- child mortality: deaths aged 1–14 years.

Early and late neonatal deaths are usually presented together as neonatal deaths, and stillbirths are often presented separately. Child mortality is commonly presented in three age groups, 1-4, 5-9 and 10-14 years.

A number of detailed analyses of factors related to mortality have been carried out, particularly by staff at ONS, but many of these analyses only cover figures for England and Wales or the whole of the UK, without disaggregation by country or region. One of the reasons for this is that when disaggregated, the numbers for each country are small, making it difficult to conduct reliable analyses.

Trends in mortality

Mortality rates are highest just after birth. They then fall in the post-neonatal period and during childhood, with the lowest rates between the ages of five and nine. Figure 4.1 shows a general downward trend in mortality. The rate of decline has been slower since the 1990s than the 1980s. The exception is the stillbirth

Figure 4.1: Stillbirths and mortality rates, England/Wales

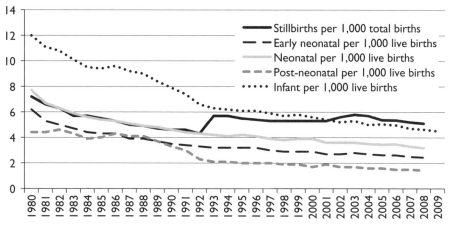

Source: ONS (2010a, Table 1; 2010b)

rate which increased in 1993 and again in 2002. The former increase is due to a change in definition – up to 1992, stillbirths were foetal deaths at or over 28 weeks gestation, and from 1993 at or over 24 weeks gestation. The increase in 2002 occurred in all countries except Scotland. An investigation (ONS, 2003) found this was due to a sharp increase in stillbirths to sole registration births outside marriage, but the reasons for this are not known.

A similar trend is observed in Figure 4.2 for child mortality – a downward trend with smaller rates of reduction since the early 1990s.

Figure 4.2: Child mortality per 100,000 of the same age, England/Wales, 2008

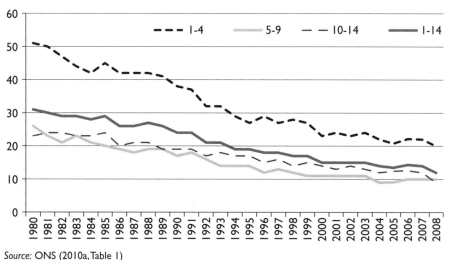

Source: ONS (2010a, Table 1)

Table 4.1 compares the stillbirth, infant mortality and child mortality rates in the countries of the UK. Scotland has a slightly higher rate of stillbirths and Northern Ireland a slightly higher rate of infant deaths, but these rates fluctuate from year to year and are not consistently different. However, Northern Ireland has a higher rate of child deaths.

The latest comparative data on child mortality is for 2006. Figure 4.3 shows that the UK has an infant mortality rate above the middle of the European Union (EU) distribution and nearly twice the level of Iceland, which has the lowest rate by some margin. Some of this variation in infant mortality could be the result of differences in the quality of antenatal and perinatal care and in the rates of

Table 4.1: Stillbirth, infant mortality and child mortality rates in the UK, 2008

	Stillbirths per 1,000 total births	Infant deaths per 1,000 births	1-14 mortality per 100,000 in age group
United Kingdom	5.1	4.6	13
England	5.1	4.6	12
Wales	4.6	4.0	11
Scotland	5.4	4.2	13
Northern Ireland	4.5	4.7	18

Source: ONS (2010a, Table 2)

Figure 4.3: Infant mortality rates (deaths before the age of 12 months per 1,000 births) in the EU, 2006

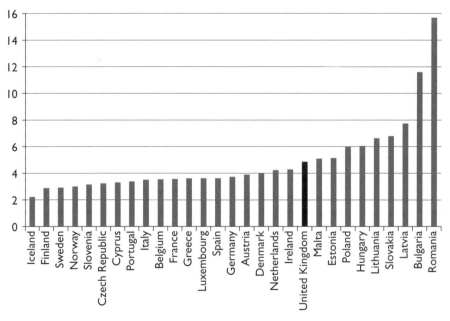

Source: World Development Indicators (WDI) 2006

—

smoking during pregnancy (Richardus et al, 2003). Child deaths are comparatively low in the UK (see Figure 4.4); this is probably attributable to relatively low rates of road traffic accidents (see below).

Figure 4.4: All under-19 deaths per 100,000 children, three year averages

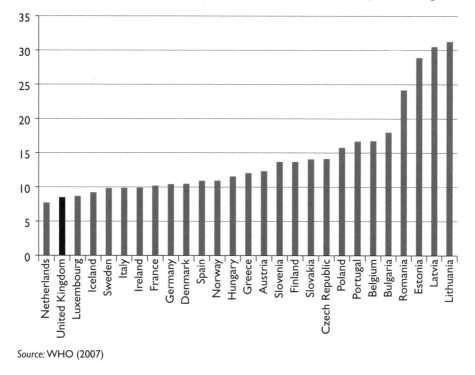

Source: WHO (2007)

There is a strong association at an international level between poverty and infant mortality. Figure 4.5 shows the association between the infant mortality rate and poverty in the EU countries using as an indicator of poverty the proportion of households lacking three or more deprivation items.

Causes of infant and child mortality

The main causes of infant deaths (under one year) are conditions in the perinatal period (related to immaturity) and congenital malformations. Sudden infant deaths have declined and were only 5.3% of all infant deaths in England and Wales in 2008 (ONS, 2010b, Table 8).

For children aged 1-14 the most common causes of death in 2008 were cancers. They have overtaken external causes (including injuries and poisonings) as the main cause of death, although both have been declining. The next most important cause is congenital malformations (ONS, 2010a, Table 4).

Figure 4.5: Association between the infant mortality rate, 2006, and percentage of households lacking three or more deprivation items

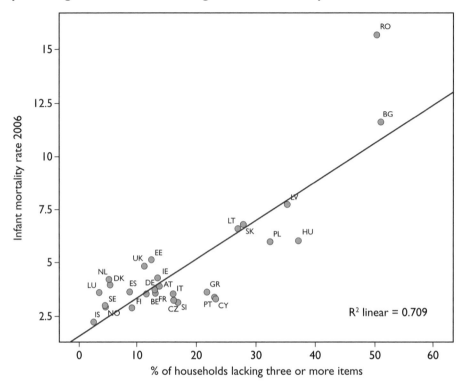

Source: Own analysis of EU-SILC 2008 and WDI 2006

Key factors associated with mortality

- Parity: overall infant mortality was 4.1 per 1,000 in 2009 for all births inside marriage. It was higher for fourth and subsequent births, at 6.1 per 1,000 (ONS, 2010b, Table 6).
- Gender: boys have higher mortality rates than girls at all ages. In 2008, the UK infant mortality rates were 5.1 per 1,000 for boys compared with 4.1 per 1,000 for girls. The child mortality rates (per 1,000,000 1–14) were 14 for boys compared to 12 for girls (ONS, 2010a, Table 2). All countries and regions of the UK show the same pattern.
- Occupational group: despite the decline in infant mortality, there is still a class gradient. Among births inside marriage the infant mortality rate in socioeconomic group 1.1[1] was 3.3 per 1,000 compared with 5.6 in the routine and manual groups (5, 6 and 7) (ONS, 2010b, Table 7). One of the *Opportunity for all* indicators was the differential in the infant mortality rate between routine and manual social groups and all other groups. The differential was falling up until 1996-98 but increased after that and the last ratio for 2003-05 was 1.18

– that is, the infant mortality for routine and manual was 18% higher than for all. The ratio in 2009 has widened further to 36%.

- Age of mother: infant mortality rates vary by mother's age and are highest for mothers aged under 20 (6.0 per 1,000 live births) in England and Wales in 2009. The next highest rates are births to mothers over 40 (5.8 per 1,000) and the lowest are to mothers aged 30-34 (3.9 per 1,000) (ONS, 2010b, Table 4).
- Marital status: infant mortality rates are higher for births to unmarried mothers (5.5 per 1,000) where the birth is a sole registration and 5.6 per 1,000 for a joint registration outside marriage at different addresses (ONS, 2010b, Table 6).
- Country of birth: Table 4.1 has already compared mortality by country in the UK, but it also varies by country of birth of the mother. The highest infant mortality is found in births to mothers born in East Africa, at 8.9 per 1,000, Caribbean, at 8.4 per 1,000 and Pakistan, at 7.9 per 1,000. The overall rate for mothers born in the new Commonwealth is 6.3 per 1,000 compared with 4.2 per 1,000 for mothers born in England and Wales (ONS, 2010b, Table 5).

Birth weight

Birth weight is one of the main indicators of the outcome of pregnancy, and low birth weight is a well-established risk factor for immediate and long-term health problems (Macfarlane et al, 2004). The World Health Organization (WHO) defines a birth weight of less than 2,500g as a low birth weight. Births under 2,500g made up 67% of all stillbirths and 61% of all infant mortality in England and Wales in 2009 (ONS, 2010b, Table 2).

Compared with other countries, the UK has a comparatively high rate of low birth weight, although there is generally an increasing proportion of babies being born with low birth weight in most other countries (see Figure 4.6). One factor contributing to this variation and to the trend is likely to be the increasing survival rates of pre-term infants. However, as the gestational age of live births is not recorded, it is not possible to explore this association.

Factors associated with low birth weight

Unsurprisingly, given the association between low birth weight and stillbirth and infant mortality, the factors associated with low birth weight are very similar. Overall 7.1% of live births were under 2,500g. But the proportion was higher for:

- births to mothers under the age of 20 (8.1%) and over 40 (8.8%);
- births to mothers born in the new Commonwealth (9.3%), in Bangladesh (10.7%), Pakistan (9.7%) and the Caribbean (9.8%);
- jointly registered births with a socioeconomic classification of 1.1, the percentage of low birth weight is 5.5, the proportion rises for each social group, and is 8.7% for socioeconomic groups 7 and 8. It is 7.7% for sole registrations.

Figure 4.6: Low birth weight births (<2,500g), European OECD countries, ranked by 2000

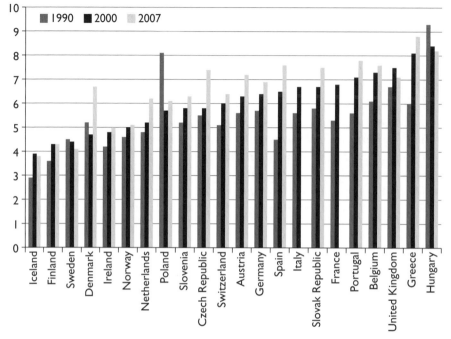

Source: OECD (2010a)

Analysis of the Millennium Cohort Study (MCS) on birth weight is in line with these findings. Bradshaw and Mayhew (2005) found that after controlling for other factors, the risk of low birth weight was higher for mothers in poverty, underweight mothers, mothers who smoked in pregnancy, first births and mothers from minority ethnic groups. However, having controlled for these factors, marital status and where they lived in the UK were not associated with low birth weight.

Infant feeding

The benefits of breastfeeding to a baby's health are well documented and include increased immunity to infection and hence lower susceptibility to illness, which in turn results in reduced mortality. Breastfed babies are less likely to suffer from conditions such as gastroenteritis, chest infections, ear infections, diabetes in childhood and childhood obesity (Ip et al, 2007; Quigley et al, 2007). In addition, breastfeeding offers protection against chronic conditions such as atopic disease, inflammatory bowel disease and childhood leukaemia (Ip et al, 2007), and there is increasing evidence of improved cognitive and behavioural outcomes (see, for example, Kramer et al, 2008). The current policy on breastfeeding is that breast milk is the best form of nutrition for infants; exclusive breastfeeding is recommended for the first six months of life and that it should continue beyond the first six months of life.

There have been slight improvements in the incidence of initial breastfeeding (that is, breastfed at birth, even if only on one occasion) in the UK since 1990. The latest data (DH, 2010) indicates that breastfeeding was initiated in 72.6% of maternities in England, but at the six to eight weeks check, only 29.4% of mothers were totally breastfeeding and 12.8% were partially breastfeeding. The latest Infant Feeding Survey for 2005 (Bolling et al, 2007) found initial breastfeeding rates were 78% in England, 70% in Scotland, 67% in Wales and 63% in Northern Ireland, and the incidence had increased more rapidly in Scotland and Northern Ireland than in England since 2000. Breastfeeding rates were higher among mothers from higher socioeconomic groups, those aged over 30 and first-time mothers. In the UK 48% of all mothers were breastfeeding at six weeks and 25% at six months. In the UK 45% of mothers were exclusively breastfeeding at one week and 21% at six weeks.

Analysis of the MCS in which low-income families were over-sampled (Mayhew and Bradshaw, 2005) found that 71% of mothers had ever tried to breastfeed their babies and that controlling for other factors, the odds of breastfeeding were higher for married mothers, older mothers, home owners, only children, mothers of minority ethnic groups and mothers in England. Poor mothers were less likely to breastfeed but this association disappeared when controlling for other factors such as marital status, mother's ethnicity, paid work status, number of siblings of the baby, tenure, country or region (within the UK) and mother's age at birth.

International comparative data is probably not very reliable as data are not consistently collected. Figure 4.7 presents some breastfeeding initiation rates from the OECD that show that the UK has a comparatively low proportion of mothers who have ever breastfed. They also publish data showing the proportion of mothers exclusively breastfeeding at three, four and six months and the UK comes at the bottom of this league table of 20 countries (OECD, 2009a, CO1.5.B).

Immunisations

Routine immunisation of babies and young children benefits the health of children and their communities where immunisation rates are high – so-called 'herd immunity' (Nicoll et al, 1989). In 1997, almost all two-year-old children in the UK had been immunised against diphtheria, tetanus and polio (96%), whooping cough (94%) and measles, mumps and rubella (MMR) (91%). However, following the publication of a flawed study in *The Lancet* (since retracted by the journal) that associated the MMR vaccine with bowel disease and autism, immunisation rates began to fall. Rates of MMR vaccination fell from 91.8% in 1995/96 to 79.9% in 2003/04. They have since recovered, and Table 4.2 summarises the immunisation rates for children in the countries of the UK.

Immunisation rates in England are lower than the other countries and especially low for MMR. Figure 4.8 shows the immunisation rates for measles for three years: in 1996 the UK was in the middle of the league table. By 2001 it had

Figure 4.7: Proportion of mothers who have ever breastfed, around 2005

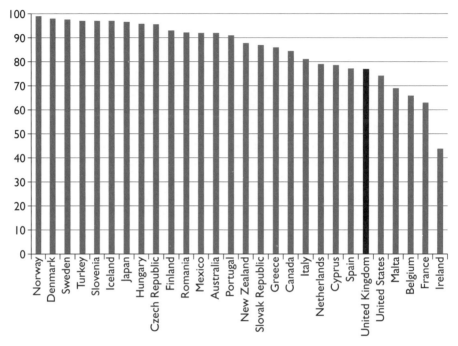

Source: OECD (2010) Family Data Base COI 5.A

Table 4.2: Percentage immunised by their 2nd birthday, 2009/10

	Diptheria, Tetanus, Polio, Pertussis, Hib (DTaP/IPV/Hib) (%)	MMR (%)	MenC (%)	Hib/MenC (%)	PCV (%)
United Kingdom	95.7	88.9	94.5	90.6	88.6
England	95.3	88.2	94.2	90.0	87.6
Northern Ireland	98.5	92.2	96.8	93.9	92.8
Scotland	98.4	93.7	96.4	94.0	94.2
Wales	97.5	92.2	96.2	93.9	96.3

Source: NHS Information Centre (2010c, Table 5b)

fallen back and in 2008 the UK had the second lowest rates in the countries for which we have data.

The introduction of the MMR vaccination programme in the late 1980s resulted in a significant decrease in notifications of cases of measles, mumps and rubella among children. However, the difficulty of consistently achieving very high levels of vaccination coverage (Nicoll et al, 1989), in addition to the impact of the vaccine scare, led to a decrease in coverage, and herd immunity of children against these three infectious diseases has been threatened. In England and Wales there was an epidemic of mumps around 2005 and very high levels of measles in 2008 and 2009 (HPA, 2010a).

Figure 4.8: Percentage of children immunised against measles, ranked by 2008

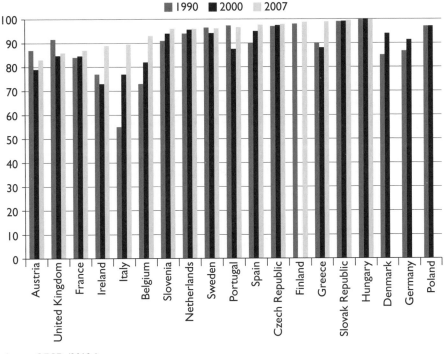

Source: OECD (2010a)

Self-assessed health

The Health Survey for England (HSE) indicates that the vast majority of children rate their health as good or very good, and the proportion increased from 91% in 1995 to 95% in 2009. The proportion reporting a limiting longstanding illness fell from 9% in 1996 to 7% in 2008 (see Figure 4.9).

The British Household Panel Survey (BHPS) youth panel (of 11- to 15-year-olds) has included a subjective health questionnaire since 1994. Unfortunately, there are gaps in the series as well as a change to the question. Table 4.3 summarises the trend – the proportion disagreeing that their health was very good fell between 1994 and 1998 (implying health improvements), and the proportion saying their health was poor or very poor was very small and may also have fallen between 2004 and 2008.

Table 4.4 is from the Health Behaviour of School-aged Children (HBSC) 2006 (Brooks et al, 2009), and compares the percentage of young people reporting good or excellent health by age and gender in the different countries of Great Britain and Ireland (Northern Ireland is not included in the HBSC). Overall, the vast majority report good or excellent health. The proportion is highest in Ireland and lowest in Wales. In all countries and at all ages the proportion is lower for girls than boys, and in all countries and for both genders it declines with age.

Figure 4.9: Percentage of all children aged 0-15 with general health good or very good, longstanding illness and limited longstanding illness

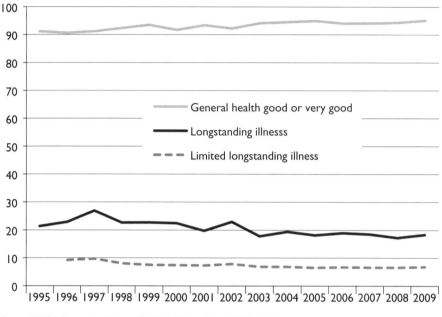

Source: NHS Information Centre (2010d, *Children Trends*, Tables 8, 9)

Table 4.3: Subjective health: BHPS youth panel, 1994-2008

	On the whole my health is very good:						Compared to people of own age would you say that your health has been:				
	1994	1995	1996	1997	1998		2004	2005	2006	2007	2008
Disagree	9.8	12.1	12.1	8.5	7	Poor	2.2		3.1	3	2
Strongly disagree	1.7	1.3	1.2	0.4	1.7	Very poor	0.7		0.6	0.5	0.6
Both	11.5	13.4	13.3	8.9	8.7		2.9		3.7	3.5	2.6

Source: Own analysis of the BHPS

Table 4.4: Percentage of young people who reported good or excellent self-rated health by gender, age and country, 2005/06

	Male				Female				Both genders			
Age	11	13	15	All	11	13	15	All	11	13	15	All
England	89.3	81.4	81.9	84.2	87.3	79.3	68.3	78.8	88.3	80.3	75.0	81.4
Ireland	94.9	90.0	84.9	89.3	93.9	88.1	80.5	87.5	94.4	89.1	82.9	88.4
Scotland	87.2	83.6	82.0	84.0	86.1	75.0	66.4	75.2	86.6	79.3	74.3	79.5
Wales	82.7	80.3	79.8	80.9	77.4	69.5	67.2	71.5	79.9	74.8	73.5	76.1

Source: www.hbsc.org/downloads/YoungPeoplesHealth_GB&Ireland.pdf Table 1.1

The Children's Society survey (Rees et al, 2010a) of a large sample (nearly 7,000) of children aged 10, 12 and 14 collected subjective health data in a number of different ways. There were five questions relating to health. The first was an 11-point Likert scale on happiness with health. The results are summarised in Table 4.5 and confirm that happiness with health is negatively skewed, with only 7.6 responding 4 or lower.

The second question was a five-point self-rating Likert scale. The results are summarised in Table 4.6. Again only 4.8% classified their health as bad or very bad.

The third question asked about the extent to which health problems caused them to miss doing things. In Table 4.7 only 7.6% said that they missed doing things because of health problems more than about once a week.

The fourth question asked about any longstanding illness of disability. In this case, 12.9% said that they had a longstanding illness or disability (and another 11% said that they were not sure) (see Table 4.8).

Table 4.5: Level of happiness with health

	n	%
0 very unhappy	102	1.5
1	52	0.8
2	62	0.9
3	112	1.7
4	181	2.7
5 not happy or unhappy	420	6.3
6	371	5.5
7	634	9.4
8	1,131	16.8
9	1,543	23.0
10 very happy	2,107	31.4
Total	6,715	100.0

Source: Own analysis

Table 4.6: Self rated health

Would you say your health is:	n	%
0 very bad	48	0.7
1 bad	270	4.1
2 fair	1,363	20.9
3 good	2,973	45.6
4 very good	1,872	28.7
Total	6,526	100.0

Source: Own analysis

Table 4.7: Health problems/miss doing things

In the last month how often did a health problem cause you to miss doing things? (reverse coded)?	n	%
0 every day	36	0.8
1 almost every day	60	1.4
2 about once a week	183	4.2
3 just a few times	1,851	42.8
4 never	2,199	50.8
Total	4,329	100.0

Source: Own analysis

Table 4.8: Longstanding illness or disability

Do you have any longstanding illness/ disability?	n	%
Yes	765	12.9
No	5,174	87.1
Total	5,939	100.0
Not sure	742	

Source: Own analysis

Finally, the young people were asked whether they were disabled – only 2% said that they were but another 2.6% said that they were not sure (see Table 4.9).

Table 4.9: Would you say you were disabled?

Would you say that you are disabled?	n	%
Yes	118	2.0
No	5,891	98.0
Total	6,009	100.0
Not sure	178	

Source: Own analysis

Variation in subjective health

Needless to say there is a good deal of overlap between the responses to these questions. Using the scale variable '*How happy are you with your health?*', Rees et al found that mean scores were significantly higher (better) for:

- boys (8.2) than girls (7.9);
- Year 6 (8.4) than Year 10 (7.8);
- those living with both parents (8.1) than those living with a lone parent or step parents (7.9);
- how well-off you felt – well-off (8.3), not well-off (6.8);
- also health correlated $r=0.48$*** with the composite subjective well-being score.

But there was no difference by:

- ethnicity
- region
- number of siblings
- number of workers in the family and
- whether or not they were receiving free school meals.

Parents' reports on child health

In Great Britain, the General Household Survey (GHS) has collected data (from parents) on the longstanding illness of their children since the 1970s. In 1972 parents reported that 4% aged 0-4 and 8% aged 5-15 had a longstanding illness. These proportions rose rapidly and were 15% and 20% by 1996. However, in recent years they have fallen back, and in 2008 they were 8% of those aged 0-4 and 12% of those aged 5-15. Similar but not such acute changes are observed for limiting longstanding illness and restricted activity in the last 14 days (see Table 4.10).

Comparative studies of self-assessed health

The best source of comparative data on child health is the HBSC that is carried out every four years on a large school-based sample of children. Figure 4.10 compares the proportion of children in EU countries who describe their health as only fair or poor; Great Britain has the third highest proportion.

—

Table 4.10: Parents' assessment of child health

	1972[a]	1996	2008
		Longstanding illness	
0-4	4	15	8
5-15	8	20	12
		Limiting longstanding illness	
0-4	2	4	3
5-15	5	8	6
		Restricted activity in the last 14 days	
0-4	6	10	7
5-15	6	10	6

Note: [a] 1975 for limiting longstanding illness.

Source: General Lifestyle Survey 2008 (www.statistics.gov.uk/downloads/theme_compendia/GLF08/GeneraLifestyleSurvey2008.pdf)

Figure 4.10: Proportion of children who rate their health as fair or poor

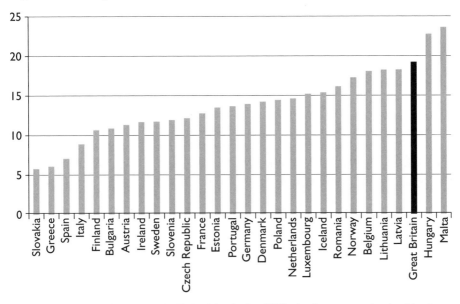

Source: Own analysis of HBSC. Data for England, Scotland and Wales has been averaged and weighted to produce a GB indicator

Types of longstanding illness

Although the GHS collects information about the types of longstanding illness reported by a participant, it does not ask this about children. However, the 2002 HSE did collect this data. The most common forms of longstanding illness found among children were conditions of the respiratory system and skin complaints. Both these types of conditions increase in prevalence with increasing age. A later section in this chapter looks more closely at respiratory health.

Factors associated with a longstanding illness

The HSE 2002 (DH, 2003) reported the outcome of a regression analysis used to identify the independent factors associated with having longstanding illness. The following were identified:

- Age: the odds of reporting longstanding illness increased significantly with age for boys and girls.
- Self-assessed general health: boys who rated their health as 'bad'/'very bad' were 11 times more likely to have a longstanding illness than those who rated their health as 'good'/'very good'; similarly girls were 23 times more likely.
- Income: the probability of reporting longstanding illness increased with decreasing income.
- Government Office Region: boys living outside London were more likely to report a longstanding illness than boys living in London; this association was not found for girls.

It should be noted that measures of area deprivation and socioeconomic category were not significantly associated with having a longstanding illness.

Ethnicity and health

In 2004 the HSE focused on the health of minority ethnic groups. There were differences between ethnic groups in the prevalence of longstanding and limiting longstanding illness (see Table 4.11). Irish and Black Caribbean boys and girls, and Chinese boys, reported similar rates of longstanding illness to the general population, but all other minority ethnic groups reported lower

Table 4.11: Self-reported longstanding illness and limiting longstanding illness among children (aged 0-15), by minority ethnic group and sex

| | Observed percentage | | | |
| | Boys | | Girls | |
Minority ethnic group	Limiting longstanding illness	Any longstanding illness	Limiting longstanding illness	Any longstanding illness
Black Caribbean	7	21	8	22
Black African	5	11	2	7
Indian	6	18	3	9
Pakistani	7	18	6	13
Bangladeshi	5	14	3	10
Chinese	10	17	3	13
Irish	7	23	4	17
General population 2001/02	8	24	7	20

Source: HSE 2004, chapter 12

—

rates of longstanding illness (HSE 2004). The most commonly reported illness was respiratory disease. Black Caribbean, Irish and Chinese boys, and Black Caribbean and Irish girls, reported similar levels of respiratory illness to the general population; all other minority ethnic groups were lower. The next highest prevalence conditions were skin complaints and mental disorders.

Common chronic conditions with increasing prevalence

There are two common conditions in childhood where increases in prevalence have been reported – diabetes and asthma.

Diabetes

Type 1 or insulin-dependent diabetes is one of the most common chronic conditions to emerge in childhood. It is a condition which requires daily management, and poor management threatens both current and future health. The cause of type 1 diabetes is not fully understood, but it is thought to be due to a genetic predisposition coupled with exposure to 'environmental risk factors' including perinatal infection and rapid growth rate in early life, although these have yet to be definitely identified. The incidence of type 1 diabetes is growing across Europe, and a recent study (Patterson et al, 2009) suggests that if present trends continue, there will be a doubling of new cases of type 1 diabetes in European children younger than five years old between 2005 and 2020, and a 70% increase in the total number of cases in young people under 15. The prevalence of type 1 diabetes is not associated with disadvantage, and some research suggests that there is a higher prevalence of type 1 diabetes among the least deprived groups (ONS, 1998).

There remains insufficient national data on diabetes in children, despite the launch of the Diabetes Audit that began in 1999 and a national recording system that began in July 2004. The most recent *National diabetes paediatric report 2008/09* remains partial in its coverage, obtaining data from less than half of all known paediatric units in England and only a quarter of the participating units being able to submit the full dataset (NHS Information Centre, 2010a).

Type 2 diabetes usually occurs in adults, but it is now beginning to be diagnosed in children. Ehtisham et al (2000) published the first case report of the incidence of type 2 diabetes in UK children at the same time as reports of its occurrence in children in North America emerged. The onset of type 2 diabetes in children appears to be linked to obesity and a family history of the condition, and certain minority ethnic groups are particularly at risk. In the *National diabetes paediatric report 2008/09* (NHS Information Centre, 2010a), 98.6% of the recorded cases of diabetes in children had type 1 diabetes and 1.4% had type 2 diabetes. The overall percentage of registrations with type 2 diabetes have not changed noticeably over the last five years, but type 2 diabetes is more common in females (2% of registrations compared with 0.8% in males) and in some minority ethnic groups (type 2 diabetes represents only 0.85% of white children with diabetes, but 5.8% of black children with diabetes and 9.2% of Asian children with diabetes). Type 2 diabetes is of concern, as it is a new chronic condition for children, and as it is thought to be associated with obesity, there is an expectation that the prevalence rate will rise.

The UK has a high prevalence of diabetes in children compared with other countries (see Figure 4.11, from the OECD Family Database [OECD, 2010], which uses data from the International Diabetes Federation).

Figure 4.11: Prevalence diabetes type I among children aged 0-14 per 100,000 of the population age group, 2000/03

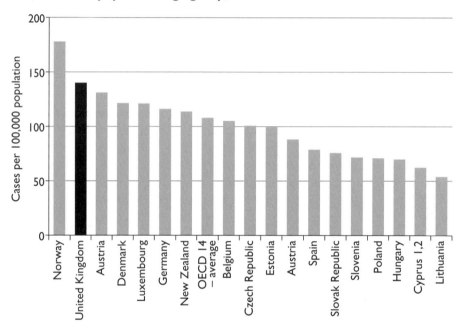

Source: IDF (2006), cited by OECD (2009a, Table CO1.6) (www.oecd.org/dataoecd/31/22/43138119.xls)

Asthma

Asthma is one of the most common non-communicable childhood illnesses around the world (Lai et al, 2009). From the International Study of Asthma and Allergies in Childhood (ISAAC), the UK has a high prevalence of asthma symptoms compared with other countries, with reported asthma symptom prevalence of 20.9% in the 6-7 year age group and 24.7% in the 13-14 year age group (Asher et al, 2006) (see Figure 4.12). This compares with global prevalence of reported symptoms of 9.4% in the 6-7 year age group and 12.6% in the 13-14 year age group (Lai et al, 2009). In the UK, asthma symptoms increased over a five-year period in the 6-7 year age group but decreased in the 13-14 year age group (Asher et al, 2006). In general, asthma symptoms tend to be more prevalent

Figure 4.12: Proportion of children who ever had asthma, 2002

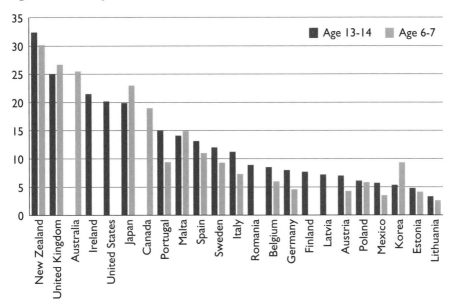

Source: ISAAC, cited by OECD (2010a) (www.oecd.org/dataoecd/31/22/43138119.xls)

in more affluent countries, like the UK, but they also appear to be less severe (Lai et al, 2009), presumably reflecting better treatment and symptom control.

The HSE 1997 and 2002 provided data on the prevalence of doctor-diagnosed asthma and showed that there had been an increase in the percentage of children aged seven and over with a medical diagnosis of asthma. The increase was bigger for boys than girls. Among children aged two to six there was a decrease in the medical diagnosis of asthma. The HSE 2002 explored the association between asthma and a number of factors thought to be associated with its presence. The findings were that overall, doctor-diagnosed asthma was 23% for 0- to 15-year-old boys and 18% for girls in the same age range. Doctor-diagnosed asthma varied by:

• Social class: the prevalence of asthma was higher for boys and girls from households where the reference person was in a semi-routine or routine occupation.
• Income: the prevalence of doctor-diagnosed asthma decreased as income increased.
• Region: the North East was the region with the highest rates and there were generally higher rates in the North than the South.
• Indoor risk factors: the prevalence of doctor-diagnosed asthma in children aged 0–15 was significantly higher in children exposed to cigarette smoke than those not exposed (boys: 28% versus 21%; girls: 22% versus 16%). However, the use of domestic gas appliances and keeping household pets did not show a significant association with doctor-diagnosed asthma.

- Degree of urbanisation: there was no significant tendency for doctor-diagnosed asthma to be more common among children living in urban areas.

The HSE 2004 explored the health of minority ethnic groups including children (DH, 2006), and found 33% higher rates of doctor-diagnosed asthma among Black Caribbean children, but the other ethnic groups had lower rates than the general population in 2001–02.

In general, prevalence of asthma in the UK and elsewhere rose over the 1980s and 1990s, particularly in younger age groups, and has since flattened or even fallen. Various explanations for the trends have been proposed, including air pollution, smoking, diet and infections in early life, but none of these explanations cover both the rise and flattening or decrease, and the changes in prevalence cannot be accounted for adequately on the basis of current epidemiological knowledge (Anderson, 2005).

Injuries and accidents

As we have seen above, injury is the second main cause of deaths in childhood (ages 1–14) in the UK (ONS, 2010a). In England, Wales and Scotland in 2008, there were 252 deaths of children aged between one month and 15 years resulting from external causes (accidents, injuries, poisoning, drowning and assault) (GRO, 2010; ONS, 2010a). Table 4.12 shows that boys are more likely than girls to die from accidental injuries and other external causes.

The most common cause of accidental death in children is transport accidents, which account for around half of the deaths in 5- to 14-year-olds in England and Wales (12 deaths per million boys aged 5–14 and 8 deaths per million girls aged 5–14). In 2009, there were 81 deaths and over 2,500 serious injuries of road users aged 0–15 (DfT, 20010a). There has been a downward trend of fatal and serious injuries of children in road traffic accidents over time (see Figure 4.13). Internationally, Great Britain's fatality rate from road traffic accidents (of those aged 0–14) per 100,000 population is relatively low (see Figure 4.14).

While childhood deaths from injuries and accidents are highly unusual, it has been estimated that for every death due to injury, there are numerous non-fatal accidents, including 5,000–6,000 minor injuries, 630 consultations with a doctor and 45 hospital admissions (Conway and Morgan, 2001). In 2009/10 in

Table 4.12: Post-neonatal (one month to one year) and childhood (1-14 years) deaths from external causes (accidents, injuries and assault), England, Wales and Scotland, 2008, by gender

	<1 year	1-4 years	5-9 years	10-14 years	1 month-14 years
Boys	26	40	30	61	157
Girls	19	36	15	28	95

Source: GRO (2010), ONS (2010a)

—

Figure 4.13: Child casualties in reported road accidents, Great Britain, 2008

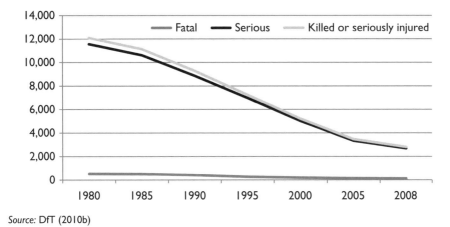

Source: DfT (2010b)

Figure 4.14: Road user fatalities, aged 0-14, per 100,000 population

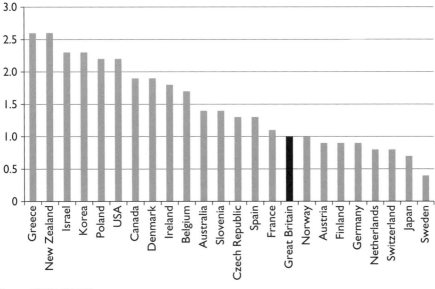

Source: OECD (2010b)

England there were 127,190 in-patient hospital episodes of children aged under 15, including around 10,000 episodes related to transport accidents, over 47,000 falls and over 5,000 accidental poisonings (for example, involving medicines) (NHS Information Centre, 2010b). In 2008/09 there were estimated to be over 3.8 million attendances at Accident and Emergency (A&E) of children and young people (aged 0-19, around half of these aged 0-9 and half aged 10-19) (NHS Information Centre, 2010b). As centrally collected A&E data are experimental at this stage, this is likely to be an underestimate.

Injuries and accidents in children are a major area of socioeconomic inequality in the UK. Where fire was the cause of death, the death rate for children was estimated at 15 times higher in the lowest socioeconomic group compared with the highest, and for child pedestrian deaths the mortality rate in the lowest socioeconomic group was five times that of the highest (Towner, 2002; Licence, 2004).

Health behaviours in children

Obesity, diet and exercise

There is widespread concern over childhood obesity, and increasing evidence that this can be linked with long-term and immediate health risks (HSE 2008). This has led to numerous national, regional and local initiatives to improve the diet of children and to increase levels of exercise, and to a Public Service Agreement (PSA) target to 'reduce the proportion of overweight and obese children to 2000 levels by 2020 in the context of tackling obesity across the population'. Strategies to achieve this target include the 'Change4Life' campaign (see www.nhs.uk/ change4life). Children who are overweight and obese have an increased risk of becoming overweight and obese adults, with the associated implications for health risks (including increased risks of heart attack, stroke, type 2 diabetes, bowel cancer and hypertension). Being an overweight child can also be associated with psychological stress, confidence and lack of self-esteem (Young-Hyman et al, 2006).

Reports of obesity in the HSE 2009 were 16% of boys and 15% of girls, and around 30% of children aged 2-15 were classified as overweight or obese (see Figures 4.15 and 4.16). Although this data source showed substantial increases from 1995 to 2004, since 2004 this trend appears to have flattened and slightly reduced.

Figure 4.15: Children's overweight and obesity prevalence by survey year and sex, age 2-15

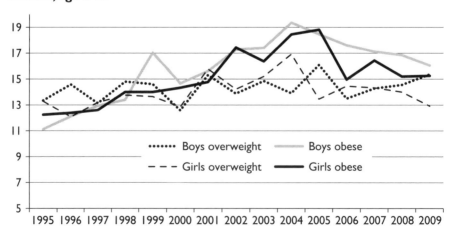
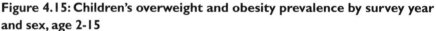

Source: HSE 2009

Figure 4.16: Overall overweight and obesity prevalence, children aged 2-15, by survey year

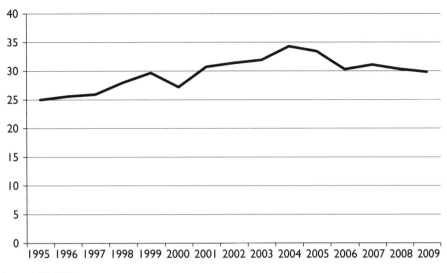

Source: HSE 2009

The HBSC 2006 includes questions on self-reported height and weight, from which body mass index (BMI) can be calculated to determine overweight and obesity prevalence in the constituent countries of the UK (see Table 4.13). There was a high proportion of missing data, but of those who answered, the highest percentage of young people who reported that they were overweight was found in Wales (19.1%), followed by Scotland (15.3%), Ireland (13.5%) and England (11.9%). Across all four countries, young people with low family affluence (81.0%) were significantly less likely to report that they were overweight compared to those with medium (84.5%) and high family affluence (85.5%) (HBSC 2006).

The HBSC is undertaken in a large number of countries around the world. Using this methodology, childhood obesity levels appear relatively high in the UK compared with internationally (see Figure 4.17).

Table 4.13: Percentage of young people who reported overweight by gender, age and country

	Male				Female				Both genders			
Age	11	13	15	All	11	13	15	All	11	13	15	All
England	13.2	14.1	12.6	13.3	9.6	13.6	8.1	10.4	11.4	13.9	10.5	11.9
Ireland	19.7	13.4	14.9	15.0	12.6	13.5	9.6	11.5	16.1	13.5	12.6	13.5
Scotland	21.9	16.4	14.4	16.8	15.2	14.7	12.0	13.7	18.7	15.6	13.3	15.3
Wales	18.9	18.3	21.1	19.5	21.2	16.6	18.4	18.5	20.1	17.5	19.8	19.1

Source: HSE 2009

Figure 4.17: Children who are overweight according to BMI

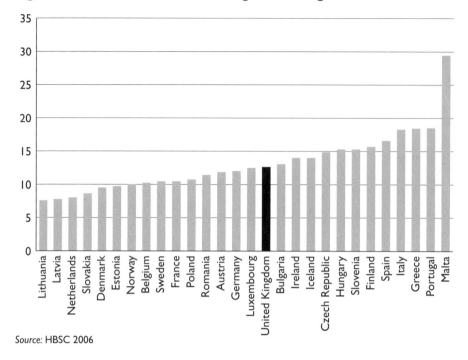

Source: HBSC 2006

The HBSC asked children if they were 'on a diet or doing something else to lose weight'. In all four countries of the UK, a positive response was significantly more likely from those aged 15 compared with younger ages, and from girls compared with boys. Children were also asked about their rates of consumption of fruit, vegetables, sweets, soft drinks and crisps. In general, girls were more likely than boys, and children in more affluent families more likely than those in less affluent families, to report at least daily consumption of fruit and vegetables. Fruit and vegetable consumption has been increasing over time, at least in England (see Figure 4.18). Patterns were slightly less clear in reports of daily consumption of sweets, soft drinks and crisps – boys were more likely than girls to have soft drinks every day, but girls were more likely to eat crisps every day, and there was no gender difference for sweets. Children in less affluent families were more likely to report daily consumption of sweets and soft drinks, but there was no difference in consumption of crisps. Age and country patterns were mixed.

With regard to physical activity, it appears that boys were significantly more likely than girls to report undertaking vigorous activity for two or more hours a week, but boys were more likely to report playing on a computer or games console for two or more hours a day (see Figure 4.19). There were no consistent differences between age group or country for physical activity, but there were differences in computer or games console use between countries (Scotland being highest and

Figure 4.18: Trends in fruit and vegetable consumption by children aged 5-15, mean portions per day

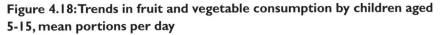

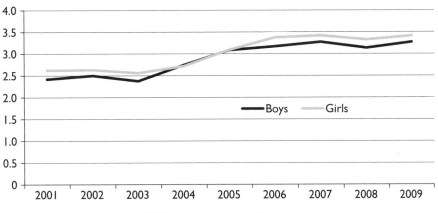

Source: NHS Information Centre (2010d, *Children Trends*, Table 7)

Figure 4.19: Percentages of young people who reported vigorous activity for two or more hours per week, and playing on a computer or games console for two or more hours a day, by gender and country

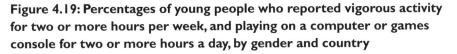

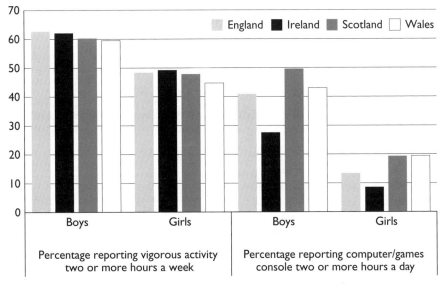

Source: HBSC 2006

Ireland lowest) (HBSC 2006). Across the four countries, children living in more affluent families were significantly more likely to engage in vigorous physical activity than those in less affluent families, and those with low family affluence were more likely to play computer games.

Smoking

The prevalence of smoking in children appears to be declining over time, at least in England (Fuller and Sanchez, 2010). The percentage of children who have ever smoked (29%) is the lowest since the survey of smoking, drinking and drug use in England began in 1982. Figure 4.20 illustrates the percentage of 11- to 15-year-old pupils who were 'regular' smokers (defined as at least one cigarette per week). Girls were more likely than boys to smoke regularly (7% versus 5%) and older children were more likely to smoke than younger children (15% of 15-year-olds, less than half a per cent of 11-year-olds) (Fuller and Sanchez, 2010). This survey also found that pupils who received free school meals (as a proxy for household income) had an increased risk of being regular smokers compared with those who did not (odds ratio 1.61). Social class, as proxied by number of books at home, was not significantly linked with the odds of being a regular smoker (Fuller and Sanchez, 2010). Other factors that predicted regular smoking included ethnicity (black pupils and those of mixed ethnicity were less likely to smoke than white pupils) and use of alcohol and drugs, which was strongly linked with likelihood of smoking. Young people classified as regular smokers smoked an average of 38 cigarettes a week (about 5-6 per day) (Fuller and Sanchez, 2010).

The HBSC 2006 permits comparisons between the constituent countries of the UK with regard to daily smoking. Differences in smoking rates between countries were not consistent across age and gender groups, and were not statistically significant overall (HBSC 2006). Young people with low family affluence were more likely to report daily smoking compared to those with medium or high affluence, particularly girls. The UK has fewer 15-year-olds reporting daily smoking than many international comparators (see Figure 4.21).

Figure 4.20: Prevalence of regular cigarette smoking by sex, 1982-2009, England

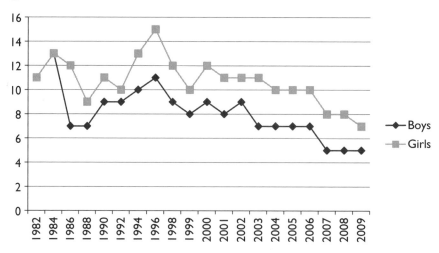

Source: NHS Information Centre (2009); Fuller and Sanchez (2010)

Figure 4.21: Percentage of 15-year-olds who smoke at least once a week, 2005/06

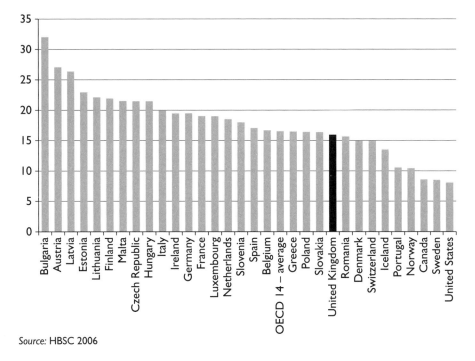

Source: HBSC 2006

Alcohol

Prevalence of children ever drinking has been declining in England since 2000 (see Figure 4.22). In 2009, the mean consumption by pupils who had drunk alcohol in the last week was 11.6 units per week (median 7 units). There was no significant difference in the amount consumed by boys and girls, and mean and median consumption of alcohol increased with age (mean 9.3, median 5 units per week for 11- to 13-year-olds, mean 13.2, median 8.5 units per week for 15-year-olds) (Fuller and Sanchez, 2010). Factors associated with having drunk alcohol in the last week included age (odds ratio 1.79 for each additional year); ethnicity (mixed ethnic background and Asian children were less likely to have drunk alcohol in the last week, odd ratios 0.61 and 0.15 respectively); and socioeconomic factors (those who received free school meals were less likely to have drunk in the last week, odds ratio 0.66).

The HBSC 2006 permits comparisons between the constituent countries of the UK with regard to drunkenness (having been drunk four or more times in their lifetimes). Boys were significantly more likely than girls to report that they had been drunk four or more times. The highest percentage of young people who had been drunk at least four times was found in Wales and Scotland, followed by England and Ireland (HBSC 2006). Young people with low family affluence were more likely to report being drunk at least four times, followed by those with

Figure 4.22: Prevalence of ever drinking alcohol by sex (all pupils), 1988-2009, England

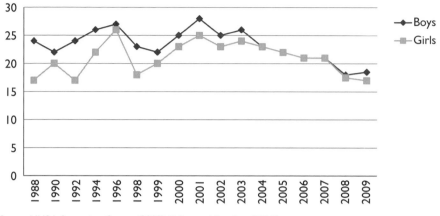

Source: NHS Information Centre (2009); Fuller and Sanchez (2010)

high and medium family affluence (HBSC 2006). The UK has a high percentage of 13- and 15-year-olds reporting that they had been drunk two or more times compared with other countries (see Figure 4.23).

Figure 4.23: Percentage of 13- and 15-year-olds who have been drunk at least twice, 2005/06

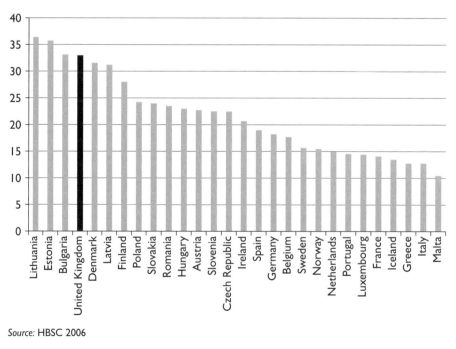

Source: HBSC 2006

Sexual health and health behaviours

While adolescence is a time when physical sexual maturity is acquired, some features of adolescence, such as social immaturity, spontaneity and risk taking, generate risks in terms of sexual and general health. For adolescents, two of the key health issues are teenage pregnancy and sexually transmitted infections (STIs). We deal with both these issues in this section. Data on adolescent sexual health are typically reported for young people under 16 years and those aged 16-19. Thus, while in much of this chapter we have restricted our data reported to children aged 15/16 years and under, in this section we have extended the upper age limit for data to 19 years so as to give as complete a picture as possible of adolescent sexual health in the UK today.

There are a number of ways to look at sexual health behaviours, including age at first sexual intercourse, use of condoms/contraception and number of sexual partners. Collecting such data from children and young people is ethically fraught and researchers often rely on retrospective accounts of adolescent sexual activity. The National Survey of Sexual Attitudes and Lifestyles (NATSAL) takes place every 10 years and is currently in process. From the previous survey, in the period 1999-2001, 30% of men and 26% of women reported first heterosexual intercourse at younger than 16 years, with the median age being 16.

The HBSC asked 15-year-olds if they had ever had sexual intercourse, and if so, their age at first sexual intercourse. Girls were significantly more likely to report having had sex by age 15 than boys, but differences between countries and family affluence groups were not significant. In terms of international comparisons, experience of sexual intercourse at age 15 varies considerably, from 12% in Slovakia to 61% in Greenland (see Figure 4.24). In most countries, boys are more

Figure 4.24: Fifteen-year-olds who have had sexual intercourse

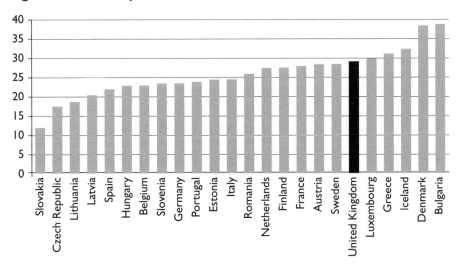

Source: HBSC 2006

likely to report sexual intercourse, but in Britain and some other countries this is reversed. In general, as in Britain, family affluence is not a strong predictive factor.

Having multiple partners and not using contraceptives and/or condoms increases the risk of early pregnancy and contracting an STI. The Contraception and Sexual Health Surveys (ONS, 2009a) provide annual data on the number of sexual partners in the previous year reported by young people aged 16-19 (see Table 4.14).

Table 4.14: Number of sexual partners in the previous year among 16- to 19-year-olds by gender, 2000-08/09

	2000	2001/ 02	2002/ 03	2003/ 04	2004/ 05	2005/ 06	2006/ 07	2007/ 08	2008/ 09
Men									
None	31	34	45	34	34	38	44	27	31
One	38	26	27	34	28	26	26	40	44
Two or three	22	25	19	21	29	26	22	19	17
Four or more	9	14	9	11	9	10	7	14	8
Women									
None	33	27	36	35	28	36	34	20	16
One	44	46	39	42	50	48	35	57	60
Two or three	20	23	22	18	16	12	23	17	19
Four or more	4	4	4	5	6	4	8	6	5

Source: ONS (2009a)

Table 4.14 shows fluctuations but no discernable trends in the proportion of young people with multiple sexual partners, or those who were not sexually active. This data source also collects information on the use of contraception by young people, which can be collated over time (see Table 4.15).

The HBSC questions 15-year-olds about condom use and contraception. Sexually active 15-year-old boys (82.4%) were more likely to report that they used a condom during their last sexual intercourse than sexually active 15-year-old girls (75.0%) (HBSC 2006). There were no significant differences between countries but those with high family affluence were more likely to report condom use at last intercourse than those with low family affluence.

Young people are vulnerable to acquiring STIs as they tend to have more sexual partners and to change partners more frequently than older age groups. The increasing incidence of STIs in the population as a whole (HPA, 2010b) only serves to increase this risk for adolescents. Table 4.16 shows the number of

Table 4.15: Percentage of 16- to 19-year-olds using at least one method of contraception

	Age 16-17	Age 18-19	Age 16-19
2000	43	68	
2001/02	61	69	
2002/03	39	64	
2003/04	50	71	
2004/05	57	76	
2005/06	51	67	
2006/07			63
2007/08			56
2008/09			57

Source: ONS (2009a)

Table 4.16: Number of new episodes of STIs by age band, gender and year, UK

		Age	2001	2002	2003	2004	2005	2006	2007	2008	2009
Syphilis	Males	<16	0	1	0	1	4	2	2	2	1
		16-19	12	29	33	35	75	68	50	59	49
		≤19	12	30	33	36	79	70	52	61	50
	Females	<16	1	2	3	2	12	9	4	5	1
		16-19	13	16	22	28	31	48	43	28	44
		≤19	14	18	25	30	43	57	47	33	45
Gonorrhea	Males	<16	57	67	59	54	49	34	38	31	31
		16-19	2,060	2,241	2,078	1,969	1,593	1,575	1,668	1,408	1,382
		≤19	2,117	2,308	2,137	2,023	1,642	1,609	1,706	1,439	1,413
	Females	<16	271	277	266	217	185	175	205	172	166
		16-19	2,598	2,761	2,807	2,500	1,999	1,888	2,069	2,044	1,935
		≤19	2,869	3,038	3,073	2,717	2,184	2,063	2,274	2,216	2,101
Chlamydia	Males	<16	93	104	135	131	145	161	201	171	139
		16-19	4,495	5,596	6,498	7,534	8,151	8,810	9,866	9,978	9,083
		≤19	4,588	5,700	6,633	7,665	8,296	8,971	10,067	10,149	9,222
	Females	<16	968	1,099	1,323	1,354	1,305	1,343	1,527	1,505	1,293
		16-19	14,070	16,292	18,222	19,762	20,525	20,204	21,499	21,884	19,994
		≤19	15,038	17,391	19,545	21,116	21,830	21,547	23,026	23,389	21,287
Genital herpes	Males	<16	9	9	8	7	10	8	10	20	14
		16-19	415	430	415	455	561	603	720	782	771
		≤19	424	439	423	462	571	611	730	802	785
	Females	<16	156	161	172	155	159	153	232	239	235
		16-19	2,274	2,147	2,246	2,330	2,395	2,754	3,255	3,576	3,445
		≤19	2,430	2,308	2,418	2,485	2,554	2,907	3,487	3,815	3,680
Genital warts	Males	<16	63	75	104	78	75	116	108	85	81
		16-19	3,598	3,638	3,966	4,428	4,496	4,804	5,220	5,554	5,514
		≤19	3,661	3,713	4,070	4,506	4,571	4,920	5,328	5,639	5,595
	Females	<16	499	540	552	599	530	611	750	723	728
		16-19	9,385	9,412	9,909	10,649	11,138	11,691	12,591	13,141	12,710
		≤19	9,884	9,952	10,461	11,248	11,668	12,302	13,341	13,864	13,438

Source: HPA (2010b)

83

new episodes of five of the most commonly occurring STIs among adolescents in the UK (HPA, 2010b). The most commonly occurring STI is genital Chlamydia, and there have been substantial increases in the number of new episodes reported in recent years. Chlamydia can result in pelvic inflammatory disease, with associated reproductive health concerns, and can increase the risk of ectopic pregnancy. There are also increasing numbers of cases of genital warts among adolescents, and cases of gonorrhoea and genital herpes are lower in number but relatively stable (see Figure 4.25). Cases of syphilis are rare in this age group but are apparently increasing.

Figure 4.25: Number of new episodes of STIs in young people (up to age 19), UK

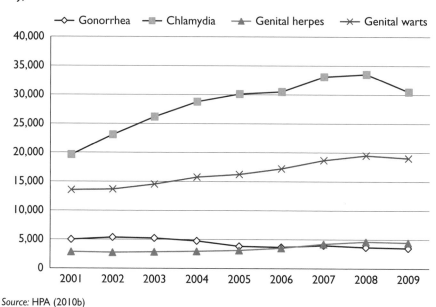

Source: HPA (2010b)

Teenage conceptions and abortions

Teenage conception is discussed in this chapter because of evidence that teenage births are associated with poor outcomes for the teenager and her child, including health outcomes, both in the short and long term. This evidence was reviewed in *Teenage pregnancy* (Social Exclusion Unit, 1999) and in a previous edition of this book (Tabberer, 2002) in more detail than is included here. Teenage pregnancies are more likely to result in low birth weight babies, infant and child mortality, hospital admissions of children, postnatal depression and low rates of breastfeeding. Bradshaw and Mayhew (2005), using the MCS, found that:

• teenage mothers were over three times more likely to be poor;
• the odds of a low birth weight baby were 40% higher for teenage conceptions;

- teenage mothers were 50% more likely to be depressed;
- and were 100% were less likely to breastfeed.

We also know that teenage mothers are less likely to complete their education and more likely to be not in employment and live in poverty, and their children are more likely to experience these disadvantages and twice as likely to become teenage parents in their turn (Rendall, 2003).

UNICEF published Innocenti Report Card no 3 (2001b) on teenage births and found that the under-20 birth rate in the UK was the second highest out of 28 OECD countries (only less than the US), and even in affluent areas, the teenage birth rate in the UK was higher than the average for the Netherlands or France. Figure 4.26 shows that in 2005 the UK had the fourth from highest teenage fertility rate in the OECD (excluding Turkey and Mexico).

The government's Teenage Pregnancy Strategy targets (Social Exclusion Unit 1999) were to:

- halve the under-18 conception rate by 2010, taking 1998 as a baseline year;
- increase the proportion of teenage parents in education, training or employment to reduce their risk of long-term social exclusion.

The Strategy is monitored by statistics on teenage conceptions produced by combining birth registrations and notifications of legal abortions, and so excludes miscarriages and illegal abortions. The latest data in Figure 4.27 shows that teenage conceptions have declined since 1998, but that the target to reduce teenage conceptions by half by 2010 is not likely to be met. By 2008 the conception rate had fallen by only 13.7% between 1998 and 2008. The number of teenage births is

Figure 4.26: Teenage fertility rate, 2005

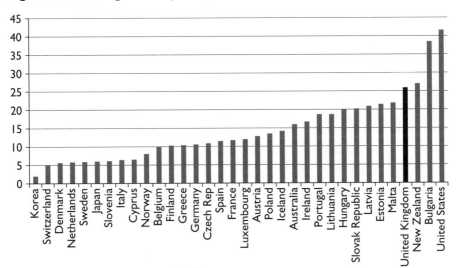

Source: OECD (2010) Family Database SF2.4D

Figure 4.27: Under-18 conception rate and % leading to abortion in England and Wales

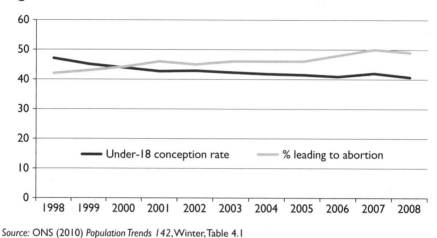

Source: ONS (2010) *Population Trends 142,* Winter, Table 4.1

a function of the proportion of conceptions that end in abortion. It can be seen that the proportion of conceptions aborted rose between 1998 and 2008, and nearly half (49.4%) of under-18 conceptions end in abortion; the proportion is higher for under-16 conceptions (61.5%) and lower for under-20 conceptions (42.7%).

In England and Wales the under-16 conception rate fell from 8.5 per 100 in 1998 to 7.6 per 1,000 in 2008, but the under-20 conception rate rose from 101.6 to 103.2 over the same period (ONS, 2010, *Population Trends 142,* Winter, Table 4.1).

The Scottish teenage pregnancy target was to reduce by 20% the pregnancy rate (per 1,000 population) in under-16-year-olds from 8.5% in 1995 to 6.8% in 2010. But they are also struggling to meet this target – the under-16 pregnancy rate was 7.9% in 2008 (www.isdscotland.org/isd/2071.html).

There are considerable variations by region and local authority in the conception rates and the proportions leading to abortion. In 2007 in England and Wales the North East region had the highest under-18 conception rate (53.2 per 1,000), but Wales had the highest proportion leading to maternities (58.4) because it had the lowest abortion rate. London had by far the highest abortion rate of 62.5% (ONS, 2010c). There are also substantial variations by local authority. Between 2006 and 2008, the teenage conception rate varied in England between 14.9 per 1,000 in Brentwood and 74.8 per 1,000 in Lambeth. The proportion of teenage conceptions that ended in abortion varied from 34% in Bolsover to 77% in Epping Forest. These variations have been shown to be very closely associated with the level of deprivation in an area – the conception rate is higher and the proportion ending in abortion is lower in deprived areas (Bradshaw et al, 2005). The result is that the teenage birth rate is closely associated with deprivation (Lee et al, 2004). Berthoud (2001) found that teenage motherhood was associated with ethnicity: Caribbean, Pakistani and Bangladeshi women had much higher rates than white women, but Indian women much lower rates than white women.

International comparisons of overall child health

In the health domain of the International Index of Child Well-being (Bradshaw and Richardson, 2009), the UK came 24 out of 29, and the OECD (2009a) showed the UK 20 out of 29 in the health domain. The Bradshaw and Richardson (2009) health domain was made up of health at birth (infant mortality and low birth weight), immunisation rates and health behaviours (assessed by five questions in the HBSC). The UK did slightly better than average on health behaviours but well below average on health at birth and immunisation rates. The subjective well-being domain contained HBSC data on self-defined health (of 11-, 13- and 15-year olds) – the UK came 26 out of 29 on the proportion defining their health as fair or poor. The UK teenage fertility rates are notoriously high – third from highest in the EU29 in 2006. The UK also came well down the international league table on risky behaviours. The only health indicator in which the UK did comparatively very well is child accidental death rates.

Conclusion

There is a fairly consistent pattern to these results on health and health behaviour. The health of UK children is comparatively poor and so is their health behaviour. However, on most indicators, the health of children and their health behaviour has been improving.

The NHS received a huge increase in national resources during this period but it is not at all clear that children were a major beneficiary of this largesse. There have been many child-related initiatives, including Sure Start, the reintroduction of nutritional standards in school meals, the fruit scheme, investment in children's sports, smoking and drinking campaigns, Healthy Start, Health in Pregnancy Grants, Sure Start Maternity Grants and Child Benefit paid to pregnant mothers. Despite the *Every Child Matters* agenda, children only belatedly became the focus of health policy. The DH and the DCSF (2009) published a statement on child health. The fact that it did not emerge until 2009 perhaps illustrates the problem of child health in this country.

It could be argued that child health is impervious to the activities of health professionals – child health outcomes are about poverty and inequality, parental and child behaviour, driven by popular culture and advertising. Perhaps there is not much that the NHS can achieve for children. This was one conclusion that could have been drawn from the statement on child health which was preoccupied with ensuring 'support for families in securing world class health and well-being outcomes for their children' (DH and DCSF, 2009, p 8).

A more structural interpretation was presented by the Marmot Review *Fairer society, healthy lives* (2010), which concluded:

> Disadvantage starts before birth and accumulates throughout life.
> Action to reduce health inequalities must start before birth and be

followed through the life of the child. Only then can the close links between early disadvantage and poor outcomes throughout life be broken. That is our ambition for children born in 2010. For this reason, giving every child the best start in life is our highest priority recommendation (Marmot Review, 2010, p 20).

Note

[1] Large employers and higher managerial.

FIVE

Subjective well-being and mental health

Jonathan Bradshaw and Antonia Keung

Key statistics

- Over 80% of children have above average life satisfaction.
- Boys' subjective well-being is higher than that of girls.
- Subjective well-being declines with age.
- Welsh children have the lowest life satisfaction in Great Britain.
- British children's life satisfaction is in the middle of the international league table.
- Subjective well-being does not vary very much with the usual socioeconomic factors.
- Relationships with family and the choices that children have are the domains that matter most to subjective well-being.
- Around 1 in 10 children aged 5-16 had a clinically diagnosed mental disorder in 2004.
- Boys are more likely than girls to have a mental disorder.
- The older age group has a higher prevalence rate of any mental disorder than the younger age group.
- Conduct disorders (5.8%) and emotional disorders (3.7%) are the two most common forms of mental disorder.

Key trends

- Subjective well-being has improved since 1994.
- Girls have closed the gap in subjective well-being with boys
- The improvement seems to be focused on relationships with friends and school.
- The level of mental illness among children and young people in the UK peaked in the 1980s and 1990s, but then showed signs of levelling off by mid-2000.
- Prevalence of emotional disorders among young boys declined from 3% in 1999 to 2% in 2004.
- Between 2002 and 2008 there was a 14% reduction in the number of youth suicides and undetermined deaths in the UK.

Key sources

- British Household Panel Survey (BHPS)
- Health Behaviour of School-aged Children (HBSC)
- The Children's Society surveys
- Health Survey for England (HSE)
- Office for National Statistics (ONS) 1999, 2004 and 2007 surveys on mental health of children and young people
- ONS mortality statistics: deaths registered in England and Wales (Series DH2 and DR)
- Registrar General Annual Reports (2002-09)
- General Register Office (GRO) for Scotland

Introduction

Subjective well-being and mental health are not the same things. Indeed, as we shall see, there is some evidence that child subjective well-being and adolescent mental health have been moving in different directions over time. However, they are dealt with together in this chapter on the grounds that they are both concerned with emotional or psychological domains of life and there is some evidence that low subjective well-being may merge into mental illness (Valois et al, 2004).

Well-being is multidimensional. Not one domain affects a child's life, but many. Some of them may be described as 'objective', such as the material resources of the child or housing and environmental conditions, and there are chapters containing these and other objective indicators in this book. In those chapters we have also reviewed evidence on what children say they feel about those aspects of their lives. In Chapter Four we reviewed a body of evidence of the self-assessed health of children. These are 'subjective' in the sense that they are what children say about their lives and what they think and feel about those domains of their lives. In the first part of this chapter, we focus on *overall* subjective well-being, although we also explore how that subjective well-being is influenced by well-being in relation to different domains.

Concept of subjective well-being

There is a vast literature on subjective well-being, although much less work has been done on the subjective well-being of children. Those who have studied subjective well-being have defined their interest variously as:

- happiness
- life satisfaction
- self-esteem
- positive affect

and many scales and measures have been adopted to represent these constructs (see Rees et al, 2010a, for a discussion of these). Without wishing to ignore the important distinctions between these concepts, we are concerned here with the expressed views of children about personal well-being.

Why be concerned about subjective well-being?

Promoting the subjective well-being of children seems to us to be a reasonable goal for any society. As David Cameron has said:

> 'It's time we admitted that there's more to life than money, and it's time we focused not just on GDP but on GWB – General Well Being. It's about the beauty of our surroundings, the quality of our culture and above all the strength of our relationships. There is a deep satisfaction which comes from belonging to someone and to some place.' (David Cameron, May 2006)

Indeed, David Cameron has recently encouraged the Office for National Statistics (ONS) to go beyond gross domestic product (GDP) in measuring the well-being of the UK. It is very good news that the ONS, as part of this brief, have started work on child well-being (Thomas, 2009).

The UN Convention on the Rights of the Child article 12[1] says 'States Parties shall assure to the child who is capable of forming his or her own views the right to express those views freely in all matters affecting the child, the views of the child being given due weight in accordance with the age and maturity of the child.' What children say about their lives matters.

Sources of data on subjective well-being

Until recently, there was rather scant evidence on the subjective well-being of children. There was no indicator of the subjective well-being of children in the *Opportunity for all* series, and the *Every Child Matters* Outcomes Framework under the 'Be healthy' domain listed young people's perception of their emotional health and well-being as an indicator. The Department for Children, Schools and Families (DCSF) sought to operationalise this indicator through the TellUs surveys that asked five simple questions covering happiness and relationships with friends and family. The key subjective well-being question was 'Do you feel happy with life at the moment?'. In TellUs 3 (2008) 69% of children in Years 6, 8 and 10 agreed with this statement. TellUs has now been abandoned by the new Coalition government.

There are three other sources of data on children's subjective well-being:

- The Health Behaviour of School-aged Children (HBSC) survey undertaken every four years has a variety of questions related to well-being and mental health including a question on life satisfaction. It enables us to compare variations within the UK and between the UK and other countries.

- The youth questionnaire of the British Household Panel Survey (BHPS) has asked children aged 11-15 about their happiness and self-esteem every year since 1994, and it enables us to compare trends over time.
- The Children's Society has been undertaking research on the subjective well-being of children in England since 2005, and their large sample enables us to explore variations in subjective well-being and what influences it.

Subjective well-being in the UK

The HBSC used 'Cantril's ladder' to measure young people's global assessment of their lives. Young people were asked to indicate the step on the ladder which best reflected their life at the moment: 'Here is a picture of a ladder. The top of the ladder, 10, is the best possible life for you and the bottom, 0, is the worst possible life for you. In general, where on the ladder do you feel you stand at the moment?'. A score of six or above was defined as a positive level of life satisfaction. Table 5.1 presents the results for the countries of Great Britain and Ireland (Northern Ireland was not included). Overall life satisfaction was very high – in all countries over 80% scored six or more (out of 11).

- Boys (87.7%) were more likely than girls (81.5%) to report that they have positive life satisfaction.
- There was a significant difference between all age groups in the percentage of young people who reported having positive life satisfaction. Positive life satisfaction was lowest among the 15-year-olds (81.9%) followed by 13- (84.4%) and 11-year-olds (87.7%).
- The percentages of young people who reported having positive life satisfaction was highest in Ireland (87.4%), followed by England (85.3%), Scotland (84.2%) and Wales (81.2%). All countries differed significantly from each other.
- The HBSC uses a 'family affluence' scale based on access to a number of assets. They found that high family affluence was associated with higher proportions of children that had life satisfaction of 6 or above.

The HBSC also asked the young people whether they had 'felt low at least weekly in the last six months'. The results were similar:

- girls were more likely than boys to have felt low;
- the proportion feeling low increased with age;
- young people in Scotland (19.3%) and Ireland (21.9%) were less likely to feel low than in England (30.6%) and Wales (23.2%);
- feeling low was more prevalent the lower the family affluence.

Table 5.1: Percentages of young people who reported a positive life

	Male				Female				Both genders			
	Age 11	Age 13	Age 15	All	Age 11	Age 13	Age 15	All	Age 11	Age 13	Age 15	All
England	88.4	86.5	88.9	87.9	87.7	81.0	79.4	82.9	88.1	83.7	84.0	85.3
Ireland	92.0	89.5	86.7	89.1	91.6	87.1	78.2	85.7	91.7	88.3	82.8	87.4
Scotland	87.9	88.8	87.4	88.1	86.3	80.6	75.8	80.5	87.1	84.7	81.6	84.2
Wales	86.3	84.6	86.1	85.6	82.2	75.7	72.2	76.8	84.2	80.1	79.1	81.2

Source: Brooks et al (2009), Table 1.3)

The HBSC is also really the only source of comparative data on subjective well-being. Figure 5.1 presents the relationship between the proportion of young people reporting high life satisfaction in HBSC 2001-02 and 2005-06. The position of children in Great Britain is in the middle of the international distribution, with perhaps a small increase in life satisfaction between the two surveys.

Levin et al (2009) also used HBSC data to explore trends in 'mental well-being' (based on four positive subjective outcome indicators: 'happiness', 'confidence', 'never feel helpless', 'never feel left out') of Scottish children. Their analysis showed an overall increase in mental well-being of both boys and girls between 1994 and 2006. They also suggested that the odds of good mental well-being had risen at a faster rate for girls than boys for all four indicators.

Trends in subjective well-being

An alternative and perhaps better source of data on trends in subjective well-being is the BHPS. This has been used for cross-sectional analysis of subjective well-being (see, for example, Clarke et al, 2000; Quilgars et al, 2005; Robson, 2009). It is an annual survey of a panel of households, which began in 1991. From 1994 the survey included a separate questionnaire administered to 11- to 15-year-olds known as the British Youth Panel Survey (BYPS). The survey asks respondents to score how they feel about their:

• school work
• appearance
• family
• friends
• life as a whole

on a six-point Likert scale, where 0 = not happy at all and 6 = very happy, making a total 'happiness' score of 30.

This data has recently been analysed by Bradshaw and Keung (2011). They found that the mean score in 2008 (24.8) was statistically significantly higher than 1994 (23.9). They also analysed trends in the proportion of young people with very

Figure 5.1: Proportion of 11-, 13- and 15-year-olds reporting high life satisfaction, 2001-02 and 2005-06

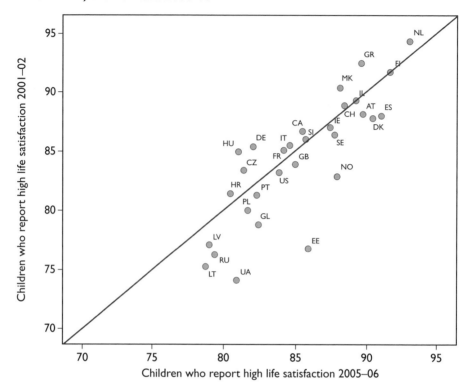

Source: Own analysis of HBSC data (www.hbsc.org/index.html)

low happiness scores, those in the tail of the distribution who might present the highest cause for concern. The proportion in the tail of the distribution declined from 24.4% in 1994 to 17.7% in 2008.

Figure 5.2 shows the trend in mean happiness with the 95 per cent confidence intervals (CI) plotted. A clear upwards trend is evident over the period. Happiness was significantly higher in 2008 than in all the previous years, except for 2007.

They also looked at those with very low subjective well-being by plotting the percentage of young people at the tail of the distributions for each year. Figure 5.3 shows a clear downwards trend in the proportion of young people with low happiness over time.

Figure 5.4 presents the components of happiness. It indicates that young people are happier with their family and friends than their school work and appearance. All of the happiness components have very slightly higher scores in 2008 than they did in 1994, but only happiness with friends, school work and life as a whole are statistically significantly better. Since 2002, the BYPS also asked young people how happy they felt about school, and over time there has also been an upwards trend.

Figure 5.2: Mean happiness of 11- to 15-year-olds with 95% CI

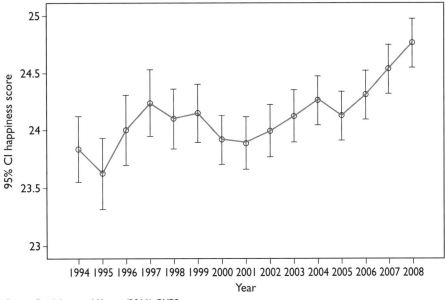

Source: Bradshaw and Keung (2011); BYPS

Figure 5.3: Trends in the percentage of young people with low happiness

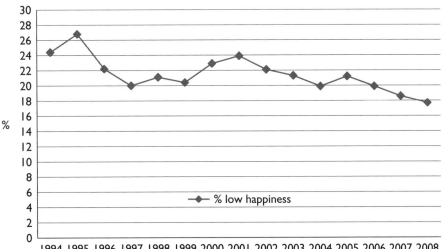

Source: Bradshaw and Keung (2011)

Bradshaw and Keung (2011) found it difficult to draw any firm conclusions about the causes of this improvement. It has occurred after controlling for changes and/or differences in the age and gender and country of the young people and despite (and in addition to) the changes in the circumstances of their families.

Figure 5.4: Trends in the mean component scores of happiness of 11- to 15-year-olds

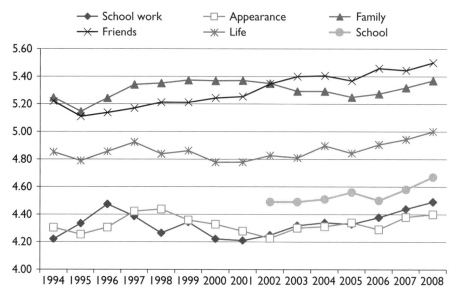

Source: Bradshaw and Keung (2011); BYPS

For example, poverty may have fallen over the period or maternal employment may have increased, but even controlling for these changes, happiness increased. There is also no evidence of the time series being interrupted by a specific event. Mean happiness scores were lower in the Tory years than the Labour years, but happiness fell after 1997 (when Labour came to power) and did not recover until after 2001. There is some evidence that happiness with school may be driving some of the increase. As well as evidence of increased happiness with school work and school, there was a remarkable increase in the proportion of young people in the UK 'liking school a lot' in the HBSC between 2002 and 2006. It also appears that happiness with friends improved markedly, particularly for girls, which may point to the positive impact of social networking websites (see, for example, Lenhart and Madden, 2007).

Variations in subjective well-being

For a greater insight into the nature of subjective well-being we turn to The Children's Society surveys (The Children's Society, 2006; Rees et al, 2010a, 2010b). The latter study was based on a school-based sample of 7,000 10- to 15-year-olds in England. Three separate measures of subjective well-being were used: Cantril's ladder of life satisfaction, an 11-point Likert scale measuring happiness with life as a whole and a version of Huebner's scale. After exploring the overlaps between these scales, they were combined into a composite measure of subjective well-being.

Figure 5.5 shows that, as with other studies, subjective well-being was negatively skewed – most children were happy and only 7% scored below the mean.

They then sought to explain variations in subjective well-being. Starting with the characteristics of the child, they found that subjective well-being was higher for:

- younger children
- boys
- where there was no disability
- for children with a religious affiliation
- for certain ethnic groups.

There was no variation by country of birth. Although these differences were significant, they were all very small, and together these factors only explained 3-4% of the variation in well-being.

They then looked at family factors and found that subjective well-being was lower if the child was poor and not living with both parents. But again the differences were very small, and together they only explained 1-2.5% of the variation. There was only one factor that seemed to be strongly related to subjective well-being and that was the experience of bullying. Figure 5.6 shows a consistent relationship between overall subjective well-being and the frequency of bullying in the last 12 months.

They then explored the make-up of well-being. Figure 5.7 gives the percentage of children who were unhappy about elements of their lives. In respect of each element, the majority were happy. This gives the proportion that were below the mid-point of an 11-point scale. The lowest levels of unhappiness were with their

Figure 5.5: Distribution of composite subjective well-being

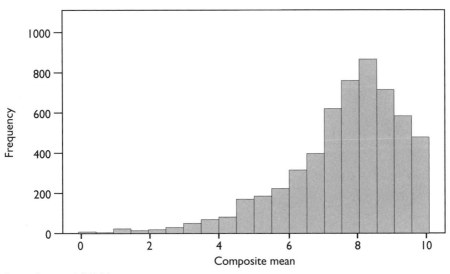

Source: Rees et al (2010a)

Figure 5.6: Overall subjective well-being (score out of 10) by frequency of bullying in the last 12 months

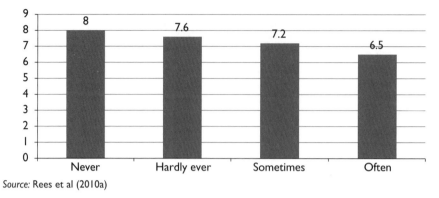

Source: Rees et al (2010a)

Figure 5.7: Percentage unhappy with elements of their well-being

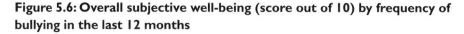

Source: Rees et al (2010a, Table 8)

friends, their home, their family and their 'things' or belongings. The highest levels of unhappiness were with their appearance and their confidence. In the case of appearance, girls were much less happy than boys, especially in the older age groups.

Using data from another survey, Rees et al (2010b) also explored the associations between the domains of well-being and overall well-being. Table 5.2 summarises the results of a regression showing the relationship. The second column provides an indication of the influence of each domain on overall well-being while holding the other domains constant. The domains are in rank order. Family, choice and money and possessions made the largest contribution to explaining variation in overall well-being. Three domains – local area, friends and safety – did not make a significant contribution.

These domains explained over half (52%) of the variation in overall well-being. There is evidence that personality traits and genetics may also be important determining factors in subjective well-being (Diener and Lucas, 1998; Diener et al, 1999). Rees et al (2010a) did not include questions on personality, although we will do this in future research. Another possible explanation of these results is the theory of dynamic equilibrium, or homeostasis. Cummins (2009) argues that subjective well-being is an innate personal characteristic, managed by

Table 5.2: Associations between domains of well-being and overall well-being

	Beta	Sig
Family	0.178	0.000
Choice	0.163	0.000
Money and possessions	0.139	0.000
Health	0.091	0.000
Time use	0.086	0.000
The future	0.081	0.000
Appearance	0.078	0.000
School	0.074	0.000
Home	0.055	0.009
Local area	0.031	0.118
Friends	0.024	0.221
Safety	0.012	0.221

Source: Rees et al (2010b, Table 4)

a system of psychological devices (not personality) that have evolved to ensure a homeostatically protected mood. If this is true, we do not pick up variation associated with sociodemographic differences or life events because they have been mitigated by the automatic processes of adaptation and habituation. These issues are discussed further in Bradshaw et al (2010).

Inequalities in subjective well-being

In the UNICEF (2010a) Innocenti Report Card no 9, HBSC data was used to explore inequalities in what was described as self-reported health but actually resonates better with subjective well-being or even mental illness. A scale was produced based on how often in the previous six months children had experienced the following problems:

• headache
• stomach ache
• feeling low
• feeling irritable
• feeling bad tempered
• feeling nervous
• having difficulty getting to sleep
• feeling dizzy.

Inequality was measured by comparing a country's median score with the average score of those below the median – the UK came 8th out of 24 countries.

Bradshaw and Richardson (2009), in their comparison of child well-being in Europe, compared the relationship between overall well-being, which was based on 43 indicators in seven domains, and the percentage of children reporting high life satisfaction. The results are shown in Figure 5.8 – high life satisfaction explains 59% of the variation in overall well-being. The UK is one of the countries with low overall well-being given its level of life satisfaction. From this we might conclude that children are happier than they should be!

Figure 5.8: Overall well-being by life satisfaction

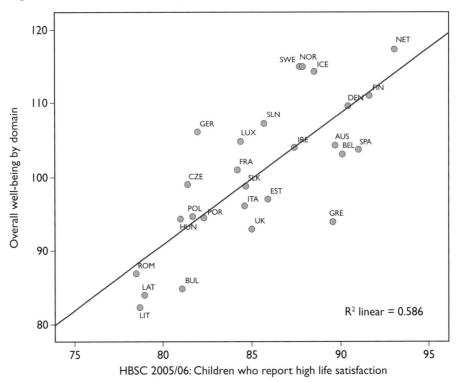

Source: Own analysis of Bradshaw and Richardson (2009) data

Mental health

The following sections focus primarily on clinically measured mental 'disorders'. We review the trends and prevalence of mental illness among children and young people in the UK, drawing mainly on findings from the ONS Mental Health of Children and Young People Survey reports for 1999, 2004 and 2007. Discussion of factors associated with the onset and persistence of mental health problems are also provided. The last section considers suicide among children and young people, its prevalence in the UK and time trends in 15 European countries.

Prevalence of mental disorders among children and young people

The first national survey of the mental health of children and young people in the UK was carried out by the ONS on behalf of the Department of Health in 1999. The aim of the survey was to provide data on the prevalence rates of the three main childhood mental disorders: conduct disorder, hyperactivity and emotional disorder. Two follow-up surveys and reports were published in 2004 and 2007 providing data on changes in mental health over the surveyed periods and factors associated with the onset and persistence of mental ill health among children and young people.

The latest findings on the prevalence rate of childhood mental disorders are provided in *Mental health of children and young people in Great Britain, 2004* (Green et al, 2005). Overall this suggests that 1 in 10 children aged 5-16 has a clinically diagnosed mental disorder. It can be seen in Table 5.3 that in general boys are more likely than girls to have a mental disorder, although it is noted that the gender ratio is greater among the younger age group than the older one. The findings also indicate that the older age group has a higher prevalence rate of any mental disorder than the younger. Conduct disorders (5.8%) and emotional disorders (3.7%) are the two most common forms of disorder. Boys are more likely to have conduct disorders whereas girls are more likely to have emotional disorders.

Table 5.3: Percentage of children with each disorder by age and sex, 2004, Great Britain

	Age 5-10		Age 11-16		
	Boys	**Girls**	**Boys**	**Girls**	**All**
Emotional disorders (anxiety or depression)	2.2	2.5	4.0	6.1	3.7
Conduct disorders	6.9	2.8	8.1	5.1	5.8
Hyperkinetic disorders	2.7	0.4	2.4	0.4	1.5
Less common disorders (including autism, tics, eating disorders and selective mutism)	2.2	0.4	1.6	1.1	1.3
Any disorder	10.2	5.1	12.6	10.3	9.6

Source: Green et al (2005)

Data from 1999 and 2004 suggest that there is no significant difference in the overall prevalence rate of mental disorders among children and young people. However, it was noted that the percentage of boys aged 5-10 who had an emotional disorder declined from 3% in 1999 to 2% in 2004 (Green et al, 2005).

The annual Health Survey for England (HSE) also provides data on the proportion of 13- to 15-year-olds who may have mental ill health. It uses the 12-item General Health Questionnaire (GHQ12) to access the mental health of children through a self-reported questionnaire. This is a widely used and clinically validated screening instrument for psychiatric morbidity. The 12 items measure general levels of happiness, depression and anxiety, sleep disturbance and ability to cope over the last few weeks. In general a GHQ12 score of 4 or more is considered a 'high GHQ12 score', indicating probable psychological disturbance or mental ill health. The latest finding of the GHQ12 of 13- to 15-year-olds is available from the HSE 2009, and it suggests that girls are more likely than boys to score highly, 16% compared to only 5% respectively. The pattern observed appears broadly similar to that of adults (NHS Information Centre, 2010d). Evidence from the above sources would suggest that older girls are more prone to suffer from mental ill health.

Profiles of children and young people with mental disorders

The prevalence of mental disorders is clearly linked to children's socioeconomic backgrounds. Results from the ONS 2004 Survey report (Green et al, 2005) show that mental disorder is more common among children:

- in lone-parent families (16% versus 8% in two-parent families);
- in reconstituted families (14% versus 9% in intact families);
- whose parent had no qualifications (17% versus 4% of those who had a degree);
- in families with unemployed parents (20% versus 8% with both parents employed);
- in families with a low household income (16% versus 5% with a relatively high household income);
- in households with someone receiving disability benefit (24% versus 8% with no disability benefit);
- in families from a lower social class background defined by occupational group (15% versus 4% from a higher social class group);
- living in the private/social rented sector (14-17% versus 7% in owned accommodation);
- living in a deprived area (15% versus 7% in a well-off area).

Additionally, earlier findings suggest that parental mental health, family functioning, level of family discord and stressful life events are all linked to mental ill health in children. Results from the ONS 1999 Survey report (Meltzer et al, 2000) indicate that a higher rate of mental disorders is found among children:

- whose parents scored highly in GHQ12 (18% versus 6% with low GHQ12);
- living in poorly functioning families (18% versus 7% in well functioning families);
- living in a discordant family (35% versus 19% with a low level of family discord);
- who have experienced three or more stressful life events (31% versus 13% reported less stressful events).

Factors associated with the onset of mental disorders

The report of the ONS 2007 Survey on the emotional development and well-being of children and young people (Clements et al, 2008) explored factors that are linked to emotional and conduct disorders. It followed a sample of almost 5,000 children and young people from the 2004 Survey sample and among those who did not have a disorder in 2004 (Time 1), around 3% developed an emotional disorder and/or conduct disorder by 2007 (Time 2).The results of the 2007 Survey suggest that there are a number of factors associated with the onset of the disorders, including child, family and household characteristics (Clements et al, 2008).

The findings from logistic regression analysis (odds ratio is only shown for factors that are statistically significant) give the odds of developing emotional disorder among children decreasing in families with two (odds ratio 0.6) or more children (odds ratio 0.8). However, it was noted that children with the following characteristics were more likely to have developed an emotional disorder by Time 2 if they:

• were older (odds ratio 2.2);
• had a physical illness (odds ratio 1.7);
• were girls (odds ratio 1.6);
• lived in lone-parent families;
• lived in families that became lone-parent families (odds ratio 4.5);
• were in (persistent) workless households (odds ratio 4.4);
• were in rented accommodation;
• were in lower income households;
• were from a lower social class background defined by the household occupational status;
• had mothers who scored highly in GHQ12 (odds ratio 2.2);
• had mothers whose GHQ 12 'remained high' (odds ratio 3.5);
• had mothers reporting three or more stressful life events (odds ratio 1.5-2.7).

Next we consider factors associated with the onset of conduct disorders. The research findings suggest that being a girl reduces the odds of such an onset (odds ratio 0.7). However, the findings show increased likelihood of developing conduct disorders among children and young people:

• with physical illnesses (odds ratio 2.9);
• with special educational needs (SEN) (odds ratio 3.7);
• living in reconstituted families;
• whose families became lone-parent families (odds ratio 2.9);
• in families with more than one child;

- whose mothers had no qualifications;
- in (persistent) workless households;
- (continuously) living in rented accommodation (odds ratio 3.5);
- from a lower social class background;
- whose mothers scored highly and/or remained highly scored in GHQ12 (odds ratio 3.5 and 2.3);
- experienced three or more stressful life events (odds ratio 2.7).

Factors associated with persistence of mental disorders

The same research (Clements et al, 2008) also shows that in a sub-sample of around 400 children and young people who have emotional disorders recorded in the last interview in 2004 (Time 1), 30% were also assessed as having an emotional disorder three years later in 2007 (Time 2). In terms of conduct disorders, around 43% of children and young people who were assessed with a disorder in 2004 were also assessed with it in 2007. Again, in the research a number of factors, including characteristics of children, their families and households, as well as social factors, were explored in relation to the persistence of the emotional and/ or conduct disorders.

The results of logistic regression analysis suggest that only the mother's mental health, in particular if the mother had a persistently high GHQ12 score (odds ratio 3.4) and children and young people being in households where occupational status was defined as 'intermediate and small employers' (odds ratio 5.3), were significantly associated with an increased likelihood of having a persistent emotional disorder.

Turning to factors related to the persistence of conduct disorder, the findings show that the odds of persistent conduct disorder decreased if the mother's GHQ score reduced. Factors associated with higher odds were found among:

- the older age group (odds ratio 2.1);
- those who had SEN at Time 1 (odds ratio 2.1);
- those in households being classified as 'of lower supervisory, semi-routine and routine occupations' (odds ratio 2.3);
- those living in a household with three or more children (odds ratio 2.54);
- those living in rented accommodation (odds ratio 5.9);
- those living in low-income families (odds ratio.2);
- those whose mothers' GHQ scores were persistently high (odds ratio 6.9) or became high (odds ratio 2.5).

Trends in mental health

Although recent ONS Surveys suggest that the prevalence rates of childhood mental disorders remained largely stable between 1999 and 2004 (Green et al,

2005), earlier research by Collishaw et al (2004) and later Maughan et al (2008), suggests that the recent level indicates a levelling off when compared to the high levels observed between mid-1970 and the end of the 20th century.

Collishaw et al (2004) studied time trends in adolescent mental health over a period of 25 years based on three large-scale national samples from the National Child Development Study, the 1970 Birth Cohort Study and the 1999 British Child and Adolescent Mental Health Survey (Meltzer et al, 2000). Comparable questionnaires were completed by parents of 5- to 16-year-olds describing their children's symptoms at 1974, 1986 and 1999. They found overall increases in the proportions of conduct, hyperactive and emotional problems observed over the period. The proportions of conduct problems, hyperactivity problems and emotional problems in 1974 versus 1999 were respectively: 7% versus 15%, 9% versus 12% and 10% versus 17% (Collishaw et al, 2004). It was noted that overall upwards trends in mental ill health over the past decades were also evident in countries such as Scotland (Sweeting et al, 2009), the US (Twenge, 2000), Finland (Sourander et al, 2004), Iceland (Sigfusdottir et al, 2008) and the Netherlands (Tick et al, 2007).

Maughan et al (2008), building on Collishaw et al (2004), in a follow-up study of Green et al (2005), shows that the parent ratings of most 'problem' scores either remained stable, or showed small declines among both children and young people between 1999 and 2004. This finding complemented Green et al's (2005) finding that childhood mental disorders remained largely stable over the period, although a small decline was noted for emotional disorders among boys aged 5-10. Results from the recent studies perhaps indicate that the level of mental ill health among children and young people in the UK after it had peaked in the 1980s and 1990s has begun to show signs of decline.

Suicide

The ONS, Registrar General for Scotland and Registrar General for Northern Ireland publish annual statistics on suicide. Table 5.4 reports the time series on suicide and undetermined death among children and young people in the UK and by countries. It can be seen that there has been a decline in the number of suicides among young people under 25 in the UK. Between 2002 and 2008 there was a 14% reduction in the number of youth suicides and undetermined deaths in the UK – from 720 to 621. However, suicide remains more prevalent among boys than girls and increases with age. The number of suicides among 15- to 24-year-olds has seen an overall reduction for boys and girls, 10% and 16% respectively, between 2002 and 2008.

Table 5.5 reports the suicide rates per 100,000 15- to 24-year-olds in the UK by country and sex. It can be seen that Scotland and Northern Ireland have a much higher suicide rate among this age group than England/Wales. Within England and Wales, the suicide rates either declined slightly or remained relatively stable,

Table 5.4: Number of suicide and undetermined deaths[a] in the UK among 0- to 24-year-olds by age group, country and sex

	2002	2003	2004	2005	2006	2007	2008	2009
0-14 years								
England/Wales								
Males	19	28	23	22	30	12	12	na
Females	28	19	17	10	19	7	11	na
Scotland								
Males	3	1	2	2	2	3	3	2
Females	2	0	0	2	1	2	0	3
Northern Ireland								
Males	1	1	0	2	1	3	1	1
Females	1	0	0	0	2	1	2	0
15-24 years								
England/Wales								
Males	407	426	384	353	398	323	364	na
Females	109	113	128	93	101	72	88	na
Scotland								
Males	97	72	78	70	75	93	71	74
Females	30	31	21	32	12	22	24	21
Northern Ireland								
Males	21	18	18	30	45	29	38	34
Females	2	5	4	3	12	8	7	7
All under 25 in the UK	**720**	**714**	**675**	**619**	**698**	**575**	**621**	**na**
Males aged 15-24	525	516	480	453	518	445	473	na
Females aged 15-24	141	149	153	128	125	102	119	na

Note: [a] Defined as 'intentional self-harm' and event of undetermined intent with inquest verdict 'open' (International Classification of Diseases [ICD]10 coding).

Sources: ONS mortality statistics: deaths registered in England and Wales (Series DH2 and DR); General Register Office (GRO) for Scotland (Vital events reference tables 2002-09); Northern Ireland Registrar General Annual Reports (2002-09)

at around 9-11 men and 2-3 women per 100,000 population between 2002 and 2008. Over the same period, the suicide rate among young Scottish men saw a 30% reduction, from 30 per 100,000 population in 2002 to 21 in 2008. Suicide rates among young women in Scotland fluctuated, between 6 and 10 per 100,000 population over the same period, with an exception for 2006 which has a record low at only 3 per 100,000 population. The suicide rate among young people in Northern Ireland, however, has seen marked increases for both sexes – 17 men per 100,000 population in 2002 compared to 26 men in 2009 and over the same period an increase from 2 to 6 women per 100,000 population.

Table 5.5: Rate[a] of suicide and undetermined deaths[b] in the UK among 15-to 24-year-olds, by country and sex

	2002	2003	2004	2005	2006	2007	2008	2009
England/Wales								
Males	11	11	9	9	9	9	10	na
Females	3	3	3	2	3	2	3	na
Scotland								
Males	30	22	23	21	22	27	21	21
Females	9	10	7	10	3	7	7	6
Northern Ireland								
Males	17	14	14	23	34	22	29	26
Females	2	4	3	2	10	6	6	6

Notes: [a] Rates per 100,000 population aged 15-24. [b] Defined as 'intentional self-harm' and event of undetermined intent with inquest verdict 'open' (ICD10 coding).

Sources: ONS mortality statistics: deaths registered in England and Wales (Series DH2 and DR); GRO for Scotland (Vital events reference tables 2002-09): Northern Ireland Registrar General Annual Reports (2002-09)

International comparisons on suicide rates among 15- to 24-year-olds

According to Greydanus and Calles (2007), worldwide there are approximately 200,000 adolescents and young adult suicides each year. In Europe, suicide has been listed as the second leading cause of death among young people aged 15-29 (Blum and Nelson-Mmari, 2004). The European Commission funded the European Alliance Against Depression (EAAD) project, including 17 European countries and set up in 2004, aiming to prevent and reduce suicide cases. Using data from the project, Värnik et al (2009) analysed the trends in suicide rates among 15- to 24-year-olds from 15 EAAD project countries during 2000-05. This involved a total number of 14,739 suicides in this age group, of which around 80% were men and 20% women.

Table 5.6 summarises Värnik et al's (2009) findings on suicide rates and trends by country and sex. It can be seen that the average suicide rate among young men was 11 per 100,000 in the 15 countries combined. Estonia, Finland and Ireland showed the highest rates per 100,000 males, with the lowest rates found in Portugal, England and Spain. Among females, the average suicide rate per 100,000 was 3. Finland, Scotland and Slovenia showed the highest suicide rates per 100,000 females, with the lowest rates again found in Portugal, England and Spain. In all EAAD countries, it was noted that the suicide rate of 15- to 24-year-olds was almost four times higher for males than females (Värnik et al, 2009). Table 5.6 also illustrates that the suicide rate among young men in most EAAD countries has seen a reduction since 2000. It was noted that the decline of the suicide rate was statistically significant in Germany, Scotland, Spain and England. Among females, suicide trends remained relatively stable over the same period, except for Ireland, where a significant increase in suicide rates was noted during 2000-04 (Värnik et al, 2009).

Table 5.6: Suicide rates per 100,000 in the age group 15-24 in 15 EEAD countries (2000-05)

Gender	Country	2000	2001	2002	2003	2004	2005	Mean
Males	Belgium	25.5	18.4	16.4	17.6	20.1	n/a	19.6
	England	7.6	6.8	6.5	6.2	6.1	n/a	6.6
	Estonia	29.6	35.1	32.8	29.5	29.1	25.2	30.2
	Finland	31.2	27.8	29.2	28.6	33.0	20.3	28.3
	France	12.1	11.1	11.9	12.5	12.2	n/a	12.0
	Germany	12.2	12.4	12.5	10.9	10.5	9.7	11.4
	Hungary	17.2	17.7	17.0	14.4	16.5	n/a	16.6
	Ireland	25.9	27.7	27.6	29.5	27.1	n/a	27.6
	Luxembourg	12.0	11.6	23.2	26.7	22.5	22.1	19.8
	Netherlands	9.4	7.3	8.2	6.9	7.3	7.9	7.8
	Portugal	3.8	5.7	7.1	5.6	5.5	n/a	5.5
	Scotland	28.9	22.0	17.3	15.2	17.2	14.9	19.1
	Slovenia	22.0	24.5	17.3	24.5	21.6	n/a	22.0
	Spain	8.2	7.0	7.0	6.9	6.3	5.9	6.9
	Switzerland	18.6	21.7	17.8	18.0	14.4	n/a	18.1
	Total EAAD countries	11.9	11.3	11.3	10.8	10.6	n/a	11.0
Females	Belgium	5.4	6.0	4.6	7.1	4.9	n/a	5.6
	England	2.4	1.4	1.7	1.5	1.7	n/a	1.7
	Estonia	6.1	6.1	4.0	5.9	5.9	4.9	5.5
	Finland	8.1	6.9	7.2	8.5	9.7	10.3	8.5
	France	3.6	3.6	3.1	3.7	3.5	n/a	3.5
	Germany	3.0	2.7	3.0	3.3	2.7	2.5	2.9
	Hungary	3.9	4.3	3.6	3.4	3.2	n/a	3.7
	Ireland	6.8	5.1	4.7	5.0	2.9	n/a	4.9
	Luxembourg	4.1	4.0	4.0	4.0	0.0	0.0	2.7
	Netherlands	1.9	3.4	2.8	3.1	2.6	3.4	2.9
	Portugal	1.0	1.1	1.5	1.6	1.2	n/a	1.3
	Scotland	5.8	6.4	8.2	8.2	5.9	8.3	7.1
	Slovenia	9.2	7.2	2.2	6.7	9.1	n/a	6.9
	Spain	1.6	1.5	1.7	2.1	2.1	1.4	1.7
	Switzerland	4.9	4.8	6.7	4.9	4.9	n/a	5.2
	Total EAAD countries	3.1	2.9	2.9	3.2	2.9	n/a	3.0

Source: Värnik et al (2009, Table 1, p 219)

Conclusion

Research on child subjective well-being is less developed, with measurement difficulties and curiously inconsistent results. For example, why are boys more likely to exhibit mental health problems when subjective well-being and unhappiness is more common in girls? There is good evidence that mental ill health is more common among children in families with lower incomes living in poverty. There is some very slight evidence that subjective well-being is also associated with socioeconomic status. Results are more consistent for age – older children exhibit more mental ill health and lower subjective well-being. There is some evidence that the subjective well-being of children has been improving recently, and also that the mental health of children has stopped deteriorating. National statistics suggest that overall, suicide rates among children and young people in the UK reduced between 2002 and 2008. International research on suicide rates among children and young adults has also shown signs of decline in many European countries since 2000.

Notes

[1] http://www2.ohchr.org/english/law/crc.htm

SIX

Education

Antonia Keung

Key statistics

- Around 80% of pupils achieved Level 4 or above in English and Mathematics by the end of Key Stage (KS) 2 in 2008/09.
- Of pupils in the last year of compulsory education, 65% achieved five GCSEs at grade A*-C or equivalent in England in 2007/08.
- Over 90% of A Level pupils achieved two or more A Levels or equivalent in England in 2007/08.
- In PISA (Programme for International Student Assessment) 2006, UK students achieved results similar to their OECD peers in Reading and Mathematics but outperformed the OECD average in Science, which put the UK among the top six in the EU countries.
- In 2008, 46% of schoolchildren in England agreed they 'like being in school'; 42% agreed that 'school is interesting; and 36% agreed that they 'look forward to going to school'.
- In England in 2008/09, the rate of overall absence in primary schools was 5.5%; the rate for all secondary schools was 7.3%. Wales has the highest overall absence rates in both primary and secondary school – 6.8% and 9% respectively.
- About 5% of the school population in England was excluded from school over a fixed period, and 0.09% (or 9 in 10,000 pupils) was permanently excluded.
- In 2009, there were around 183,200 16- to 18-year-olds not in education, employment or training (NEET) in England, representing 9.2% of all 16- to 18-year-olds.
- In 2009 some 221,670 pupils across all schools in England had statement of SEN (special educational needs), representing 2.7% of all pupils.

Key trends

- The proportion of 19-year-olds obtaining at least a Level 2 qualification or equivalent in England increased from 67% in 2004 to almost 79% in 2009.
- The proportion of all 16- to 18-year-olds remaining in education and training increased from 75% in 2002 to almost 83% in 2009.
- The percentage of the school population being excluded from schools declined between 2007 and 2009.
- The proportion of young people aged 16 to 18 NEET increased from 8.9% in 1997 to a record high of 10.7% in 2005 and has since declined, with a provisional figure for 2009 of 9.2%.

> - The proportion of statemented SEN pupils in all schools in England reduced slightly, from 2.9% in 2006 to 2.7% in 2009.
>
> **Key sources**
>
> - The Children's Society National Child Well-being Survey in England
> - Department for Education (DfE) (former Department for Children, Schools and Families, DCSF)
> - Department of Education in Northern Ireland (DENI)
> - Health Behaviour in School-aged Children (HBSC) survey
> - Northern Ireland Statistics and Research Agency (NISRA)
> - Office for National Statistics (ONS)
> - Scottish Government
> - Programme for International Student Assessment (PISA) 2000, 2003 and 2006
> - Welsh Assembly Government

Introduction

This chapter reviews the educational attainment of children across the countries in the UK and over time and, where possible, puts this in a wider international context. It focuses on the formal qualifications attained by children in compulsory schooling and up to A Level, and explores how attainment varies by age, gender, ethnicity and social class. The chapter also refers to the findings from the Programme for International Student Assessment (PISA 2006). Rather than looking at the success rates in formal examinations, PISA evaluates the performance of school leavers of participating countries by assessing the ability of the 15-year-olds to use their knowledge and skills to meet the challenges of adult life. As such, PISA assessments do not intend to match the curriculum of any participating country (OECD, 2007). Additionally, the chapter reviews how schoolchildren feel about their well-being at school by drawing attention to the research findings from The Children's Society survey on young people's well-being (Rees et al, 2010a) and the Health Behaviour in School-aged Children (HBSC) survey (Currie et al, 2008a). Research findings on the relationship between social background and educational outcome are discussed briefly. The chapter then explores the prevalence of educational disaffection through reviewing the data on truancy, school exclusion and young people not in education, employment or training (NEET). The final section examines the latest data and analysis on special educational needs (SEN).

Context of school types

All children of compulsory school age between 5 and 16 across the UK are entitled to free, full-time education, although it is worth noting that in England, the *Education and Skills Act 2008* (DCSF, 2008a) will raise the school leaving age to 18 from 2015. There are many different types of schools in the UK – grammar schools, community schools, foundation schools, trust schools, voluntary (aided or controlled) schools, and some special schools are state schools maintained by the Local Education Authority (LEA). Schools that are not maintained by the LEA include independent (private) schools, city technology colleges, academies and also some special schools. The majority of the children in the UK are in state-(maintained) schools; in 2009 there were approximately 7.3 million pupils in state-funded primary, secondary and special schools (DCSF, 2009a). Data provided by the Independent Schools Council (ISC) shows that there are about 628,000 schoolchildren in independent (private) schools in the UK, approximately 6.5% of all schoolchildren in the UK and over 7% of all schoolchildren in England (ISC, 2010).

The way schools are funded and governed and how the pupils are selected and taught differs by the type of school. Under the Labour government the education systems remained diverse and divisive. Tomlinson (2005) illustrates how the current school system continues to mirror the social class structure and how it is associated with variations in levels of achievement. For instance, statistics suggest that pupils who attend an academy are more likely to be eligible for free school meals (FSM), have special educational needs (SEN) and have lower Key Stage (KS) 2 attainments compared to those entering other types of school. They are also more likely to have come from a minority ethnic background and speak English as an additional language (DCSF, 2008b). However, in grammar schools the incidence of FSM and SEN is below the national average, and pupils from minority ethnic groups are under-represented (DCSF, 2008b).

Although the government was keen to break the intergenerational cycle of disadvantages and poverty, for example, the End Child Poverty Campaign, and related policy showed the greatest efforts ever made in contemporary Britain, the continuous segregation of the schooling system and lack of intergenerational educational mobility among the very poor may curb the effectiveness of such efforts. Nevertheless, as shown in the following sections, there are signs of improvement in the general levels of educational attainment of children and young people, after huge investment on the part of the Labour government.

Education attainments of children at the end of KS2

All children in maintained primary schools in England, Wales and Northern Ireland are required to take part in the National Curriculum tests in English and Maths before they move on to secondary schools. The National Curriculum tests assess children's achievements against a set of attainment targets determined by the National Curriculum. By the end of KS2 pupils are expected to have achieved at least Level 4 in both English and Maths. Figure 6.1 reports the time trend of pupils' attainments by KS2 in both subjects in England. The proportions of pupils achieving the expected level reported an overall increase over the period and the

Figure 6.1: Percentage of pupils achieving Level 4 or above in KS2 tests for English and Mathematics, England, 1997-2010[a]

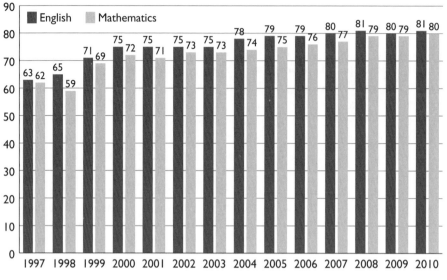

Note: [a] Figures for 2010 are based on provisional data. Figures for all other years are based on final data.

Source: DfE (2010a)

proportion of the last three years' figures remain largely stable, at around 80% for both subjects. This compares to less than 65% of pupils in 1997.

There has been a significant gender gap in KS2 attainment, particularly in the English tests. Figure 6.2 shows that girls continue to outperform boys in English,

Figure 6.2: Percentages of pupils achieving Level 4 or above in KS2 tests, by subjects and sex, 2010[a]

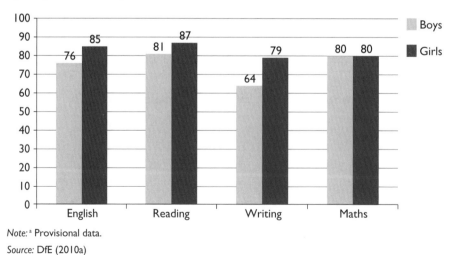

Note: [a] Provisional data.

Source: DfE (2010a)

Reading and Writing. It is worth noting that the percentage of girls at the expected level in Maths is equal to that of boys for the first time since 2004 (DfE, 2010a).

Attainments at the age of 15+

Governments in the UK regularly publish data on the educational attainments of children at the end of compulsory schooling. As revealed in Figure 6.3, there have been overall increases in the proportion of pupils achieving good results in public examinations and the participation rate in education and/or training under the Labour government. In England, there have been steady increases in the proportions of 15-year-olds with at least five GCSEs at grades A*-C or equivalents between 1996 and 2008. Figure 6.3 shows that 64.8% of the pupils achieved five GCSEs at grades A*-C or equivalent in 2008 compared to only 45.1% in 1997, indicating a huge increase in the numbers of pupils achieving good GCSE qualifications.

However, there are some variations in GCSE performance by regions. Figure 6.4 shows that the North East of England has the highest proportion of pupils with good GCSE qualifications (66.4%), whereas Yorkshire and the Humber regions (62.1%) and East Midlands (63%) have some of the lowest proportions.

Comparing across the UK, Figure 6.5 shows that girls consistently outperformed boys. Pupils from Northern Ireland have the highest proportion, attaining five or more GCSEs A*-C, followed by pupils from England.

Figure 6.3: Percentage of 15-year-olds with at least five GCSEs at grades A*-C or equivalents, England, 1995-2008

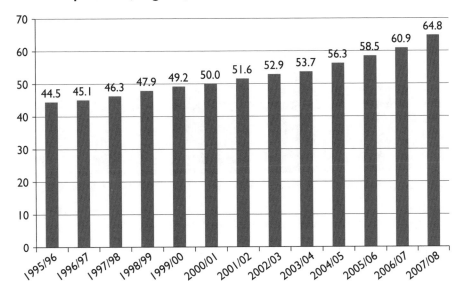

Source: DfE (2010d)

Figure 6.4: Percentage of 15-year-olds with at least five GCSEs at grades A*-C or equivalents by English regions, 2007/08

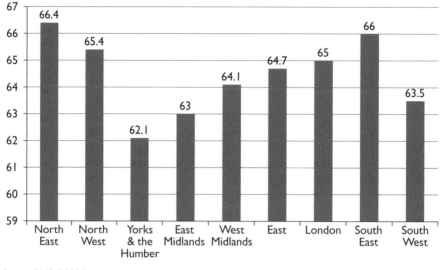

Source: ONS (2010c)

Figure 6.5: Percentage of pupils in their last year of compulsory education achieving five or more GCSEs A*-C or Scottish National Qualifications (NQs), 2007/08

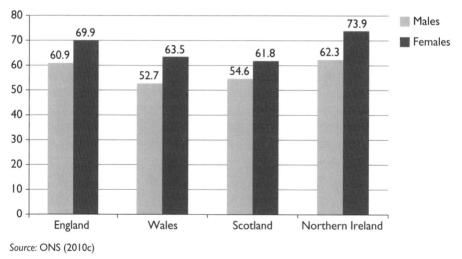

Source: ONS (2010c)

Except for Scotland, the gender gap of attainment is much narrower with higher qualifications, although Figure 6.6 shows that still slightly more girls than boys achieved two or more A Levels or equivalent in 2007/08. It should be noted that the Scottish education system is very different from the education system

Figure 6.6: Percentage of candidates achieving two or more A Levels or equivalent, 2007/08

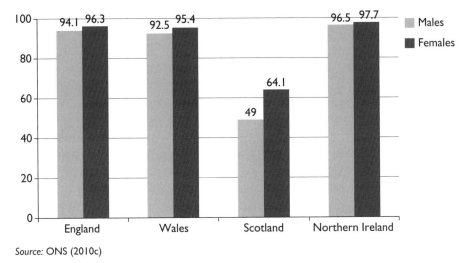

Source: ONS (2010c)

in England, Wales and Northern Ireland. In Scotland, the post–16 qualifications include Highers and Advanced Highers, making direct comparison impossible between Scotland and the rest of the UK.

There were some small variations in the proportions of pupils achieving two or more A Levels or equivalent among Northern Ireland, England and Wales, with pupils from Northern Ireland having the highest percentages of achievement for both boys (96.5%) and girls (97.7%).

Since 1998, the Department for Work and Pensions (DWP) has published an annual report, *Opportunity for all*, setting out the progress made by the government in tackling poverty and social exclusion against a set of national indicators. One of the indicators relating to young people was the proportion of '19-year-olds with at least a Level 2 qualification'. This indicator was last published by DWP in 2007 and subsequently discontinued. However, the Department for Children, Schools and Families (DCSF) continued to collect data on this indicator and the 2008 and 2009 data are presented in Figure 6.7. The trend shows a steady increase in the proportion of young people achieving at least a Level 2 qualification, with 78.7% in 2009 compared to 66.7% in 2004.

Another relevant indicator reported by *Opportunity for all* was '16- to 18-year-olds in learning', also referred to as 'in education or training'. Figure 6.8 shows an overall increase in the proportion over the period from 1997 to 2009, although there were fluctuations prior to 2002 because of some reported under-estimations. Comparing the latest data in 2009 to the previously published data in 2007, it appears that there are greater increases in the percentages in the last three years than in any previous years observed.

Figure 6.7: Percentage of 19-year-olds with at least a Level 2 qualification or equivalent, England

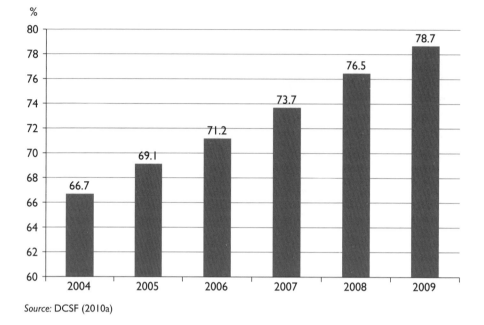

Source: DCSF (2010a)

Figure 6.8: Percentage of all 16- to 18-year-olds in education and training, England

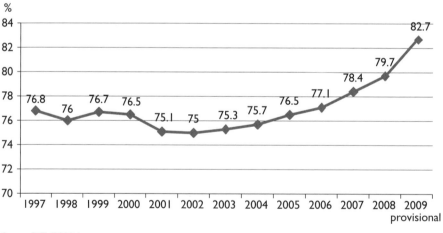

Source: DfE (2010c)

Competences at the age of 15

The OECD undertakes a comparative study on the knowledge and skills of 15-year-olds through PISA. The PISA survey has been conducted every three years since 2000 on the competencies of students on Reading, Mathematics and Science. PISA measures student performance on all three subject areas in each cycle of its survey, but with a particular focus on one subject at a time. The intention of the PISA Reading test is to assess the ability of the students to understand, use and reflect on information from texts in situations encountered in life. The Mathematics test aims to assess the ability to apply mathematical knowledge to functional use in different situations in adult life. And the Science test measures scientific knowledge and concepts as well as understanding of scientific processes and contexts needed in adult life (OECD, 2007).

All three subject areas are scored on a points scale constructed to produce an average of 500 points across all students in all participating countries and with a standard deviation of 100 points. Internationally, about two thirds of students scored between 400 and 600 points. So far, the OECD has published three PISA survey reports. The first survey in 2000 focused primarily on Reading (OECD, 2001), the second one in 2003 on Mathematics (OECD, 2004) and the third one in 2006 on Science (OECD, 2007). There were over 400,000 students from 57 countries, inclusive of all 30 OECD member countries, participating in the PISA survey 2006. This compares to a total of 43 countries that took part in the first cycle and 41 countries in the second cycle, which represents a significant increase in the number of participating countries.

In the UK, eligible schools from the main samples of all four countries participated in a two-hour assessment in PISA 2006. This involved a total of 4,935 students from 169 schools in England (Bradshaw et al, 2007c), 3,044 students from 124 schools in Wales (Bradshaw et al 2007d), 2,728 students from 107 schools in Northern Ireland (Bradshaw et al 2007e) and around 2,700 students from 101 schools in Scotland (Scottish Government Social Research, 2007). Data on student performance collected in the last three cycles provided a valuable source that allowed progress of individual countries to be compared and monitored. However, as a result of non-response bias identified in the UK samples at the student level in PISA 2000 and 2003, the UK results cannot be compared with those of other participating countries, as is also the case with comparing the UK results from PISA 2006 with those from 2000 (OECD, 2007).

This section presents the performance results from PISA 2006 relating to England, Wales, Northern Ireland and Scotland. It also compares the UK results with the other PISA participating countries. It should be noted that the rankings presented in the tables that follow are merely for the purpose of demonstration, and differences between countries may not be statistically significant unless otherwise specified in the text. Table 6.1 summarises the student performance in Science literacy of the top 30 countries based on the mean performance score.

The UK achieved a mean score of 515 in Science literacy, which was higher than the OECD average of 500. In Table 6.1 countries that have a ranking from 1 to 7 are countries that have significantly outperformed England, whereas countries that have a ranking beyond 25 are significantly below the English scores. The rest of the countries are not significantly different from England. Thus, it can be

Table 6.1: Comparison of mean Science literacy proficiency and distribution for 15-year-old sample population in OECD countries

Rank	Countries	Mean score	Standard deviation	Score difference between sex (M-F)	Score difference between bottom 5% and top 5%
1	Finland*	563	86	−3	281
2	Hong Kong-China	542	92	7	301
3	Canada	534	94	**4**	309
4	Chinese Taipei	532	94	7	307
5	Estonia*	531	84	−4	276
6	Japan	531	100	3	328
7	New Zealand	530	107	−4	352
8	Australia	527	100	0	328
9	Netherlands*	525	96	**7**	313
10	Korea	522	90	−2	296
11	Liechtenstein	522	97	−11	317
12	Slovenia*	519	98	−8	322
13	England	516	107	**11**	350
14	Germany*	516	100	7	328
15	Scotland	515	100	4	330
16	United Kingdom*	515	107	**10**	348
17	Czech Republic*	513	98	5	322
18	Switzerland	512	99	**6**	325
19	Austria*	511	98	8	321
20	Macao-China	511	78	4	257
21	Belgium*	510	100	1	323
22	Northern Ireland	508	113	2	367
23	Republic of Ireland*	508	94	0	309
24	Wales	505	102	**10**	334
25	Hungary*	504	88	6	288
26	Sweden*	503	94	1	308
27	OECD average	500	95	**2**	312
28	Poland*	498	90	3	293
29	Denmark*	496	93	**9**	305
30	France*	495	102	3	333

Notes: Values that are statistically significant are indicated in bold. Countries not in the OECD are presented in italic. EU countries are starred *. Only results of the top 30 countries are shown.

Source: Bradshaw et al (2007c)

seen that England, although not one of the highest achieving of the countries, is doing relatively well internationally.

Furthermore, significant gender difference in Science literacy is noted in some of the countries presented, including the UK, and particularly England and Wales, with males significantly outperforming their female counterparts. Overall, the UK nations except for Scotland have shown a higher spread in the attainment scores than the OECD average, as indicated by the size of the standard deviation. Northern Ireland in particular has the highest standard deviation of the presented countries in Table 6.1, which means a much larger spread of abilities than in other countries. This could be related to the selective schooling system in Northern Ireland. The performance gap between the top 5% and bottom 5% in Northern Ireland was 367 points, the highest among all the participating countries, and way above the OECD average, suggesting the presence of a huge inequality in Science attainment.

Results of the Mathematics literacy test are given in Table 6.2. Students from England achieved a mean score of 495 for Mathematics, which was not statistically different from the OECD average of 498. Countries with a ranking from 1 to 17 and including Slovenia significantly outperformed England in Mathematics. The rest of the countries presented in Table 6.2 are not significantly different from England. Countries that are significantly below England are not presented. Males significantly outperform females in Mathematics in most countries including the OECD. The gender gap in Mathematics performance is wider in England, Scotland and Wales than the OECD average. It is interesting to note that while there is a wide gap between the highest and the lowest achieving groups in Northern Ireland, the gender gap in Mathematics is not statistically significant. Except for Northern Ireland, all the other three nations of the UK have a smaller attainment gap between the highest and the lowest achieving groups than the OECD average.

Results of the Reading literacy test are given in Table 6.3. England's performance in reading is not significantly different from the OECD average, nor is the UK as a whole. Countries that significantly outperform England include those shown with a ranking from 1 to 7. The rest of the countries are not significantly different from England except for Iceland, which is significantly below. Other countries that performed significantly less well than England are not presented.

Furthermore, England has a rather large variation around the mean and is above that of the OECD average. Scotland and Wales are below the average. There is a significant gender difference in Reading attainment. Females do significantly better in Reading than males in all participating countries. Although compared with the OECD average, the UK as a whole shows a smaller gender gap in Reading performance. Among the four UK nations, Scotland has the smallest gender difference, while Northern Ireland has the biggest. Comparing the highest and the lowest achievers, the attainment gap in England is wider than the OECD average and is only slightly smaller than Northern Ireland. Both Scotland and Wales have a smaller attainment gap than the OECD average.

Table 6.2: Comparison of mean Mathematics literacy proficiency and distribution for 15-year-old sample population in OECD countries

Rank	Countries	Mean score	Standard deviation	Score difference between sex (M-F)	Score difference between bottom 5% and top 5%
1	*Chinese Taipei*	549	103	13	333
2	Finland*	548	81	12	266
3	*Hong Kong-China*	547	93	16	306
4	Korea	547	93	9	302
5	Netherlands*	531	89	13	290
6	Switzerland	530	97	13	320
7	Canada	527	86	14	281
8	*Liechtenstein*	525	93	0	310
9	*Macao-China*	525	84	11	276
10	Japan	523	91	20	298
11	New Zealand	522	93	11	306
12	Australia	520	88	14	289
13	Belgium*	520	106	7	341
14	*Estonia**	515	80	1	264
15	Denmark*	513	85	10	278
16	Czech Republic*	510	103	11	337
17	Iceland	506	88	−4	289
18	Scotland	506	85	16	279
19	Austria*	505	98	23	319
20	Germany*	504	99	20	325
21	*Slovenia**	504	89	5	292
22	Sweden*	502	90	5	295
23	Republic of Ireland*	501	82	11	268
24	OECD average	498	92	11	300
25	France*	496	96	6	312
26	England	495	89	17	293
27	Poland*	495	87	9	285
28	United Kingdom*	495	89	17	292
29	Northern Ireland	494	93	7	306
30	Slovak Republic*	492	95	14	308
36	Wales	484	83	16	270

Notes: Values that are statistically significant are indicated in bold. Countries not in the OECD are presented in italic. EU countries are starred *. Only results of the top 30 countries are shown.

Source: Bradshaw et al (2007c)

Table 6.3: Comparison of mean Reading literacy proficiency and distribution for 15-year-old sample population in OECD countries

Rank	Countries	Mean score	Standard deviation	Score difference between sex (M-F)	Score difference between bottom 5% and top 5%
1	Korea	556	88	−35	289
2	Finland*	547	81	−51	265
3	Hong Kong-China	536	82	−31	270
4	Canada	527	96	−32	316
5	New Zealand	521	105	−37	344
6	Republic of Ireland*	517	92	−34	303
7	Australia	513	94	−37	307
8	Liechtenstein	510	95	−45	321
9	Poland*	508	100	−40	328
10	Netherlands*	507	97	−24	317
11	Sweden*	507	98	−40	324
12	Belgium*	501	110	−40	360
13	Estonia*	501	85	−46	279
14	Scotland	499	96	−26	316
15	Switzerland	499	94	−31	311
16	Japan	498	102	−31	337
17	Chinese Taipei	496	84	−21	278
18	England	496	102	−29	337
19	Germany*	495	112	−42	359
20	Northern Ireland	495	106	−33	348
21	United Kingdom*	495	102	−29	335
22	Denmark*	494	89	−30	293
23	Slovenia*	494	88	−54	287
24	Macao-China	492	77	−26	250
25	OECD average	492	99	−38	324
26	Austria*	490	106	−45	353
27	France*	488	104	−35	341
28	Iceland	484	97	−48	318
29	Norway	484	105	−46	342
30	Czech Republic*	483	111	−46	363
32	Wales	481	96	−31	323

Notes: Values that are statistically significant are indicated in bold. Countries not in the OECD are presented in italic. EU countries are starred *. Only results of the top 30 countries are shown.

Source: Bradshaw et al (2007c)

Children's well-being at schools

In addition to assessing children's educational performance both nationally and internationally, there has been a growing interest in how children feel about their well-being. In 2008, The Children's Society and the University of York conducted a national survey on the well-being of children and young people. The survey involved a sample of 7,000 children aged 10-15 in England and asked about their well-being regarding various aspects of their lives (Rees et al, 2010a). One aspect was how children felt about their well-being at school. Figure 6.9 shows that in the survey most children agreed that their 'schools are interesting' (42%) and they 'like being in school' (46%). However, a significant minority of children said they were not 'looking forward to going to school' (27%).

Figure 6.9: Percentage of schoolchildren on their views about schools

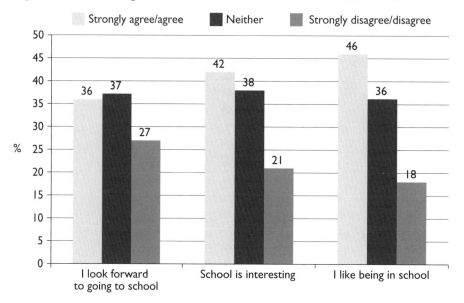

Source: The Children's Society Survey data 2008 (Rees et al, 2010a)

The HBSC conducted by the World Health Organization (WHO) provides comparative data on school well-being. With reference to the most recent data (2005/06), Figure 6.10 compares the proportion of children from the UK and the OECD who reported that they 'like school a lot'. Significantly, more girls than boys reported positively to the question. Children in England were significantly more likely to report that they liked school a lot than those in the other four UK nations as well as the average of the OECD countries.

Figure 6.10: Percentage of 11-, 13- and 15-year-olds who reported that they like school a lot, by sex and countries

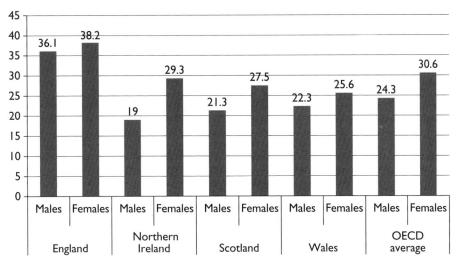

Source: HBSC 2005/06

Education disaffection

It is encouraging to see that most children in the UK are doing well and are happy in school. However, a minority of children still might find themselves disengaged or have difficulty in fully engaging in education. This section reports relevant statistics in relation to education disaffection, including truancy and school exclusion and young people not in education, employment or training (NEET) and those with special educational needs.

Truancy

Research highlights the negative impacts on educational attainments of absentees, their social development as well as future employment prospects. Persistent truancy is found to be associated with a range of social problems, for example, teenage pregnancy, drug taking and engaging in criminal activities (Wilson et al, 2008). The truancy rate was taken as one of the key indicators in *Opportunity for all* to measure the progress of the government in tackling poverty and social exclusion.

Truancy rates are calculated from absenteeism rates (the percentage of half-days of school attendance missed) collated via the School Census. A distinction is made between authorised and unauthorised absences. Truancy is defined as unauthorised absence from school and research suggests a possible link between truancy and behavioural problems. Furthermore, there is evidence of parentally condoned absenteeism, where children are being kept away from school by their parents, for example, to look after a sick parent/sibling or go shopping (Wilson et al, 2008).

Table 6.4 reports the absenteeism rates by school levels and by countries in 2008/09. Rates for unauthorised absences in primary schools are around one half that of secondary schools, with a slightly smaller difference noted in Wales. Secondary schools in all countries reported a higher rate of overall absence than primary schools. The highest overall absence rates were reported in Wales, with 6.8% of the total half-days absence in primary school and 9% in secondary schools. This compares with 5.5% and 7.3% respectively in England. It should be noted that caution must be exercised when comparing the data across countries, owing to possible differences in the way absence is being interpreted by schools.

The overall absence rates in primary and secondary schools in England remain at similar levels in the period from 2007/08 and 2008/09 (DCSF, 2009d).

Table 6.4: Percentage of total half-days absence in the UK, 2008/09

	Primary schools		Secondary schools	
	Unauthorised absence	Overall absence	Unauthorised absence	Overall absence
England	0.7	5.5	1.5	7.3
Wales	1.0	6.8	1.7	9.0
Northern Ireland	1.2	5.1	2.5	7.7
Scotland	n/a	4.8	n/a	8.8

Source: DENI and NISRA (2009)

School exclusion

School exclusion data are collected by government departments in all four nations of the UK. Distinction is made between fixed period and permanent exclusion. The former refers to pupils who are excluded from school but remain on the school register because they are expected to return when the exclusion period is completed. Permanent exclusion refers to pupils who are excluded and their names removed from their school registers. Pupils who are permanently excluded would be educated at another school, or some other type of provision made. It should be noted that the terms 'suspension' and 'expulsion' are used in Northern Ireland.

Data collection on school exclusions has improved markedly in recent years. Previously only permanent exclusion data was collected, but since 2003/04 data on fixed period exclusion has also been collected. The data coverage has also been extended to include city technology colleges and academies from 2000/01 on permanent exclusions and from 2005/06 on fixed period exclusions. The School Census is now the main vehicle for relevant data collection; it has replaced the former Termly Exclusion Survey since 2005/06.

Table 6.5 reports the numbers and rates of school exclusions in all schools in England. It is difficult to compare the rates of fixed period exclusions of recent years to those reported before 2007 because of the change in data coverage, as mentioned earlier, but there is evidence to suggest that the percentage of fixed

Table 6.5: Number of fixed period and permanent exclusion in all schools, England, 2003/04 to 2008/09

	2003/ 04	2004/ 05[c]	2005/ 06[d]	2006/ 07	2007/ 08	2008/ 09
Number of fixed period exclusions	344,510	389,560	n/a	425,600	383,830	363,280
% of school population[a]	4.49	5.12	n/a	5.66	5.14	4.89
Number of permanent exclusions	9,990	9,570	9,330	8,680	8,130	6,550
% of school population[b]	0.13	0.13	0.12	0.12	0.11	0.09

Notes:

[a] The number of fixed period exclusions expressed as a percentage of the number (headcount) of all pupils (excluding dually registered pupils) in January each year.

[b] The number of permanent exclusions expressed as a percentage of the number (headcount) of all pupils (excluding dually registered pupils) in January each year.

[c] Information on fixed period exclusions was collected from city technology colleges and academies for the first time in 2005/06.

[d] Data is not available for the 2005/06 school year as information on fixed period exclusions from primary schools and special schools was not available due to the change in the method of data collection.

Source: DfE (2010b)

period exclusions has declined steadily, from 5.66% in 2007 to 4.89% in 2009. Table 6.5 also shows that the percentage of permanent exclusions in England has also declined over the period from 2004 to 2009, the latest record of 0.09% being the lowest figure since the record began in 1997/98.

The majority of school exclusion involves secondary students, and boys in particular. The latest data provided in 2008/09 by the Department for Education (DfE) indicates that 78% of the total number of permanent exclusions and 75% of all fixed period exclusions were boys (DfE, 2010b). Boys are much more likely than girls to be excluded from school at a younger age, with very few girls being excluded during primary years. However, the likelihood of exclusion increases for both boys and girls at Years 9 and 10, which accounts for about 54% of all permanent exclusions recorded in 2008/09 (DfE 2010b). The most commonly quoted reason for exclusion (both permanent and fixed period) was 'persistent disruptive behaviour', and this was associated with nearly 30% of permanent exclusions and about 23% of fixed period exclusions (DfE, 2010b).

Those with special educational needs (SEN) are over-represented among the excluded pupils. Compared with non-SEN pupils, SEN pupils including those with and without statements are over eight times more likely to be permanently excluded and over six times more likely to be temporarily excluded (DfE, 2010b). With reference to the DfE figures reported for the school population in 2008/09, pupils of Black origin (0.18%) were twice as likely than White pupils (0.09%) and over three times more likely than Asian pupils (0.05%) to be excluded from school permanently. Of all pupils of Black origin, Black Caribbean pupils reported the highest percentage of permanent exclusion (0.30%). Of White pupils, Gypsy/ Roma reported the highest percentage (0.38%), followed by Travellers of Irish heritage (0.30%). Within the Mixed category, White-and-Black Caribbean has the highest rate (0.25%), and among the Asian category, Pakistani has the highest rate (0.07%) and Indian the lowest (0.03%). As for the percentage of fixed period exclusions, again Black pupils (7.74%) reported a higher rate than White (5.58%) and Asian pupils (2.65%). Similar to the pattern reported above for pupils excluded permanently, the following ethnicities showed a higher rate within the classification of each ethnic group: Black Caribbean pupils (11.24%), Travellers of Irish heritage (17.06%), Gypsy/Roma (15.7%), White-and-Black Caribbean (11.44%) and Pakistani (3.55%) (DfE, 2010b). Statistics also show FSM pupils to be about three times more likely to be excluded from school either permanently or over a fixed period than non-FSM pupils (DfE, 2010b).

To see how the incidence of permanent and fixed period exclusions in England compared with the other three UK nations, Table 6.6 provides an overview of the figures reported for the 2006/07 school year within the UK. It should be noted that Northern Ireland's figures are not directly comparable to the other countries because of variations in the way exclusion is defined. As shown in Table 6.6, England has the highest rate of permanent exclusions and the second highest rate of fixed period exclusions. Scotland has the highest rate of fixed period exclusions, but has only about one third of the rate of permanent exclusions reported in England. These variations are likely to be attributable to different school policies and legislation regarding exclusion in different countries.

Table 6.6: School exclusion recorded in all schools in the UK, 2006/07

		Permanent	Fixed period
England[a]	Number of exclusions	8,680	425,600
	Rate per 1,000 pupils	1.1	52.2
Wales	Number of exclusions	291	20,096
	Rate per 1,000 pupils	0.7	48.2
Northern Ireland[b]	Number of exclusions	45	4,981
	Rate per 1,000 pupils	0.1	15.1
Scotland	Number of exclusions	248	44,546
	Rate per 1,000 pupils	0.4	64.5

Notes: [a] Pupil numbers for England are rounded to the nearest 10. [b] Permanent exclusions data for Northern Ireland is the total of pupils excluded rather than the total number of exclusions.

Source: Welsh Assembly Government (2010b)

Not in education, employment, or training (NEET)

NEET is another indicator of educational disaffection. The data reported in this section relates to England only. The Labour government previously set up a target of reducing the proportion of 16- to 18-year-olds NEET by 2 percentage points from 9.6% in 2004 by 2010. Figure 6.11 presents the time series of NEET percentages and it indicates that the proportions of NEET fluctuated between the end of 2004 and 2009. The proportion of NEET in 2005 increased to a record high at 10.7%, and since then it more or less declined but picked up again

Figure 6.11: Percentage of all 16- to 18-year olds NEET, England

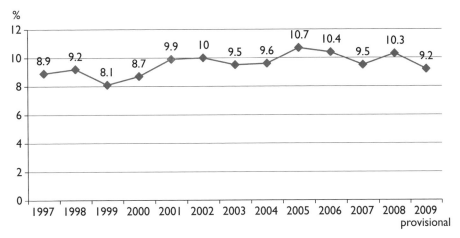

Source: DfE (2010c)

in 2008. In 2009, 9.2% of all those aged 16-18 were NEET, lower than 10.3% previously recorded in 2008. The recent reduction in the proportion of NEET is attributable to the increase in the proportion of young people who choose to remain in education and training. Given these persistently high rates reported over the last couple of years, it was clear that the Labour government would have been unable to meet their target.

By the end of 2009 there were as many as 183,200 16- to 18-year-olds NEET. A detailed breakdown of the statistics by age and sex for 16- to 18-year-olds is available for the earlier release of NEET data. Figure 6.12 reports statistics in 2008, and it shows that the proportion of young people NEET increases as they become older and boys outnumber girls in all age groups.

Figure 6.12: Percentage of 16- to 18-year-olds NEET in England, by sex and age

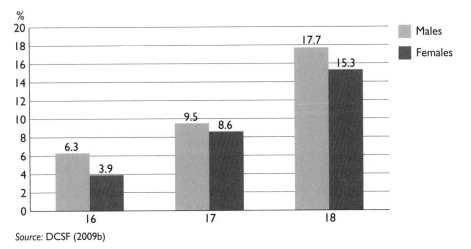

Source: DCSF (2009b)

The OECD published a set of international data regarding the proportion of young people aged 15-19 not in education and unemployed or not in the labour force in 2007 (OECD, 2009b). The data provides the closest indicator of NEET and this section looks at how the level of young people NEET in the UK compared internationally. In most countries, 15- to 19-year-olds are still in full-time education, although there may be small variations in terms of the age range due to various education systems in different countries. Figure 6.13 presents the percentage of these age groups NEET in the OECD and partner countries.

Figure 6.13 shows that in 2007, 10.7% of 15- to 19-year-olds in the UK were not in education and unemployed or not in the labour force. This figure was substantially higher than the EU19 average of 5.9% as well as the OECD average of 7.4%. Early experience of exclusion from education and the labour market is often linked to a series of disadvantages, including teenage parenting, leaving care, homelessness, drug abuse and youth offending. The high rate of inactivity among the young people in the UK is certainly an area of concern, as research demonstrates that it is very costly to both individuals as well as society as a whole in terms of lost contribution and welfare expenditure (Coles et al, 2010). As many countries are still being affected by the global economic recession that started in around 2008, it is very likely that the proportions of NEET might have increased in more recent years.

Special educational needs (SEN)

In England, the DfE (and the former DCSF) collected information on SEN in all schools. Conditions leading to the identification of SEN include: visual, hearing or other physical impairments; speech, language and communication needs; cognitive disorders and learning difficulties; and behavioural, emotional and social difficulties. The most acute needs are given a formal statement of SEN. The most common condition reported among the primary school-age pupils was speech, language and communication needs, and among the secondary school-age pupils, learning difficulties was the most prevalent type of SEN (DfE, 2010e). This section focuses mainly on statemented SEN pupils.

In 2009, some 221,670 pupils across all schools in England had SEN statements, representing 2.7% of all pupils. The incidence of SEN was greater in state-funded secondary schools (2%) than in maintained primary schools (1.4%). There were also some variations in the incidence of SEN by sex, age, FSM status and ethnicity. Boys were over 2.5 times more likely than girls to be identified with SEN. The rate of pupils with SEN in mainstream primary schools increases with age, ranging from 1.3% for 6-year-olds to 2.2% for 10-year-olds. For secondary school-age pupils in state-funded secondary school, the rate of pupils with SEN has remained largely stable, at around 2%. The proportion of pupils known to be eligible for FSM is about twice as likely to be identified with SEN. In 2009, 28.4% SEN pupils were known to be eligible for FSM in mainstream primary schools compared with 13% of pupils with no SEN. In mainstream secondary schools the

Figure 6.13: Percentage of 15- to 19-year-olds NEET in 2007

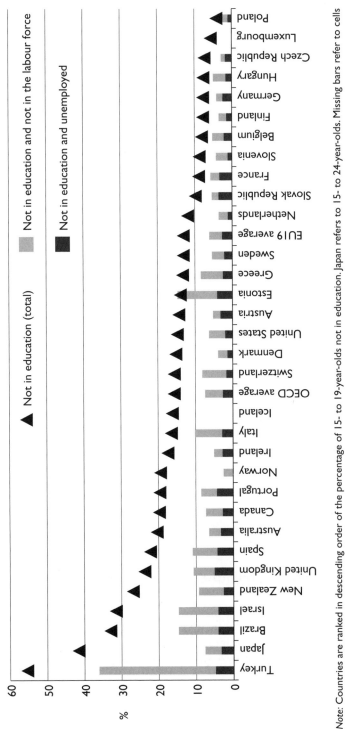

Legend:
- ▲ Not in education (total)
- Not in education and not in the labour force
- Not in education and unemployed

Note: Countries are ranked in descending order of the percentage of 15- to 19-year-olds not in education. Japan refers to 15- to 24-year-olds. Missing bars refer to cells below reliability thresholds.

Source: OECD (2009b)

figures were 24.6% for SEN pupils and 10.4% for non-SEN pupils. In mainstream primary schools, Black pupils (2%) showed a higher incidence rate of SEN than White or Mixed-race pupils (both at 1.7%). In secondary schools, similar rates were reported among White, Black and Mixed-race pupils, at around 2%. The lowest occurrence of SEN in both mainstream primary and secondary schools was generally found in pupils of Chinese or Asian ethnic origin (DCSF, 2009c).

Table 6.7 compares data of SEN from all four UK nations from 2006 up to 2009. There are large variations in the SEN rates within the UK, although such variations are mainly due to variations in the way SEN is defined and local government policies. Table 6.7 shows that the proportion of pupils with SEN remained largely stable over the period in England, Wales and Northern Ireland. However, there were signs of increases in the SEN rate in Scotland over the same period, although the increases could be the result of improved recording practices.

Table 6.7: Pupils with SEN statements (or additional support needs in Scotland)

		2006	2007	2008	2009
England[a]	Number	236,750	229,110	223,610	221,670
	%	2.9	2.8	2.8	2.7
Wales[b]	Number	16,183	15,579	14,994	14,832
	%	3.3	3.2	3.1	3.1
Northern Ireland[c]	Number	n/a	n/a	n/a	n/a
	%	4.0	3.8	4.0	4.1
Scotland[d]	Number	29,173	29,833	31,960	37,504
	%	4.2	4.4	4.8	5.6

Sources and notes:

[a] DfE (2010e). Figures show statemented pupils in all schools in England.

[b] Welsh Assembly Government (2009b). Figures show statemented pupils in all schools in Wales.

[c] DfE (2010). Figures show statemented pupils in all schools but excluding hospital and independent schools.

[d] Scottish Government (2009). Figures show statemented pupils in all mainstream primary and secondary schools. Increase in 2009 statistics is due to improved recording.

Impact of social background: evidence from national and international studies

Earlier research shows that growing up poor significantly reduced young people's chances of achieving A Level or higher qualifications (Ermisch et al, 2001). Recent research suggests that poverty has a greater impact on the academic performance of White British children than children from most minority ethnic groups. Research led by the Institute of Education found that 63% of White pupils who do not receive FSM achieved five A*-C GCSE grades compared to only 31% of FSM pupils. The performance gap of 32 percentage points was far higher than that of any of the other ethnic group, including Bangladeshi (7% points) and Chinese (5% points). The research also found bigger differences in academic performance between White pupils from middle and working-class families, as defined by their parents' occupations, than was the case for other ethnic groups. Cultural aspirations and expectations as well as support from parents are considered to be contributing factors for such differences (Institute of Education, 2010).

A longitudinal study by Ermisch and Del Bono found that in England the negative intergenerational link in education outcomes of children from poorly educated households persisted over generations (The Sutton Trust, 2010). The study showed that of children from the 1990 cohort and whose parents left school without any O Levels or equivalent qualifications, only 33% obtained at least five GCSEs at A*-C grades compared with 79% of children whose parents were educated to degree level – a gap of 46 percentage points. In the cohorts born in 1970 and 1958, the equivalent achievement gap in O Levels was 44 percentage points. Ermisch and Del Bono's study also shows that, internationally, educational mobility in England was comparatively restricted compared to similar countries. They pointed out that in England an achievement gap at the top 25% of tests between children (1990 cohort) from degree-educated parents (56%) and those without any O Levels (9%) was as wide as 47 percentage points. This was substantially higher than Australia (23 percentage points), Germany (37 percentage points) and the US (43 percentage points) (The Sutton Trust, 2010).

Thus, socioeconomic backgrounds remain important predictors of educational outcomes of children in England. Research reviewed shows no sign of improvement in educational mobility of children from the lower social class background, and this in turn is likely to work against the government's efforts in promoting social mobility.

Conclusion

Pupils' levels of attainment in England improved steadily under the last Labour government. There was evidence of significant increases in the proportion of pupils achieving the attainment targets across the board. Recent data within the UK shows a higher proportion of pupils achieving good results in GCSE, A Level or equivalent exams in England compared to Wales and Scotland. Gender inequality in terms of Reading literacy remained. Girls continued to outperform boys in English, Reading and Writing. However, the attainment gap in Mathematics showed the first indication of closing of the gap, as girls for the first time since 2004 did just as well in the latest Mathematics assessment in England.

Internationally, pupils in the UK competed relatively well with the other PISA participating countries. Pupils in England and Scotland in particular generally did better in PISA 2006 than pupils in Northern Ireland and Wales. The UK as a whole performed best in Science literacy, which was above the OECD average. As for Reading and Mathematics, the UK's average performance was not significantly different from that of the OECD. The quality of school life enjoyed by children in England was also relatively high by OECD standards, with most agreeing that they liked school a lot.

In England, there were also some signs of reduction in the number of permanent and fixed period school exclusions. Truancy rates have remained stable over the last two years. However, despite the government's efforts in trying to reduce the NEET rate, it has increased in recent years and the proportion of young people NEET in the UK was higher than that of the EU, as well as the OECD average, which certainly requires serious government attention.

Although the overall level of attainment has risen among children and young people over the period, the educational mobility among those from poorly educated households and lower social class backgrounds remains stubbornly low. However, new research shows that pupils of different ethnicity in similar poor backgrounds do not appear to be equally affected by their circumstances. Poor White pupils were shown to be particularly susceptible to their disadvantaged background. Cultural aspirations and expectations and parental support are suggested to be key to successful achievement among some poor minority ethnic groups.

SEVEN

Housing and the environment for children

Deborah Quilgars

Key statistics

- Poor families and lone parents are more likely to live in poor housing and in poor neighbourhoods than other households.
- Children who live in bad housing for a longer period of time are more likely to experience negative outcomes.
- Both positive and negative outcomes are associated with being re-housed under the homelessness legislation.
- At the EU level, UK households are more likely to be satisfied with their housing, but they are also more likely to report problems with crime, violence and vandalism in their environment.

Key trends

- UK-wide, housing conditions continue to improve over time.
- Officially measured homelessness has reduced in the last few years in England, partly explained by a growing emphasis on preventing homelessness.
- Poor households and lone parents continue to be more likely to live in poor environments.

Key sources

- English Housing Survey (previously English House Condition Survey) and other house condition surveys
- Save the Children surveys of severe poverty
- CLG survey of family homelessness and 16- and 17-year-olds
- Academic studies

Introduction

This chapter reviews the evidence of the link between housing, homelessness and the environment and the well-being of children in the UK. The previous Labour government placed a high priority on the creation of '*sustainable communities*'

(ODPM, 2003), acknowledging the role of both good quality housing and cohesive neighbourhoods in achieving this. The new Coalition government, with its policy focus on increasing localism and the development of the Big Society, has signalled that neighbourhoods will be the 'building blocks' for public sector reform more generally (Pickles, 2010). The Department for Communities and Local Government's (CLG) resource settlement, however, was the severest, with a budget decrease of 33% by 2014-15, increasing to 51% when the devolving of funds to local government is taken into account (HM Treasury, 2010b). The role of social housing has received greatest attention to date, with the government currently consulting on its future, including reviewing aspects of the present legislation on homelessness and overcrowding (CLG, 2010a). Interestingly, this review did not consider any specific impacts on children or families.

This chapter begins by reviewing the nature of poor housing and the type of housing that children, and particularly poor children, currently live in, as well as the potential impacts of poor housing on the lives of children. The chapter then examines the scale of homelessness affecting families and young people, as well as its impact on their lives. A third section examines the evidence on poor neighbourhoods and children.

House conditions

The condition of housing is recognised as a key variable in ensuring that all households, irrespective of background, can enjoy a home that is in good repair, fit for use and has adequate facilities. In particular, the previous Labour government established a policy that aimed to ensure that all social rented homes should reach the 'Decent Homes standard'[1] by 2010. The new Coalition government has recently signalled that they intend to complete the Decent Homes programme (CLG, 2010a).

The respective governments/assemblies in England, Scotland, Wales and Northern Ireland all undertake regular house condition surveys. The surveys, however, are undertaken using different measures, making comparisons between countries problematic. Table 7.1 shows the proportions of houses which fall below certain nationally prescribed house condition standards in the four countries. As can be seen, 35% of dwellings in England currently fail the Decent Homes standard. In Scotland, a high proportion of dwellings (71%) fail the Scottish Housing Quality standard, mainly on poor energy efficiency (57% of dwellings not meeting this standard). However, only 1% of dwellings fail the basic definition of being a dwelling 'below tolerable standard'.[2] Table 7.1 also shows that approximately 5% of Welsh dwellings were defined as unfit in 2007, and just over 3% of Northern Irish dwellings were also described as unfit in 2006. House conditions tend to vary by tenure across the UK. For example, 26% of social housing failed the Decent Homes standard (using the new Housing Health and Safety Rating System [HHSRS]) in 2008, but 44% of private rented housing did not meet the standard (and 32% of owner-occupied housing). While there were no tenure differences

Table 7.1: Housing failing nationally prescribed house condition standards

	Number of dwellings (000s)	% of dwellings failing specified standards
England	5,890	35% of properties not meeting the Decent Homes standard (2008)
Wales	57	4.8% of properties unfit (2004)
Scotland	20	0.9% of dwellings below tolerable standard (2007)
		71% failing the Scottish Housing Quality standard (serious disrepair, energy efficiency, lack modern facilities or services and/or not healthy, safe and secure) (2007)
Northern Ireland	24	3.4% unfit dwellings (2006)

Sources: Wilcox (2010, Table 23a/b: data from English Housing Survey Headline Report 2008-9; Table 27a: Northern Ireland House Condition Survey, 2006; Table 25a: Living in Wales 2004 – Report on unfitness and repairs; Table 26a: Data from Scottish House Condition Survey, 2007)

in Scotland for houses 'below tolerable standard', in Wales 12% of private rented housing was unfit compared to only 4% of owner-occupied housing and 3% of local authority housing.

National surveys show that house conditions have improved considerably over the last two decades. Under the original Decent Homes standard (fitness-based definition), improvements were recorded for England from 45% of properties in 1996 failing the standard to only 27% of properties in 2006 (equating to 35% of properties under the new HHSRS-based measure). In Wales, unfitness rates reduced from 13% of stock in 1993 to 5% in 2004. In Northern Ireland, the proportion of unfit properties reduced from 7% in 1996 to 3% in 2006. The proportion of properties 'below tolerable standard' remained about the same from 1996 to 2007, but some improvements have been recorded under the Scottish Housing Quality standard (77% failed in 2002 compared to 71% in 2007).

In terms of the previous Labour government's *Opportunity for all* indicator to reduce the proportion of children who live in a home that falls below the set standard of decency (England), this has been achieved year on year since the baseline year of 1996 (41% living in non-decent homes) to 2005 (23% living in non-decent homes) (DWP, 2007).

Household characteristics

Some types of household are more likely to live in poor housing than others. The most comprehensive, up-to-date data[3] on household characteristics is found in the English Housing Survey 2008 (CLG, 2010b). This Survey demonstrated that households on lower incomes[4] were more likely to live in homes in serious disrepair or problems with condensation or mould, although there was no association between income and HHSRS excess cold or falls hazards. Minority ethnic households were also much more likely to be living in homes in serious disrepair (18% compared to 12% of white households) or ones that had serious condensation (11% compared to 4%). Differences were also evident on some measures between households with children and those without children. Table 7.2 shows that households with children were almost twice as likely to be living in homes with serious condensation compared to other households. However, they were less likely to live in cold homes, and there was little difference between those with and without children with respect to living in homes in serious disrepair, with the exception of lone parents who were more likely to live in this type of poor housing. Table 7.2 also shows that households with children living in poverty were substantially more likely to be living in homes in serious disrepair (19% compared to 12% of households with children not living in poverty), or homes with serious condensation (10% compared to 5%%). Lone parents were the most likely type of household to live in homes in serious disrepair whether they were living in poverty or not. Households with children living in the private rented sector were also more likely to live in homes in serious disrepair than those in other tenures, particularly those living in poverty.

Save the Children-commissioned surveys on severe poverty in Great Britain and Northern Ireland (Adelman et al, 2003; Monteith and McLaughlin, 2004) also provide comparable data on housing quality from the perspective of families, highlighting how children living in poor households[5] are more likely to be living in poor housing. In the British study, three quarters (73%%) of non-poor children lived in homes described as in good repair, compared to just over two fifths (42%) of severely poor children and a half (48%) of non-severely poor children. Children in severe and non-severe poverty experienced an average of 1.38 and 1.31 housing problems respectively, compared to an average of 0.49 problems for non-poor children. Children in Northern Ireland were less likely to live in accommodation where housing problems were reported, with an average of 1.19 problems being reported for those in severe poverty, 0.98 problems for non-severe poverty and 0.47 – about the same as Britain – for non-poor children.

European comparisons

At a European level, EU-SILC (Statistics on Income and Living Conditions) collects information on housing conditions and facilities on an annual basis utilising four basic indicators: leaking roof or damp; bath or shower in dwelling; indoor toilet for sole use of household; dwelling too dark. In addition, in 2007 a special module on housing also examined a number of other dimensions including shortage of space, facilities including heating and an overall measure of satisfaction with the dwelling. Analysis allows a comparison between those households at risk of poverty (defined as those with incomes under 60% of the national median) and households not at risk of poverty. Across Europe, including in the UK, households at risk of poverty are generally more likely to suffer from poor housing conditions than those not at risk of poverty (EC, 2010). Table 7.3 suggests a relatively high level of overall satisfaction with housing compared to

Table 7.2: Households with children (0-15) by poor living conditions

	HHSRS excess cold	HHSRS falls	Serious disrepair	Serious condensation	Worst neighbourhoods	Number of households (000s)
				% of group living in homes with:		
All households						
Households with children:						
Lone parent	4.5	12.3	17.3	7.0	19.8	1,241
Couple or multi-person household	7.0	12.5	12.0	5.3	10.2	4,475
All households with children	6.4	12.5	13.1	5.7	12.3	5,716
Households with no children	9.1	12.6	12.1	3.3	9.2	15,691
All households	**8.4**	**12.6**	**12.3**	**3.9**	**10.0**	**21,407**
Households in poverty						
Households with children:						
Lone parent	5.7	11.9	20.7	10.2	24.8	452
Couple or multi-person household	7.3	14.8	18.6	10.0	20.7	714
All households with children	6.7	13.7	19.4	10.1	22.3	1,166
Households with no children	9.8	12.7	16.8	4.5	13.7	2,635
All households in poverty	**8.8**	**13.0**	**17.6**	**6.2**	**16.3**	**3,801**
Households not in poverty						
Households with children:						
Lone parent	3.8	12.6	15.3	5.1	16.9	790
Couple or multi-person household	6.9	12.1	10.7	4.4	8.2	3,761
All households with children	6.4	12.2	11.5	4.6	9.7	4,550
Households with no children	9.0	12.6	11.1	3.0	8.3	13,056
All households not in poverty	**8.3**	**12.5**	**11.2**	**3.4**	**8.6**	**17,606**

Source: English Housing Survey 2008, household sub-sample

Table 7.3: Proportion of people with income above and below the at-risk-of-poverty threshold with housing problems according to different measures, 2007

	Deprived of one of three indicators and overcrowded[a]		Reporting three of five 'module problems'[b]		Overall dissatisfied with housing[c]	
	Not at risk	At risk	Not at risk	At risk	Not at risk	At risk
Luxembourg	1.1	8.4	2.9	13.0	4.3	15.5
UK	1.5	3.5	3.3	5.3	5.8	8.6
Cyprus	0.6	2.2	10.2	16.7	13.1	22.7
Austria	3.0	9.3	1.0	5.0	7.0	20.0
Ireland	1.0	2.3	1.4	4.9	14.6	27.0
Netherlands	0.4	3.2	1.7	3.9	2.8	6.8
Germany	0.6	2.8	3.5	8.5	16.0	21.3
Denmark	1.2	5.7	2.5	7.0	5.2	14.9
Belgium	0.9	5.1	1.7	8.3	9.6	22.5
Sweden	0.7	3.6	1.8	2.8	4.2	9.2
France	2.4	8.1	5.0	11.9	7.8	22.1
Finland	0.5	2.3	3.0	6.8	6.2	10.1
Italy	5.4	13.8	5.6	16.4	12.2	28.8
Slovenia	10.7	22.3	1.0	3.3	10.5	19.3
Spain	1.2	3.9	3.2	9.6	10.1	16.6
Greece	6.6	14.1	6.4	12.6	11.3	18.6
Portugal	6.2	13.3	15.0	26.8	16.2	25.9
Czech Republic	6.2	25.3	4.3	11.1	13.1	31.9
Slovakia	3.4	12.3	5.9	11.3	22.4	36.1
Estonia	12.2	23.8	5.9	10.4	29.1	34.5
Hungary	12.0	29.3	2.2	7.5	36.6	50.6
Lithuania	18.3	35.3	8.9	10.2	37.2	41.7
Poland	21.5	45.9	7.4	16.5	19.6	32.2
Latvia	24.8	34.5	10.0	19.5	30.2	39.6

Notes:

[a] Indicates having at least one of a leaking roof, damp walls, etc, no bath and indoor toilet, too dark a house plus a shortage of space as measured by the number of rooms relative to the number of people.

[b] Indicates having at least three out of five of the aspects covered by the EU-SILC housing module – inadequate electrical installation, inadequate plumbing/water installations, dwelling not comfortably warm during winter, dwelling not comfortably cool during summer, shortage of space in dwelling.

[c] Indicates those reporting being either greatly dissatisfied or somewhat dissatisfied with their dwelling.

Source: EU-SILC data reported in EC (2010, Table 26, p 155)

most countries among those at risk of poverty, with only a lower proportion of households at risk of poverty in the Netherlands reporting dissatisfaction with housing than the UK. Only a small proportion of those at risk of poverty were also likely to be reporting a number of 'module problems' (see Table 7.3), or being deprived, based on a leaking roof, damp, no bath and toilet and a shortage of space; however, on both these accounts, the UK ranked 6th of the 24 countries.

A recent UNICEF Innocenti Research Centre report (Adamson, 2010) focused on inequalities in the well-being between children within individual countries. This study included a measure of 'living space' as one of three aspects of material well-being.[6] Table 7.4 shows that while the UK average (median of 1.20 rooms per person in households with children) for living space was above average among the OECD countries (median of 1.07), the inequality gap (as a percentage of the median) was higher than the average (at 24.4% compared to the OECD average of 20.8%), placing the UK 17th out of 24 on this measure.

Table 7.4: Inequality in material well-being: house living space (rooms per person)

Living space – rooms per person	Median	Average below the median	Average absolute gap	Gap between the average below the median and the median (as % of median)
Iceland	1.00	0.91	0.09	8.8
Germany	1.00	0.91	0.09	8.9
Switzerland (2007)	1.00	0.91	0.09	9.1
Greece	0.80	0.69	0.11	14.0
Spain	1.25	1.08	0.18	14.5
France (2007)	1.00	0.85	0.15	14.5
Netherlands	1.25	1.03	0.23	17.6
Ireland	1.25	1.03	0.23	17.7
Norway	1.20	0.97	0.23	18.8
Belgium	1.20	0.97	0.23	19.0
Finland	1.20	0.97	0.23	19.3
Portugal	1.00	0.80	0.20	19.6
Czech Republic	0.80	0.62	0.18	22.2
Austria	1.00	0.77	0.23	22.9
Denmark	1.20	0.92	0.28	23.0
Sweden	1.20	0.91	0.29	24.4
United Kingdom	1.20	0.91	0.29	24.4
Slovakia	0.75	0.56	0.19	24.9
Luxembourg	1.25	0.93	0.33	26.2
Canada (2006)	1.50	1.10	0.41	27.5
Poland	0.67	0.47	0.19	28.6
United States (2007)	1.25	0.89	0.36	29.3
Italy	1.00	0.68	0.32	31.8
Hungary	0.75	0.50	0.25	33.4
OECD average	1.07	0.85	0.22	20.8

Notes: The OECD average is an unweighted average for the 24 countries included in the main league table.

Sources: EU-SILC 2008. Data for France are from EU-SILC 2007, reported in Adamson (2010, Figure 2c, p 7)

Impact of poor housing on children

The relationship between health and housing has been the subject of numerous individual studies, although few large-scale comprehensive studies have been undertaken.

A number of studies in the 1980s found links between dampness and hydrothermal growth and children's poor respiratory health in Scotland and London (Strachan, 1988; Platt et al, 1989). The Scottish House Condition Survey 2002 tested this association, finding that significant predictors of whether a child had symptoms of respiratory health problems included: dwelling type (house or flat); level of heating usage; presence of a smoker in the household; tenure (private or social); whether adult respondent had respiratory health problems; and satisfaction with heating. The most significant factor was whether or not the adult had respiratory problems him/herself. The predictive power of the logistic regression model was very weak – only predicting whether a child had respiratory symptoms 5% of the time. Overcrowding and dampness both appeared to be associated with poor respiratory health, but these variables were not included in the final regression model as they had no power to predict children's respiratory health.

Research also indicates the long-term effects of poor housing on children. An analysis of the National Child Development Study found that three housing variables increased the odds of ill health over the period 1958-91: living in non-self contained accommodation; past experience of homelessness (see next section); and dissatisfaction with area (see last section) (Marsh et al, 1999).

The most robust recent research on the impact of poor housing used the Families and Children Study (FACS)[7] to look at the impact of three types of bad housing over time: overcrowded accommodation (using the bedroom criteria); accommodation in a poor state of repair (adult respondent's self-reported assessment); and inadequately heated accommodation (also self-reported assessment) (Barnes et al, 2008). In 2005, 25% of children were living in housing which qualified as 'bad' on at least one of these three measures, with 5% living in bad housing using more than one measure. Over a five-year period (2001-05), the study found that 13% of children persistently (that is, for at least three or more years) lived in overcrowded accommodation, 6% persistently lived in poorly repaired accommodation and 4% persistently lived in inadequately heated accommodation. The study found that some types of families/children were more likely to experience certain types of bad housing. First, larger families and Asian families were more likely to experience persistent overcrowding; children living in the most deprived areas and/or in households below the poverty line or in families with a number of debts were more likely to experience a persistent poor state of repair; and those children from Black families, lone-parent families and families with a number of debts were more likely to experience persistent inadequate heating. Importantly, this study found that children who persistently lived in bad housing were more likely to face a range of other negative outcomes (when controlling for other factors):

- feeling unhappy about their own health (overcrowding);
- having no quiet place at home to do homework (overcrowding and inadequate heating);
- having a longstanding illness or disability (poor state of housing repair);
- having chest or breathing problems, or stomach, liver or digestive problems (poor state of housing repair);
- being bullied in or out of school (poor state of housing repair);
- feeling unhappy about their family health life (poor state of housing repair);
- getting into trouble with the police (poor state of housing repair);
- having four or more of these negative outcomes (inadequate heating).

Homelessness

In the UK, local authorities have a legal responsibility to re-house (and find temporary accommodation in the meantime) for families with children who are found to be 'statutorily homeless'. Households are considered homeless if they have no accommodation, or none they can reasonably occupy (for example, without threat of violence or abuse). Under the homelessness legislation in England, Scotland, Wales and Northern Ireland, homeless families with dependent children are accepted as being in priority need and therefore receive assistance with re-housing, providing they can also demonstrate a local connection (unless they are moving as a result of violence) and that they are not homeless intentionally. Following legislative change in the early 2000s, 16- and 17-year-olds and care leavers aged between 18 and 20 years are now considered to be in priority need in England, Wales and Scotland.[8] Other young people between 18 and 25 may be accepted as being in priority need only if they can demonstrate that they are 'vulnerable'.[9] From 2012, Scotland will also abolish priority need categories, effectively giving all homeless people, including young people, the right to permanent re-housing.[10]

While the majority of families with children, and 16- to 17-year-olds, should be protected from long-term homelessness by the UK homelessness legislation, it is important to note that some children are not covered by this provision. This includes children living in families who have been deemed to be unintentionally homeless, that is, that they have caused their own homelessness, for example because of anti-social behaviour. Local authorities will not provide settled accommodation in these cases, although they will still find temporary accommodation for the family until they can make alternative arrangements. The legislation also does not cover asylum seekers or immigrants whose status does not give them recourse to public funds. Young people over the age of 17 are also accepted as homeless under certain circumstances, as described above. Extensive provision does exist for young people who are not statutorily homeless in the form of hostels and supported accommodation, but access to settled housing is often constrained (Quilgars et al, 2008).

Incidence of family homelessness in the UK

The main statistical sources on the incidence of family homelessness in the UK are the returns submitted quarterly by local authorities to the CLG, the Welsh Assembly Housing Directorate, the Scottish Government and the Northern Ireland Housing Executive.

Table 7.5 shows homelessness acceptances in England, Scotland and Wales since 1996. The number of total acceptances in the three countries peaked in the early 1990s (179,410 in 1992), before declining to 129,000 in 1997. The number then started to gradually increase again to a new height of 188,162 in 2003. However, it can be seen that a considerable decrease in homelessness acceptances then occurred in the late 2000s, to just over 100,000 in 2008, with indications of further likely decreases for 2009. Examining homelessness acceptances for the three countries separately, it can be seen that this trend has been driven largely by changes in the levels of homelessness acceptances in England, which peaked in 2003 at 147,820 and had fallen to 66,400 by 2008. A similar pattern was observed in Wales, with the highest number of acceptances in 2004 at 10,993. The pattern is different in Scotland, however, with the number of acceptances doubling over the period 1997 to 2008 from 17,400 to 34,701. Unfortunately, it cannot be presumed that the incidence of homelessness has increased to a greater extent in Scotland than England and Wales, as there has been considerable policy change over the period. First, the introduction of more generous homelessness legislation, particularly the extension of priority need categories in the early 2000s, will have accounted for some of the rises at this time. Second, in England (and to a lesser extent, Wales), a prevention agenda has been actively pursued with local authorities attempting to assist (potentially) homeless households through a 'housing options' approach that obviates the need for a homelessness assessment to be undertaken (Fitzpatrick et al, 2009).

Table 7.6 shows the homeless presentations and acceptances in Northern Ireland from 2000/01- 2009/10.[11] As can be seen, there was a significant increase in the number of presentations over this period, from 12,694 in 2000/01 to a height of 21,013 in 2006/07, with a small decrease in the last few years. The number of households awarded priority status also increased, but at a slower pace, from 6,457 households in 2000/01 to over 9,000 from 2005/06. Approximately a third (6,122, or 33%) of the 18,664 households presenting as homeless in 2009/10 included children.

CLG homelessness statistics[12] indicate that homeless families have represented a majority of homeless households accepted as in priority need over the last decade in England. In 2008, 60% of households were accepted as a result of having dependent children, with a further 11% of households containing a pregnant woman. A further 8% of households were young people aged 16- or 17- or 18- to 20-year-old care leavers. Similar proportions of families were accepted in 1998 (59% with dependent children and 10% containing a pregnant woman),[13] but only 3% of households were young people in 1998. In Wales, from April to June 2010,

Table 7.5: Homelessness acceptances, England, Scotland and Wales (number of households)

	1996	1997	1998	1999	2000	2001	2002	2003	2004	2005	2006	2007	2008	2009
Not held to be intentionally homeless														
England	113,590	102,000	104,630	105,370	111,340	117,830	123,840	135,590	127,760	100,170	76,860	64,970	57,520	41,790
+ Scotland	15,500	15,600	16,500	18,000	18,200	24,900	27,506	29,995	30,032	31,700	31,326	31,214	33,156	
+ Wales	8,334	4,297	4,371	3,695	4,156	5,181	6,437	8,512	10,071	8,376	6,974	6,339	6,226	
= Great Britain	137,424	121,897	125,501	127,065	133,696	147,911	157,783	174,097	167,863	140,246	115,160	102,523	96,892	
Held to be intentionally homeless														
England	5,070	4,960	6,120	7,330	8,860	8,420	9,490	12,230	13,640	13,830	11,410	9,920	8,890	6,870
+ Scotland	1,700	1,800	1,900	2,300	2,400	2,000	1,435	1,146	1,099	1,230	1,430	1,461	1,545	
+ Wales	815	343	380	476	510	555	608	657	921	976	865	797	627	
= Great Britain	7,585	7,103	8,400	10,106	11,570	10,975	11,533	14,033	15,660	16,036	13,705	12,178	11,062	
All homeless acceptances														
England	118,660	106,960	110,750	112,700	120,200	126,250	133,330	147,820	141,400	114,000	88,270	74,890	66,400	48,660
+ Scotland	17,200	17,400	18,400	20,300	20,600	26,900	28,941	31,141	31,131	32,930	32,756	32,675	34,701	
+ Wales	9,149	4,640	4,751	4,171	4,666	5,717	7,045	9,201	10,993	9,352	7,839	7,136	6,853	
= Great Britain	145,009	129,000	133,901	137,171	145,466	158,867	169,316	188,162	183,524	156,282	128,865	114,701	107,954	

Notes: The 1990 figures for Wales include 2,000 households made homeless in Colwyn Bay by flooding in February of that year. Scottish figures are for priority need homeless and potentially homeless cases only, and figures from 2000 onwards are for financial years (that is, 2000/01 etc). The England and Wales figures for 1997 and later years reflect the changes in homeless legislation, and no longer include 'non-priority acceptances': in 1996 these accounted for 3,310 acceptances in England and 3,501 acceptances in Wales.

Source: Wilcox, S. (2010, Table 90); data from CLG, Scottish Government and Welsh Assembly Government

Table 7.6: Homeless presenters and acceptances, Northern Ireland, 2000/01-2009/10

	2000/ 01	2001/ 02	2002/ 03	2003/ 04	2004/ 05	2005/ 06	2006/ 07	2007/ 08	2008/ 09	2009/ 10
Presenters	12,694	14,164	16,426	17,150	17,362	20,121	21,013	19,030	18,076	18,664
Awarded priority status	6,457	7,374	8,580	8,594	8,470	9,749	9,744	9,234	8,934	9,914

Source: Northern Ireland Housing Executive statistics (www.dsdni.gov.uk/index/publications/housing_stats.htm)

47% of those households in priority need included dependent children, with a further 10% being 'young people at risk'.[14] In Scotland, 35% of those households found priority homeless in 2009-10 included children, with a further 6% of priority need acceptances being single people under the age of 18.[15]

Number of children in temporary accommodation

Statistics are collected on the number of families and other households who are living in temporary accommodation while awaiting re-housing under the homeless legislation. Figure 7.1 charts the increase in the number of households in temporary accommodation in England in the late 1990s and early 2000s to a height of 100,000 households in 2004/05. It also shows a halving of the numbers in the last five years of the decade, to 50,000 in 2010. Approaching three quarters of households in temporary accommodation at any one time in England contain dependent children. For example, in the second quarter of 2010,[16] of 50,400 households, 12,910 (26%) were couples with dependent children or expecting a child and 23,630 (47%) were lone-parent households with dependent children/ expecting a child. Since 2002, data has also been collected on the number of households with children/expected children living in different types of temporary accommodation in England. Since March 2004, English local authorities have only been able to place families in Bed and Breakfast (B&B) accommodation in emergency situations and for up to six weeks.[17] While 6,820 such families were in B&B accommodation in the second quarter of 2002, this had reduced to 1,100 in the second quarter of 2004 and was only 740 households in the second quarter of 2010. The vast majority of households with children are temporarily housed in private sector-leased accommodation (25,210 households), with a relatively small number in hostels (including women's refuges), (2,380 in the second quarter of 2010).

In terms of the previous Labour government's *Opportunity for all* indicator to reduce the number of families with children in temporary accommodation (England), this was not achieved over the period 2002-07 (54,660 families in 2002 and 65,210 families in 2007) (DWP, 2007). However, it is likely to have been achieved more recently, although unfortunately monitoring of this target has ceased.

Figure 7.1: Homeless households in temporary accommodation as at the end of each quarter, by type of accommodation, England

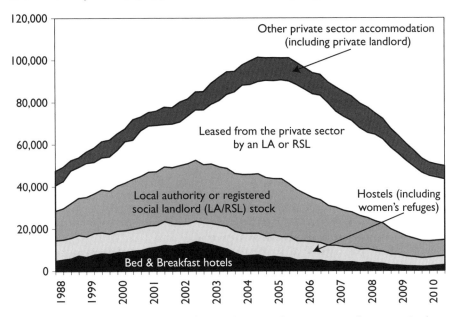

Note: From March 2002 onwards, some self-contained accommodation in annex-style units previously recorded under B&B now more appropriately attributed to private sector accommodation.

In Scotland, of the 10,815 households in temporary accommodation at the end of March 2010, a much smaller proportion (34%, or 3,724) compared to England were families with children. Only 53 households (1%) were in B&B accommodation, with 3,308 (86%) in social sector accommodation, 71 (2%) in hostels and 391 (10%) in other forms of accommodation. The total number of children in temporary accommodation was 6,132 at the end of March 2010.

In Wales, the number of households accommodated temporarily peaked in 2005 and has fallen slowly in the last five years, with 2,558 homeless households in temporary accommodation at the end of June 2010.[18] As in England, most households are accommodated temporarily in private sector-leased housing. At the end of June 2010 there were only 15 families in B&B accommodation.

Causes of family/child homelessness

It is widely acknowledged that the causes of homelessness among all households are multifaceted and complex. Homelessness statistics in England record three key reasons for loss of last home: parents, relatives or friends no longer willing or able to accommodate (36%, 2009); breakdown of relationship with partner (20%, 2009); and loss of private dwelling (22%, 2009, including end of assured short-hold tenancy, 11%). These key reasons are similar across the UK.

A recent representative survey of statutorily homeless families and 16- and 17-year-olds in England (Pleace et al, 2008) confirmed that the immediate causes of homelessness were predominantly the breakdown of social relationships and/ or experience of housing pressures. Just over half (55%) of families applied as homeless from somewhere other than their last settled accommodation, indicating that many families make temporary arrangements of their own before applying to the local authority for assistance. Nearly four in ten (38%) cited relationship breakdown as the main reason for applying as homeless, with 13% citing violent relationship breakdown. Other reasons included the end of a tenancy or eviction (26%), overcrowding (24%) and 'outstaying their welcome/could no longer be accommodated' (20%). Eviction/loss of private dwelling was most commonly reported as the reason for applying as homeless in areas of highest housing stress. For 16- and 17-year-olds, the overwhelming reason for applying as homeless (70%) was relationship breakdown, almost always with parents/step parents. Of some concern was the finding that 41% of young people reported that violence was involved in relationship breakdown with parents.

This study also documented how 16- and 17-year-olds had often had traumatic childhoods and frequently had a range of support needs that may have contributed to the circumstances that led to their homelessness. This was much less likely to be the case for homeless adults. A recent review of evidence on youth homelessness in the UK (Quilgars et al, 2008) indicated that young homeless people, particularly 16- and 17-year-olds, were likely to have:

- experienced family disruption (due to parental separation or divorce and/or the arrival of a step parent);
- had difficulty getting on with parents;
- witnessed or experienced violence within the family home;
- lived in a family which experienced financial difficulties;
- run away from home;
- spent time in care;
- been involved in crime or anti-social behaviour;
- had their education severely disrupted (for example, been suspended or excluded from school).

Research often identifies one or more of the above characteristics as 'risk factors' that heighten a young person's likelihood of experiencing homelessness (see, for example, Craig et al, 1996; Bruegel and Smith, 1999; Scottish Homes, 2001; Smith, 2003). Research in London demonstrated that young homeless people originate disproportionately from the most deprived wards (Bruegel and Smith, 1999).

Impact of homelessness on children

In the 1980s and 1990s, a number of small-scale studies investigated the impact on families of living in temporary accommodation, with a particular focus on the role of B&B accommodation. Some temporary accommodation was found to be below standard, overcrowded, dangerous, lacking facilities for cooking and washing and being located outside the home borough (GLA, 2001a, 2001b). High levels of illnesses, infections and a range of respiratory problems were also found (see, for example, Royal College of Physicians, 1994; Sawtell, 2002). As a result of these findings, as indicated above, policy changed in the early 1990s to end the use of B&B accommodation, apart from for a very short period in emergencies. Research has also suggested that the experience of homelessness, even in self-contained accommodation, may have significant effects resulting from people's loss of control over their lives, especially where this means a move of schools and the loss of networks of friends and family (Sawtell, 2002; Shatwell, 2003), with implications for educational progress and emotional health.

The recent survey of family homelessness (Pleace et al, 2008) provided robust statistical evidence on the impact of homelessness on homeless adults and children.[19] Families in settled housing (following re-housing) reported a consistently better quality of life than families still living in temporary accommodation, with 64% of adult respondents considering their lives to be 'on hold' compared to only 18% of those in settled housing. Children in temporary accommodation, particularly shared forms of accommodation, consistently had poorer outcomes than re-housed children. However, the net effect of homelessness on children, compared to their last settled home, was quite balanced. Negative outcomes included a reduction in participation in clubs/activities (45% had decreased participation; 25% halted), increased loneliness (29% of children reporting this compared to 17% in their last home) and ruptured peer relationships. However, more encouragingly, a number of positive outcomes were also reported for children when compared to their last settled accommodation – school performance improved for some (parents reporting improvements in 34% of cases, compared to only 7% reporting poorer performance), as did relationships with parents (41% of young people interviewed reported an improvement, with only 10% reporting deterioration), and overall health (20% of children's physical health had improved). Overall, the disruption of homelessness was believed by families to have had more of a negative impact on children than the experience of homelessness.

The survey also provided insights into the net effect of homelessness on young people aged 16 and 17. As with homeless adults, young people were more likely to report that life was better overall (52%) rather than worse (25%) than it had been in their last settled accommodation. There was a net reduction in young people's contact with family and friends since leaving their home, but their access to emotional and instrumental support (someone to help them in a crisis) appeared to have improved. However, as with adults, young people in temporary accommodation were more likely to report that their lives were on hold than those in settled housing. There was also evidence of a substantial net deterioration in the economic position of young people, with 34% having discontinued education, employment or training and only 4% taking up one of these activities, and 56% reporting their ability to manage financially had declined.

European comparisons

The European Observatory on Homelessness has produced a number of reviews of statistics on homelessness across the EU, the latest being in 2009 (Edgar, 2009). These provide detailed information on a country-by-country basis, utilising a conceptual framework, the European Typology of Homelessness and Housing Exclusion (ETHOS). However, a lack of data on homelessness, combined with the use of different measures in the data that does exist, means that comparison across Europe is highly problematic. This may change partially with the 2011 Census, as EU directives require member countries to enumerate all citizens, including homeless people. Two recent publications have reviewed the limited evidence on child homelessness (FEANTSA, 2007) and youth homelessness (Quilgars, 2010) across Europe. Both these publications indicate that disadvantaged children and young people are at continued risk of homelessness across Europe, and there is an urgent need for better information on the precise nature of this social problem.

Poor neighbourhoods

The English Housing Survey (CLG, 2010b, 2010c) appears to provide the most comprehensive, up-to-date data on disparities in living conditions, including neighbourhood issues. Two measures of poor neighbourhoods are incorporated into the English Housing Survey. First, the *Housing stock report*, using professional surveyors, records the 10% of households whose 'neighbourhoods' (defined as the public and private space/buildings in the immediate environment of the dwelling) are assessed to be the most neglected, poorly maintained and/or vandalised (CLG, 2010b). Second, the *Household survey* asked respondents to rate the levels of satisfaction with their local area as a place to live using a five-point scale (1 = very satisfied to 5 = very dissatisfied) (CLG, 2010c). In addition, respondents were presented with a series of nine issues and asked whether these issues were 'a serious problem', 'a problem but not serious' or 'not a problem'.

As with poor housing, certain types of household were more likely to be living in poor neighbourhoods than others. Households that made up the poorest fifth were more than three times as likely to live in neighbourhoods with worst upkeep problems, and minority ethnic households were twice as likely to live in such areas. Table 7.2 (see earlier in this chapter) showed that households with children were slightly more likely to be living in the worst neighbourhoods compared to households without children (12% compared to 9%). A much greater difference was observed between poor and non-poor households with children, with 22% of the former living in the worst neighbourhoods compared to 10% of the latter (see Table 7.2). Households with children living in local authority accommodation were also much more likely than those in other tenures to live in neighbourhoods with the worst upkeep problems.

When households were asked to rate their satisfaction with their local area, those unemployed or otherwise economically inactive respondents were more likely to be dissatisfied than retired and working households (CLG, 2010c). Table 7.7 shows that there were some differences by household type, with lone parents much more likely to be dissatisfied with their local area than other household types (16% compared to 9% of all households). Couples with dependent children were no more or less likely to be dissatisfied with their area than all households. A similar finding was found for reports of serious issues in the local area with lone parents (and single people under 60) most likely to report issues as being a problem.

The Save the Children surveys on poverty in Great Britain and Northern Ireland (Adelman et al, 2003; Monteith and McLaughlin, 2004) also provided information on households' experiences of their neighbourhoods. In the British study, children in severe poverty were found to be three times as likely as children in non-severe poverty to live where parents were (slightly or very) dissatisfied with the area (41% compared to 13%), while children in non-severe poverty were twice as likely to live in areas where parents were dissatisfied compared to non-poor children (13% compared to 8%). In the Northern Irish study, 9% of severely poor children lived in an area that their parents considered 'a fairly/very bad place to live', compared to 6% of children in non-severe poverty and 1% of non-poor children. As with housing quality, overall, a lower proportion of families in Northern Ireland considered they were living in poor neighbourhoods compared to British families, and over half of all children (57%) in Northern Ireland lived in areas where no problems with the area were reported compared to a quarter (26%) of all children in Britain. Table 7.8 shows the mean number of problems reported by parents were also higher in Britain, and that households in severe poverty reported more problems than those in non-severe poverty, and

Table 7.7: Household type of those satisfied/dissatisfied with local area

	Very satisfied	Fairly satisfied	All satisfied	Neither satisfied nor dissatisfied	Slightly dissatisfied	Very dissatisfied	All dissatisfied
All households[a]							
Household type							
Couple under 60	48.9	38.3	87.2	4.7	6.1	2.0	8.1
Couple aged 60 or over	60.8	30.2	91.0	2.5	4.6	1.9	6.5
Couple, dependent child(ren)	50.4	36.3	86.7	5.1	5.5	2.7	8.2
Lone parent, dependent child(ren)	40.6	36.4	77.0	6.9	8.7	7.4	16.1
Other multi-person households	48.0	36.0	83.9	6.2	6.8	3.1	9.8
One person under 60	46.2	39.2	85.4	5.6	6.3	2.7	9.0
One person aged 60 or over	60.7	29.2	89.9	3.0	5.2	1.8	7.1
Total	51.9	35.0	86.9	4.6	5.8	2.7	8.5

Note: [a] Excludes households that did not respond to question. Base = 21,530 households (100%).

Source: English Housing Survey 2008-09, full household sample, reported in CLG (2010c, Annex tables)

Table 7.8: Number (mean) of problems with area, by poverty status, Northern Ireland and Great Britain

	Mean number of common problems with areas experienced	
	Northern Ireland	**Great Britain**
No poverty	1.12	1.59
Non-severe poverty	2.66	2.94
Severe poverty	3.29	4.83
All children	1.94	2.34

Note: Base for Northern Ireland = 1,195; Great Britain = 766.

Source: Monteith and McLaughlin (2004, Table 5.5)

in turn, less than those in no poverty. The most commonly reported problems (from a list of potential issues) in Britain were 'teenagers hanging around the streets' (40% of all children; 76% of those in severe poverty) and 'dogs and dog mess' (40% of all children; 56% of those in severe poverty). In Northern Ireland, the most common problems were 'dog mess' (20% and 33% of all children and those in severe poverty, respectively), 'drunkenness' (12% and 21% respectively), 'graffiti' (11% and 17%) and 'joyriding' (10% and 15%). Children in severe and non-severe poverty in Northern Ireland were more likely to live in areas that experienced problems with paramilitary behaviour and sectarian harassment than non-poor children, although these problems were relatively rare overall (3-4% of all children). It is important to note that there was a greater difference between 'severely' poor and 'non-severely' poor children in terms of likelihood of living in a poor neighbourhood compared to likelihood of living in poor housing.

European comparisons

At the European level, the EU-SILC collects respondent experiences of three types of environmental problems: noise, pollution, and crime, violence or vandalism (EC, 2010). As with house conditions, analysis allowed a comparison between those households at risk of poverty (defined as those with incomes under 60% of the national median) and households not at risk of poverty. Table 7.9 shows that, in most member states, between 15% and a quarter of the population report that they suffer from noise problems (with the UK within this range). Somewhat fewer people report problems with pollution or safety (crime, violence or vandalism) in their neighbourhood. However, it is notable that the highest proportion of people in the UK at risk of poverty reported crime, violence or vandalism as a problem (and the UK was the second highest on this measure for people not at risk of poverty). The EU report (EC, 2010) concluded that there was no clear link between these three problems and the average level of income in the country, nor did people on incomes below the poverty threshold appear to be much more exposed to these problems than those on higher incomes. The report concluded

Table 7.9: Proportion of people with income above and below the at-risk-of-poverty threshold reporting environmental problems, 2007

	Noise		Pollution		Crime, violence or vandalism	
	Not at risk	At risk	Not at risk	At risk	Not at risk	At risk
Luxembourg	20.7	30.0	15.9	18.5	9.7	9.7
UK	19.3	22.0	13.2	12.2	26.5	28.2
Cyprus	36.7	37.1	26.3	23.0	13.6	13.3
Austria	19.1	25.4	7.6	10.4	11.4	11.6
Ireland	12.3	16.0	8.8	11.8	14.1	21.1
Netherlands	31.9	34.0	13.6	15.2	17.6	18.2
Germany	25.8	34.7	21.1	25.6	11.4	18.3
Denmark	18.9	27.0	7.2	14.2	13.5	17.6
Belgium	22.3	25.9	16.7	21.0	16.7	20.9
Sweden	12.4	15.6	7.2	5.3	12.6	16.5
France	18.0	25.4	16.5	18.0	15.6	21.9
Finland	15.6	18.9	14.2	12.5	12.3	16.4
Italy	25.1	26.5	21.3	20.4	15.5	18.3
Slovenia	18.3	21.6	19.7	20.8	10.2	10.0
Spain	26.1	25.5	16.5	15.8	18.0	18.1
Greece	22.6	18.4	19.8	14.6	10.8	8.7
Portugal	28.2	24.4	21.8	23.3	12.4	13.5
Czech Republic	18.3	20.0	16.7	20.2	12.6	17.9
Slovakia	18.5	22.1	17.9	20.4	9.3	7.5
Estonia	23.8	18.8	27.3	22.8	21.1	22.7
Hungary	14.3	17.9	13.5	12.9	12.1	18.4
Lithuania	19.2	15.4	15.9	13.6	7.8	4.1
Poland	19.3	19.7	13.2	11.3	7.8	8.5
Latvia	22.6	19.3	37.4	34.6	30.6	25.2

Source: EU-SILC 2007 reported in EC (2010, Table 30, p 157)

that this might reflect a tendency for people with lower incomes to be more tolerant of such problems rather than a genuine lack of a relationship.

Conclusion

Overall, housing conditions have improved significantly over time and households with children per se do not tend to live in poorer housing than others. However, families on lower incomes and lone parents do appear to be at much greater risk of living in poor housing. The best data on homelessness in the UK derives from local authority homelessness determinations; this data shows some reductions in recorded homelessness in recent years in England and Wales, although not in

Scotland and Northern Ireland. The available evidence suggests that the effects of poor housing and homelessness on children may be considerable, although new evidence indicates that the circumstances leading up to homelessness may have a greater impact on children than living in temporary accommodation. Households with children are no more likely to live in poor neighbourhoods than other types of household although, as with poor housing, lone parents are over-represented in these areas as well as those in poverty (particularly severe poverty).

Notes

[1] A decent home is one that: (a) meets the current statutory minimum for housing, which was the 'Fitness Standard' until April 2006, which was then updated to reflect the Housing Health and Safety Rating System (HHSRS); (b) is in a reasonable state of repair – a home which fails to meet this criterion will have either one or more 'key' building components that are old and in poor condition or two or more 'other' building components that are old and in poor condition; (c) has reasonably modern facilities and services – homes which fail to meet this criterion lack three or more of a specified list of facilities; and (d) provides a reasonable degree of thermal comfort, that is, it has effective insulation and efficient heating. See CLG (2006).

[2] A house meets the 'tolerable standard' if the house: (a) is structurally stable; (b) is substantially free from rising or penetrating damp; (c) has satisfactory provision for natural and artificial lighting, for ventilation and for heating; (d) has an adequate piped supply of wholesome water available within the house; (e) has a sink provided with an adequate supply of both hot and cold water within the house; (f) has a water closet or waterless closet available for the exclusive use of the occupants of the house and suitably located within the house; (g) has a fixed bath or shower and a wash-hand basin, all with a satisfactory supply of hot and cold water suitably located within the house; (h) has an effective system for the drainage and disposal of foul and surface water; (i) has satisfactory facilities for the cooking of food within the house; and (j) has satisfactory access to all external doors and outbuildings.

[3] Relatively limited data in this area is available from the most recent Scottish and Welsh House Condition Surveys.

[4] Households below average income using equivalised income before housing costs.

[5] Child poverty was measured using a combination of three definitions: the child's own deprivation (child going without one or more 'necessities'); parents' deprivation (parents going without two or more 'necessities'); and the income poverty of the family (income of below 40% of median). Children were defined as being in 'severe' poverty if they were poor on all three measures, and 'non-severely poor' if poor on one or two of the three measures.

[6] House living space was defined as the number of rooms per person in households with children (not counting corridors, kitchens and bathrooms). Inequality was measured by the

gap between the score at the median (column 2 of Table 7.4) and the average score of all children below the median (column 3). Column 4 shows the difference between the two.

[7] FACS is a series of annual surveys that investigate the lives of British families with dependent children commissioned by the Department for Work and Pensions. In 2005 (Wave 7), 6,976 families took part, covering 13,814 children.

[8] England – Homelessness (Priority Need for Accommodation) (England) Order 2002); Wales – Homeless Persons (Priority Need) (Wales) Order 2001); and Scotland – Homelessness etc (Scotland) Act 2003. It should also be noted that England defines people aged 21 who are 'vulnerable as a result of having been looked after, accommodated or fostered' as a priority need group, whereas Scotland, Wales and Northern Ireland do not. In Scotland, Wales and Northern Ireland young people who are at risk of financial or sexual exploitation are also described as a priority need group by guidance to legislation. However, while Wales defines this group as also being aged 18-20, neither Northern Ireland nor Scotland set a specific age limit. Further, Scotland also includes those aged 18-20 who are involved in substance misuse as a priority need group.

[9] The *Homelessness code of guidance for local authorities* (ODPM, 2002) defines 'vulnerability' as whether, when homeless, 'the applicant would be less able to fend for himself than an ordinary homeless person so that he would be likely to suffer injury or detriment, in circumstances where a less vulnerable person would be able to cope without harmful effects'.

[10] Homelessness etc (Scotland) Act 2003. There will be an exception for intentionally homeless households.

[11] These statistics are collected using different measures and therefore are presented separately for England, Wales and Scotland.

[12] www.communities.gov.uk/housing/housingresearch/housingstatistics/housingstatisticsby/homelessnessstatistics/livetables/

[13] Although it should be noted that in 2003 and 2004 households with dependent children represented 51% of homeless priority need acceptances.

[14] Homelessness, April to June 2010, first release of statistics: http://wales.gov.uk/topics/statistics/headlines/housing2010/100922/?lang=en

[15] www.scotland.gov.uk/Topics/Statistics/Browse/Housing-Regeneration/hmlss0910

[16] Provisional data.

[17] There is also a target to reduce B&B use to emergency situations for 16- and 17-year-olds by 2010.

[18] Homelessness, April to June 2010, first release of statistics: http://wales.gov.uk/topics/statistics/headlines/housing2010/100922/?lang=en

[19] A total of 2,053 adults participated in the main survey, reporting on a total of 3,272 children. In addition, 450 children aged 8-15 were interviewed separately.

EIGHT

Children's time and space

Antonia Keung

Key statistics

- One in four schoolchildren disagreed that there were places for them to go in their local area.
- In the UK, over 90% of pupils have access to the internet at school; 87% also have access to a computer at home and among these, 71% have access to the internet.
- Of 8- to 17-year-olds in the UK in 2007, 42% had a social networking profile.
- Of children aged 12-15, 37% visited a social networking site (SNS) on a daily basis and girls (41%) were more likely than boys (32%) to visit these sites every day.
- Of around 149,000 schoolchildren surveyed in 2008, 36% had engaged in sport activities for six or seven days over the previous week; 35% said they had done so for three to five days; 21% said they had done so for only one or two days; and 4% said they had not pursued any sport or active engagement in the last week.
- Of just under 7,000 schoolchildren surveyed in 2008, around 9% felt unhappy about how they spent their time.
- Of an estimated population of 3.5 million 11- to 15-year-olds in England and Wales, around 2.3 million children will have worked at some point before their school-leaving age.
- Of around 6,000 young carers aged under 18 surveyed, over 50% were girls and half of all the young carers were from single-parent families.

Key trends

- Children are increasingly spending more time indoors than outdoors, and have less opportunities for independent mobility compared to their parents' generation. Similarly, reductions in children's use of outdoor spaces and independent mobility have also been reported in countries such as the Netherlands, Australia and the US.
- Children nowadays also have much less time to play freely, and they spend more time on structured activities associated with education and learning.
- There has been a rapid rise of SNSs in the past few years and a growing number of children and young people in the UK and worldwide using these sites.

Key sources

- Office for National Statistics (ONS)
- British Household Panel Survey (BHPS) youth panel

> • The Children's Society national well-being of young people survey 2008
> • The National Survey of Culture, Leisure and Sport: Child Survey 2007
> • TellUs3 Survey
> • UK 2000 Time Use Survey
> • Playday 2009 opinion poll
> • Academic research papers and reports

Introduction

The aim of this chapter is to provide a broad picture of children's time and space in England. It provides a review of children's access to private, public and virtual spaces and factors associated with their spatial patterns. The chapter then looks into children's use of time in various activities, including paid work and provision of unpaid care. The main sources of reference include the UK 2000 Time Use Survey, The Children's Society Survey on well-being of children, the Playday 2009 opinion poll and the youth panel of the British Household Panel Survey (BHPS). In addition to quantitative data, information on children's experience and use of time and space are provided by qualitative studies on a local or regional level.

Children's spaces

Home(s)

Other than school, the home and family are the main physical and social spaces in which most children spend their childhood. However, Britain, like many other western developed countries, has witnessed substantial changes in the patterns of marriage and divorce, which mean that many children in the country today have experienced rather different home and family lives than previous generations. Statistics suggest as many as one in five children live in a lone-parent family and more than one in ten in a stepfamily (see Chapter Two). These changes imply that many children may have two homes and alternative living arrangements with their separated or divorced parents.

There are no guidelines on the amount of time non-resident parents should spend with their children after separation or divorce. The majority of parents make their own arrangements for sharing time with their children but statistics from a recent Omnibus survey show that 1 in 15 children whose parents are separated/divorced had the contact arrangements with their non-resident parent negotiated by mediators or lawyers. Seventeen per cent of children from the non-resident parent sample and 8% of children from the resident parent sample had their contact arrangements ordered by court (ONS, 2008).

The family life of children whose parents are separated/divorced can get very complicated at times, as their lives are no longer lived in one place but scattered between several locations. Data from the ONS Omnibus Survey (ONS, 2008) show that over 70% of children meet their non-resident parent at the non-resident parent's home and around one third of these stay at their non-resident parent's home over night at least once a week. Other common locations where contact takes place also include 'place of leisure', 'at resident parent's home', 'at a relative's or friend's home', 'school' or at a 'contact centre' (ONS, 2008).

Children often feel they do not have much say regarding contact arrangements (Smart et al, 2001), but older children have more influence and hence may have different arrangements from younger children (ONS, 2008). Nonetheless, children who have to experience this are increasingly aware of the effort involved in maintaining a life across two households (Smart et al, 2001), and in some cases running between two homes can be a source of stress for those less organised.

Private space at home

The child's bedroom is no longer just a space where he/she gets rest, but to many it has became a central location of leisure and the mediation of everyday life. For older children in particular, their bedrooms provide them with much needed space, not only for individual privacy but also for the construction of personal identity, styles and tastes. Livingstone (2007) argues that 'bedroom culture' has emerged at the turn of the 21st century as part of the process of 'individualisation' and the increasing concern of children's safety in a 'risk society'. Crucially, parents consider home spaces as havens of safety for their children (Livingstone, 2007). There are, however, cases of child abuse and domestic violence, which mean home may not necessarily be safe for some children (see Chapter Ten, this volume).

Increasingly, children are spending more time indoors than outdoors and this is implicitly linked to the perceived danger of public outside spaces by both parents and their children. A similar shifting from 'outdoors' to 'indoors' is also experienced by Dutch children. Karsten and van Vliet (2006; cited in Lester and Russell, 2008) describe the emergence of 'indoor children' as a new phenomenon in Dutch history.

With multimedia becoming more affordable to many families, children's bedrooms are now often filled with all kinds of electronic gadgets, including personal televisions, internet-connected personal computers, music media and so on. Livingstone (2007) points out that the media-rich lifestyle lived by many young people reflects not only their fascination with the media technologies but also the extent to which young people today have little satisfactory alternatives.

The quality and quantity of home space is linked to socioeconomic factors. Overcrowding is endemic among poor families, and children of low-income families are likely to have to share their bedrooms with their siblings. Save the Children's research shows that 41% of families live in severe poverty and do not have enough bedrooms for each child of 10 or over of a different sex (Save the Children UK, 2007). Often these children live in the most deprived neighbourhoods and it is also these children who perceive the greatest risks to playing in public outdoor spaces (Farmer, 2005).

Public outdoor spaces

Children generally like playing in public outdoor places as it provides spaces for them to meet and 'hang out' with friends and to get away from adult supervision. Outdoor play is important for child development and keeping children active and healthy (Gleave, 2009). Research found parental anxiety about safety has restricted children's ability to play outside the home with friends (Mhonda, 2007). Gill (2007) argues that a number of social and cultural changes might have caused parents to be overprotective of their children, one of which is the danger of traffic. The increased volume of traffic has left most residential streets more dangerous and unpleasant. Other factors include concerns about bullying, fear of crime and strangers, concerns about gangs, activities associated with the illegal drugs market and other less specific fears. These have made all public outdoor places feel less safe, and this is especially the case among children living in very deprived or troubled estates (Matthews, 2001; Gill, 2007).

The societal expectations of good parenting also mean that children are expected to be under the active care and guidance of their parents or other responsible adults. These expectations stigmatise as irresponsible those who try to let children out to play unsupervised (Furedi, 2001). Additionally, the disproportionate focus of media on risk and stories of tragedy have also been blamed for cultivating the 'fear culture' and 'risk aversion' in Britain (Gill, 2007).

There is a range of factors affecting the means and extent to which children and young people can access public outdoor places. A study conducted by Mackett et al (2007b) found that in a sample of 330 primary school children aged 8-11 from Cheshunt, Hertfordshire, 56% of the children were allowed out without an adult. Table 8.1 presents further results and shows that the proportion generally increases with age, and boys are more likely to be allowed out than girls.

Table 8.1: Percentage of children aged 8-11 allowed out without an adult

Year groups	Boys	Girls	All
Year 4 (age 8-9)	52	33	44
Year 5 (age 9-10)	50	44	47
Year 6 (age 10-11)	86	69	78
Total	**63**	**48**	**56**

Source: Mackett et al (2007b)

Other research found that children from minority ethnic groups appeared to be more restricted in their use of urban space, which may be attributable to greater and stricter parental control and fear of racism (O'Brien et al, 2000). Level of income and family type are found to be associated with children's independent mobility. Mackett et al (2007a) point out that children in higher-income families seem to be more protected by their parents and are more likely to travel by car for safety and security reasons. It has also been suggested that children in lone-parent families are significantly more likely to be the most independent, as they do not get the same level of supervision and control as their two-parent peers.

Furthermore, Mackett et al (2007a) found that the nature of the environment and the neighbourhood's surrounding areas are also linked to whether children were allowed out alone. More specifically, their research findings suggest that children who live in urban areas, like Lewisham, are less likely to be allowed out without an adult, which is probably the result of greater perceived risk related to local traffic and street crime. On the other hand, children who live in suburban areas like Hertfordshire, with more open green space, good access to local shops and strong social support networks, are more likely to be allowed out without an adult. Other research showed that the seasons and associated weather and duration of daylight (Matthews, 2001), and the attractiveness of potential play places (Lester and Russell, 2008), could all influence the extent to which children play out in public spaces.

Sutton (2008), in a qualitative study, compared the use of free time and style of play between 'estate' and private school children and found marked differences between the two groups. From the perspective of the estate children, street play and/or outdoor socialising are deemed important and they spend most of their free time 'hanging out' with friends at various places in their neighbourhoods. On the other hand, those private school children in the study spent more time in organised leisure activities. The study found that the estate children's preference for street play was mainly owing to financial constraint and lack of available transport to get to activity venues. Sutton (2008) illustrated that playing outside is fundamentally linked with disadvantage, as the estate children have little space at home, and few opportunities for alternative leisure activities.

Overall, research evidence from the UK and other industrialised societies such as the Netherlands, the US and Australia, clearly indicates that the opportunities for independent mobility and free play has significantly reduced for many children (Lester and Russell, 2008). This trend is particularly worrying as it means that many children and young people are missing out on their outdoor unsupervised play experience and associated benefits. Further discussion of children's play and benefits are provided in a later section in this chapter.

Spaces for teenagers

A national survey of children's well-being conducted by The Children's Society in 2008 suggests that as many as one in four school-aged children surveyed either 'disagreed' or 'strongly disagreed' that there were places for them to go in their area. Figure 8.1 presents details of the statistics.

There is generally a lack of suitable public spaces for teenagers to use for meeting and 'hanging out' with friends. It has been highlighted in a review by Lester and Russell (2008) that most of the parks and outdoor spaces and play facilities are designed for younger children, and such provisions are unattractive and do not meet the needs of the teenage groups. Thus, teenagers tend to meet on the street simply because there is a lack of alternatives. This is especially the case for those from a less affluent background, as alternatives are often unaffordable for them.

In a large-scale public consultation carried out in 2005 for the policy initiative of *Youth matters*, many young people expressed that they would have liked

Figure 8.1: Proportion of young people aged 10-15 who agree/disagree with the statement 'There are places for me to go in my area'

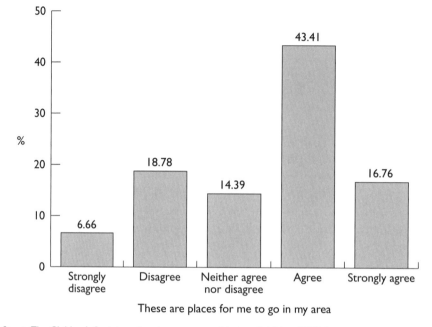

These are places for me to go in my area

Source: The Children's Society national survey on well-being of children 2008 data

somewhere to go and something to do (DfES, 2006). Of the young people who responded to the consultation, 73% thought that 'having more places for young people to go would stop some teenagers getting into trouble' (DfES, 2006, p 9). This suggests that boredom may be the cause of trouble making among some young people in public areas.

Teenagers' activities and movements on the street are often unwelcome to neighbours and local community members, as group behaviour can sometimes be intimidating to others. Consequently, young people may feel that they are being restricted from using much of the public realm and confronted by the intolerance of local adults (Lester and Russell, 2008). Sanction and control by the police authority, such as the use of the Anti-social Behaviour Order and Curfew Order, is another example of denying some young people the use of public spaces.

It was clear from a public consultation on *Youth matters* that there was a high demand for 'things to do, places to go' from children and their parents (DfES, 2005, 2006). The Labour government was committed to addressing the issue of inadequate provision of facilities and positive activities to keep children active and healthy, in particular children from disadvantaged backgrounds. *Aiming high for young people* (HM Treasury and DCSF, 2007) and the Department for Children, Schools and Families' (DCSF) 2008 Play Strategy were the two main policy documents detailing the government's plan, and a financial commitment of over £200 million to ensure that children and young people have opportunities to engage in more physical activities through play and to help them develop new skills and raise their aspirations.

Virtual space

Many children and young people would have access to the internet, providing them with a virtual space for leisure, education and learning activities. A recent research project, UK Children Go Online (UKCGO), carried out by Livingstone and Bober, looked into the internet use of a representative sample of around 1,500 9- to 19-year-olds in the UK. The review provided here is mainly based on the findings in their final report (Livingstone and Bober, 2005). It is suggested that over 90% of pupils have access to the internet at school. The majority of children (87%) also have access to a computer at home, and among those children, 71% have access to the internet at home. Households with children are more likely to acquire multiple computers and be connected to the internet/broadband.

A significant digital divide remains an important issue. Researchers found that 88% of middle-class compared to only 61% of working-class children have access to the internet at home. Around one fifth of the children in the UKCGO study had access to the internet in their bedrooms. Whether internet is available in children's bedrooms is associated with the child's sex, social class and age. Twenty-two per cent of boys versus 15% of girls, 21% of middle-class versus 16% of working-class children and 10% of 9- to 11-year-olds versus 26% of 16- to 17-year-olds have internet access in their bedrooms. Most children who are frequent users of the internet use it for homework (90%), or to get information for other things (94%), as well as for sending emails (72%) and to play online games (70%). Time spent online is still less than time spent watching television or with the family, but is similar to that spent doing homework and playing computer games. Research evidence also suggests that children often lack the skills to evaluate online content and do not receive sufficient training in how to judge the reliability of online information. The UKCGO study found that 38% of pupils trust most of the information on the internet, and only 33% of 9- to 19-year-olds who go online at least once a week say they have been told how to judge whether they can trust online information (Livingstone and Bober, 2005). The UK Council for Child Internet Safety (UKCCIS) launched an internet safety campaign 'Click Clever, Click Safe' in early 2010, which aims to increase public awareness about online risks and safety, and provide guidance to parents, children and young people on how to protect themselves in an online environment (Directgov, 2010a).

It is also worth noting the rapid rise of social networking sites (SNSs) in the past few years and the increasing numbers of children and young people who use SNSs for a host series of online activities such as: expressing themselves, enjoying entertainment, keeping in touch with friends and meeting new people. As cited from comScore (2008) in a research review, 42% of UK 8- to 17-year-olds had a social networking profile in 2007, including 27% of 8- to 12-year-olds and 55% of 13- to 17-year-olds. It was also cited that similar figures are recorded in other countries, and the use continues to grow worldwide (comScore, 2008, cited in Livingstone and Brake, 2010). It is cited by the ONS that in the UK in 2007, 37% of children aged 12-15 visited an SNS on a daily basis and girls (41%) are more likely than boys (32%) to visit these sites every day. Children from this age group used SNSs mainly as a communication tool for talking to friends or family they either saw a lot (75%) or rarely saw (45%). Over a third of children used SNSs for entertainment or to look up information and at other people's pages without leaving a message (36%), while nearly a quarter of children used these sites to look for old friends or people with whom they had lost touch (2%) (Ofcom data, cited in ONS, 2009b). Research evidence from the US suggests that gender differences exist concerning the motivation of SNS use. For girls, SNSs are primarily places to reinforce existing friendships, whereas for boys, they use them for flirting and making new friends (Lenhart and Madden, 2007). There is other evidence from abroad which points out that while girls use SNSs mainly for maintaining offline contacts, boys are more likely to use SNSs for entertainment purposes (Shi et al, 2009).

Children's play

Article 31 of the United Nations Convention on the Rights of the Child (UNCRC) states that children have the right to rest and leisure, to engage in play and recreational activities appropriate to their age, and to participate freely in cultural life and the arts (UN, 1989). However, recent research suggests that the nature and amount of free play for children has changed. Compared with the previous generations, children nowadays have much less time to play freely in outdoor spaces and they spend more time on structured activities associated with learning (Lester and Russell, 2008). The benefits of play are well researched and there is ample research evidence which supports play as important for children's physical, mental, emotional and social well-being (Lester and Russell, 2008). The values of free or unstructured play are illustrated in much research literature. Burdette and Whitaker (2005), in their literature reviews, highlighted that unstructured free play in outdoor spaces is beneficial to child development in a variety of ways. Cognitive benefits include concentration, self-discipline, problem solving and creativity. Social benefits include self-awareness, flexibility and cooperation. Emotional benefits include becoming happier, reduced mental health problems such as anxiety, depression and aggression. Burdette and Whitaker (2005) further point out that if children are given regular opportunities to engage in free and unstructured play in an outdoor environment, they can become brighter, better able to get along with others, healthier and happier.

In an opinion poll conducted by Play England in 2009, over half of 1,030 children aged 7-14 interviewed over the telephone said they needed more time to play. 'Doing homework' and going to 'extra lessons, organised activities and out-of-school clubs' were the common reasons quoted in the findings as having a big impact on children's time for free play. It has also been suggested that driving children to or from school stops or limits the time children have to play. Among a random sample of 1,037 parents interviewed, half of them said 'there aren't enough places where they live, for their children to play safely without an adult. This is particularly true amongst low-income families (67%)' (Play England, 2009).

Children's time use

Statistics collected by the National Survey of Culture, Leisure and Sport 2007 (DCMS, 2009) show that the majority of children and young people spend their free time with their friends and family, and watching television and/or listening to music. Table 8.2 presents the proportions of children aged 11-15 engaging in various kinds of free time activities in 2007. Apart from spending free time with friends and family, most children also spend their free time doing homework (71%), sports activities (69%) and playing computer games (65%) and/or a range of online activities (64%).

Table 8.3 presents the proportion of young people aged 16-24 engaging in free time activities. It can be noted that besides spending time with friends/family and on media entertainment, most young people from this age group spend their free time shopping (69%) and online activities (69%). Only 59% of this age group would spend their free time engaging in sports/doing exercises (compared with 69% of 11- to 15-year-olds).

The UK 2000 Time Use Survey (ONS, 2002) provides data regarding the amount of time children spend on various activities. It is suggested that children aged under 16 spend only 2% of their time on their own, and most of their time is

Table 8.2: Free time activities performed by children aged 11-15, England, 2007

Activities	%
Spending time with friends	89
Watching television	87
Listening to music	76
Spending time with family	71
Homework	71
Sports activities	69
Playing computer games	65
Internet/emailing/instant messaging	64
Shopping	58
Going to the cinema	56
Going on days out or visits to places	49
Reading	44
Arts and craft	27
Other	8

Notes: The category 'Other' includes playing musical instruments and participation in drama and dance.

Sources: DCMS (2009), cited in ONS (2009) *Focus on Children and Young People.* Data available at www. statistics.gov.uk/StatBase/Product.asp?vlnk=15232)

Table 8.3: Selected free time activities performed by 16- to 24-year-olds, England, 2007/08

	%
Spending time with friends/family	83
Listening to music	83
Watching television	82
Shopping	69
Internet/emailing	69
Going to cinema	64
Going to pubs/bars/clubs	61
Sport/exercise	59
Eating out at restaurants	55
Days out	50
Reading	47
Playing computer games	43

Sources: DCMS (2009), cited in ONS (2009) *Focus on Children and Young People.* Data available at www.statistics.gov.uk/StatBase/Product.asp?vlnk=15232)

spent in the company of their parents, siblings, friends, classmates and/or teachers. Table 8.4 shows children's average daily use of time in hours by age groups. It can be seen that both 8-11 and 12-15 age groups spend most of their waking time in school and doing reading/homework (around 30 hours per week) and watching television (15.9 hours for ages 8-11 versus 18.2 hours for ages 12-15). The younger age group spends much more time on games/hobbies (11.3 hours)

Table 8.4: Average hours per week (including school holidays) children spent on various activities by age groups, 2001

	Age 8-11	Age 12-15
Television/media	15.9	18.2
Computer use	3.3	4.4
Cinema etc	1.9	3.7
Games/hobbies	11.3	4.5
Shopping	2.0	1.6
Sports/walking (non-school)	3.3	4.2
Social visits	3.0	3.8
Travel (not to school)	6.6	6.3
Conversation	0.6	1.5
Eating	8.0	7.6
Unpaid work	2.8	4.5
Paid work	0.3	1.0
Reading/homework	3.0	4.9
School (including travel)	26.1	27.7
Washing/dressing	5.7	5.7
Sleep	73.7	68.0
Other	0.6	0.6
Total	168.0	168.0

Source: UK 2000 Time Use Survey, cited in Layard and Dunn (2009)

than the older age group (only 4.5 hours). It is worth noting that children of these age groups were spending relatively little time outside school on sports or physical activities (3.3 and 4.2 hours respectively among both the younger and the older children).

TellUs3 Survey data in 2008 asked around 149,000 Year 6, 8 and 10 schoolchildren about how many days in the last seven that they had engaged in at least 30 minutes of sport or other active pursuits. The TellUs3 Survey data shows 36% had engaged in sports activities for six or seven days over the previous week; 35% said they had done so for three to five days; 21% said they had done so only one or two days; and 4% said they had not pursued any sport or active engagement in the last week (Ofsted, 2008).

How children feel about their time use

The Children's Society national survey on the well-being of children aged 10-15 asked how children felt about their use of time in various activities – whether it was 'too much', 'just right' or 'too little'. Table 8.5 presents the findings and it shows that over half of the children surveyed said that they thought they had spent 'about the right' amount of time with friends, family, by themselves and engaging in activities. Only around 41% of the children thought they had spent 'about the right' amount of time on doing homework, 21.5% thought they spent 'too much time' and around 37% thought they spent 'not enough' time on it.

Table 8.5: Children's view on their use of time on different activities

How do you feel about the amount of time you spend on:	Too much	About right	Not enough
Spending time with friends	6.6	71.2	22.2
Spending time with family	11.0	67.6	21.4
Time to yourself/relaxing	11.3	56.7	32.0
Activities (hobbies, clubs, sports, etc)	12.4	55.5	32.1
Doing homework	21.5	41.3	37.2
Helping round the home	10.5	48.5	41.0

Source: The Children's Society national survey on well-being of children 2008 data

Furthermore, in the same survey children were also asked to rate how happy they felt about their overall time use on a scale of 0-10. Figure 8.2 shows that the majority of schoolchildren were happy with how they spent their time, although there were still around 9% of children who were unhappy about it.

Figure 8.2: Children's rating of their level of happiness regarding their time use

Source: The Children's Society national survey on well-being of children 2008 data

Children's employment

Research into the impact of child employment on well-being and achievement remains scarce, although it is largely deemed by parents and government as acceptable for school-aged children to engage in part-time employment (Hobbs et al, 2007) as a result of the perceived potential benefits associated with preparation for adult life. Data on child employment are very difficult to access as government employment surveys typically do not extend below people under 16 years of age. Recent figures provided by the Better Regulation Task Force (2004) suggest that work by school-aged children is widespread. Of an estimated population of 3.5 million 11- to 15-year-olds in England and Wales, around 2.3 million children will have worked at some point before their school-leaving age (Better Regulation Task Force, 2004).

Research suggests that there are a number of reasons for children to do part-time work. These include: gaining financial independence from parents, acquiring work experience, combating boredom, earning money to buy consumer goods (Davies, 1999), and for those who live in a poor family, contributing towards family income (Stack and McKechnie, 2002). There is a range of part-time work undertaken by children and the most common types of work quoted include: newspaper delivery, shop floor work, waiter/waitressing, hotel and catering, agricultural work, office work and cleaning (Davies, 1999).

To explore the extent of employment among school-aged children in the UK and to see whether children's employment varies by a number of demographic and economic variables, a secondary analysis of the BHPS youth panel (2008/09), based on a sample of over 1,000 11- to 15-year-olds, has been undertaken for this chapter. Table 8.6 presents the results of the analysis. It can be seen that boys and girls are just as likely to do paid work, with 14.3% of the children reporting that they did paid work in the last week. It is noted in the sample that a small number of cases reported extreme values regarding the numbers of hours worked and the amount of earnings received. So for the analysis, cases with reported working time exceeding 17 hours per week and/or earning over £40 per week were excluded.

The analysis results show that the average number of hours children spent working per week was around 4.6 hours and they earned on average £13.60 per week. No significant differences were noted regarding the average number of hours spent working and mean earnings between boys and girls. Significant differences were, however, noted with children's ages. The results in Table 8.6 show that the proportions of children engaged in paid work increased across the older age group. The proportions of children's employment varied, from 2.9% among the 11-year-olds to 26.6% among the 15-year-olds. Age is also a significant influence on the number of working hours engaged and amount earned among children. It can be seen that older children worked for longer and also earned more than the younger ones. It is noted that family type, parental employment, number of siblings and Income Support were not significantly associated with children's employment, length of working hours or levels of earning. Although a previous study based on the BHPS data found no significant association between receiving pocket money and children's work (Mayhew et al, 2005), the current analysis was not able to re-explore the relationship because a question about pocket money was not included in the latest survey.

It is worth noting that further analysis based on the sample found no significant association between children's employment and their self-esteem or happiness.

Present child employment legislation

In England, the rules that apply to the employment of children under school-leaving age are mainly found in the Children and Young Persons Act 1933. The Act sets out the minimum age at which children may be employed, and allows local authorities to enact byelaws. Young people are also protected by the terms of the European Directive on the Protection of Young People at Work, implemented into UK legislation within the Working Time Regulations. According to the present legislation, as illustrated in the Directgov website (2010b), children may not work:

- if under the age of 13;
- without an employment permit (if this is required by local byelaws);
- in any industrial setting such as a factory or industrial site;
- during school hours;

- before 7am or after 7pm;
- for more than one hour before school (if allowed by local byelaws);
- for more than four hours without taking a break of at least one hour;
- in any occupations prohibited by local byelaws or other legislation;
- in any work that may be harmful to their health, well-being or education;
- without having a two-week break from any work during the school holidays in each calendar year;
- for more than a maximum of 12 hours per week during term time;
- for more than 25 hours per week if they are 13- to 14-year-olds or more than 35 hours per week for 15- to 16-year-olds during school holidays.

Table 8.6: Percentages of children who did paid work last week, hours spent per week and mean weekly earnings, 2008/09

	% with earnings	Hours spent working per week (SD)	Mean earnings £ per week (SD)
Gender	ns	ns	ns
Boys	14.5	4.45	13.05
Girls	14.0	4.86	14.21
Age	***	*	**
11	2.9	1.00	5.67
12	6.5	3.62	6.92
13	15.9	3.72	12.43
14	21.2	5.40	14.17
15	26.6	5.28	16.59
Family type	ns	ns	ns
Couple	14.6	4.33	12.84
Lone parents	13.3	5.42	15.72
Parents' employment	ns	ns	ns
Two earners	15.0	4.32	14.66
One earner	14.1	4.29	10.91
No earner	17.1	6.50	7.50
Number of siblings	ns	ns	ns
0	12.8	4.70	15.10
1	17.3	4.66	11.31
2	12.5	3.50	13.83
Parents receiving Income Support	ns	ns	ns
Yes	13.4	4.27	12.80
No	14.4	4.68	13.63
All	14.3	4.64 (3.65)	13.59 (9.77)

Note: *$p < 0.05$; **$p < 0.01$; ***$p < 0.001$; ns = not significant.
Source: Secondary analysis of the BHPS youth panel (2008/09) by author

It is noted that children of compulsory school age are not entitled to the National Minimum Wage, but young people aged 16 and above are entitled to it. Employers who wish to hire a child must obtain a permit from the Local Education Authority (LEA). Without a permit, children are working illegally. An LEA has the power to supervise the employment of schoolchildren in its area and may require particulars about a child's employment. However, the legislation put in place to protect working children has been criticised as ineffective, as research shows that the majority of working children are unlikely to hold a permit either because they are not aware of the requirement or simply ignore it (Hobbs and McKechnie, 1997; Hobbs et al, 2007). Consequently, child workers in the UK are largely hidden, as most are unregistered with the authorities. In 2004 the Better Regulation Task Force proposed reforms to the child employment law, a consultation of the recommendations was followed, but according to Hobbs et al (2007), the results of the consultation have not been made public. However, it was noted that government's decision to refuse the proposed recommendations is evident in a written answer provided in *Hansard*, 22 June 2006 (Hobbs et al, 2007).

There are concerns about the potential risks and dangers involved in children's work and a general fear that working may have a negative impact on schooling (see Hobbs et al, 2007). Although it appears that working children as a whole do not perform less well academically, it has been argued against in research conducted by McKechnie and Hobbs (2001) that long working hours, especially by those who work more than 10 hours per week, tend to result in children performing less well in school than those who work five hours per week or less.

Children as carers

The situation of children undertaking long-term care for their family members has been a major child welfare concern since early 1990. Young carers are recognised in parliamentary legislation in the Carers (Recognition and Services) Act 1995, and they have been widely accepted as meeting the definition of children in need in the Children Act 1989. Under the Labour government, there were a number of related pieces of legislation concerning young carers, including the National Strategy for Carers 1999, the Carers and Disabled Children Act 2000 and Carers (Equal Opportunities) Act 2004. More recently, the *Every Child Matters* initiatives (2004) and *The Children's Plan* (2007) also provided important policy and guidance on supporting young carers.

However, there is no standard definition of the term 'young carer'. The Social Care Institute for Excellence (SCIE) cited the National Strategy for Carers as referring to young carers as 'persons under the age of 18 who have caring responsibilities for another family member who is either unwell (from either mental or physical illness) or disabled' (SCIE, 2005). The type of caring provided by young carers is very broad and can include household tasks, sibling care or general care, emotional support or intimate care.

Number of young carers

It is difficult to know how many young carers there are in the UK, given the variations in the way 'young carers' are defined and the fact that many are not known by the local authorities or organisations that support and provide them with services (Dearden and Becker, 2004). This suggests that there may be substantial numbers of 'hidden' young carers in the UK. The official figure provided by the 2001 Census suggests that there were around 175,000 young carers nationally (cited in Dearden and Becker, 2004). The BBC, in collaboration with the University of Nottingham, conducted a survey on young carers and based on this they found that about 1 in 12 of around 4,000 schoolchildren surveyed said they had caring responsibilities such as carrying out personal care for someone at home. This latest survey finding provides an estimate of 700,000 young carers in the UK (Howard, 2010). There are a number of reasons identified for young people to become carers, including: a lack of good quality, appropriate, affordable and accessible health and community care services; a lack of information about how to get assistance; and in some cases, a general reluctance to seek formal help, particularly among the minority ethnic groups because of the fear of stigmatisation or separation on the part of those needing care (SCIE, 2005).

Characteristics of young carers

With reference to a large-scale national survey of young carers (who are supported by young carers projects across the UK) carried out by researchers from Loughborough University in 2003/04, it was found that the average age of the carers was 12 and more girls than boys acted as young carers (56% girls versus 44% boys based on a sample size of over 6,000 young carers). The study shows over half of the sampled young carers were living in lone-parent families, 70% of which were caring for their mothers in need. In contrast, of the young carers living in two-parent families, about half were caring for their siblings. The study also suggests that young carers were more common in poor families – with unemployed parents or on low income (Dearden and Becker, 2004). With reference to the care provided by young carers, the same study shows that half of all those needing care had conditions of a physical health nature, 29% with mental health problems, 17% had learning difficulties, and 3% had sensory impairments (Dearden and Becker, 2004). The study shows that young carers performed a range of caring tasks, and Table 8.7 summarises the statistics regarding the types of caring roles young carers performed. It can be seen that providing emotional support was the most common type of caring role provided by young carers (82%), followed by household chores (68%) and nursing tasks (48%).

Research also shows that young carers provide more care as they grow older. The amount of time young carers spend on performing caring tasks also varies. Just under half of the carers surveyed spent 10 hours or less per week caring; around 30% spent 11-20 hours; and around 20% spent over 21 hours (Dearden and Becker 2004).

Table 8.7: Percentage of young carers providing different caring tasks, 2003

Caring tasks	%
Domestic (for example, cooking, cleaning, washing, etc)	68
Nursing-type (for example, giving medication, assisting with mobility, etc)	48
Emotional support	82
Intimate care (for example, bathing, dressing, etc)	18
Child care (that is, caring for younger siblings)	11
Other (for example, bill paying, accompanying to hospital, etc)	7

Note: Valid sample size = 5,116. Figures do not add up to 100% since most carers do several caring tasks.

Source: Dearden and Becker (2004)

Impacts of caring on young carers

Not all young carers consider their caring roles to be negative or damaging to their well-being. A number of studies cited in SCIE (2005) showed that many young carers think that 'caring gives them feelings of maturity, and a sense of closeness to both parents and family; they also value their responsibilities and consider them to be a source of practical life skills' (SCIE, 2005). However, without appropriate support, long-term demanding caring roles can impact negatively on carers' own well-being.

Often young carers feel tired as a result of their caring roles, and some may experience physical problems, for instance as a result of lifting parents with physical disabilities. Studies also show that young carers often feel concerned and worried about their parent's welfare when they are not around. Substantial numbers of young carers are suffering from stress, feeling anxious, are depressed and report low self-esteem. However, it is hard to gauge the effect of caring alone on the psychological health of young carers, as it has been pointed out that many of the studies did not control for the effect of socioeconomic factors (see SCIE, 2005).

Additionally, negative impacts on schooling have also been reported. Young carers often experience difficulties in attending school and finding time and energy to do homework on top of their demanding caring routines. Young carers have also reported feelings of isolation from their peers and being excluded from the opportunities to socialise, given their demanding caring responsibilities. Many also report being bullied or fearful of bullying, which in turn has negative impacts on their social development (SCIE, 2005).

Conclusion

Research findings reviewed in this chapter show that children spend most of their free time with families and friends. Doing homework is the second most free time consuming activity reported by most school-aged children. Children and young people nowadays spend much less time playing out but more time in structured activities associated with learning. Owing to urban planning and development, a lot of green open spaces have disappeared and the increasing volume of road traffic has also made most outdoor spaces unpleasant and unsafe for play. Parental anxiety over the potential dangers associated with public outdoor places also limits children's independent mobility and opportunities to play outside. Overall, children are spending more time indoors.

Home is the space where children spend most of their childhood time. One of the most observable changes in children's home space is their bedrooms. Media, telecommunications and in particular the internet technologies have transformed the lifestyles of many children and young people over the last decade. Personal televisions, internet-connected computers, music media and video game consoles are just a few of the common electronic gadgets that children have in their bedrooms. The online virtual spaces also offer today's young people a new way of expressing themselves and a range of online activities from leisure and entertainment to education and learning.

In the UK, most schoolchildren have a part-time job at some point, and yet the majority of children's employment is unnoticed by the local authorities, which have the statutory duty to supervise and protect children from potential risks or harm while working. Demand from the public for the government to reform the employment laws concerning children has been low. It might be argued that the common perception held by parents and government about the benefit of work experience for future adult life has outweighed the concerns about the health and safety issues of child employment. Another possible reason is that most child workers are employed by small businesses, and reforms might increase the financial burdens of these fragile small enterprises, which certainly is not in the interests of the government. Furthermore, there are potentially hundreds of thousands of children who are undertaking unpaid domestic care, although many are not known by the authorities and/or the professional groups. This puts at risk the young carer's rights as a child being denied as research shows negative impacts of demanding caring roles on young carers' own development and well-being.

NINE

Children and young people in and leaving care

Gwyther Rees and Mike Stein

Key statistics

- In 2009, over 83,000 children and young people were looked after by the state in the UK.
- In 2009, Scotland had the highest rate of looked after children and Northern Ireland the lowest (although there are definitional differences between the four nations).
- During a 12-month period, 2008-09, 36,000 children and young people started to be looked after and 32,000 ceased to be looked after.
- Over 11,000 young people aged 16 and over ceased to be looked after in the UK in 2009.
- Looked after children aged 11-15 are four to five times more likely to have mental health problems than children of the same age group living in private households.
- Looked after children aged 10 and over are twice as likely to be cautioned or convicted of an offence than their peers.
- Less than one in five looked after children aged 15-16 achieves five A*-C grades at GCSE compared to around 70% of the general population.
- Those ceasing to be looked after, compared to young people in the general population, are at substantially higher risk of not being in education, training or employment (NEET), of experiencing homelessness and of having mental health problems as adults.

Key trends

- The number of children in the UK looked after at any given point has increased by over 10,000 over the last decade. This increase has been greatest in Wales and Scotland.
- There has been an increase in the number of children becoming looked after due to abuse or neglect in England over the last five years.
- There is evidence of increased educational attainment among looked after children over the last decade.

Key sources

- Office for National Statistics (ONS)
- Department for Education (DfE), England
- Statistical Directorate, Welsh Assembly Government

- Analytical Services Unit (Children, Young People and Social Care), Scottish Government
- Department of Health, Social Services and Public Safety (DHSSPS), Northern Ireland

Introduction

At the end of March 2009 over 83,000 children were 'looked after' in the UK. In all four countries of the UK, the aims of official policy are to improve the well-being of these children and to help those young people who leave the care system in their often difficult transition to adulthood.

Against this background this chapter is divided into two sections. The first provides descriptive information about numbers and trends and covers the following topics:

- the number of children in care and time trends in these statistics;
- the reasons that children are admitted to care;
- the characteristics of children who spend time in care;
- the experiences of, and lengths of time that children spend in, care;
- the routes through which they leave care.

The second half presents a summary of evidence on the well-being of children in care, or who have been in care, during childhood, in the transition to adulthood and in later life.

The evidence presented in this chapter is based on statistics that are routinely produced in all four countries of the UK, and on a growing body of research evidence about the experiences and well-being of children in and leaving care.

Definitional note: Throughout this chapter we use the term 'looked after' to describe children and young people in public care in the UK.

Statistical note: Unless otherwise stated, all official statistics in this chapter are for the most recent year available. At the time of writing this was the year ending March 2010 in England and Wales and the year ending March 2009 in Scotland and Northern Ireland.

Number and trends for children in care

Number of children in care

At the end of March 2009 there were over 83,000 looked after children in public care in the UK (see Table 9.1), amounting to a rate of 6.4 per 1,000 of the child population. The rate of looked after children per 1,000 of the child population varies somewhat between the four countries of the UK. The rates are lowest, and relatively comparable (5.5 and 5.7 per 1,000 respectively), in England and Northern Ireland. Wales has a higher rate of children in care (7.5 per 1,000). Scotland has the highest rate at 14.7 per 1,000.

Table 9.1: Numbers and rates of looked after children by country, 31 March 2009

	Numbers	Child population[a] (000s)	Rate per 1,000	Adjusted rate per 1,000 (see below)
England	60,900	11,012	5.5	5.1
Wales	4,704	629	7.5	6.7
Scotland	15,288	1,042	14.7	9.0
Northern Ireland	2,463	432	5.7	4.6
Total	**83,355**	**13,115**	**6.4**	**5.5**

Note: [a] These are ONS population estimates for mid-2009 for the 0-17 age group. Note that some looked after young people are aged 18 and over, so the rates are approximations.

However, these comparisons are distorted by the extent that Scotland counts as 'looked after' children who were at home on supervision orders,[1] who would not be counted as looked after in the rest of the UK. A more valid yardstick for comparison may be the rate of children who are looked after and not placed with parents. On this basis, the approximate rates per 1,000 are 4.6 in Northern Ireland, 5.1 in England, 6.7 in Wales and 9.0 in Scotland.

Trends in the number of children in care

Table 9.2 shows time trends in rates of children in care over the last decade. There are quite different patterns to these trends in the four countries of the UK.

In England, after a gradual increase in the number of looked after children in the late 1990s and early 2000s (see Rowlands and Statham, 2009 for a long-term analysis of these trends), the numbers were fairly steady between 2003 and 2009. However, the numbers rose from 60,900 in 2009 to 64,400 in 2010. In Wales there was a 44% increase in the number of looked after children over the last decade, from 3,574 children in 2000 to 5,162 in 2010. In Scotland the numbers have also increased substantially (by around 35%) over the last decade. In Northern Ireland, the numbers in care have been relatively steady over recent years.

Table 9.2: Trends in numbers of children in care by country, selected years, 2000-10

Year	England	Wales	Scotland	Northern Ireland	UK total
2000	58,100	3,574	11,309	2,422	75,405
2005	60,900	4,380	12,185	2,531	79,996
2006	60,300	4,530	12,982	2,436	80,248
2007	60,000	4,640	14,060	2,356	81,056
2008	59,400	4,633	14,888	2,433	81,354
2009	60,900	4,704	15,288	2,463	83,355
2010	64,400	5,162	—[a]	—[a]	

Note: [a] 2010 statistics for Scotland and Northern Ireland were not available at the time of writing.

Reasons that children are admitted to care

Statistics are available on broadly defined categories of need for children admitted to care in England. Current numbers and trends in these statistics for children starting to be looked after in a given year are shown in Table 9.3.

Table 9.3: Numbers and trends in categories of need for children starting to be looked after in England, 2006-10

	2006	2007	2008	2009	2010
Abuse or neglect	11,500	11,400	11,300	12,700	14,500
Child's disability	830	740	690	690	700
Parent's illness or disability	1,500	1,300	1,200	1,200	1,200
Family in acute stress	2,800	2,800	2,700	2,800	3,100
Family dysfunction	3,200	3,300	3,100	3,700	4,600
Socially unacceptable behaviour	1,300	1,200	1,100	1,100	1,100
Low income	70	80	60	70	110
Absent parenting	3,400	3,100	3,200	3,500	2,500

The previous edition of this edited collection noted a long-term increase in the proportion of children looked after for reasons of abuse and neglect between 1994 and 2003. From 2003-09, the proportion of children starting to be looked after due to abuse or neglect stayed relatively constant, at between 47% and 49%, although there was a noticeable increase to 52% in 2010. Similarly, the proportions starting to be looked after due to family dysfunction increased from 14% in 2009 to 17% in 2010. Meanwhile, there was a fall in the proportion becoming looked after due to 'absent parenting', from 14% in 2009 to 9% in 2010. This decrease appears to be partly attributable to a decline in the number of unaccompanied asylum-seeking children (UASC) looked after who primarily appear in this category of need.

For Wales, four official categories are published, of which the largest is 'abuse or neglect' – 59% of cases in 2010, an increase from 52% in 2008.

Background and characteristics

Age

There is an uneven age distribution of children who are looked after. For example, in England in 2010 there was a greater representation in the under one year (6%), 10-15 (39%) and 16 and over (21%) age groups than in the intervening age groups – 1-4 (17%) and 5-9 (17%). In terms of trends over the last five years, there has been a decrease in the proportions in the 5-9 and 10-15 age groups and increases in the 1-4 and 16 and over age groups. In Wales and Scotland the highest proportions of being looked after are in the 10-17 and 12-15 age groups, respectively. In Northern Ireland, there is a similar proportion (20%) of looked after children aged 16 and over to that in England – higher than in Wales or Scotland.

Gender

In England, around 56% of looked after children are male and around 44% are female. This balance has been fairly consistent over the past five years. The proportions of males in Wales, Scotland and Northern Ireland are 54%, 55% and 53% respectively.

Disabled children

There is long-standing evidence that disabled children and young people are over-represented in the care system (Berridge, 1997). In England, for looked after children at the end of March 2010, 2,200 (4%) had a need category of 'child's disability' relating to the point when they started to be looked after. However, the total number of disabled looked after children is likely to be substantially higher than this figure. In addition, 8,300 children with this need category had been looked after under at least one agreed series of short-term placements in the 12 months to March 2010.

In Scotland, official statistics are available on the number of disabled looked after children. In 2009, 1,641 (11%) looked after children were categorised as having one or more disabilities. The largest groups were social, emotional and behavioural difficulties (644), learning disabilities (277) and multiple disabilities (239).

Baker (2007, p 1173) compares the experiences of disabled and non–disabled foster children and proposes the idea that disabled children may experience a '"reverse ladder of permanency"; being less likely than their peers to receive permanent placements such as adoption and return home'.

Ethnic origin

In England in 2010, 76% of children in care were of White origin, 8% were of Mixed origin, 5% were Asian or Asian British, 7% were Black or Black British, and 3% from other ethnic groups. There appears to have been some increase in the number and proportion of looked after children of Asian origin, from 2,100 (3%) in 2005 to 3,200 (5%) in 2010. In Wales, 4,830 (94%) of looked after children were of White origin and 305 (6%) were from Black and minority ethnic groups. In Scotland, 13,918 (91%) looked after children were of White origin, 432 (3%) were of Asian, Black, Mixed or other origins; the ethnic origins of the remainder (6%) were not disclosed or not known.

Unaccompanied asylum-seeking children (UASC)

The large majority of UASC – that is, those arriving in the UK unaccompanied by a parent or responsible adult – are referred to local children's services departments for help. Their numbers in some authorities represent a substantial proportion of the care population. There were 3,400 UASC looked after in England in March 2010 – a decrease of 500 from the previous year. The figures for 2003 and 2006 were 2,200 and 3,400 respectively. In 2010, 89% of these children were male and 71% were aged 16 and over.

Young mothers

In England, there were 350 mothers aged 12 and over looked after in March 2010. This number is 17% higher than in 2006. Almost half (48%) of these young people were under 16 at time of the birth of their first child.

Experiences of care

There is a huge diversity of experience of care in terms of age of entry to care, type and stability of placement(s) and lengths of time spent in care. A recent study of over 7,000 children in the English care system (Sinclair et al, 2007) identified six groups of children for whom there were different patterns of care experiences: young entrants (under the age of 11); adolescent graduates (those who entered care before the age of 11 and were still looked after aged 11 and over); abused adolescents; other adolescent entrants; young people seeking asylum; and disabled children. The study found that the first two and last of the above groups had a higher chance of achieving a stable placement (or adoption) than the other three groups. Adoption was almost exclusively reserved for those children who first entered care under the age of five.

Numbers entering care

In England, 27,800 children started to be looked after in the year ending 31 March 2010. This is an increase of 8% on the previous year. The corresponding numbers for Wales, Scotland and Northern Ireland were 2,018, 5,194 and 1,041 respectively (the latter two figures being for 2009). The 2010 figure for Wales was 40% higher than in 2008. The figure for Scotland has increased by around 11% since 2001. There is no evidence of a clear trend in Northern Ireland.

Placement type

Statistics are available on the types of placements in which children are looked after for each of the four countries of the UK. However, each set of statistics uses slightly different categorisations and so it is difficult to make direct comparisons. These include the different legal provisions in Scotland relating to supervision at home that have already been discussed above (see endnote 1). With the exception of Scotland, where the majority (59%) of looked after children are placed with parents or with friends or relatives, most looked after children live in foster care.

———

Based on the most recent available statistics, the proportion living in foster care is highest in Wales (78%), followed by England (73%) and Northern Ireland (65%). In contrast, relatively few looked after children are placed in residential care (with the highest proportion being around 15% in England).

Lengths of time in care

Many periods of being looked after are relatively short-lived. In a study of over 7,000 looked after children, Sinclair et al (2007) estimated that just under half of those in the sample who started to be looked after left the care system within one year. Of these children, 63% returned home to parents or relatives. After one year, the likelihood of leaving care diminishes substantially. For children aged 11 and over who remained looked after for a year or more, only 5% left care within the subsequent year.

In England, figures are available for the number of looked after children under 16 who had been looked after continuously for at least two-and-a-half years. There was a total of 20,800 of these children in 2010. There has been a small gradual decline in this figure since 2006 (23,000).

In Scotland, the most recent statistics show that 34% of children ceasing to be looked after had been looked after for less than one year. Notably, almost half (47%) of those under the age of one were looked after for less than six weeks.

In Northern Ireland, 44% of children were discharged from care within three months and a further 16.5% within one year.

Placement stability and change

Stability and continuity of care placements have been shown to be key predictors of the well-being and longer-term outcomes of looked after children (see, for example, Biehal et al, 1995, 2010; Sinclair et al, 2007), and so statistics on these aspects of care provision have come to be seen as important indicators.

In England, the number of looked after children who had three or more placements during the year ending 31 March 2010 was 7,000 or around 11% of all looked after children. This number was broadly the same as the previous two years but lower than the comparable figure of 7,800 in 2006. For Wales, the proportion of looked after children having three or more placements during the same year was 10%.

Official statistics in England are also available on the number of children under 16 looked after for at least two-and-a-half years who had been looked after in the same placement for at least two years. In 2010 this amounted to 14,100 – the same figure as the previous year and slightly lower than 2006 (14,600). However, because of the decline in longer-term stays as outlined in the previous section, the proportion in stable placements for two years increased from 63.5% in 2006 to 68% in 2010.

Routes out of care

Looked after children and young people who are accommodated in foster care, residential care and other settings ceased to be looked after through four main routes – returning home to live with parents or relatives, through adoption, through special guardianship or residence orders, or to live independently (at age 16 and over).

In the most recent years for which statistics are available, the numbers of children ceasing to be looked after in each country were as follows – England (25,100), Wales (1,568), Scotland (4,386) and Northern Ireland (921).

Returning home to live with parents or relatives

This is the most common pathway out of the looked after system. In England it accounted for 9,800 cases (39%) in 2010. This is a decrease from 42% in 2006. In Wales and Scotland[2] the proportions leaving care through this route were 47% and 64% respectively.

Adoption

The number of children adopted from care in the most recent year for which statistics are available for each country was 3,200 in England, 229 in Wales, 203[3] in Scotland and 64 in Northern Ireland.

In England, there has been a decrease in looked after children being adopted over the last five years – from around 3,700 in 2006 to around 3,200 in 2010. This decrease was primarily between 2006 and 2007 (3,300).

Special guardianship

The Adoption and Children Act 2002 introduced a new legal option of special guardianship. A special guardianship order, made by a court, provides a legal status for adults (other than parents) to look after a child. Unlike adoption, the birth parents also retain legal status in relation to the child. In England in 2006, when this option first became legally available, 70 looked after children ceased to be looked after through a special guardianship order. This number increased substantially to 760 in 2007 and then continued to grow to over 1,200 children in 2009 and in 2010.

Leaving care at 16 and over

A total of 9,100 young people aged 16 and over ceased to be looked after in England in 2010. This is an increase from 8,200 in 2006. Of these young people, 21% were aged 16 (down from 27% in 2006), 16% were aged 17 (down from 18% in 2006), and 63% were aged 18 and over (up from 54%). These statistics show a trend of greater numbers legally leaving care at the age of 16 and over, and of these, young people leaving care at an older age. The most common final placements for these young people were foster care (39%), parents (5%), other placements in the community (26%) and children's homes and other residential settings (28%).

In the other three countries, the numbers of young people aged 16 or over ceasing to be looked after in the most recent year for which statistics are available was 503 in Wales, 1,396 in Scotland and 299 in Northern Ireland. In Northern Ireland, two thirds of looked after young people aged 16 and over remained in care until they were 18.

Well-being of children in care

In this section we summarise recent evidence on the well-being of children in care across a number of domains. Overall, there are indications that, viewed as a whole group, children in care fare less well than the average for the general population of children in a number of areas including health, education and longer-term outcomes as young adults. However, there are three important overarching points to bear in mind when reviewing this evidence.

First, indicators of 'well-being' should not be seen as synonymous with 'outcomes' of being looked after. In all domains, the well-being of children in care will have been influenced by various factors that occurred before their entry into the care system. Inevitably, children who enter the care system will, by and large, have already experienced considerable adversity in their lives. For example, in early childhood many of these children will have experienced abuse or neglect that is known to have serious consequences for mental health. They may also have been less likely to receive standard healthcare and a good start in relation to their education. It is clear then that comparing the well-being of these children with the general population is not particularly meaningful and is certainly not an indicator of the 'outcomes' of the care system. The question for the care system is how well they are able to compensate children for these adverse experiences and, in this respect, more needs to be done.

Second, many of the official statistics and research findings for looked after children relate specifically to that group of children who were either in care at a given moment or who remained in care until after the age of 16. These findings are, therefore, about specific sub-groups of children who experience care at some point in their lives. They may not accurately reflect 'outcomes' for all children who have spent time in care.

Finally, research studies have highlighted the considerable diversity that exists within the care system across a range of short-term and longer-term well-being measures. Overall, a number of studies (see, for example, Sinclair et al, 2007) have demonstrated the importance of quality and stability of placements for maximising the well-being of looked after children. Space does not permit a detailed summary of these findings under each heading below, so we briefly draw out a few examples of overarching findings here. A study of adoption and long-term foster care (Biehal et al, 2010) found that stable, long-term foster care could be very successful in providing positive outcomes for children. Where this form of stability was achieved, emotional, behavioural and educational outcomes were relatively similar to those achieved through adoption. Wade et al (2010) found that among a sample of maltreated children in the looked after system, there were better follow-up outcomes in terms of well-being and stability for those children who remained within the care system than for those who returned home.

Subjective well-being

There is relatively little evidence on the subjective, self-reported well-being of the general population of looked after children. Some studies of specific samples have developed such measures. In one recent study of a sample of 150 young people in foster care, children's homes and residential special schools (Berridge et al, 2008), the young people were asked to rate their well-being in six areas – schooling, family relationships, friendships, staying out of trouble, achieving goals and general happiness. This study found that young people's ratings regarding schooling, friendships and general happiness were negatively associated with changes in placements. Currently, there appears to be a significant gap in more widespread measurement of the subjective well-being of looked after children, including comparisons with the child population as a whole. As Stein (2009, p 116) argues, young people's own perspectives are 'central to identifying the quality of services that will enhance their well-being'.

Mental health

A study for the Office for National Statistics (ONS) (Meltzer et al, 2003) found that among children looked after by local authorities, 5- to 10-year olds were five times more likely to have a mental disorder than children living in private households, and 11- to 15-year-olds were four to five times more likely. The differences in rates of conduct disorder were particularly high – for example 40% of 11- to 15-year-olds who were looked after compared to 6% of those living in private households. Similarly, higher rates were also reported in companion studies in Wales and Scotland (Meltzer et al, 2004a, 2004b). Further analysis of these data (Ford et al, 2007) also showed significantly higher rates of disorder for looked after children than for children living in disadvantaged private households.

The above findings related to children already being looked after. A study by Sempik et al (2008), based on analysis of case files, highlighted the already extensive emotional and behavioural difficulties of children at the point of entry into care.

In the last two years, the emotional and behavioural health of looked after children has been monitored in England through the use of the Strengths and Difficulties Questionnaire (SDQ). In 2010, an SDQ score was gathered for 68% of eligible children. The mean score was 14.2.

Physical health

Meltzer et al (2003) found that two thirds of all looked after children were reported by carers to have at least one 'physical complaint'. This included a number of categories that were higher than those in the general population: eye and/or sight problems (16%); speech or language problems (14%); bed wetting (13%); difficulty with coordination (10%); and asthma (10%).

The most recent government indicators reported that 84–86% of looked after children had up-to-date immunisations, had received a dental check and an annual health assessment. There has been an improvement in these statistics over the last decade. Comparable figures for the year 2000 were in the region of 67% to 71%.

Education

Children who are looked after tend to have lower levels of educational achievement than other children. As with other areas of well-being discussed in this section, the educational attainment of looked after children needs to be viewed within the overall context of their lives. Children's experiences before entering care and their experiences in care (for example, placement instability) can adversely affect their educational attainment (O'Sullivan and Westerman, 2007). A report by the Social Exclusion Unit (2003) highlighted the fact that children in care were nine times more likely to have a statement of special educational needs (SEN) than children in the general population. In the most recent government statistics in England (DCSF, 2010b), around 27% of children who had been looked after continuously for a year or more had a SEN statement. Over 11% had missed at least 25 days of school during the previous school year.

In terms of attainment, in England in 2009, at 10–11 years of age, 46% of children looked after continuously for at least 12 months achieved at least Level 4 in both Key Stage 2 English and Mathematics (increasing from 42% and 38% respectively in 2005). However these statistics compare to 80% and 79% respectively for the general population in 2009. Similarly, in 2009, 15% of children looked after continuously for at least 12 months and aged 15–16 obtained five A*–C grades in GCSEs or GNVQ equivalent – an increase from 11% in 2005 and from around 7% in 2000. The 2009 figure compares approximately with 70% for all children although the latter figure also includes other GCSE equivalents not included in the statistics for looked after children. In Wales, statistics show an increase over the last three years in looked after children achieving specified levels in core National Curriculum subjects at Key Stage 2 (from 38% in 2008 to 44% in 2010) and Key Stage 3 (from 18% in 2008 to 25% in 2010) and in average external qualifications point scores at the age of 16.

In England, at the end of school Year 11, 73% of looked after children remained in full-time education and 14% were unemployed in the September after leaving school. These figures show some improvements compared to 2008 (69% and 16% respectively).

However, there is some evidence from research that those looked after children who fare better educationally tend to be female, to have been looked after longer, most often in foster settings, to have had fairly settled care careers and active encouragement from primary caregivers, teachers and social workers (Biehal et al, 1995; Wade and Dixon, 2006).

Offending

Young people who are looked after have a higher than average likelihood of being involved in the youth justice system. The most recent government indicators report that around 9% of looked after children aged 10 and over were cautioned or received a conviction for an offence during the year ending 30 September 2009 – over twice the rate for all children of this age in the population. However, three points should be borne in mind on this issue. First, as with other well-being areas, given the histories of many children in care, comparisons with the general population are probably not that meaningful. Second, many of these children may have been involved in the youth justice system prior to entry into the care system. Third, it has been suggested that young people in care may become criminalised because of behaviour in care, particularly in children's homes, or due to their increased visibility or surveillance (NACRO, 2005).

Running away

There is evidence of relatively high rates of young people in the care system going missing and running away. A study of young people in children's homes and foster care (Wade and Biehal, 1998) found that rates of going missing varied considerably across four local authority areas. Two national surveys of young people (Safe on the Streets Research Team, 1999; Rees and Lee, 2005) have reported significantly higher than average rates of running away among young people currently living in care and among the larger group of young people who have lived in care at some point in their lives. However, these studies have also indicated that as many as half of the young people who run away from care had started to run away prior to becoming looked after, so again this issue needs to be viewed within a broader context.

Substance misuse

The most recent government statistics on substance misuse among looked after children show that around 2,200 children (5%) who had been looked after continuously for at least 12 months in England had been identified as having a substance misuse problem during the last year. Research has shown that compared with the general population, children in care and young people leaving care have relatively high levels of tobacco, alcohol and drug use (Meltzer et al, 2003).

However, it should not be assumed that these difficulties are attributable to the care system.

Well-being of young people from care to adulthood

For most young people today, moving into their own accommodation, entering further or higher education, or finding satisfying employment, and achieving good health and a positive sense of well-being, represent important landmarks during their journey to adulthood. These pathways are also closely connected and often reinforcing. There is evidence that, as a group, care leavers face more difficulties than other young people in achieving these landmarks, although there are differences in outcomes between different groups of care leavers (Stein, 2009).

Moving into settled, safe accommodation

Young people leave care to live independently at an earlier age than other young people leave home. Some young people may feel they have been forced to leave care before they are ready, at just 16 or 17 years of age, find themselves in unsuitable accommodation, move frequently and experience homelessness (A National Voice, 2007; Stein, 2010).

In a 2001 Scottish survey, 61% of care leavers had moved three or more times, and 40% reported having been homeless since leaving care (Dixon and Stein, 2002). In a study of 106 care leavers in England, Wade and Dixon (2006) reported that, 12-15 months after leaving care, 64% of the sample had made either no or one move in accommodation since leaving care. Over half (56%) of young people were considered to have a 'good' housing outcome and a further third (31%) a 'fair' outcome. However, more than one third (35%) of the young people had some experience of homelessness after leaving care. Also of note, a study (Simon, 2008, p 91) comparing 80 care leavers and a comparison group of 59 other disadvantaged young people found that the care leavers had 'fewer crisis transitions and less experience of homelessness' than the comparison group. This was attributed to preparation and support offered by leaving care teams.

The accommodation needs of care leavers has been a focus of policy attention, and recent official statistics for England show that the numbers of care leavers living in suitable accommodation after their care placement increased from 77% in 2004 to 90% in 2009. In Scotland, in 2009, 12% of young people eligible for aftercare services had experienced one or more periods of homelessness since becoming eligible for these services. There is also recent evidence that the proportion of rough sleepers in London with a care background fell, from 17% in 2001-02 to 7% in 2007-08: 'The findings do suggest an improvement in the way young people and children in care are provided with the skills for independent living and advice and support with housing when they become adults and leave care' (Savage, 2009, p 4).

Entering further or higher education, finding satisfying employment

Official data and research studies have consistently shown poor post–16 educational and employment outcomes for young people leaving care (Dixon and Stein, 2005; Barn et al, 2005; Mallon, 2005; Stein, 2005; Wade and Dixon, 2006; Cameron et al, 2007; Cashmore et al, 2007).

In England, among care leavers now aged 19, 37% were still in education and 25% were in training or employment. Since 2005, there has been a rise in the proportion still in education and a roughly equal drop in the proportion in training or employment. The overall percentage in education, employment or training has fluctuated a little over the last five years but was broadly similar in 2010 (62.1%) to 2006 (62.7%). The proportion of care leavers aged 19 who were not in education, training or employment (NEET) (for reasons other than illness or disability) was 28% in 2010. In Wales, 49% of care leavers aged 19 in 2010 were in education, training or employment.

In Dixon et al's (2006) study of care leavers, around two fifths of young people were NEET at the first and second waves of data collection. This study found that a positive career outcome was associated with greater placement stability while looked after and this finding is supported by other studies (Allen, 2003; Jackson et al, 2003, 2005; Merdinger and Hines, 2005).

Achieving good health and a positive sense of well-being

As detailed above, on entering care children and young people have often experienced high levels of psychological adversity and have far higher rates (three to four times) of mental health problems than those not living in care. Young people living in residential care also have poorer mental health than those living in foster care, which may reflect different pre-care family experiences and care histories. There is evidence of associations between poor mental health, poor physical health and lower educational attainment for young people living in care than for their peers.

Transitions from care

Many care leavers have to cope with major changes in their lives, in leaving foster care or residential care and setting up home, in leaving school and entering the world of work, or post–16 education or training, or being parents at a far younger age than other young people. These compressed and accelerated transitions to adulthood represent a barrier to promoting their well-being in that they are denied the psychological opportunity to deal with issues over time which is how most young people cope with the challenges of transition (Stein, 2008).

A follow-up study of 106 young people leaving care at the age of 16 and above (Dixon et al, 2006) found an increase in self-reported physical and mental health problems among the sample approximately a year after leaving care. Analysis of the data from this study showed that both physical and mental health problems increase at the time of transition and may combine with earlier pre-care and in-care difficulties or new challenges during transition, in affecting their overall health and well-being (Dixon, 2008).

Research by Sinclair et al (2005) into the outcomes for young people leaving foster care has identified key variables that distinguished those 'doing well' from those who were less successful: a strong attachment with a family member, partner or partner's family or foster carer was associated with a good outcome. Conversely, those young people who were assessed as 'disturbed' at first contact – and this correlated with other key variables including performance at school, placement disruption and attachment disorder – had poorer outcomes. Young people being seen as ready and willing to leave was also associated with the 'doing well' outcome measure.

Adult outcomes

In the UK, there is very little research, either follow-up or retrospective studies, of adults who have been in care. Analysis of UK data from the National Child Development Study indicates a higher risk of depression at age 23 and 33, a higher incidence of psychiatric and personality disorders, and greater levels of emotional and behavioural problems among those who had been in care, than for the same-age population who had not (Cheung and Buchanan, 1997; Buchanan, 1999).

More recently, using longitudinal data from the 1970 British Cohort Study, Viner and Taylor (2005) have shown that at 30 years old and after adjustment for social class, those with a history of care were significantly less likely to achieve high social status and significantly more likely to have psychological morbidity, poor general health, have been homeless and have a conviction. Their data analysis showed that such adversity related to being in care per se, rather than to wider aspects of childhood and then adult disadvantage. However, Pritchard and Williams (2009) found lower rates of offending in early adulthood among a sample of males who had been looked after as adolescents than among a comparison group of socially disadvantaged males who had no statutory right to social work support.

International comparisons

A review of the international evidence from 16 countries shows that as a group, young people aged 16 and over leaving care in the transition to adulthood, have a high risk of social exclusion. However, there are differences in outcomes between those who successfully 'move on', those who 'survive' and those who 'struggle', and that these differences are associated with the quality of care they receive, the nature of their transitions from care and the support they receive after they leave (Stein and Munro, 2008). A literature review drawing on research from five EU countries (Denmark, England, Hungary, Spain and Sweden), collaborating in the 'young people from a public care background pathways to education in Europe'

(YIPPEE) project, showed that the participation rates of young people from care were much lower than those in the general population (Hojer et al, 2008).

Conclusion

The number of looked after children in the UK has increased over the last decade, with the largest increases being seen in Wales and Scotland, although it should be noted that there are some definitional differences between the four countries.

Research studies and official statistics have drawn attention to the higher probability of negative well-being and longer-term outcomes for looked after children in comparison with the general population. Looked after children as a group are more likely to have mental health problems, less likely to do well at school and more likely to become involved in offending and substance misuse than the average for the population as a whole. However, there are indications from recent monitoring and research that the well-being of looked after children is improving in a number of areas including educational attainment, healthcare and housing outcomes.

Additionally, in terms of well-being, comparisons between looked after children and the general population of children may not be particularly appropriate as they do not take into account the backgrounds and characteristics of children who become looked after, which often include a number of factors known to be associated with poorer well-being and outcomes. Some recent studies which have compared the outcomes for looked after children with those for other socially disadvantaged children have suggested that, under the right circumstances, being looked after can be associated with better than expected outcomes, taking into account young people's starting points before being looked after.

Stability and continuity of placement and quality of care have been shown to be key factors in promoting positive well-being of looked after children. There is some positive evidence of recent improvements in placement stability and continuity.

Notes

[1] Under Section 70(1) of the Children (Scotland) Act 1995. The overall aim of these orders is to promote beneficial changes in the lives of children while enabling them to remain at home.

[2] In Scotland this includes children who were at home on supervision orders.

[3] This is the number of children who, on ceasing to be looked after, went to stay with newly adoptive parents.

TEN

Child maltreatment

Carol-Ann Hooper

Key statistics

A survey of children, young people and caregivers (Radford et al, 2011) carried out for the National Society for the Prevention of Cruelty to Children (NSPCC) found the following rates of maltreatment (all lifetime figures):

- Physical assault by adult caregivers – 1.3% of under 11-year-olds, 6.9% of 11- to 17-year-olds, 8.4% of 18- to 24-year-olds.
- Neglect – 5% of under 11-year-olds, 13.3% of 11- to 17-year-olds.
- Sexual abuse (involving forced contact or by a family member) – 0.5% of under 11-year-olds, 4.8% of 11- to 17-year-olds, 11.3% of 18- to 24-year-olds (a broader definition gives higher figures).
- Emotional abuse –
  - exposure to domestic violence – 12.6% of under 11-year-olds, 19.8% of 11- to 17-year-olds, 27.8% of 18- to 24-year-olds
  - other aspects – 3.6% of under 11-year-olds, 6.8% of 11- to 17-year-olds, 6.9% of 18- to 24-year-olds.

Key trends

- There is some tentative evidence of a decline in fatal abuse, although there are many limitations to the available data.
- Comparison of the two NSPCC surveys (Cawson et al, 2000; Radford et al, 2011) found significant declines in prolonged smacking, pinching and slapping, physical assault, and harsh treatment of children, with neglect remaining stable.
- Safeguarding activity has increased over the last five years, but this may reflect increased activity rather than increased maltreatment.

Key sources

- Radford et al (2011) *The maltreatment and victimisation of children and young people in the UK: NSPCC research findings*, London: NSPCC – now the best source of evidence. This reports on the prevalence survey described above and gives both lifetime and past year figures for children under 11 and 11-17. The lifetime findings for 18- to 24-year-olds are compared with the 2000 NSPCC survey (Cawson et al, 2000) to consider evidence of trends.

- There are no government statistics that show the extent of child maltreatment. Statistics on safeguarding activity (referrals, assessments and child protection plans) are available from the Department for Education (DfE). Recorded crime statistics are produced by the Home Office.

Introduction

Definitions of child maltreatment are variable and contested. While harm attributable to specific individuals is a common defining characteristic, and a common core includes physical abuse, neglect, sexual abuse and emotional abuse, some definitions are broader – child poverty, for example, covered in Chapter Three, can be argued to be a form of societal neglect, given its impact on children (Hooper et al, 2007). When new forms of harm to children are discovered, it is now common to claim that they are 'a form of child abuse', and definitions are sometimes, but not always, revised to include such harms. (Recent examples of those forms of harm not included so far include parental smoking and drinking). This chapter takes government definitions, given in the inter-agency guidance, *Working together to safeguard children* (HM Government, 2010), as its territory. Under the *Every Child Matters* programme, for the first time local authorities have had an implicit duty to prevent child maltreatment (rather than to prevent the demands on services associated with it) since 'Staying safe' is one of the five domains of child well-being that authorities are required to promote. It is clear that the quality of children's family and peer relationships are among the strongest influences on their well-being (ESRC, 2010; Hobcraft and Kiernan, 2010; Rees et al, 2010a) and, unsurprisingly, maltreatment increases the risk of a wide range of other negative outcomes, including poor emotional well-being/mental health, further victimisation, delinquency, drug and alcohol abuse, teenage pregnancy and homelessness (Radford et al, 2011). In this chapter, however, it is considered as an outcome in its own right.

Sources of data

There are no government statistics that show the number of children who have experienced maltreatment. While there are data on crimes recorded by the police and on convictions (criminal statistics), and on cases referred, assessed and subject to a child protection plan by children's social care departments (safeguarding statistics), research consistently shows that only a small minority of incidents reported to researchers were ever reported to any agency (Cawson et al, 2000; Sidebotham and the ALSPAC Study Team, 2000). Reported cases are commonly described as the tip of the iceberg (Creighton, 2004). Trends in these official statistics tell us something about agency workloads, but it is not possible to tell whether changes are the result of changing levels of need/incidence of maltreatment, of public and professional awareness and reporting, of professional anxiety or activity, or some combination of them all. Furthermore, crimes recorded by the police are organised by offence category, and do not always allow easy identification of those offences involving children; convictions are the outcome of an attrition process influenced by many factors other than whether maltreatment has occurred; and trends in the number of children subject to a child protection plan (which have gone down and then up again since 1997) have been influenced by changes in the policy context (including the introduction of targets involving registration) as well as other factors.

Fatal abuse is an exception, as there are two sources of statistics on homicides involving children, although neither is wholly reliable. The international World Health Organization (WHO) mortality statistics are most commonly used in research on child homicide, although studies vary as to whether figures for those deaths classified as homicides only are used (see, for example, Hunnicutt and LaFree, 2008), or whether other categories which may include some cases of fatal abuse not identified as such are also included (for example, cases where it is undetermined whether injuries were accidental or purposely inflicted, as in Roberts et al, 1998, UNICEF, 2003; suicides, also in Roberts et al, 1998; other external causes of death, accidents and adverse events, as in Pritchard and Williams, 2010). Both strategies have limitations, since using only the homicide figures gives an unrealistically low figure – there is widespread agreement that maltreatment tends to be underrepresented in mortality statistics worldwide – and adding other categories gives an overly inflated figure. The second source is Home Office data on homicides, which have been used in the previous two editions of this work and are considered below, along with cross-national research. Again, these are not wholly reliable since cause of death is sometimes contested – as evident in cases of convictions for murder that have been overturned on appeal – and for this reason recent figures are least reliable. To some extent, aggregating data for several years overcomes this difficulty, and the often erratic nature of trends where numbers are small. In addition to WHO and Home Office statistics, all child deaths where abuse or neglect are known or suspected to be a factor should be subject to a serious case review, and the development of local multiagency death review teams, required by the Children Act 2004, might be expected to reduce the number of unidentified cases and result in more accurate figures in the future (Jenny and Isaac, 2006). In the meantime, a recent increase in the number of serious case reviews involving child deaths may be the result, at least in part, of changing practices (Brandon et al, 2010).

To establish the extent and patterns of non-fatal child maltreatment it is necessary to turn to research. The existing research falls into two main categories – incidence studies and prevalence studies – although there is now some overlap between the two. Incidence studies focus on the number of cases reported per year (in which abuse may have occurred that year and/or earlier). While such studies still exclude unreported abuse, the collection of data directly from agencies, for example, the police or NHS emergency departments, allows its organisation according to the researchers' criteria and extends our knowledge of agency workloads beyond the police and children's social care. Prevalence studies ask adults or children and young people directly about their experiences of childhood (or sometimes parenting) to establish the proportion of the population affected. At the time of writing for the previous two books, the most comprehensive and methodologically sophisticated prevalence study in the UK was Cawson et al's *Child maltreatment in the UK* (2000), for which 2,689 18- to 24-year-olds were interviewed about childhoods lived in the late 1970s, 1980s and 1990s, and its findings were given as the best available data on the extent of maltreatment. More recent data are now available from a further survey, also conducted by the NSPCC (Radford et al, 2011), which has retained some similarities to the 2000 study in order to enable trends to be established, and also incorporated changes in methodology to reflect current thinking and to enable the collection of data on maltreatment in the past year as well as over the lifetime, which is more useful for service planning. This is now the best data available, and the findings are given in some detail in this chapter.

The new survey involved 6,195 randomly selected households across the UK and included children aged 0-17, and also 1,761 young adults aged 18-24 for comparison with the previous survey. For the 2,160 children aged 0-10, parents or caregivers were interviewed as proxy reporters. In addition, 2,275 children and young people aged 11-17 were interviewed directly, with a primary caregiver also interviewed. Interviews were conducted in 2009, using computer-assisted interviewing (with questions heard through headphones as well as read on the screen) and a validated instrument, the Juvenile Victimisation Questionnaire, which has been used in large-scale studies in other countries. The change of approach reflects growing recognition of the limitations of retrospective surveys (where events that occurred some time ago may not be reported for a range of reasons), of the importance of direct research with young people (using age-appropriate methods) and of the value of interviewing parents about young children (which the Avon Longitudinal Study of Parents and Children [ALSPAC] has shown to reveal much maltreatment that has not been reported to agencies). The sample has similar limitations to the previous survey in that it was confined to private residential accommodation and so excluded young people in residential care, hostels and custody, all of whom are known to report high rates of abuse, although numbers are small. It has the further limitation that parental consent was required for all those under the age of 18. While parents interviewed about young children may not have known or concealed some incidents of maltreatment, it is also possible that some of those who refused consent may have been motivated to conceal maltreatment. The response rate was 60.4%, which is somewhat lower than in the 2000 survey (although not unusually low for similar surveys). Children and young people still living with their parents may also cope with maltreatment by amnesia, defensive exclusion or dissociation, only accessing memories later in life (Briere, 1992; Cameron, 2000). The figures are all likely to be underestimates, perhaps especially those for the 0-10 age group. Despite the limitations that are inevitable in such research, the survey has produced a wealth of information, much of which is yet to be analysed, and gives a picture of children's very recent experiences of maltreatment which has not been available before.

Some trends can now tentatively be identified in relation to maltreatment (from the two NSPCC surveys), and in relation to fatal abuse (from mortality data and homicide statistics), and these are discussed in the relevant sections below. Meaningful comparisons between the different countries of the UK are possible only for bullying (using the WHO international Health Behaviour in School-aged Children [HBSC] survey) and internationally only for bullying and homicide, and these are treated similarly. While prevalence studies have been conducted in many countries, especially on child sexual abuse, differences of definition, methodology, awareness and cultural context make comparisons difficult, and the most comprehensive overview, the UN *World Report on Violence against children* (2006), which gathered data from over 130 countries, refrains from any real comparison or ranking, concluding simply that child maltreatment is widespread and a global problem. Some studies have used identical methodologies in several countries, in relation to the sexual abuse of girls (the WHO multi-country study on women's health and domestic violence, 2005) and in relation to physical punishment (the WorldSAFE study, Runyan et al, 2010) but so far, the UK has not been included in these.

Extent of child maltreatment

Fatal abuse

The number of fatal abuse cases is widely thought to have remained fairly stable over decades, with the child protection system developed in the 1970s making little, if any, difference (see, for example, Lonne et al, 2008). The conclusions reached in the previous two chapters, after examining Home Office data, were in line with this belief. Infant and child homicide rates in England and Wales appeared to have been fairly stable in the 1980s and 1990s (Hooper, 2002), and to have increased slightly between 1992-97 and 1997/98-2002/03, although that apparent increase could well have been the result of improved identification (Hooper, 2005). Roberts et al (1998) also found no reduction in intentional injury death rates among 0- to 19-year-olds (using WHO data and including suicides and deaths where it was undetermined whether they were accidental or purposely inflicted) between 1980 and 1995, although there was a substantial fall in unintentional injury death rates over this period. Pritchard and Williams (2010), however, again using WHO data, including homicide and other categories that might include possible child abuse related deaths (CARD) and comparing figures aggregated for two three-year periods, 1974-76 with 2004-06, argue there are grounds for cautious optimism. CARD rates, both for babies under one and for children up to 14, were found to have declined significantly over that period, and more in England and Wales than in many other countries. Pritchard and Williams (2010) further argue that since England and Wales are in the four major developed countries in which CARD (the responsibility primarily of the child protection system) have gone down more than all deaths (the responsibility primarily of medicine), social workers should be encouraged that child protection work may have had a more significant impact in reducing child deaths than is often recognised. These arguments are somewhat undermined, first, by the fact that it is impossible to tell how much of the decline is accounted for by accidental deaths which are included in the figures and where it is known that the UK, along with many other countries, has made very significant progress (WHO and UNICEF, 2008), and second, by evidence from other studies that both child mortality overall and child homicide are associated with economic inequality (Roberts et al, 1998, Hunnicutt and LaFree, 2008) as much as, if not more than, either medical or social work intervention. Nevertheless, Home Office data also now suggest grounds for cautious optimism. While five years ago the average risk of homicide for babies under one over the previous 10 years was 47 per million per year in England and Wales, it is now 40 per million (Smith et al, 2010). The average number of children under 16 killed by their parents has also gone down, from an average of 50 per year 1999/2000-2003/04 to an average of 32 per year 2004/05-2008/09. Given the growth of economic inequality in Britain since the 1970s (Dorling, 2010), it may be that even a steady state is an achievement and a small decline more of an achievement than it at first appears. It is clear that intensive family assessment and support can reduce risk levels or at least stop child protection concerns escalating (Kendall et al, 2010), although many child deaths occur in families not currently perceived by agencies as high risk (Brandon et al, 2010).

Given the different ways in which the available data are used, it is not surprising that international comparisons give varied results. Hunnicutt and LaFree (2008) place the UK fairly low in a comparison of 39 countries on infant homicides (27th for females and 25th for males, based on WHO data for deaths classified as homicide only), behind countries including Spain, Greece, Italy, Belgium, Norway, Ireland, France, Sweden, Australia and Canada, and ahead of New Zealand, Germany, the US, Japan, Austria, Finland and Hungary. UNICEF (2007), who aggregated mortality statistics for accidents, murder, suicide and violence in relation to 0- to 19–year-olds to give a measure of children's safety as part of a broader analysis of children's well-being in 25 high-income countries, place the UK much higher, with the second lowest level after Sweden, although this may largely reflect the success in reducing accidental deaths. In an earlier UNICEF study (2003), comparisons based on homicide and deaths where the cause was 'undetermined' only resulted in the UK being placed 14th in a ranking of 27 OECD countries. Earlier comparative research (summarised in Hooper, 2002) has found child homicide rates associated with high female labour force participation (where it is accompanied by low status of women and low investment in welfare spending), high divorce rates and a culture of violence. The most extensive and recent study (Hunnicutt and LaFree, 2008) again found women's labour force participation together with economic inequality to be the two most significant factors, suggesting that the former may be significant because of its association with economic stress and lack of resources. The quality of bureaucracy was also found to be significant, although only in relation to male infant deaths, suggesting that efficient organisations may be better at detecting risk and make some contribution to improved outcomes.

Physical abuse and punishment

Physical abuse, as defined in government guidance, 'may involve hitting, shaking, throwing, poisoning, burning or scalding, drowning, suffocating or otherwise causing physical harm to a child', and may also include fabricating or deliberately inducing illness in a child (HM Government, 2010, p 38). In the new NSPCC survey, 8.4% of the 18- to 24-year-olds had experienced physical assault by adult caregivers in their childhoods (7% of young men and 9.9% of young women). Of the under 11-year-olds, 1.3% had been physically assaulted (with 0.7% experiencing it in the past year) as had 6.9% of the 11- to 17-year-olds (with 2.4% in the past year) (Radford et al, 2011). Clearly, lifetime figures are likely to rise with age as experience accumulates, and the reliance on caregiver accounts for younger children may also underrepresent abuse, but these figures also highlight the importance of the growing awareness of the abuse of adolescents (Rees and Stein, 1999). The lifetime and past year prevalence of physical violence by other adults, from peers and from partners, is given in Table 10.1.

While such assaults will undoubtedly cause distress, not all incidents result in injury, although a significant proportion do, as shown in Tables 10.2 and 10.3.

Table 10.1: Findings on physical violence, lifetime (LT) and past year (PY) figures

Age group	Physical assault by adult caregivers	Physical violence by other adults	Peer victimisation physical violence	Physical violence in intimate partner relations
<11s	1.3% LT, 0.7% PY	0.6% LT, 0.2% PY	16.9% LT, 11.8% PY	
11-17	6.9% LT, 2.4% PY	3.3% LT, 1.1% PY	42.7% LT, 23.0% PY	5.2% LT, 2.9% PY
18-24	8.4% LT	5.8% LT	46.2% LT	9.8% LT

Source: Radford et al (2011)

Table 10.2: Percentage hit, beaten, kicked or physically hurt by an adult who looked after them, LT figures

Age group	Boys experienced	Of these boys hurt/injured	Girls experienced	Of these, girls hurt/injured
<11s	0.7	23.8	0.4	26.8
11-17	4.0	57.1	4.6	64.3
18-24	4.2	61.3	6.4	73.5

Source: Radford et al (2011)

Table 10.3: Percentage shaken or shoved very hard by a caregiver, LT figures

Age group	Boys experienced	Of these boys hurt/injured	Girls experienced	Of these girls hurt/injured
<11s	0.5	0	0.4	44.9
11-17	4.3	26.6	4.2	43.3
18-24	4.0	31.3	5.9	43.4

Source: Radford et al (2011)

Further evidence comes from hospitals. An incidence survey conducted by the NSPCC found 5,871 children had been taken to hospital with deliberately inflicted injuries in 2008, including 318 aged two or under and 177 with head injuries. In other words, each week roughly three babies or toddlers were admitted to hospital with deliberately caused head injuries (NSPCC press release, 14.4.09). An annual survey of Accident and Emergency (A&E) departments conducted by the Cardiff Violence and Society Research Group further suggests an overall decline since 2001 in children attending with violence-related injuries, but an increase of 7.5% in 2009 over 2008 among children aged 0-10 (Sivarajasingam et al, 2009, 2010).

A certain level of physical violence to children, in the name of punishment or discipline, is much more widespread. Radford et al (2011) found 39.4% of parents or guardians reported using physical punishment in the past year with under 11-year-olds, and 45.9% with 11- to 17-year-olds. While physical punishment has been thought to peak in early childhood and decline with age, this data suggests otherwise. A review of previously available research found between 48% and 71% of parents reporting they had ever used physical punishment (Bunting et al, 2010). While a distinction is commonly made between physical punishment and physical abuse, there is a clear association between them, and Radford et al (2011) report significant declines both in prolonged smacking, pinching and slapping (which probably includes both) and in physical assault. Evidence of a decline in the frequency of physical punishment between the 1960s and 1990s was given in a previous chapter in Hooper (2002). The Children's Society (2010) also report a significant change of attitude across generations, with younger people seeing 'slapping children on the legs as a standard punishment' as a higher risk practice than those over the age of 65. Despite growing pressure for a universal prohibition on corporal punishment, both internationally and within the UK, and a growing trend among other countries to comply with the principles of the UN Convention on the Rights of the Child in this respect and give children equal rights to protection from assault with adults, the UK has not yet abolished altogether the defence of 'reasonable chastisement'. Public and parental attitudes remain ambivalent, with many parents recognising the ineffectiveness and negative consequences of physical punishment but continuing to smack nevertheless, usually when stressed, angry, frustrated, worried or tired. While most do not fully defend smacking, viewing it as a last resort, only a minority yet support an outright ban, suggesting that a children's rights framework, combined with a public health approach (based on the evidence of negative effects), are more likely to achieve change than reliance on public opinion (Reading et al, 2009; Bunting et al, 2010).

Neglect

Neglect is 'the persistent failure to meet a child's basic physical and/or psychological needs, likely to result in the serious impairment of the child's health or development' (HM Government, 2010, p 39). Physical neglect includes failing to provide adequate food, clothing or shelter, failing to protect the child from harm or danger, failing to ensure adequate supervision or failing to ensure appropriate medical care or treatment. Emotional neglect involves neglecting or failing to respond to the child's basic emotional needs. Radford et al (2011) note that it is harder to measure in a self-report survey what has not been done than what has been done, and difficult also to capture what is often an ongoing condition rather than an event. Questions covering physical neglect, lack of supervision and monitoring, emotional neglect and educational neglect were combined for lifetime measures of neglect, but past year figures are based on a measure of physical neglect only. Exposure to domestic violence is addressed separately (see the section on emotional abuse below) to avoid the implicit blaming of mothers for men's violence often involved in judgements of 'failure to protect'. Despite the limitations of the data, neglect was the most common form of maltreatment identified by the survey (as it is also in cases subject to a child protection plan). Of children under 11, 5% were judged to have experienced neglect over their lifetimes (0.1% had experienced physical neglect in the past year), and 13.3% of 11- to 17-year-olds over their lifetimes (0.4% had experienced physical neglect in the past year).

There has been a steady rise in the number of children subject to a child protection plan under the category of neglect (a more than 30% increase between 2004 and 2009) (DCSF, 2007/08/09), an increase in cases of 'cruelty to and neglect of children' reported to the police (the average of 5,431 cases per year over the last five years is 47% higher than the average for the preceding five years; Home Office, 2003, 2010) and a similar increase in calls to ChildLine relating to neglect (NSPCC, press release 25.2.10). However, the data that allows for comparison between the 2000 and 2010 NSPCC surveys suggest prevalence has remained fairly stable over the period. The discrepancy may be because the experience of agencies and professionals reflects increased awareness and reporting, as discussed above, although it may also be that it is forms of neglect not covered by the NSPCC survey measures that are rising.

Maternal substance abuse during pregnancy is now included in the definition of neglect, and the author's chapter in the previous volume of this book (see Hooper, 2005) noted the increasing number of children born to drug-using parents and living with parents misusing drugs. Over the four years 2004/05-2007/08 in

Britain, consultants recorded around 1,200 babies a year as suffering neonatal withdrawal symptoms from being born to mothers who were drug dependent (personal communication, National Treatment Agency for Substance Misuse). In 2003, the Advisory Council on the Misuse of Drugs estimated that between 41,000 and 59,000 children in Scotland (4-6% of all children under the age of 16) and between 200,000 and 300,000 children in England and Wales (2-3% of all children under the age of 16) may be affected by parental drug misuse. More recent reliable figures are not available. Although not all children in such situations suffer adverse effects, it is clear that the risks of both physical and emotional neglect are increased by the impact of drug use (for example, loss of contact with reality) and the lifestyle associated with it.

Sexual abuse

Sexual abuse includes a wide range of activities, some involving physical contact (including assault by penetration, masturbation, kissing and touching) and others not (including showing children sexual imagery, involving them in watching sexual activity or grooming them in preparation for abuse). There may or may not be force or violence involved, but in the absence of coercion, sexual activity is nevertheless abuse by virtue of the inability of children to give informed consent within relationships of unequal power. Unlike other forms of abuse, sexual abuse is perpetrated by people in a wide range of relationships, with only a small minority of cases involving parents. In Radford et al's (2011) survey, 1% of the 18- to 24-year-olds reported sexual assault by an adult caregiver during their childhoods (a similar figure to the previous survey). The figures are much lower among the under 11-year-olds and 11- to 17-year-olds (0.1% for both groups), but while lower rates would to an extent be expected among younger children, this is also more likely to reflect underreporting than a real trend. The need for parental consent may have skewed the sample, parents and caregivers involved in the survey may not know of all incidents for younger children (since most sexual abuse occurs in secrecy and children often tell no one), and older children may dissociate from such experiences of abuse while still dependent on their parents and only recall or recognise them later (Cameron, 2000).

Using a broad definition including contact and non-contact abuse, and including all perpetrators, 24.1% of 18- to 24-year-olds reported sexual abuse during their childhoods, 16.5% of 11- to 17-year-olds and 1.2% of under 11-year-olds (Radford et al, 2011). A total of 11.3% of 18- to 24-year-olds, 4.8% of 11- to 17-year-olds and 0.5% of under 11-year-olds had experienced sexual abuse that involved forced contact or abuse from a family member. Further details are given in Table 10.4. Much of what is included in the broad definition involves peers and intimate partners. Overall, other children and young people were the most common perpetrators (59.1%), adults not living with the children (known or unknown) the next most common (21.8%), followed by intimate partners (14.6%), parents or guardians (3%), and siblings (1.4%). Teenage girls were at greatest risk.

Table 10.4: Findings on sexual abuse, LT and PY figures

Age group	Broad definition – contact and non contact	Forced contact sexual abuse or abuse by a family member[a]	Sexual abuse by adult caregivers	Sexual abuse by siblings	Sexual victimisation by other adults	Peer sexual victimisation	Sexual victimisation by intimate partners
<11s	1.2%	0.5%	0.1% LT, 0 PY	0.1% LT, 0.1% PY	0.3% LT, 0.2% PY	0.7% LT, 0.3% PY	
11-17	16.5%	4.8%	0.1% LT, 0% PY	0.3% LT, 0.1% PY	1.4% LT, 0.3% PY	9.5% LT, 5.9% PY	2.2% LT, 1.6% PY
18-24	24.1%	11.3%	1.0% LT	0.1% LT	5.3%	12.7% LT	4.1% LT

Note: [a] This included rape or attempted rape by an adult, sexual abuse by a caregiver or sibling to a young person under 18, sexual abuse by an adult relative to a person under 16 and sexual abuse by an adult to a person under 13.

Source: Radford et al (2011)

The number of cases made subject to a child protection plan registered under the category of sexual abuse has been declining steadily in recent years. The reason for this is unclear; it may be that since the perpetrator of sexual abuse is usually excluded from further contact with the child, ongoing concerns are more likely to be framed as neglect or emotional abuse. Finkelhor and Jones (2006), in an examination of similar trends in the US where a wider range of sources of data are available, concluded there was clear evidence of a real decline in sexual abuse (as well as physical abuse and homicide) there. The data for the UK is more ambiguous, since a change in the questions between the two NSPCC surveys means of three composites (unwanted sexual exposure, attempted forced or coercive sexual acts, forced or coercive sexual acts), only the last can be compared. This does give tentative indication of a decline – in the 2000 survey, 6.8% reported forced or coercive sexual acts under the age of 16; in the 2010 survey, 5% of the comparable sample reported such experiences under the age of 16 and 6.8% under the age of 18 (Radford et al, 2011). At the same time, there has been a small increase over the last two years in cases reported to the police. An incidence survey conducted twice so far by the NSPCC found 20,758 cases of sexual offences involving children reported to the police in 2008 in England and Wales, rising to 21,618 in 2009 (an average of 60 per day). While this may reflect increased reporting rather than increased incidence, such data collected from the police are a useful addition to crime statistics. In 2009, 3,035 reported cases involved children under 10, and 1,000 children under five. Girls were six times more likely than boys to be involved. The number of cases involving an offender known to the victim was four times higher than the number involving strangers (NSPCC press releases, 19.1.09 and 25.2.10). Reports of incidents involving the internet, made to the Child Exploitation and Online Protection

Centre (CEOP), are also increasing, with 6,291 reports in the last reporting year, about a quarter involving grooming, and another quarter relating to the possession and distribution of images (CEOP, 2010).

Emotional abuse

Emotional abuse even more than other forms comes in many guises, since what is hurtful to a particular child is an individual matter, although common forms include rejection, persistent criticism, silencing, ridiculing and imposing expectations inappropriate to the child's age and development (HM Government, 2010). Exposure to domestic violence has been included in definitions of emotional abuse since the 1990s, while also being associated with an increased risk of all other forms of abuse (including fatal abuse – see Brandon et al, 2010).

The first NSPCC survey (Cawson et al, 2000) assessed emotional abuse on seven dimensions: psychological control and domination; psycho/physical control and domination (for example, being locked in a cupboard or room); humiliation/ degradation; withdrawal (absence of affection or exclusion from family activities); antipathy; terrorising and proxy attacks (including domestic violence between parents); and attacks on pets and valued possessions. Using a scoring system with a cut-off point that represented adverse experiences on at least four of the dimensions, 6% of the sample was judged to have experienced emotional maltreatment, with another 6% coming close to this level.

In the second survey (Radford et al, 2011), exposure to domestic violence and damage to the child's property were considered separately from other aspects of emotional abuse. Currently, findings for the other aspects are only given for two screening questions about being 'scared by a parent or guardian' and being 'threatened by a parent or guardian'. Of the 18- to 24-year-olds, 6.9% reported experiencing these in childhood, while 6.8% of the 11- to 17-year-olds (with 3% experiencing it in the past year), and 3.6% of the under 11-year-olds (1.8% in the past year) reported these experiences. When directly comparable questions in the two surveys of 18- to 24-year-olds were examined, harsh treatment by adults at home, at school or elsewhere, was found to have declined significantly.

The figures are considerably higher for exposure to domestic violence. Of the 18- to 24-year-olds, 27.8% were found to have experienced this at some point in childhood, with 19.8% of the 11- to 17-year-olds (2.9% in the past year) and 12.6% of the under 11-year-olds (3.3% in the past year) also reporting this experience. The vast majority of this occurred between parents, although some violence to a sibling or another adult was included. The vast majority, 96%, of the perpetrators were male (Radford et al, 2011). Although no trends are identified between the two NSPCC surveys on this issue, the British Crime Survey shows a continuing decline in partner abuse reported by both men and women in England and Wales over the last five years, from 4.1% men and 5.4% women reporting partner abuse over the last year in 2004/05 to 2.6% men and 4.3% women in 2008/09 (Smith et al, 2010). Although the British Crime Survey findings suggest greater gender symmetry, it is clear from more detailed analyses of such data that the gender gap is greater at the more severe, chronic end, with women much more likely to be hurt or injured by domestic violence than men (Dobash and Dobash, 2004). Only about one in six incidents in the recent British Crime Survey was reported to the police (the same proportion at the beginning and end of the period) (Smith et al, 2010). In Scotland, reported incidents continue to increase steadily, although it is not known whether this reflects increased awareness or confidence in the police, increased incidence, or both (Scottish Executive, 2009).

Serious bullying (including cyberbullying) is also now included in the definition of emotional abuse (HM Government, 2010), but it is more commonly addressed separately, so it is covered in the next section.

Bullying and abuse by peers

Many of the behaviours covered in the sections on physical, sexual and emotional abuse above are labelled bullying when they occur between peers. Bullying comes in a variety of forms, although verbal abuse is the most common. Since children identify relationships with peers and with their families as equally important (Featherstone and Evans, 2004), it is unsurprising that bullying has many similar consequences to child maltreatment, although it is more likely to be a matter for schools than for child protection intervention. Bullying remains very widespread, and James (2010) concludes that most children will experience bullying at some point, either as bullies, victims or witnesses. Many studies have also found children from families where parenting is inconsistent or abusive at greater risk of being bullied, becoming bullies or both, than those who are not (Cawson, 2002; WHO, 2004; James, 2010), and bullying also occurs between siblings at home (ESRC, 2010). The experience of being bullied is significantly associated with poorer well-being (Rees et al, 2010a), poorer performance in GCSE exams and not being in employment, education or training (NEET) at age 16 (EHRC, 2010), drug and alcohol abuse, criminal convictions, later violence (including against partners and children), and attempted and actual suicide (Beatbullying, 2010; James, 2010). Children bullied both at home and at school are particularly vulnerable to unhappiness (ESRC, 2010).

Prevalence figures vary, affected as always by different definitions, methodology, samples and timeframes. The Equality and Human Rights Commission (EHRC) (2010) draw on available longitudinal surveys of young people to conclude that 66% of them reported being bullied at some point over the three-year period 2004-06. Rees et al's (2010a) survey of children's well-being found that 23% said they had been bullied often or sometimes in the last 12 months. The international HBSC survey found 9.7% of young people in England, 8.6% in Ireland, 9.4% in Scotland and 11.4% in Wales, reported being bullied at least twice at school in the last two months (WHO Europe, 2006). Radford et al (2011) include bullying, community and gang violence in a wider measure of victimisation by peers (excluding siblings) and found that 28% of under 11-year-olds, 59.5% of

11- to 17-year-olds and 63.2% of 18- to 24-year-olds reported experiencing one or other form over their lifetimes. Bullying by siblings is also widespread – a survey of 2,500 young people, conducted as part of the Understanding Society study, found 31% of children reported being hit, kicked or pushed by a brother or sister 'a lot' or 'quite a lot' (ESRC, 2010). Radford et al (2011) give a broader measure of lifetime experiences of sibling victimisation (which includes physical, emotional and sexual abuse), reported by 28.5% of under 11-year-olds, 31.8% of 11- to 17-year-olds and 25.2% of 18- to 24-year-olds (Radford et al, 2011).

New forms of bullying have emerged, with the increasingly widespread use of electronic communication, and cyberbullying (involving the use of internet, email and mobile phones) is a growing concern. Again this comes in a range of forms, with hoax calls to mobile phones and the use of social networking sites being particularly common (NFER, 2010; Welsh Assembly Government, 2010a). It is often an extension of bullying offline, and as James (2010) notes, can be particularly vicious as messages and images can be spread quickly to many people. A recent review of available evidence by NFER (2010) cites Cross et al's (2009) survey as the best data on prevalence – 30% reported some form of cyberbullying, with 1 in 13 persistently cyberbullied in the last year. The new NSPCC survey found little cyberbullying known to parents or guardians against under 11-year-olds, but that 'someone had used a mobile phone or the internet to harass, spread pictures or videos, sexually abuse or groom' them was reported for 10.6% of 11- to 17-year-olds (5.5% in the past year) and 8% of 18- to 24-year-olds (Radford et al, 2011).

Bullying has been widely found to decrease with age, after a peak during the transition from primary to secondary school (James, 2010; Welsh Assembly Government, 2010a; WHO Europe, 2006), although there are some exceptions to this. While physical aggression tends to decrease with age, verbal aggression tends to increase (Craig et al, 2009). Less decline with age has been found in cyberbullying than in other forms, and in severe or persistent bullying than in bullying overall (Welsh Assembly Government, 2010a). And Radford et al (2011), using a broader definition of peer victimisation, found that although sibling violence declined after the age of 12, peer victimisation increased for both boys and girls and did not decline until the late teens.

While in many countries, boys are more involved in bullying and girls more likely to be victimised, in the UK fairly similar rates of being bullied have been found among boys and girls (WHO Europe, 2006; EHRC, 2010). Boys are more likely to report physical bullying (James, 2010), including physical violence and property victimisation from peers (Radford et al, 2011). Girls are more likely to report verbal, relational, less direct forms of bullying (including exclusion from activities on purpose) (Craig et al, 2009; Welsh Assembly Government, 2010a), sexual victimisation from peers (Radford et al, 2011), and cyberbullying, the latter attributed to their greater use of social networking sites and instant messaging via the internet (NFER, 2010; Welsh Assembly Government, 2010a).

Bullying overlaps with and contributes to a variety of forms of discrimination. Disabled children, especially those with learning disabilities, have been consistently found to be more vulnerable (EHRC, 2010) as have LGBT (lesbian, gay, bisexual and transgender) young people (Stonewall, 2007; EHRC, 2010), and girls are particularly vulnerable to sexual bullying (Radford et al, 2011). There are more mixed findings on socioeconomic status, some research finding higher rates among children from lower income groups (Welsh Assembly Government, 2010a; WHO Europe, 2006), and some not (EHRC, 2010). There are also mixed findings on ethnicity – the EHRC (2010) report white pupils slightly more likely to report bullying than those from black and minority ethnic groups. The Welsh Assembly Government (2010a), however, found more children reporting others being bullied because of 'race' or ethnicity than report experiencing it, and suggests that children experiencing it may not always recognise it for what it is. Children from white, non-British, ethnic backgrounds reported more persistent cyberbullying than others in Cross et al (2009, cited in NFER, 2010). There is also some evidence of, and growing concern about, faith as a basis for bullying.

All schools in England, Wales and Northern Ireland are now required by law to have an anti-bullying policy and it is highly recommended in Scotland (James, 2010). While a range of approaches are taken, there is some evidence both of effective school-based programmes (Farrington and Ttofi, 2009) and of declining levels of bullying, at least of the offline kind (Welsh Assembly Government, 2010a), but bullying clearly remains widespread. No clear trend is evident in the proportion of children reporting worrying about being bullied at school, either a lot or a bit, in the British Household Panel Survey (BHPS) data over the last 13 years (33.2% in 2008/09; personal communication, Antonia Keung). A comparison of 40 countries using HBSC survey data (Craig et al, 2009) places the countries of the UK around the middle in relation to the bullying of girls (with Ireland 8th lowest, Scotland 17th, England 18th and Wales 20th, in a range from 4.8% in Sweden to 35.8% in Lithuania), and somewhat better in relation to boys (with Wales, Ireland and Scotland 7th, 8th and 9th lowest respectively and England 13th lowest in a range from 8.6% in Sweden to 45.2% in Lithuania). An analysis of cross-national data correlated with income inequality suggests that children experience more 'bullying, fights and conflict' in more unequal societies (Wilkinson and Pickett, 2009). A significant minority of pupils still report not knowing who to talk to if they are being bullied and dissatisfaction with school responses (Welsh Assembly Government, 2010a).

Multitype maltreatment and polyvictimisation

Different forms of maltreatment and victimisation have been discussed separately so far, but they are not necessarily experienced as such. Some level of emotional abuse is involved in all forms (HM Government, 2010), and exposure to one form of maltreatment often increases the risk of another, and/or of other forms of victimisation. In the new NSPCC survey, children and young people exposed to domestic and family violence were up to 4.4 times more likely to experience physical violence and/or neglect from a parent or guardian. Those who had experienced physical violence from a parent or guardian, or from a non-caregiver, were also at increased risk of sexual violence (Radford et al, 2011).

Radford et al (2011) give overall rates for maltreatment and direct victimisation by a caregiver (of all forms but not including physical punishment) as 8.9% of under 11-year-olds affected over their lifetimes (2.5% over the past year), 21.9% of 11- to 17-year-olds (6% over the past year) and 24.5% of 18- to 24-year-olds. Table 10.5 also gives two rates calculated for severe maltreatment, one including non-caregivers, such as siblings and peers, the other confined to maltreatment by caregivers. Judgements of severity were made on the basis of chronicity (repeat abuse), multiple forms, injury, weapons involved and self-definition as abuse. These are the experiences that have the strongest associations with worse emotional well-being, and with delinquency.

A further highly vulnerable group of polyvictims, for whom victimisation is more a condition than an event, and among whom trauma-related symptoms tend to be highest, was first identified in the US by Finkelhor et al (2007a). Radford et al (2011) identify polyvictims as those with the highest 10% exposure at each age – for 0- to 2-year-olds, this meant two or more reported experiences, for 0- to 10-year-olds seven or more, for 11- to 17-year-olds 12 or more, and for 18- to 24-year-olds, 15 or more. Physical assault and victimisation by peers and/ or siblings were the most common form of abuse among polyvictims of all ages. Polyvictims tended to be older and to come from the lowest socioeconomic groups, and were more likely to have special educational needs (SEN) or a long-standing disability or illness, a parent with enduring physical, learning or psychiatric problems and higher rates of exposure to other (that is, non-victimisation) forms of adversity than the rest of the sample (Radford et al, 2011). In the US, where longitudinal data is available, polyvictimisation at one point in time has been found to increase the risk of polyvictimisation a year later, with high levels of anger and aggression and moving to a worse neighbourhood, contributing to persistence, and more good friends and a lower level of adversities to desistance (Finkelhor et al, 2007a, 2007b).

Table 10.5: Findings on aggregate measures for maltreatment by caregivers and severe maltreatment, LT and PY figures

	Maltreatment and direct victimisation by caregiver	Severe maltreatment and/ or contact sexual abuse from any perpetrator	Severe maltreatment (caregiver perpetrated)
<11s	8.9% LT, 2.5% PY	5.9%	5%
11-17	21.9% LT, 6% PY	18.6%	13.4%
18-24	24.5% LT	25.3%	14.5%

Source: Radford et al (2011)

———

Patterns and social dimensions

Child maltreatment is a complex phenomenon, which comes in many diverse forms, and it is not possible in a chapter of this kind to cover its causes fully. An ecological framework is now widely accepted, which draws attention to different levels of context, including the child's family relationships, their social networks and community context, and the social, political, economic and cultural context. Some patterns have been discussed already. The risk and resilience factors identified in relation to child maltreatment by quantitative research have been summarised recently by Sidebotham and Heron (2006) as follows, in Table 10.6.

Such lists conceal as much as they reveal, however. Poverty is invisible, although many of the conditions identified are associated with it (including large families, families with disabled children, parents with low educational achievements, unemployment, lone parenthood and young parents). Most of the negative outcomes for children associated with lone parenthood have been found to be attributable to poverty, conflict prior to separation and the disruption of transitions rather than lone parenthood per se (Burghes, 1994). Many of the negative outcomes associated with young parents disappear when the social disadvantage that is the common context of teenage parenthood is controlled for (Duncan, 2007). Gender is also largely invisible, although it is common to distinguish between male and female employment/unemployment (the latter

Table 10.6: Risk and resilience factors identified in relation to child maltreatment

Risk factors	Resilience factors
• Young parents • Lone parents • Presence of a step parent (especially for child sexual abuse) • Large families • Domestic violence • Parents with low educational achievement • Parents with adverse childhood experiences (including abuse) • Parents with a psychiatric history (including a history of alcohol or drug abuse) • Paternal unemployment • Poor social networks • Unwanted children/children whose parents report few positive attributes to them • Babies of low birth weight • Children with health, behaviour or developmental problems • Disabled children • Maternal employment/unemployment	• Social support from partner, relatives or friends • Perceptions of availability of support • Satisfaction with support

Source: Sidebotham and Heron (2006)

increasingly found associated with risk for women as well as men). Yet some of these conditions are highly gendered phenomena, for example, lone parenthood and domestic violence. There is also a tendency in such lists to focus attention on individual and household factors and to take for granted a given policy and political context. Parents with adverse childhood experiences and/or a psychiatric history appear, but not the long waiting lists both children and adults often face when they seek help for trauma-related and mental health problems. A recent comparative study focusing on children's violence, including its association with maltreatment, found significantly higher levels among children in the US than in Nordic countries, where political culture is more child and family-friendly, and there is a stronger commitment to children's rights in policy (Covell and Howe, 2009).

The social divisions of age, gender, ethnicity and income form part of the context in which child maltreatment occurs and influence patterns in ways which are discussed further below.

Age: babies are still at greatest risk of homicide, and most vulnerable also to some forms of severe physical abuse (Sibert et al, 2002). While, unsurprisingly, lifetime rates of maltreatment increase with age, the risks also change as children grow older and, for some forms, the frequency also increases. As children and young people spend more time outside their families, the opportunities for access by other perpetrators increase, but physical assault and physical punishment, neglect, sexual abuse and emotional maltreatment within families, and physical violence, sexual abuse, bullying and exposure to community violence outside them, also continue into adolescence. Alongside increased awareness of adolescent abuse (Rees and Stein, 1999), there is now also growing evidence of abuse by partners among young people as young as 11-14 (Radford et al, 2011). Prevalence rates for physical violence from the new NSPCC survey were given in Table 10.1 above, but overall, 7.9% of 11- to 17-year-olds were found to have experienced violence and abuse within an intimate relationship, and 13.4% of 18- to 24-year-olds had done so before the age of 18 (Radford et al, 2011). Other surveys report varying prevalence rates, influenced once again by methodology and samples (Barter et al, 2009; Wood et al, 2011: forthcoming), but it is clear (i) that a significant minority of young people experience abuse in early partner relationships; (ii) that girls are particularly vulnerable to sexual victimisation, more often report being hurt or injured, and have more trauma-related symptoms; (iii) that this occurs in same-sex relationships as well as heterosexual ones; and (iv) that sexual and physical assault by a partner are associated with worse mental health for both young men and young women (Radford et al, 2011). Barter et al (2009) found young people with experience of family violence more likely to experience all forms of partner violence, and girls with older partners (that is, at least two years older) at particularly high risk. Wood et al (2011: forthcoming) found especially high rates of intimate partner violence among disadvantaged young people, including those excluded from school, pregnant teenagers and young mothers, young offenders and young people in care.

Gender: girls are significantly more vulnerable to sexual abuse – at all ages, the gap increasing with age (Radford et al, 2011) – and, some studies have also found, to emotional abuse (Cawson et al, 2000), while boys have commonly been found most vulnerable to physical abuse. In the new NSPCC survey, fairly similar levels of physical hurt and injury by an adult looking after them were reported for boys and girls, with slightly more boys hurt in the under 11 age group, and slightly more girls hurt in the 11-17 age group. Among the young adult sample, girls were found more vulnerable than boys to severe maltreatment, both overall (30.6% versus 20.3%) and by caregivers (17.5% versus 11.6%), with the most pronounced difference in relation to sexual violence.

Males are the majority of perpetrators of domestic violence and of physical and sexual violence against children and young people, both within and outside the family. While the most recent definition of sexual abuse includes recognition that women and other children may be perpetrators as well as men, in the new NSPCC survey, perpetrators were males in all cases involving under 11-year-olds, in four out of five cases among 11- to 17-year-olds, and in six out of seven cases among young adults (Radford et al, 2011). Female parents/guardians are also frequently involved in the maltreatment of children, however. Radford et al (2011) found the most frequently reported direction of abuse among children under 18 was female parent to female child, followed by male parent to male or female child, with female parent to male child the least frequent (especially in the older group, where boys may often be physically stronger than their mothers). The gender dimensions of maltreatment are discussed more fully in Hooper (2010).

Ethnicity: while it is well established that black children (especially those of mixed parentage) are over-represented in the care system, UK research has not shown any significant 'race' differences in the prevalence of abuse. Black and minority ethnic children are likely to be more exposed to racial abuse and harassment, however, both from outside and within families.

Income/class: all forms of abuse occur across all socioeconomic groups, but poverty increases the risk of physical abuse and neglect, although not necessarily of sexual or emotional abuse. This association has been found both at household level (Cawson et al, 2000) and at neighbourhood level (Drake and Pandey, 1996; Gillham et al, 1998). Analyses of the ALSPAC data have also found child protection registration (with no distinction made between different forms of abuse) significantly associated with indicators of social deprivation (Sidebotham et al, 2002), and the first NSPCC survey found domestic violence more frequent among lower socioeconomic groups, although to what extent this was, because income had dropped when relationships broke down, is not clear (Cawson et al,

2002). The association between poverty and maltreatment is explored more fully in Hooper (2005) and Hooper et al (2007).

Family versus non-family members: one final pattern worth mentioning is the identity of the perpetrators of maltreatment. There remains a strong emphasis both in the media and in policy on the 'dangerous stranger', and on the threat of his or her infiltration into positions of trust with children and young people, with much less recognition of the risks within families and their informal networks. The new NSPCC survey shows parents and caregivers, siblings, other relatives, peers, known and unknown adults all involved as perpetrators. Adults in a position of trust via an organisation or by private arrangement account for only a small minority of incidents, suggesting that increased vetting and barring is unlikely to increase children's safety significantly (Radford et al, 2011).

Conclusion

The data reviewed in this chapter suggest grounds for cautious optimism on trends in child deaths, physical abuse and punishment, harsh treatment and perhaps bullying. However, there are many uncertainties in the data. Far too many children are still harmed by maltreatment, any gains made could easily be reversed, particularly in worsening economic conditions, and there is no room for complacency. The findings of the new NSPCC survey suggest that the upwards trend in referrals, assessments and children made subject to a child protection plan evident in safeguarding statistics over the past five years (DCSF, 2007/08/09; DfE, 2010f) may owe more to an expansion of activity by children's services than to trends in maltreatment itself.

Whether this expansion of activity is a positive or negative development, or perhaps most likely a mixed picture, is unclear. While the majority of children are protected from further abuse by social work intervention, questions are increasingly being asked about whether the heavily proceduralised child protection system developed in Anglophone countries, which persists relatively unchanged despite the broader *Every Child Matters* agenda, may do more harm than good (Children's Commissioner, 2010; Lonne et al, 2008; Macdonald and Macdonald, 2010; Munro, 2010a, 2010b). That debate is beyond the scope of this chapter, but the extent of maltreatment revealed in it (which goes far beyond the families caught up, for better or worse, in the child protection system) and the societal costs likely to be associated with it,[1] highlight the importance of maintaining and developing a broader preventative agenda (Macmillan et al, 2009). Programmes with proven effectiveness such as the Nurse Family Partnership are a welcome development, but that agenda must also reflect a societal commitment to children's rights (to provision and participation as well as protection; Reading et al, 2009), and to supporting the healthy family relationships so important to children's development and well-being, for which a wide range of services, including housing and mental health services (adult, child and adolescent), are relevant.

Notes

[1] The costs to society of child maltreatment have not been calculated in any reliable way. An estimate of £1 billion made by the National Commission of Inquiry into the Prevention of Child Abuse in 1996 now seems absurdly conservative, given both some of its assumptions (for example, 10% of mental health service costs) and the results of a more comprehensive approach to the costs of domestic violence which calculated them as £23 billion per annum in 2001.

ELEVEN

Childcare and early years

Christine Skinner

Key findings

- Some experience of formal early years care prior to school age is the norm in the UK.
- The evidence on outcomes is incontrovertible; formal early years care in high quality group settings produces positive child development outcomes that are relatively long lasting (up to age 10 at least).
- The longer duration in early years care the greater the impact on positive child outcomes – except attending prior to the age of two, which potentially produces negative behavioural outcomes.
- Family and child characteristics exert a stronger influence on child development outcomes than experience of formal early years care.
- Being a girl, having parents that are educated to degree level and family income has a very strong influence on outcomes at age five as measured by Foundation Stage Profile (FSP) scores. Living in social housing has the strongest negative influence on child development outcomes.
- Some parental childrearing behaviours have a positive impact on cognitive development – reading to the child daily at age three, for example. However, some evidence suggests teaching a child the alphabet or counting daily has no positive effect and may even negatively affect some child outcomes.

Key trends

- Between 1999-2004 (a year after the National Childcare Strategy was developed) there was substantial growth in the use of formal childcare. This was mainly due to extensive take-up of free early years education for three- to four-year-olds that increased from 77% in 1999 to 94% in 2004.
- There was a doubling in take-up of out-of-school care provided by breakfast clubs and after-school clubs between 2001-04 but no growth between 2004-07 and only a slight apparent increase in 2009.
- Use of informal care has remained relatively constant throughout this time period, at around 41%.

Key sources

- Millennium Cohort Study (MCS) (UK)
- Effective Provision of Pre-school Education (EPPE) (England, Wales and Northern Ireland)
- National Institute of Child Health and Human Development study (NICHD) (USA)
- Organisation for Economic Co-operation and Development (OECD) Family database

Introduction

Over the last 12 years 'early years' policy relating to childcare and early education has progressed considerably, particularly in England. In 2004 a 10-year strategy provided much needed policy coherence (HM Treasury, 2004). The policy 'vision' was for each child to be given a 'sure start' in life and for parents to have more choices to help them balance work and family life. This represented the two key aims of early years policy: to tackle child poverty through increasing parental employment and to improve child outcomes through provision of high quality services for children aged five or less. Some elements of the strategy were devolved requiring consultation regarding implementation in Wales, Scotland and Northern Ireland, but others were 'reserved' and would cover the whole UK (for example, funding of services and childcare subsidies for parents). Unless otherwise stated, this chapter refers to the strategy for England as this underpinned the policy direction for all countries in the UK.

This chapter is divided into two sections. The first provides a review of the policy framework to help set the context and assess the current policy direction. The second provides research evidence on the benefits of formal childcare services for child development.

Childcare strategy in the UK

The 10-year strategy published in December 2004 built on the initial 1998 National Childcare Strategy. It aimed to further improve the availability, the quality and the affordability of childcare and early education. However, it was also a landmark policy that introduced the first ever Childcare Act 2006, giving local authorities a legal duty to ensure that sufficient services were available to meet local demand.

The first column in Table 11.1 describes the 2004 policy framework under three headings: improving availability and accessibility, quality and affordability. Regarding availability and accessibility, it can be seen in Table 11.1 (first row) that existing services were expanded, including:

- increasing free early education for three- to four-year-olds up to 15 hours per week;
- providing more children's centres to offer integrated childcare, early education and family support services;

• improving take-up and provision for disabled and minority ethnic groups.

The new initiatives are also shown in Table 11.1 (second row), and these include:

• a new Childcare Act 2006 imposing a 'sufficiency and information duty' on local authorities;
• an extended schools policy to provide childcare wrapped round the school day and holidays;
• a pilot of free early education and care to disadvantaged two-year-olds.

In respect of improving quality and affordability, some of the new initiatives are shown in the third and fourth rows of Table 11.1, and these include:

• setting minimum standards to improve child well-being outcomes (later known as the Early Years Foundation Stage (EYFS) framework;[1]
• unifying regulation and inspection frameworks;
• consulting on new qualifications and career structures;
• funding investment in quality services;
• increasing the value of the childcare subsidy for low-income families.

Simultaneously, while the 10-year strategy expanded and strengthened existing services, it also represented a key policy shift towards improving child outcomes rather than simply aiming to reduce poverty per se. It stated that:

> Good quality childcare and early education can have a positive effect on child outcomes, boosting cognitive development and improving social skills and confidence. (HM Treasury, 2004, p 65)

This shift was primarily the result of a renewed policy confidence founded on research evidence that was emerging from key population and evaluation studies. These confirmed that 'high quality' early years services had a positive impact on child development outcomes.

This evidence fed into recommendations made by The Equalities Review (2007). They created a strong case for the state to expand its role beyond simply promoting sufficient childcare places to meet demand, to one of ensuring 'high quality' provision to achieve the best child outcomes. In particular, provision should aim to reduce the development gap between advantaged and disadvantaged children. Thus, the EYFS framework, the plan for universal provision of 'free part-time' services for disadvantaged two-year-olds (DCSF, 2009e, pp 29, 31) and the statutory 'improvement target' and 'equalities target' for local authorities to improve development outcomes and reduce inequalities between all preschool children (DCSF, 2009e, p 60).[2] These are the main features of the progress made in the 10-year strategy as described in *Next steps for early learning and childcare* (DCSF, 2009e). This took stock of the advances made since 2004; a detailed summary of progress is provided in Table 11.1 in the second column. *Next steps*

Table 11.1: Childcare policy strategy 2004-09

Choice for parents, the best start for children: A ten-year strategy for childcare (HM Treasury, 2004)		*Next steps for early learning and childcare: Building on the 10-year strategy* (DCSF, 2009)
Policy aim	**Service provision**	**Service provision**
Improve availability and accessibility	Expand existing services: • Expand all services – private, voluntary and independent sectors • Free early education (for three- and four-year-olds) – expand to 15 hours per week by 2010 and integrate with childcare from 8am-6pm all year round • Children's centres to provide childcare and early education, family, health and parenting support. Target of 2,500 children's centres by 2008, 3,500 by 2010 • Build on Early Support Programme to improve childcare for disabled children under three years • Improve recruitment of minority ethnic groups and consult with families on service take-up	Update on service expansion: • Free offer of early education, nearly full take-up for all three- and four-year-olds of at least some of the 12.5 hours per week, 38 weeks per year. Fifteen hours of weekly flexible provision delivered in 34 areas, on track for universal implementation by September 2010 • 'Stretching' the 15 hours 'free offer' for two-, three- and four-year-olds to cover school holiday periods (that is, for more than 38 weeks per year) • 3,000 children's centres now running, on track for 3,500 by 2010 • Access for disabled children, a £640 million Capital Fund 2008-11 to all local authorities. All providers to have an inclusion policy to show how they meet all children's needs • Minority ethnic groups, take-up encouraged via national advertising campaigns. Piloting strategies with 12 local authorities to improve practice • Pilots exploring ways to make services more 'joined up' for users • Improvements to childcare information services including a national price comparison website (continued)

Table 11.1: Childcare policy strategy 2004-09 (continued)

Choice for parents, the best start for children: A ten-year strategy for childcare (HM Treasury, 2004)		*Next steps for early learning and childcare: Building on the 10-year strategy (DCSF, 2009)*
Policy aim	**Service provision**	**Service provision**
Improve availability and accessibility	New initiatives: • Extended schools: to offer childcare all year round (including school holidays) from 8am-6pm weekdays (for children aged 5-14) • New legal 'sufficiency duty' on local authorities to ensure enough places to meet families' needs (including disabled children), enshrined in the first ever Childcare Act 2006 (implemented April 2008) • 'Information duty' in the Childcare Act to ensure effective family information services • Pilot of 12,000 two-year-olds living in disadvantaged areas to get 'free offer' of high quality education and care	Progress on the new initiatives: • Extended schools: in 2005 15,000 schools provided core extended services childcare/post-school activities. Goal of all schools to offer extended services by 2010. Between 2008-11, £1.3 billion for development (p 32) • Encourage schools to engage with most economically disadvantaged to provide some free activities every week • Local authorities second round of sufficiency assessments due April 2011 to include action plan that prioritises holiday care and out-of-school care for 5- to 14-year-olds • An expectation for local authorities to manage the market and reduce market failures in the mixed economy of provision (p 63) • Free services for disadvantaged two-year-olds: 20,000 will receive it by 2011. Aim for 15% of most disadvantaged to get 10 hours per week in *all* local authorities. Then universal provision for all two-year-olds to be introduced in stages (p 27) • Local authorities to receive dedicated funding for outreach work with disadvantaged families

(continued)

Table 11.1: Childcare Policy Strategy 2004-2009 (continued)

Choice for parents, the best start for children: A ten-year strategy for childcare (HM Treasury, 2004)		*Next steps for early learning and childcare: Building on the 10-year strategy* (DCSF, 2009)
Policy aim	**Service provision**	**Service provision**
Improve quality	• Develop a new single 'quality framework' for services from birth to age five to ensure all providers meet minimum standards and to improve child welfare outcomes as set out in the *Every Child Matters* agenda • Reform of legal regulation and inspection framework into a unified service covering both education and childcare to be in place by 2008 • Consultation on new qualifications and career structures for early years workforce. This to be overseen in England by a new Children's Workforce Development Council (CWDC) to start in April 2005 • Transformation Fund of £125 million a year from April 2006 to support investment by local authorities in quality childcare	• In 2008 the Early Years Foundation Stage (EYFS) framework was implemented for all services from birth to age five years • Workforce – all workers to have qualifications to Level 3 (A Level standard). In 2007, 72% in 'full daycare settings' met this standard. Possibly become a requirement by 2015 • All full daycare providers to have a graduate from 2015. Early Years Professional Status (EYPS) awarded to those who meet set professional standards – 2,500 workers achieved the status in 2009. Graduate Leader Fund of £305 million available from 2008-11 • Initiatives to promote excellence and to provide career pathways, training and development
Improve affordability	• Childcare subsidy increased via the childcare element of Working Tax Credit for low-income families • Extension of free element of early education (as above) also helps reduce costs	• Access to childcare subsidy up by 72% since 2004; 460,000 families receiving it across the UK • Advertising childcare subsidy and pilots exploring how to make it easier to claim • Target more generous subsidies for all disabled children and low-income families in London • Local authorities to encourage all providers to register with Ofsted, making their services eligible for parents to claim the childcare subsidy

also made it clear that the promotion of child outcomes was now the first key objective of childcare and early years policy (DCSF, 2009e, p 8). In addition, it promoted childcare policy as being a long-term investment for the benefit of society as a whole.

> ...we believe that early learning and childcare are paramount for child development and social mobility and constitute a vital long-term investment in the well-being of our society. (DCFS, 2009e, p 68)

Next steps was one of the last key documents produced by the Labour government before losing office in May 2010. It mainly consolidated policy developments in the Childcare Act 2006 across the four areas of improving availability, accessibility, quality and affordability (see Table 11.1). In particular, a commitment was made to extend the 'free offer' of learning and play services to disadvantaged two-year-olds and in the longer term to make this universal for all. A new focus was also developed which introduced or extended various initiatives to encourage 'positive parenting' and 'outreach work' in order to help disadvantaged parents enrich their children's 'home learning environment' and thereby engage more effectively with their children's development to help prevent their later disadvantage (see DCSF, 2009e, Chapter 2; and The Equalities Review, 2007, Chapter 3). This represented a more direct interventionist approach reaching into the home itself.

In May 2010, the UK elected the first ever coalition government, whose first policy priority was to reduce the budget deficit by cutting public services. Their policy strategy for the early years has yet to be fully clarified, but some commitments have been made in the *Comprehensive Spending Review 2010* (HM Treasury, 2010b), including:

- extending the free entitlement to 15 hours per week of early education for three- and four-year-olds will go ahead by September 2010, as previously planned;
- continuing to fund early learning and childcare for the most disadvantaged two-year-olds from disadvantaged backgrounds and extending this free entitlement to 15 hours per week from 2012-13 (HM Treasury, 2010b, p 41);
- maintaining the funding for Sure Start children's centres and new investments for Sure Start health visitors. Also, to refocus Sure Start children's centres 'on its original purpose of improving the life chances of disadvantaged children' and encouraging more community providers to run Sure Start children's centres (HM Treasury, 2010b, pp 41-2);
- reducing the value of the childcare subsidy for low-income families in the tax credit system with a view to save £385 million a year by 2014-15 (HM Treasury, 2010b, p 42).

Most plans have been warmly welcomed by the childcare sector as they mainly follow what went before and recognise the value of formal services in producing positive outcomes (Daycare Trust, 2010; Defries, 2010). However, there is alarm over the cuts to the childcare subsidy that the Daycare Trust (2010) has calculated will result in a loss of up to £1,560 per year for families. It remains to be seen what the future holds under the Coalition government, although it seems that targeted rather than universal provision will be the policy aim. Even so, the policy framework to date has benefited from the research evidence. Before turning to consider the evidence, the trends in childcare are presented first.

Parental use of childcare: trends over time

Evidence on parental use of childcare has been collected via a national survey based on childcare usage during a particular reference week. These surveys began in 2004 and three further waves were conducted, in 2006, 2008 and 2009. Trends over the last 10 years are summarised in the latest survey report by Smith et al (2010). This shows that between 1999-2004 (a year after the National Childcare Strategy was developed) there was substantial growth in the use of formal childcare. This was mainly due to extensive take-up of free early years education for three-to four-year-olds that increased from 77% in 1999 to 94% in 2004 (Smith et al, 2010, p 27). There was also a doubling in take-up of out-of-school care provided by breakfast clubs and after-school clubs between 2001-04 (Bryson et al, 2006), but no growth between 2004-07 (Kazimirski et al, 2008). Table 11.2 shows these trends since 1999 by broad categories of type of care, as Bryson et al (2006, p 52) report that 'slight changes in the way that childcare and early years providers were categorised in 1999/2001 compared to 2004 means that direct comparisons of all provider types were not possible'.

The data collection methods changed in 2008, making comparisons in trends over time difficult – see Table 11.3. A small increase in the take-up of formal childcare may be evident between 2007-08, and Smith et al (2010, pp 27-8) conclude this may be due to 'higher take-up of out-of-school clubs and other activities located on a school site (which may be attributed to the growth of the Extended Schools agenda)'. Over the decade there has been some fluctuation in the use of informal care but generally trends have been static, with around 41% of families using this care type. Overall they state: 'There have been no significant changes in the take-up of childcare as a whole or of different types of childcare between 2008 and 2009. This can be interpreted positively since the economic downturn has led to an increase in unemployment (ONS, 2010) which one might have expected would reduce demand for childcare' (Smith et al, 2010, pp 27-8).

Table 11.2: Trends in childcare usage, 1999-2007 (%)

	1999	2001	2004	2007
Used childcare in the last year	87	86	86	84
Used childcare in the last week	58	56	64	63
Used formal care in the last week	28	31	41	40
Used informal care in the last week	41	36	42	39
Unweighted base all families	*4,866*	*5,416*	*7,774-7,802*	*7,136*

Sources: 1999-2004: Bryson et al (2006, p 51); 2007: Kazimirski et al (2008)

Table 11.3: Use of childcare providers, 2008 and 2009 (%)

	Survey year	
Use of childcare	**2008**	**2009**
Any childcare	73	73
Formal childcare and early years provision	56	55
Nursery school	4	4
Nursery class attached to a primary or infants school	5	5
Reception class[a]	7	8
Special day school/nursery/unit for children with SEN	1	1
Day nursery	9	8
Playgroup or preschool	6	6
Other nursery education provider	+	+
Breakfast/after-school club or activity, on school site	28	27
Breakfast/after-school club or activity, off school site	6	6
Childminder	5	5
Nanny or au pair	1	1
Babysitter who came to home	1	2
Informal childcare	**41**	**41**
Ex-partner	6	7
Grandparent	26	26
Older sibling	5	5
Another relative	6	6
Friend or neighbour	8	7
Other[b]		
Leisure/sport	9	9
Other childcare provider	5	4
No childcare used	**27**	**27**
Weighted base	7,077	6,708
Unweighted base	7,076	6,708

Notes:

[a] The data on use of reception classes should be treated with caution, as there is both under- and over-reporting of the use of this type of childcare. The under-reporting concerns four-year-olds, whose parents sometimes did not consider reception class a type of childcare, even if their four-year-olds were attending school (hence were likely to be in reception). The over-reporting concerns those five-year-olds who attended reception class as compulsory school rather than childcare, but whose parents listed it as a type of childcare.

[b] The use of other types of childcare counts towards any childcare but not towards formal or informal provision' (Smith et al, 2010, p 29).

Source: Smith et al (2010)

International comparisons

The OECD (2010) Family database publishes data on spending on childcare and early education, enrolment in childcare and preschool, informal care arrangements, childcare support, childcare benefits and fees, and the types and quality of childcare.

In terms of spending on childcare as a percentage of gross domestic product (GDP), in 2005 the UK came in the middle of the distribution. In terms of enrolment in formal early years it can be seen in Figure 11.1 that the UK comes in the top third of countries for both the 0-2 and 3-5 year groups.

In terms of the level of childcare fees, the UK is in the top third of countries.

Evidence of impact of early years experience on child outcomes

Types of evidence

Various methods have been used to collect evidence on the effects of childcare and early education on child development outcomes. Longitudinal population surveys have measured the impact of early years experiences on later child development outcomes. Such population surveys use representative samples allowing inferences to be made about typical experiences. In contrast, evaluation studies measure the impact of targeted interventions aimed at selective groups of users and do not represent a typical childhood experience. In the UK, the key evaluation studies of targeted programmes aimed at disadvantaged groups include: the National Evaluation of Sure Start local programmes 1999-2005 (Belsky et al, 2007), the Neighbourhood Nurseries Initiative (NNI Research Team, 2007); and Peers Early Education Partnership (PEEP) (Evangelou et al, 2005). However, this chapter focuses on evidence from population studies, as this helps predict the effects of early years' experiences on all children, not just specific groups. The key UK population studies assessing the impact of early years provision on child development outcomes are the Effective Provision of Pre-school Education (EPPE) Project and the Millennium Cohort Study (MCS). In the US the main population study is the National Institute of Child Health and Human Development (NICHD) study.

EPPE and NICHD

The EPPE Project is funded by the UK government's Department for Education (DfE) and is the first major longitudinal study of its kind in Europe. It has a number of phases; the first occurred between 1997-2003. It followed 3,000 children attending different childcare settings offering early education in England as well as 200 children who used only home care up to age seven (end of Key Stage 1). Its original main research question was to consider how formal childcare compared to home care in terms of the impact on child development outcomes. The study continued to follow the same children in three more phases: EPPE 3-11 (2003-08), EPPSE (Effective Pre-school, Primary and Secondary Education) 3-14 (2007-11) and EPPSE 16+ (2008-13). Respectively, these have looked at the enduring impact of preschool experiences up to age 11 (the end of primary school Key Stage 2), age 14 (end of Key Stage 3) and age 16 (the final year of compulsory

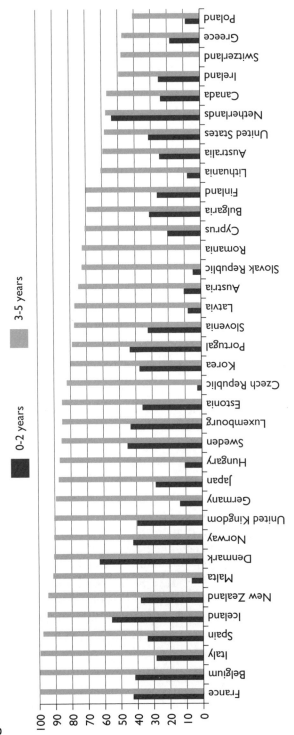

Figure 11.1: Enrolment rates of children under six in formal care or early education services, 2006

Source: OECD (2010) Family database PF.3.2.A

schooling into post-education training and employment). The NICHD study in the US was much smaller; it followed 1,000 children from birth to school age.

The findings of the first phase of the EPPE study have already been reported in more detail (Skinner, 2005) and are only briefly summarised here. Formal preschool early education (in group settings) has been shown to produce positive benefits for both cognitive and behavioural development outcomes for children aged three and four when compared to children who received only parental care. Similar research findings emerged in the US from the NICHD study. Formal preschool group care was more likely to produce better outcomes than care provided informally by relatives and friends, but greater time spent in group care increased the risk of anti-social behaviour at age four-and-a-half (Belsky, 2006, cited in Evangelou et al, 2009, p 16). The EPPE Project showed that the positive effects on development outcomes were stronger the greater the duration of early years experience, but like NICHD results, not for longer hours spent in care per week. Thus, full-time early years formal care did not produce greater benefits than part-time care, although the evidence from EPPE showed overall duration spent attending formal provision did make a difference. It was the duration of experience rather than the saturation of experience that was most important.

These benefits from preschool provision remained in place for UK children up to ages six and seven in primary school (Key Stage 1), but by that time the strength of the effects had weakened (Sammons et al, 2007a, 2007b; Sylva et al, 2007). Even so, the EPPE researchers were adamant that the beneficial effects of 'good' early years formal care still mattered; they were evident even at age 10. 'Children's abilities in reading, maths and behaviour were better if they had attended good preschool. However, it was the quality of preschool that was most significant not just attending preschool per se as attendance at poor quality preschool was associated with poorer social/behavioural development' (Sylva et al, 2007, p 9).

For children starting formal early years care below the age of two, however, there were mixed results, with gains in cognitive development but a greater risk of anti-social behaviour at ages three and five (Sammons et al, 2003; Sylva et al, 2004). But the follow-up study of EPPE 3-11 (2003-08) found that these negative effects on behaviour had gone by age 10 (Sammons et al, 2007a, 2007b; Sylva et al, 2008). Similarly, the NICHD study found that the negative effects had disappeared by Sixth grade in the US (cited by Hansen and Hawkes, 2009).

A key factor from EPPE that related to producing better outcomes was the quality of provision and also that disadvantaged children stood to gain the most beneficial outcomes. Overall, the findings show a complex interaction between quantity and quality of care, but quality remained key to the production of good outcomes, especially maintaining them over the primary school period, as they found in the EPPE 3-11 study (Sammons et al, 2008). As stated in the scoping review conducted by the Centre for Excellence and Outcomes in Children and Young People's Services:

Findings from EPPE 3–11 research (Sammons et al, 2008) show that the quality and effectiveness of the pre-school environment make a significant difference to longer term developmental outcomes. *Different aspects of quality* were found to be associated with different aspects of behaviour. Increased self-regulation is associated with academic aspects of quality pre-school, while increased pro-social behaviour and decreased hyperactivity are associated with caring and emotional relationship aspects of pre-school quality. (C4EO, 2008, p 16; original emphasis)

MCS and outcomes at age three

The MCS is the fourth national cohort study conducted in Britain. It recruited into the survey 19,000 children born at the turn of the 21st century. To date it has followed them up from birth, at age nine months (between 2001-02), age three years (the second sweep in 2004), the start of formal full-time schooling around the age of five (the third sweep in 2006) and at age seven in 2008 (a fourth sweep). A fifth interview sweep is planned when the children reach age eleven, in 2011. The latest published analysis of the MCS is on the third sweep, up to age five, and that is what is reported on here.

The second sweep of the MCS broadly coincided with the introduction of free early years education for three- and four-year-olds (introduced between 2002 and 2004). Therefore, the MCS children would have potentially benefited from the expansion of all types of childcare that began in 1998 as part of the National Childcare Strategy, including free early education. Indeed, analysis of childcare usage in the preschool years by Roberts et al (2010) led them to conclude that substantial experience of non-maternal care was the norm in the UK. Table 11.4 shows the type of childcare used, and describes the common experience at that time. It also helps to contextualise the analysis of the longer-term effects of childcare on child development outcomes at ages three and five, discussed later in this chapter.

The columns in Table 11.4 describe the types of childcare used at age nine months (the first sweep of MCS), at age three years (the second sweep of MCS), between the ages of three and four and up to starting school. The rows divide childcare into informal care types, formal care types and the mix of care used. Overall, at age nine months, the majority of children had some childcare experience other than maternal care (60%). Some 49% of children had experience of informal care (other than maternal care) and 20% of formal care; but only 10% had solely used formal care. The use of formal care increased considerably by age three years and up to starting school; overall 70% had some experience at age three rising to 96% by start of school. Sole use of this type of care also increased, up to 54% at age three, rising to 60% between ages three to four, but by start of school age this had dropped to 22%. This pattern reflects the provision of free

Table 11.4: Types of childcare usage, by MCS children, from age nine months to school age

Care type	% children making any use of childcare			
	At nine months	At three years	Between ages three to four years	All up to starting school
Partner	25	11	18	55
Grandparents	30	16	20	44
Other relative	8	3	4	15
Non-relative (including paid in the home)	4	1	3	11
Any informal care	*49*	*27*	*37*	*77*
Childminder	10	7	10	17
Day nursery	12	19	22	25
Nursery school/class	n/a	31	62	62
Playgroup	n/a	25	33	35
Preschool	n/a	15	25	25
Other	0.7	0.8	1	2
Any formal care	*20*	*76*	*96*	*96*
Informal only	39	5	1	2
Formal only	10	54	60	22
Both formal and informal	10	22	36	74
Any non-maternal care	60	81	97	99
Observations = 100%	13,392	13,372	13,391	13,391

Source: Adapted from Roberts et al (2010, p 134)

early education for three- and four-year-old children delivered prior to starting school. Ofsted (Office for Standards in Education) reports also show that take-up of this free provision has been near universal. Thus, in the UK it is a tiny minority of children that have no experience of formal care by the age of three or four. This can be seen more easily in Figure 11.2 that shows the combinations of care used as the children in the MCS study grew older.

At the second sweep of the MCS it was possible to measure the potential relationship between formal childcare experiences at age nine months and child development outcomes at age three years. Hansen and Hawkes (2009) provide an analysis of this, but only for children whose mothers worked at age nine months, as they were mainly interested in exploring the effects of maternal employment on child outcomes.[3] Table 11.5 summarises their analysis. Child development was assessed using three measures: two cognitive ability tests (vocabulary and 'school readiness') and one behavioural measure using the Strength and Difficulties Questionnaire (SDQ) (Hansen and Hawkes, 2009, p 218). Table 11.5 shows the effect of childcare type on child outcomes in the first row, and the second row shows other factors and characteristics that had a stronger impact on child outcomes than childcare type.

Figure 11.2: Combinations of any childcare used in the preschool period among MCS children

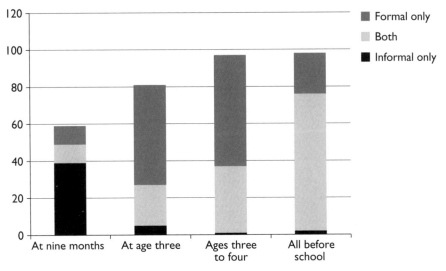

Source: Adapted from Roberts et al (2010, p 135)

Table 11.5: MCS – effect of type of childcare on outcomes for children at age three years among working mothers when child aged nine months

	Cognitive outcomes (vocabulary)	Cognitive outcomes 'school readiness'	Behavioural outcomes
Childcare type with greatest effect on child outcomes, controlling all other factors[a]	• Grandparent Care (+)	• Formal Group Care (+)	• Grandparent care (–)
Effect of other factors/ family characteristics on child outcomes. All had a stronger influence than childcare type	• Only English spoken in household (+) • Mother White (+) • Mother <5 GCSE (grades A*-C) (–) • Child is female (+) • Child is first born (+)	• Father <5 GCSE (grade A*-C) (–) • Mother <5 GCSE (grade A*-C) (–) • Only English spoken in household (+) • Child is female (+)	• Mother <5 GCSE (grade A*-C) (–) • Mother younger age (–)

Notes:

[a]Childcare types that were compared include:
- formal group care (nurseries and crèches)
- formal non-group care (childminders, nannies, au pairs)
- grandparent care
- partner care
- other informal care (relatives, friends, neighbours)

(+) Positive impact

(–) Negative impact

Source: Adapted from Hansen and Hawkes (2009)

Looking at Table 11.5, it seems that all other things being equal, formal group care (compared to the other types of care) had the most positive impact on the cognitive outcome of 'school readiness' but not for vocabulary or for behavioural outcomes. It was grandparent care that had the most positive effect on vocabulary, but it also had the most negative effect on behaviour. More fine-grained analysis of the behavioural outcome test scores showed this negative association to be mainly related to children's peer relationships (measured by a peer-relation scale) as children in grandparent care did not have as much opportunity to interact with other children their age. This result contrasts with the EPPE Project which showed greater behavioural problems associated with group care, especially if poor quality. The MCS data, however, did not collect information on quality of care or quantity of care used by these children. Even so, Table 11.5 also shows that type of care was not the most important factor impacting on child outcomes; other child and family characteristics had a greater influence.

Looking at the effect of child and family characteristics on cognitive outcomes, Table 11.5 shows that having a mother or father with less than five GCSEs at grades A*-C had a significantly negative influence (controlling for all other factors), but if English was the only language spoken in the household and/or if the child was female, this had a positive impact (being the first born also had a positive impact on vocabulary). Whereas for behavioural problems, these were significantly greater where children had a mother with less than five GCSEs at grades A*-C and where the mother was younger.

Hansen and Hawkes (2009) conclude from this analysis that it is reassuring for government to know that formal group care can reduce inequalities in cognitive outcomes (at least in 'school readiness' scores) but that policy might also need to tackle inequalities in family background characteristics (such as mothers' education and young motherhood). Moreover, support for grandparent care may help to improve the outcomes further for young children. However, they point out that the data cannot explain why there are differences in outcome by type of childcare used, but suggest it is likely to be something to do with the way children are cared for. There are no large data sets in the UK collecting that information.

MCS and Foundation Stage Profile (FSP) scores at age five

By the third sweep of the MCS it was possible to measure child outcomes using the children's Foundation Stage Profile (FSP) scores as measured by school teachers in the child's first year at school (at age five). The FSP scores cover six domains: personal, social and emotional development; communication, language and literacy development; mathematical development; knowledge and understanding of the world; physical development; and creative development (Hansen, 2010, p 202). The MCS data could also measure the impact on child outcomes of child and family characteristics as well as some parenting attitudes and behaviours (teaching children to count etc). In addition, it is possible to match the FSP scores to the cognitive and behavioural development scores as measured by the MCS instruments at age three years. Thus, the effect of children's prior abilities at age three on later outcomes at age five can also be assessed. There are three publications reporting different aspects of this FSP analysis: Cullis and Hansen (2008); Hansen and Jones (2010); and Hansen (2010). Hansen's analysis (2010) is the most comprehensive, and it is summarised here, in Table 11.6.

Table 11.6 shows models of all the factors that were significantly correlated with child development at age five across all six domains measured by FSP scores. Using Hansen's (2010) analysis of model 4, the factors that consistently affected child development positively across all six domains were:

- child being older at the end of the school year;
- child with higher birth weight;
- higher parental education qualifications;
- family income;
- some formal childcare experience up to age three;
- MCS measures of development at age three (vocabulary and 'school readiness' scores).

Other consistently positive factors across fewer domains included:

- child's gender female (five domains);
- child was read to daily at age three (five domains).

The key factors that consistently affected child development negatively across the domains were:

- living in social housing (all six domains);
- MCS measure of problem behaviour at age three (all six domains);
- child taught alphabet daily at age three (four domains);
- maternal depression (three domains).

Ethnicity was the only factor that showed a mix of positive and negative effects:

- Pakistani/Bangladeshi positive impact on four domains;
- Indian positive impact on one domain;
- Black ethnic background negative impact on two domains.

The factors that tended not to have a significant impact on development outcomes included:

- taught counting daily at age three (not significant in all six domains);
- parental attitudes at age three saying it is important to talk to the child (not significant in all six domains);

The well-being of children in the UK

Table 11.6: MCS factors related to child development using FSPs for children at age five

Full model controlling all factors including child development scores at age three	Personal, social and emotional development	Communication, language and literacy development	Mathematical development	Knowledge and understanding of the world	Physical development	Creative development
Child: older age at end of school year	+	+	+	+	+	+
Child: girl	+ S	+ S	+	n/s	+ S	+ S
Child: birth weight higher	+	+	+	+	+	+
Mother's ethnicity	+ Pakistani/ Bangladeshi	+ Pakistani/Bangladeshi + Indian	+ Pakistani/ Bangladeshi	– Black	+ Pakistani/ Bangladeshi	– Black
Higher parental qualifications	+ S	+ S	+ S	+ S	+ S	+ S
Family income	+	+	+	+	+	+
At least one parent has a professional occupation	n/s	n/s	+	n/s	n/s	n/s
Social housing	–	–	– S	– S	–	–
Maternal depression	–	–	–	n/s	n/s	n/s
Child at age three:						
– Read to daily	+	+	+	+	n/s	+
– Taught counting daily	n/s	n/s	n/s	n/s	n/s	n/s
– Taught alphabet daily	n/s	–	–	–	n/s	–
– Watch television three or more hours a day	n/s	n/s	n/s	n/s	n/s¹	–¹
Formal childcare up to age three	+	+	+	+	+	+
'School readiness' score, age three	+ W	+ W	+ W	+ W	+ W	+ W
Vocabulary score, age three	+	+	+	+	+	+
Problem behaviour, age three	–	–	–	–	–	–
Parental views at nine months:						
– Important to talk to child	n/s	n/s	n/s	n/s	n/s	n/s
– Important to stimulate child	n/s	+	+	n/s	n/s	n/s

Notes: (+) Positive impact on child development; 'S' means the strongest impact; 'L' means the weakest impact controlling for all other factors. (–) Negative impact on child development; 'S' means the strongest impact; 'L' means the weakest impact controlling for all other factors. n/s = non-significant result. ¹ At age 5.
Source: Adapted from Hansen (2010)

- child watches television three or more hours daily (not significant in five domains);
- at least one parent has a professional qualification (not significant in five domains);
- parental attitudes at age three saying it is important to stimulate the child (not significant in four domains, but positive influence for two domains of language/ literacy and mathematical development).

Overall, Table 11.6 shows that a child's personal and family characteristics exerted a strong influence on child development at age five. Being a girl had a very strong positive impact; girls outperformed boys across four domains. Children of parents with degrees outperformed all other children on FSP scores across all six domains. As might be expected, family income was important in producing positive outcomes, but having a parent with a professional qualification was generally not significant. Social housing exerted a strong negative impact, especially across two domains, and maternal depression negatively affected conceivably the most important three domains: personal development and cognitive development in Literacy and Maths. Children's experiences and parental attitudes at age three also had an influence on the FSP scores at age five. Having some formal childcare experience up to age three had a positive impact on child development at age five across all six domains, even controlling for all other factors. But, while producing a positive effect, the MCS 'school readiness' measure at age three exerted the weakest influence on child development at age five. Parenting practice at age three showed a mixed picture – reading to children daily was positive in all domains apart from physical development, whereas teaching counting daily was not significant across any domain (including Maths). Rather counter-intuitively, teaching the alphabet at age three had a significantly negative effect in four domains and was not significant in two domains (personal and physical development).

Hansen (2010, p 214) concludes that it is children from lower-income families with less educated parents who are not as advanced at age five as others with parents who have higher education levels, higher incomes and not living in council housing. But other aspects can assist in improving development at age five, specifically, experience of formal childcare up to age three and being read to by parents.

Considering all the analysis of MCS data presented here, it confirms the importance of having some formal childcare experience up to age three on positive cognitive outcomes at ages three and age five. The MCS data is, however, limited regarding childcare as it does not measure the quantity and quality of the care used, but as we have seen, it is able to assess the relative influence of early childcare experience and compare this to other important factors such as parental education and income etc.

Partly to correct this limitation, a further study was funded by the Department for Children, Schools and Families (DCSF) to look at the quality of childcare experienced by a sub-sample of MCS children at age three attending 301 childcare settings in England in 2005 (Roberts et al, 2010). This was the first study to look 'at the quality of provision for its own sake in a broadly representative sample' (Roberts et al, 2010, p 141). It took a snap-shot of families in the MCS and compared those who used or did not use centre-based care, their access to high-quality services and the quality of centre-based care used. They found that less privileged children were less likely to attend centre-based 'group' care but when they did attend, they experienced significantly higher quality care compared to more advantaged groups. For all types of care overall, the quality was scored as adequate and the authors argued there was scope for improvement. However, they could not conclude whether the investment in early years services had yet improved the prospects of both poor and privileged children (Roberts et al, 2010, p 150).

Conclusion

The analysis of the EPPE, NICHD and MCS longitudinal population surveys shows that the case for formal early years care producing positive child development outcomes is incontrovertible, especially if it is high quality care provided in group settings. Cognitive abilities seem to be particularly responsive to this type of care. However, the MCS analysis has shown that while child development outcomes by age five (using FSP scores) can be positively influenced by formal group care at age three, it was other child and family characteristics that exerted a stronger influence. Being a girl and having parents educated to degree level produced the strongest positive effect (all other things being equal). Family income level was also very important for positive outcomes. Whereas living in social housing produced a strong negative effect on all child outcomes and the strongest negative effect on two outcomes (see Table 11.6).

It seems that formal early years childcare services can only do so much to reduce inequalities in child development outcomes by the start of school at age five. At the time of writing (November 2010), the new Coalition government's approach to early years policy is not fully formed. On the one hand, it has made a commitment to continue current provision; on the other, it has cut back on the childcare subsidy for poorer families and it plans to return Sure Start children's centres 'back' to a targeted service aimed at disadvantaged families, thereby reversing the previous Labour government's attempt to build this into a universal service open to all. New resources have also been committed to recruit more Sure Start health visitors, which seems to be a highly interventionist strategy as they plan to target disadvantaged parents within the heart of the home itself in order to help them create a better 'home learning environment'. This is quite an intriguing approach given the analysis of the MCS FSP scores at age five. While the models reproduced here take account of a child's prior ability at age three, the analysis shows that all other things being equal, a parent reading to a child daily at age three has a significant positive impact on FSP scores at age five, but other parental education tactics do not. For example, parents teaching their three-year-old child counting daily has no significant effect, and teaching the alphabet daily seems to be even worse as this can produce negative outcomes. The evidence on parental education tactics is, however, relatively unsophisticated. As Hansen and Hawkes observed (2009), there is not sufficient evidence yet available that can pinpoint exactly what it is about the differential effects of types of care (both formal and informal) on numerous child development outcomes; they conclude these are probably explained by the various ways in which children are 'cared for'.

Notes

[1] A play-based curriculum published in March 2007 and implemented in September 2008 in England and Wales. It replaced a raft of previous guidance.

[2] The provisions of the Childcare Act 2006 and the free offer of care for disadvantaged two-year-olds are mostly applicable to England and Wales (WAGC, 2008); they do not extend to Scotland. According to One Parent Families Scotland (2009), there is no subsidy in place to offer free care to disadvantaged two-year-olds and there is limited means of systematically monitoring Scottish-wide provision.

[3] The sample size fitting these criteria with full data over the two sweeps was 4,800 children (Hansen and Hawkes, 2010, p 217). No analysis of the MCS has been completed measuring outcomes for children at age nine months whose parents were not working.

TWELVE

Children, crime and illegal drug use

Lisa O'Malley and Sharon Grace

Key Statistics

- Although a high proportion of young people in England and Wales commit crime, the majority is still committed by adults.
- Most juvenile crime is committed by young men.
- Most crimes committed by young people are relatively minor.
- It is mainly older teenagers who are involved in drug-related offences and the majority of even these offences are relatively minor.
- Young men are more likely to be involved in drug use than young women.
- Around a third of young people aged 10-17 are the victims of crime annually.
- Victimisation and offending rates highlight a relationship between the likelihood of being a victim and the likelihood of being an offender.
- Risk factors associated with offending cluster around deviant behaviour (such as drug and alcohol use) as well as school and family-related factors.
- Risk factors associated with drug use cluster around aspects of vulnerability, while protective factors rely on self-efficacy and interpersonal skills.

Key Trends

- Proven offences against those aged 10-17 fell in the period 2002/03 to 2008/09.
- The overall trend in drug use for all ages and all drugs is downwards.
- Fear of crime among young people is falling, but their fear of crime is out of proportion to the likelihood of victimisation, particularly in terms of being physically assaulted.

Key Sources

- (Offending) Crime and Justice Survey
- Drug Misuse Declared
- Smoking Drinking and Drug Use
- Mori Youth Survey

Introduction

This chapter reviews trends and data about how much crime is committed by children in England and Wales, it examines the types of crimes that are committed with a particular focus on illegal drug use, and considers crimes committed against children. It does not include data relating to topics covered elsewhere in this edition, specifically child abuse or neglect (see Chapter Ten, this volume) and alcohol consumption (see Chapter Four, this volume).

Definitions and indicators

Much of the available data covers age ranges starting at 10 years (the age of criminal responsibility) which leaves a gap in our knowledge about offending behaviour by those younger than 10. More problematic is the upper age limit of some data sources. These range from 17 years for most administrative data, but rise to 25 years for self-reported offending. Wherever possible, this chapter covers an age range of 10-17, making comparisons where appropriate to older age ranges. The chapter considers data from England and Wales only, within which there is little scope for regional comparison.

The chapter covers the three main types of data source available in relation to offending behaviour and illegal drug use: administrative data; self-reported crime surveys; and victimisation data. Each of these has limitations that are discussed below. A fourth section covers available data about risk and protective factors in relation to offending and drug use, drawing on nationally representative survey data.

Throughout this chapter there is an assumption that the definition of what constitutes a crime is a universal fact. Clearly, this is more straightforward when examining administrative data that uses legal definitions of crimes. However, both self-report studies and victimisation surveys often use far more flexible definitions of crime – frequently dependent on the respondent's interpretation of the event rather than any legal definition. This means that cross-comparisons between the different types of survey should be done with extreme caution.

Administrative data

Recorded crime statistics are offence-based rather than offender-based and therefore only reveal data and trends about the offences that have been reported or recorded, not details of the offender. Hence, in this section the focus is on official data relating to offenders that can only be gathered once an offence has been investigated and a suspect arrested. This administrative data regarding types of offences committed by young people is restricted to 'notifiable offences'[1] and is likely to underestimate the amount of crime committed by young people.

Overall levels of crime

As a means of setting the discussion in context, it is worth considering national trends for all crime across all age groups. In 2009/10 police-recorded crime showed that 4.4 million offences had been reported to the police, down from 4.7 million in 2008/09 (an 8% change). British Crime Survey data also show a fall in crime of 9% between 2008/09 and 2009/10, and a 24% reduction since 2001/02 (Flatley et al, 2010).

Proportion of crime committed by young people

In 2008/09, 19% of arrests involved those aged 10–17 (see Figure 12.1). This compares with 66% for those aged 21 and over and 15% for those aged 18–20. If we compare these proportions with total population estimates (see Figure 12.2), we can see that those aged 10–17 comprise 11% of the population. In other words, 11% of the population account for almost a fifth of all those arrested. This suggests that people's concerns about levels of offending are understandable, although the subsequent discussion shows that these figures belie much complexity about young people's offending behaviour.

Figure 12.1: Arrests for notifiable offences, by age group, 2008/9

Figure 12.2: Mid-year population estimates by age group, 2009

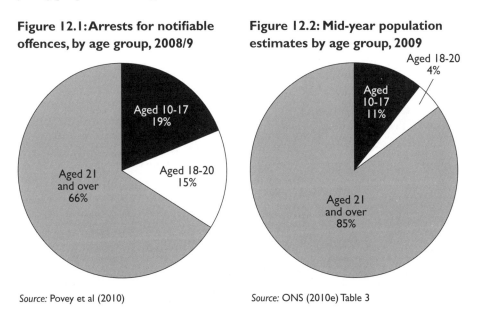

Source: Povey et al (2010)

Source: ONS (2010e) Table 3

Types of crime committed by young people

Table 12.1 shows that just over 273,000 young people aged between 10 and 17 were arrested for notifiable offences in 2008/09. The most prevalent offences for which this group were arrested were theft and handling stolen goods (26%), violence against the person (25%) and criminal damage (15%), which together

Table 12.1: People arrested for notifiable offences, by type of offence and age group, 2008/09

Notifiable offence group	Aged under 10	Aged 10-17	Aged 18-20	Aged 21 and over	Age unknown	All ages	% offence aged 10-17	Offence as % of all crime 10-17
Theft/handling stolen goods	22	70,244	44,757	210,854	749	326,626	22	26
Violence against the person	18	69,537	64,790	327,085	1,285	462,715	15	25
Criminal damage	11	41,787	24,620	72,989	341	139,748	30	15
Other	20	28,261	33,700	152,437	789	215,207	13	10
Burglary	5	26,598	17,340	51,963	185	96,091	28	10
Drug offences	3	15,710	18,871	80,304	228	115,116	14	6
Robbery	2	14,638	7,292	12,693	46	34,671	42	5
Sexual offences	2	4,387	3,293	25,887	114	33,683	13	2
Fraud and forgery		1,879	4,023	28,498	90	34,490	5	1
Total	83	273,041	218,686	962,710	3,827	1,458,347	19	100

Source: Povey et al (2010, Table 1b, p 15)

account for 66% of arrests in this age range. The data also reveal, however, that 10- to 17-year-olds are not the age group with the highest levels of arrest for these offences, accounting for 22% of all arrests for theft and handling stolen goods, just 15% for violence against the person and 30% of arrests for criminal damage. This means that although violence against the person is the second most prevalent crime for this age group, the vast majority of arrests for violence (78%) involved people aged 18 and over.

Of more interest, perhaps, are those offences for which young people represent a high proportion across all those arrested. In the case of robbery, for example, 42% of arrests were made of those aged 10-17, yet robbery only accounts for 5% of arrests in this age group. Similarly, drug offences account for only 6% of all arrests for those aged 10-17, yet 14% of all arrests for drug offences were from this group. However, many arrests among young people for drug-related offences are made for relatively minor infringements. Data about 'defendants proceeded against'[2] (see Table 12.2) show that in total, 13% of those proceeded against at all courts for drug offences were under the age of 18, but the vast majority of these were in the older age category of 15 to under 18. The predominant offence was possession of a Class C drug, with the 15 and under 18 age groups accounting for just under a quarter of all those proceeded against for this offence. Figures for all other categories were far lower, the next highest being 6% for supply of both Class A and Class C drugs. Thus, the data suggests that it is mainly older teenagers involved in drug-related offences, and the vast majority of these are relatively minor.

Further detail about offences committed by specific age ranges is available through data about 'proven offences'.[3] Proven offence data gather information

Table 12.2: Defendants proceeded against at all courts for main drug offences, by age and sex, 2008

	10-11 years	% of drug offences for 10-11 years	12-14 years	% of drug offences for 12-14 years	15-17 years	% of drug offences for 15-17 years	All ages	% of drug offences
Supply[a] of Class A	0	0	27	5.3	547	8.6	8726	15.8
Supply of Class B	0	0	2	0.4	24	0.4	999	1.8
Supply of Class C	0	0	11	2.2	378	5.9	5985	10.8
Possession[b] of Class A	0	0	16	3.2	471	7.4	15,072	27.3
Possession of Class B	0	0	10	2.0	172	2.7	3442	6.2
Possession of Class C	4	100	439	86.9	4,787	75.0	20,989	38.0
Total	4		505		6,379		55,213	
Males	4	100	458	90.7	6,068	95.1		
Females	0		45	8.9	296	4.6		

Notes: [a] The full legal offence is 'the production, supply and possession with intent to supply a controlled drug – Class A/B/C'. [b] The full legal offence is 'the possession of a controlled drug – Class A/B/C'. At this time, cannabis was a Class C drug – since January 2009 it has been reclassified as a Class B drug.

Source: Ministry of Justice (2009)

about offences and so are not comparable with arrest data, which is a count of offenders. Nonetheless, the data can indicate trends for specific ages, as shown in Table 12.3 and Figure 12.3. The data show that proven offences have fallen across all ages between 2002 and 2009, but with some variation. While proven offences have fallen by 11.5% and 14.8% for ages 10–11 and 16–17 respectively, the rates are much lower for other ages – just 1.7% for 12- to 13-year-olds and 1.1% for 14- to 15-year-olds.

Table 12.3: Trends in the number of proven offences, by age, 2002-09

Age	2002-03	2003-04	2004-05	2005-06	2006-07	2007-08	2008-09	% +/– 2002-09
10-11	6,844	6,959	7,320	8,163	8,150	7,377	6,059	−11.5
12-13	30,296	32,340	34,826	38,384	38,229	35,301	29,770	−1.7
14-15	84,943	92,752	95,065	105,454	105,334	97,184	83,990	−1.1
16-17	146,397	155,832	149,802	149,859	143,416	135,481	124,764	−14.8

Source: YJB (2004, 2005, 2006, 2007, 2008, 2009, 2010)

Sex and arrest

Table 12.4 confirms previous findings that males are more likely than females to commit crime. According to arrest data for 2008/09, this finding holds across all offence types with notable variations occurring in relation to sexual offences, where 35 times as many males as females were arrested, burglary (where males

Figure 12.3: Trends in the number of proven offences, by age group, 2002-09

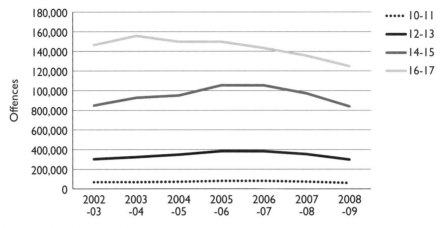

Source: YJB (2004, 2005, 2006, 2007, 2008, 2009, 2010)

Table 12.4: Persons aged 10-17 arrested for notifiable offences, by type of offence and sex, 2008/09

Notifiable offence group	Male	Female	All people	Ratio females to males
Violence against the person	51,418	18,119	326,626	1:3
Sexual offences	4,266	121	462,715	1:35
Robbery	12,958	1,680	139,748	1:8
Burglary	24,403	2,195	215,207	1:11
Theft and handling stolen goods	50,240	20,004	96,091	1:3
Fraud and forgery	1,329	550	115,116	1:2
Criminal damage	35,709	6,078	34,671	1:6
Drug offences	14,337	1,373	33,683	1:10
Other	23,291	4,970	34,490	1:5
Total	217,951	55,090	1,458,347	

Source: Povey et al (2010, Table 1b, p 15)

were arrested 11 times more frequently than females) and drug offences (10 times more males than females).

However, if we examine trends over time, in relation to arrest we find more variation beginning to occur. While it is still the case that more males are arrested for notifiable offences than females, arrests have fallen by 17.5% for the period 1999/2000 to 2008/09 for them while they have risen by 1.5% for females (see Table 12.5). Figure 12.4 shows the overall trend by year since 1999. The trends are broadly similar, both peaking in 2006/07 before beginning to fall sharply for males, but less clearly so for females.

In terms of offence types, there is considerable variation across trends for males and females, as shown in Table 12.5. Arrests for males fell overall by 17.5% in

Table 12.5: People aged 10-17 arrested for notifiable offences, by type of offence and sex, selected years, 1999/2000 to 2008/09

| Notifiable offence group | 1999/2000[a] | | 2006/07[b] | | 2008/09[c] | | % change 1999/2000 to 2008/09 | |
	Males	Females	Males	Females	Males	Females	Males (%)	Females (%)
Violence against the person	38,000	10,600	66,975	22,964	51,418	18,119	35.3	70.9
Sexual offences	3,700	100	4,466	120	4,266	121	15.3	21.0
Robbery	11,400	1,400	17,980	2,668	12,958	1,680	13.7	20.0
Burglary	33,400	3,100	30,674	3,232	24,403	2,195	−26.9	−29.2
Theft and handling stolen goods	101,800	28,100	69,900	25,820	50,240	20,004	−50.6	−28.8
Fraud and forgery	2,600	1,200	1,347	697	1,329	550	−48.9	−54.2
Criminal damage	42,000	5,300	53,653	8,831	35,709	6,078	−15.0	14.7
Drug offences	15,000	1,700	11,498	1,302	14,337	1,373	−4.4	−19.2
Other	16,200	2,800	25,682	5,561	23,291	4,970	43.8	77.5
Total	264,100	54,300	282,175	71,195	217,951	55,090	−17.5	1.5

Sources: [a] Ayres et al (2001, Table AB, p 4); [b] Ministry of Justice (2008, Table AB, p 6); [c] Povey et al (2010, Table 1b, p 15)

Figure 12.4: Arrests of those aged 10-17 for notifiable offences, by sex, 1999/2000 to 2008/09

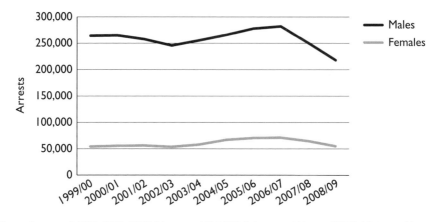

Source: Ayres et al (2001, 2002, 2003); Murray and Fiti (2004); Ayres and Murray (2005); Ministry of Justice (2007, 2008); Povey et al (2009, 2010)

the period, most notably for theft and handling stolen goods (down 50.6%) and burglary (down 26.9%). Increases in arrests have occurred for violence against the person (35.3%), sexual offences (15.3%) and robbery (up 13.7%). For females a similar pattern can be discerned, with numbers of arrests also falling for theft and handling stolen goods (down 28.8%) and burglary (down 29.2%). Arrests among females have also risen for violence against the person (up 70.9%) and for robbery (up 20%), both of which have seen higher rates of increase than for males. The only offence for which trends are opposite for males and females is criminal damage, where arrests have fallen for males by 15% since 1999/2000, but have risen among females by almost the same amount (up 14.7%).

Reprimand and warning rates as well as data about those proceeded against show that drug-related crime is predominantly committed by males. Table 12.2 (above) shows that defendants proceeded against are overwhelmingly male (over 90% for all age groups).

Ethnicity

Arrest data are not available by ethnic group, but it is possible to examine proven offence data by ethnicity to give some indication of trends over time.

The numbers of young people with proven offences from Asian and Mixed ethnic groups have both risen in the period 2002/03 to 2008/09 by 8.4% and 127.1% respectively (see Figures 12.5 and 12.6). Proven offences have fallen across all other ethnic groups including white (down 8.3%) and black (down 2.7%). It is not clear why these trends are so marked for those from mixed ethnic backgrounds; the cause is likely to be a counting/description change although the data are not clear and do not provide an explanation.

Figure 12.5: Trends in the number of young people with proven offences, by ethnicity, 2002-09

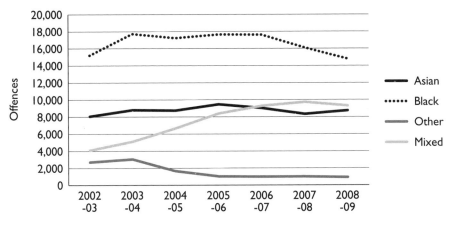

Source: YJB (2004, 2005, 2006, 2007, 2008, 2009, 2010)

Figure 12.6: Trends in the number of young White people with proven offences, 2002-09

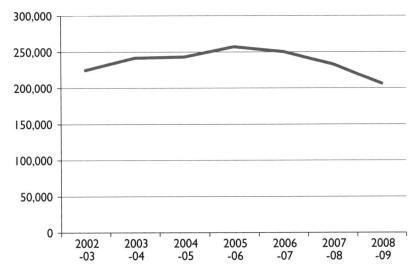

Source: YJB (2004, 2005, 2006, 2007, 2008, 2009, 2010)

Administrative data can be revealing about the prevalence of crime among young people, as well as the types of crimes they are most likely to be prosecuted for committing. However, the limitations of administrative data of this type are also numerous and depend on the willingness of people to report crime as well as on the police in successfully investigating crime. Changes in recording practices and in policing practices have regularly meant that the reliability of administrative data has been called into question. The data are limited in terms of the social characteristics of offenders and can tell us little about offending patterns among young people under the age of 10. Furthermore, data about ethnicity are of poor quality in terms of the broad categories used, which is unfortunate given levels of interest in aspects of discrimination and disproportionality that may occur in the criminal justice system.

Perhaps the most important criticism that is levied at administrative data is that it underestimates the amount of crime in society – a problem that is most frequently rectified by combining and comparing administrative data with findings from self-report surveys and victimisation surveys. The remainder of this chapter reviews the evidence about youth crime from these two very different types of sources.

Self-reporting of offending and drug use

Unlike administrative data, which can only provide data about crime that has come to the attention of the criminal justice system, self-report studies ask individuals about their offending behaviour regardless of whether this has been reported. Although the reliability of these studies can be called into question (Downes and Rock, 2003), there is broad agreement that they provide a useful and important addition to the range of data available. Furthermore, given the limited data available from administrative data and victimisation surveys on drug offences, this type of survey is often the sole source of detailed information on the nature of young people's drug use.

In this section we draw on the Offending Crime and Justice Survey to examine self-reported crime among young people, and two reports looking at drug use: the British Crime Survey's Drug Misuse Declared and the Smoking, Drinking and Drug Use Surveys:

- The Crime and Justice Survey was first undertaken in 2003. Later waves of the survey – re-named the Offending Crime and Justice Survey (hereafter OCJS) – were undertaken in 2004, 2005 and 2006. It was a random, nationally representative survey with an initial sample of 12,000 and follow-up samples of around 5,000. It was a longitudinal survey examining attitudes and experiences of offending among young people aged between 10 to 25.
- The Drug Misuse Declared Surveys (hereafter DMD) are based on British Crime Survey data and focus discussion about age and drug use predominantly on a 16-24 age group. Data have been collected since 1996 and over 26,000 respondents participated in 2009/10.
- The Smoking, Drinking and Drug Use Survey (hereafter SDDU) is a school survey of around 7,500 11- to 15-year-olds in schools in England, and trend data have been available since 2001.

The limitations of these data sources lie predominantly in respondent-related error, particularly the suggestion that respondents might conceal offending behaviour and drug use because they are not convinced that the information will remain confidential or perhaps because of the presence of others. They may also exaggerate behaviour if they believe that their social status might be increased by doing so. There will also be factual and temporal distortion of events, including recanting of admissions of drug use (Percy et al, 2005). Those who were not available to participate in these studies (which often occur during the school day) may well be those with more chaotic lifestyles, living in poorer accommodation and, perhaps, disproportionately involved in risky behaviour including truanting (Downes and Rock, 2003).

There are also relatively few studies that ask about the abuse of legal prescription drugs[4] and/or the ever increasing availability and use of so-called 'legal highs'. Recent, smaller-scale surveys have been attempting to address this (for example, the MixMag survey of 2010), but it may be important for future sweeps of both SDDU and DMD to incorporate questions about these alternative ways of 'getting high'.

Trends in offending

The trends across four waves of the OCJS show consistency both in terms of levels of offending and the types of offences committed (see Table 12.6). Around one quarter (between 25% and 26%) admitted to committing an offence in the last 12 months, meaning around three quarters of the sample did not admit to any offending behaviour. Among 10- to 17-year-olds, assault was the most common offence, at 18% for 2006, followed by other thefts at 11%, and criminal damage at 5%. Drug-related offences (1%), vehicle-related thefts (2%) and burglary (1%) were less common, with robbery extremely rare in this age group.

Table 12.6: Trends in offending by 10- to 17-year-olds in the last 12 months (%)

	2003	2004	2005	2006
Any core offence	25	26	26	26
Any property offence	13	15	13	14
Burglary	0	1	1	1
Vehicle-related thefts	2	2	2	2
Other thefts	10	13	11	11
Criminal damage	4	5	4	5
Any violent offence	19	19	18	19
Robbery	0	0	0	0
Assault	18	19	18	18
Any drug selling offence	2	2	2	1

Source: Roe and Ashe (2008, Table 2.6, p 20)

These findings confirm those from administrative data that males are more likely than females to commit offences of all types. In 2006, 30% of males aged 10-17 committed an offence in the last 12 months compared with 22% of females (see Table 12.7).

Table 12.7: Offending in the last 12 months among 10- to 17-year-olds by sex, 2006 (%)

	Males	Females
Any core offence	30	22
Vehicle-related thefts	4	1
Other thefts	13	10
Criminal damage	6	3
Assault	19	14
Selling drugs	3	1

Source: Roe and Ashe (2008, Table 2.4, p 18)

Ethnicity

The OCJS 2003 found that White and Mixed ethnic respondents were more likely to admit to offending behaviour whereas Asian respondents were the least likely (see Figure 12.7). This pattern was consistent across both the *ever* and *last year* basis and across all offence categories. It also held true for both serious and frequent offending.

The study suggests that these results might reflect the different age profile of the various ethnic groups, most particularly the higher proportion of young males in the Mixed ethnic origin group. When age was controlled for, White respondents continued to have a higher than average rate for last year offending, but the rate of those from a Mixed ethnic background did not differ from the average (Sharp and Budd, 2005).

Figure 12.7: Percentage committing any offence and any serious offence in their lifetime, by ethnic group, 2003

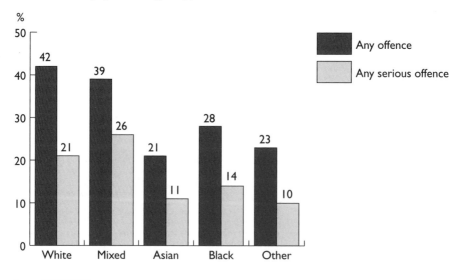

Source: OCJS 2003

Peak age and extent of offending compared with general population

The OCJS 2003 included ages 10-65 and was able to estimate the proportion of crime attributable to young people; it confirms previous evidence that younger people commit most crime. In 2003, 35% of crimes were committed by 10- to 17-year-olds who comprised just 14% of the sample (Budd et al, 2005). Furthermore, the 2003 findings reported that the peak age of offending was among 14- to 17-year-olds, followed by 12- to 13-year-olds; for males the highest rates of offending also occurred among 14- to 17-year-olds, whereas for females the rates were more even throughout the teenage years (Budd et al, 2005). Thus, the male/female ratio of offending behaviour varies with age. Later surveys reinforce the finding that offending is most prevalent among 10- to 17-year-olds, compared with other age groups. In 2006 this was reported to be the case in respect of all offence categories with the exception of drug selling offences (Roe and Ashe, 2008).

Serious and prolific offenders

The OCJS also seeks to identify those young people who can be described as 'frequent' and 'serious' offenders. Frequent offenders are defined as those who have committed six or more offences in the last 12 months. Serious offenders are defined as those who have committed one or more of the following offences: theft of a vehicle, burglary, robbery, theft from the person, assault resulting in an injury and selling Class A drugs. Frequent serious offenders are those who have committed a serious offence at least six times in the last 12 months (Roe and Ashe, 2008).

The percentages of 10- to 17-year-olds falling into these categories in 2006 are summarised in Table 12.8. A higher proportion of males aged 14-15 appears in all categories compared with other age ranges. While there are relatively few frequent serious offenders across 10- to 25-year-olds (between 1% and 3%), the proportion of those aged 14-15 engaged in frequent (15%) and serious (18%)

Table 12.8: Serious and frequent offending among 10- to 17-year-olds by sex, 2006 (%)

	Males					Females				
	10-11	12-13	14-15	16-17	18-25	10-11	12-13	14-15	16-17	18-25
Offender	22	26	37	33	21	12	24	26	23	13
Serious offender	9	12	18	16	11	4	12	14	10	5
Frequent offender	3	7	15	11	7	4	3	8	4	2
Serious and frequent offender	0	6	10	7	4	2	2	6	2	2
Frequent serious offender	0	2	3	2	1	2	1	3	1	1

Source: Roe and Ashe (2008, Table 2.5, p 19)

offending are relatively high compared with lower ages – for those aged 12-13 the proportions are 7% for frequent offending and 12% for serious offending. These data allude to questions about the age of onset of offending and the factors that lead to young people continuing to offend.

Key trends in the prevalence of drug use

According to the Smoking, Drinking and Drug Use Among Young People in England 2009 Survey (hereafter SDDU 2009), between 2001 and 2009, there was an overall decline in the proportion of pupils who reported *ever* having taken drugs (from 29% to 22%). Over the same time period, the proportions who reported taking drugs *in the last year* (from 20% in 2001 to 15% in 2009) and taking drugs *in the last month* (from 12% to 8%) also declined (see Table 12.9). However, all three measures of drug use remained unchanged between 2008 and 2009 (Fuller and Sanchez, 2010).

Table 12.9: Lifetime, last year and last month drug use from 2001 to 2009 among 11- to 15-year-olds (%)

	2001	2002	2003	2004	2005	2006	2007	2008	2009
Ever taken drugs									
Boys	30	29	31	26	28	24	26	23	23
Girls	28	25	30	25	27	24	24	21	21
Total	29	27	30	26	28	24	25	22	22
Taken drugs in the last year									
Boys	21	21	22	18	19	17	18	16	16
Girls	19	18	20	17	19	16	17	14	14
Total	20	20	21	18	19	17	17	15	15
Taken drugs in the last month									
Boys	13	13	13	11	11	10	10	9	9
Girls	11	10	12	9	10	8	9	7	7
Total	12	12	12	10	11	9	10	8	8

Source: Fuller and Sanchez (2010)

The latest Drug Misuse Declared Survey (hereafter DMD 2009-10) uncovers similar patterns for older teenagers and young adults (aged 16-24) (see Table 12.10). Since 1998, when the rate of *lifetime* drug use for this age group peaked at 53.7%, there has been a gradual decline year by year to the most recent rate in 2009/10 of 40.7%. Again, this pattern also remains true for the *last year* and *last month* measures. Of respondents aged 16-24, 31.8% claimed to have taken drugs in the *last year* in 1998 compared to 20% in 2009/10; in 1998 the rate for *last month* usage among this age group was 20.8%, but by 2009/10 this rate had dropped to 11.6% (Hoare and Moon, 2010).

Table 12.10: Lifetime, last year and last month drug use from 1998 to 2009/10 among 16- to 24-year-olds (%)

	1998	2000	2001/ 02	2002/ 03	2003/ 04	2004/ 05	2005/ 06	2006/ 07	2007/ 08	2008/ 09	2009/ 10
Ever taken drugs	53.7	52.0	49.1	48.2	47.5	46.0	45.1	44.7	42.6	42.9	40.7
Taken drugs in last year	31.8	29.9	30.0	28.5	28.3	26.5	25.2	24.1	21.5	22.6	20.0
Taken drugs in last month	20.8	19.0	19.3	18.1	17.5	16.4	15.1	14.3	12.5	13.1	11.6

Source: Hoare and Moon (2010)

Looking in more detail at age, the SDDU 2009 shows a clear and steady increase in the prevalence of drug use as pupils get older (Table 12.11). Only 9% of 11-year-olds reported ever having taken drugs compared to 40% of 15-year-olds. This pattern remained across *last year* (5% and 30% respectively) and *last month* (2% and 17% respectively) measures (Fuller and Sanchez, 2010).

Table 12.11: Lifetime, last year and last month drug use rates[a] for 11- to 15-year-old boys and girls, 2009 (%)

	Age 11	Age 12	Age 13	Age 14	Age 15	Total
Boys						
Ever taken drugs	9	14	17	27	43	23
Taken drugs in last year	5	7	10	19	32	16
Taken drugs in the last month	3	4	6	10	21	9
Girls						
Ever taken drugs	9	13	16	27	37	21
Taken drugs in last year	4	6	10	18	27	14
Taken drugs in the last month	2	3	6	11	13	7
All persons aged 11-15 years						
Ever taken drugs	9	13	17	27	40	22
Taken drugs in last year	5	7	10	19	30	15
Taken drugs in the last month	2	3	6	10	17	8
Total	1,125	1,446	1,455	1,403	1,713	7,142

Note: [a]Excludes volatile substances.

Source: Fuller and Sanchez (2010)

Only *last year* rates were available further broken down into 16-19 years and 20-24 years categories in the DMD 2009-10 and comparisons were made over time. Figures in 2001 showed 28.5% of 16- to 19-year-olds and 31.3% of 20- to 24-year-olds admitting to any drug use in the last year. By 2009/10 these rates were 22.3% and 18.1% respectively (see Table 12.12).

These overall figures for *all* drug use suggest that the younger of these two age groups now have a higher rate of drug use compared to the older group.

Table 12.12: Last year drug use for 16- to 19-year-olds and 20- to 24-year-olds from 2001/02 to 2009/10 (%)

	2001/ 02	2002/ 03	2003/ 04	2004/ 05	2005/ 06	2006/ 07	2007/ 08	2008/ 09	2009/ 10
16-19 age group	28.5	26.4	27.7	26.6	24.8	23.3	20.7	22.2	22.3
20-24 age group	31.3	30.3	28.7	26.4	25.6	24.8	22.1	22.9	18.1
All ages (16-59)	11.9	12.2	12.3	11.3	10.5	10.0	9.6	10.1	8.6

Source: DMD 2009-10, Hoare and Moon (2010)

However, this hides a more complex pattern of different rates of use for different drugs. While the rate of use of powder cocaine, ecstasy and 'Any Class A drug' is higher for the older age category, the use of hallucinogens, amphetamines and cannabis is lower, suggesting a change with age in drug use repertoire. However, for all ages and for all drugs the overall trend is downwards.

Comparing the results from both surveys, they suggest that in 2009/10 the *last year* drug use rate peaked at age 15 at a rate of 30%, dropping to 22.3% in the 16-19 category. However, comparison between the two surveys should be made with considerable caution – different samples and different methodologies may well result in non-comparable rates. In addition, without a more detailed breakdown of the 16-19 age category into individual years, it is difficult to say anything conclusive about changes year by year.

Types of drug taken

The main drug used by the 11- to 15-year-olds sampled in the SDDU 2009 survey was cannabis (see Table 12.13), with 8.9% of pupils saying they had used cannabis in the last year. However, this rate dropped from 13.4% in 2001 – reducing steadily year on year in the intervening period. Volatile substances (glue, gas, aerosols or solvents) were the next most frequently misused substances – 5.5% of students admitted to their use in 2009 – again demonstrating a steady decline from 7.1% in 2001. Poppers have also been consistently relatively popular with this group –

Table 12.13: Type of drug taken in last year by 11- to 15-year-olds, from 2001 to 2009 (%)

Type of drug taken in last year	2001	2002	2003	2004	2005	2006	2007	2008	2009
Cannabis	13.4	13.2	13.3	11.3	11.7	10.1	9.4	9.0	8.9
Glue, gas, aerosols or solvents	7.1	6.3	7.6	5.6	6.7	5.1	6.2	5.0	5.5
Poppers	3.4	4.3	4.0	3.4	3.9	4.2	4.9	2.9	1.8
Any Class A drug	4.3	3.7	4.3	3.9	4.4	4.3	4.0	3.6	3.6
Any drug	20.4	19.7	21.0	17.6	19.1	16.5	17.3	15.0	14.8

Source: SDDU 2009, Fuller and Sanchez (2010)

---

peaking at 4.9% in 2007 (from 3.4% in 2001); but use has dropped considerably since then, with only 1.8% of pupils admitting to their use in the latest survey. Class A drug use[5] is very rare in this age group – overall 3.6% of students admitted using Class A drugs in 2009, a drop from 4.3% in 2001. This rate is mainly driven by the use of magic mushrooms (1.5% in 2009), powder cocaine (1.2% in 2009) and ecstasy (also 1.2% in 2009) (Fuller and Sanchez, 2010).

Gender

In 2009, boys were more likely to have *ever* taken drugs than girls (23% compared to 21%), to have taken drugs *in the last year* (16% and 14%) and to have taken drugs *in the last month* (9% and 7%) (see Table 12.9 above). This pattern has remained fairly constant over repeated SDDU surveys (Fuller and Sanchez, 2010). The DMD 2009-10 does not offer a detailed combined breakdown for age and gender required for comparison here. However, the 2008/09 DMD does. In 2008/09, males aged 16-24 were more likely to have taken drugs in the last year than females in the same age category (27.2% compared to 17.9%). It can be seen from these figures that the gender differences are less extreme among children and younger teenagers and that the gap between male and female drug use may widen with age.

Ethnicity

The SDDU 2009 survey conducted a logistic regression analysis to explore characteristics that might have an independent association with drug use – among the factors included was ethnicity. The results of this were expressed in terms of increased or decreased levels of risk.[6] The analysis showed that pupils of Mixed (odds ratio of 1.76), Asian (2.27) and Black (2.28) ethnicity were more likely than White pupils to have used drugs. It should be noted, however, that far more significant in this analysis were factors such as regular smoking (12.09), having drunk alcohol in the last week (6.84) and having a family who did nothing to discourage or actually encouraged drug use (12.81) (Fuller and Sanchez, 2010).

Controlling for both age and gender in bivariate analysis, analysis of the OCJS 2003 found that White males and males of Mixed ethnic groups aged 10-25 had similar rates of drug use. Young Asian males were significantly less likely to use drugs than any other group, and Class A drug use was highest among White males. Among the youngest respondents aged 10-15, *last year* drug use was very similar among White, Black and Mixed ethnic groups (at around 5%), but significantly lower for the Asian ethnic group, at just 1% (Sharp and Budd, 2005).

However, when age standardisation was applied to the sample in order to control for the different age structure of the various ethnic groups, the rate for Mixed and Black respondents was no greater than average, Asian and Other groups were below average and only Whites had a higher than average rate of drug use in the last year. This suggests that sophisticated analysis is required in order to fully understand any relationship that might exist between ethnicity and drug use, and that initial patterns may well be disguising other factors with more influence, such as age and gender structures within different ethnic groups.

Victimisation data

In terms of 'crime and young people' it is offending behaviour that is most commonly studied and reported, although this focus belies the significance of victimisation for many young people. In reality, the data suggests that young people are at least as likely, if not more likely, to be a victim of crime (around 31%) than to commit crime (around 25%).

The data presented here derive from two main sources: the OCJS, which included questions about victimisation in 2005 and 2006, and the Ipsos MORI Youth Survey data for 2008, based on a sample of 4,750 young people aged 11-16 in mainstream education. The discussion is restricted to general crime and does not include drug use, which can be defined as a 'victimless crime'. Although the British Crime Survey is the most well-known victim survey, it does not regularly include young people – the exception being in 1992 (see Neale, 2006) – and is therefore not discussed here.

Findings from the OCJS

Two waves of data from the OCJS explored the victimisation of young people. Both the 2005 and 2006 waves provide data on personal victimisation in the last 12 months, using a definition consistent with the British Crime Survey by including personal theft (robbery, theft from the person, other personal thefts) and assaults (resulting in injury and without injury) (Wilson et al, 2006, p 6).

In 2005, 31% of 10- to 15-year-olds had been victims of personal theft or assault in the previous 12 months (see Table 12.14). Moreover, this age group is more likely to be victimised than those aged 16-25 (25%). Those aged 12-13 were more likely to have been victims of crime than other age ranges, the differences in rates of victimisation being largest for assault without injury (at 17% compared with 14% for the next highest rate) and other personal thefts. Those aged 10-11 were most likely to have been the victims of assault with injury (14%).

Both the nature of items stolen and the location of victimisation were found to vary by age group in the 2005 survey. Among 10- to 15-year-olds, the majority of incidents were portrayed as 'not crime' by respondents, reflecting the relatively minor nature of offences such as theft of stationery and sports items at school (Wilson et al, 2006, pp 10-11). In terms of location, 10- to 15-year-olds were more likely to be victims at school, while those aged 16-25 were more likely to mention locations such as clubs, home and in the street (Wilson et al, 2006, p 68).

Serious injury was rare for all age groups, and especially so for those aged 10-15, where most injuries were sustained as a result of being pushed, grabbed or kicked (Wilson et al, 2006, p 69). In contrast, 16- to 25-year-olds were more

Table 12.14: Proportion of young people who were victims once or more in the last 12 months, by age, 2005 (%)

	Age group					
	10-11	12-13	14-15	10-15	16-25	10-25
Any personal victimisation	31	33	29	31	25	27
Any personal theft	16	18	16	17	11	13
Robbery	3	2	2	2	2	2
Theft from person	6	6	5	6	4	4
Other personal thefts	10	13	11	11	7	9
Any assault	21	21	20	20	16	18
Assault (no injury)	12	17	14	14	10	11
Assault (with injury)	14	10	10	11	10	10

Source: Wilson et al (2006, Table 6a, p 67)

likely to be hit with a weapon and sustain more serious injuries such as broken bones (7% compared with 2% for ages 10-15). The locations of assault were also different across age groups, with assaults against those aged 10-15 most likely to happen at school (61% with injury and 68% without) (Wilson et al, 2006, p 70).

The OCJS report found the following factors to be independently statistically associated with a higher likelihood of 10- to 15-year-olds being victims:

- committing an offence in the last 12 months;
- being male;
- one or more disorder problems in the local area;
- committed anti-social behaviour in the last year;
- living in rented accommodation;
- having a bad perception of school;
- parents perceived to have poor parenting skills. (Wilson et al, 2006, Table 6b, p 72)

These factors are of interest, as they point to possible similarities between aspects of risk experienced by both offenders and victims – an issue we explore further in the final section of this chapter.

The OCJS 2006 reports very similar findings to 2005, with 30% of those aged 10-15 having been victims in the last 12 months, making this age group the most likely to be victimised. This rises to 38% for males aged 10-15 (compared with 27% for males aged 16-25). Gender differences in victimisation are also consistent with 2005 findings, with 22% of females aged 10-15 having been victims in the previous 12 months. However, the difference between age groups for females is not significant, with 20% of females aged 16-25 having been victims (Roe and Ashe, 2008).

The 2006 data provides information about the differences in victimisation between offenders and non-offenders. Among 10- to 15-year-olds, 55% of those who had committed any offence in the previous 12 months were also victims of personal crime, compared to 22% of those who had not committed any offence (see Figure 12.8). Levels of offending were similarly higher among those who had been victims (46%) compared with those who had not (16%) (see Figure 12.9).

These findings provide insights into the overlap between victims and offenders among young people that point to aspects of vulnerability and risk – these issues are further explored in the final section of this chapter.

Figure 12.8: Proportion of offenders aged 10-15 who were victims of crime in the last 12 months, 2006

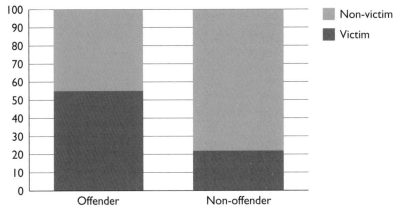

Source: Roe and Ashe (2008, Figure 4.1, pp 29, 31)

Figure 12.9: Percentage of victims aged 10-15 who offended in the last 12 months, 2006

Source: Roe and Ashe (2008, Figure 4.2, p 30)

MORI Youth Surveys

The MORI Youth Surveys are not based on representative samples of young people, focusing mostly on those attending mainstream education, and focusing on a range of crimes and age ranges that mean it is not possible to compare the findings with the OCJS. The MORI Surveys do, however, give some indication about young people's fear of crime. Table 12.15 compares the proportion of young people who were worried about particular crimes in 2000 with 2008, and indicates that concerns are declining among young people in all offence categories. In relation to experience of crime, the data indicates that 38% of young people had not been victims of any of the offences included. Increases in victimisation were reported for physical attacks, theft of mobile phones and racial abuse for the period 2006-08 (MORI, 2009, p 39).

The survey report also reinforces findings from the OCJS regarding the overlap between young victims and offenders – 'two thirds (67%) of those who have committed an offence have been the victims of crime, compared with 44% of those who have not committed a crime' (MORI, 2009, p 40).

The inclusion of data about fear of crime also allows us to consider differences between experience and fear. The largest differences occur in relation to physical assault and racism, with 21% of young people saying they were worried about being the victims of racism but only 2% having been victims and 36% reporting concern about physical assault compared with 18% who actually experienced this.

The victimisation of young people is often overlooked, yet the available data provides insight into some important contextual issues in relation to young people's offending behaviour. Overall, the data suggests that around a third of young people may be the victims of offence in any year, but there are tentative indications that among school pupils at least, far greater numbers are worried about being the victims of crime.

Most notably, the data indicates that there is a clear overlap between offenders and victims, possibly underlining the vulnerability of many young people who find themselves involved in criminal activity. The dichotomy of victim/offender does not apply to many young people who are often the same individuals. Further

Table 12.15: Experience and worry about selected crimes, ages 11-17, 2000 and 2008

	Worried about crime		Experienced crime in last 12 months
	2000	2008	2008
Being bullied at school	42	22	23
Being the victim of theft	55	35	26
Being physically assaulted	57	36	18
Being the victim of racism	40	21	2

Source: MORI (2009)

insight into the types of risk and vulnerability young offenders may experience is offered in our final section, where those factors associated with being a victim and being an offender can be seen to be very similar.

Risk and protective factors

In relation to 'risk' and 'protective' factors we are concerned with those aspects of young people's lives that might indicate links between particular factors and the risk of becoming an offender or drug user. The relationship between risk and protective factors is not always clear, although it is generally accepted that 'risk factors cluster together in the lives of the most disadvantaged children' (YJB, 2005, p 27).

Here, we review findings from the OCJS 2005 while acknowledging that there are a number of important studies that are omitted – most notably the Cambridge Longitudinal Study.

Findings from the OCJS

The risk factor analysis undertaken from OCJS data considers overall, serious and frequent offending and distinguishes between 10- to 15-year-olds and 16- to 25-year-olds. For the purposes of this discussion, findings related to the former age group are discussed in detail with salient comparison made to the older age group.

A multivariate analysis was used to 'identify characteristics which were independently statistically associated with a higher likelihood of offending for 10–15 year olds' (Wilson et al, 2006, p 34). These are summarised in Table 12.16, which also provides the odds ratio for each factor across three offender types 'offender', 'serious offender' and 'frequent offender'. These factors can be clustered together across three main areas: first, there are a number of factors associated with 'deviant behaviour' – most notably committing anti-social behaviour, drinking alcohol and taking drugs; a second group of factors clusters around school and family life; while a third reflects attitudes and behaviours of others – most notably friends and parents. These broad types mirror findings in previous studies where 'domains' of risk have been identified as important (see Neale, 2006).

The OCJS data, however, differs from previous studies by examining the differences in risk factors across offender types. While many factors remain salient for all types, there are some notable exceptions. In the case of serious offenders, for example, the influence of parents is not significant, while for frequent offenders poor relationships with parents feature prominently in the likelihood of offending. Thus, the data reveals that risk factors are likely to differ across groups of young people depending on the seriousness and frequency of their offending.

If we consider the factors themselves, we can also see that some factors become more important in relation to some types of offending. Drug use, for example, increases the odds of a young person offending once in the last 12 months by 2.1, but this rises to 4.1 for frequent offenders. So, not only do risk factors cluster

Table 12.16: Factors associated with offending for 10- to 15-year-olds, by type of offender

Factors showing association	Odds ratio offenders	Odds ratio serious offenders	Odds ratio frequent offenders
Committed anti-social behaviour in the last 12 months	2.9	3.3	2.6
Victim of personal crime	3.4	3.7	3.1
Has been drunk once a month or more in the last 12 months	2.3	1.6	1.4
Friends/siblings have been in trouble with the police	1.6	–	2.1
Has taken drugs in the last 12 months	2.4	3.3	4.1
Has been suspended or expelled from school	2.1	1.9	1.8
Parents have been in trouble with the police	1.3	1.5	–
More likely to agree criminal acts are okay	1.8	1.6	2.5
Spends little or no time with parents/guardians	1.2	–	–
Schooling thought to be fairly, not very or not at all important	–	1.4	–
Gets on badly with at least one parent	–	–	3.7

Source: Data extracted from Wilson et al (2006, Table 3a, p 35, Table 3.3, p 44 and Table 3.4, p 44)

together differently across different 'types' of offending, the importance of these also changes depending on the severity and frequency of crimes committed.

Risk and protective factors for drug use

Following Lloyd's 1998 review, which identified a number of groups who may be at a greater risk of developing problem drug use, a considerable body of work has been conducted to further examine the relationship between what Lloyd termed 'vulnerable' young people and drug use.

Using Lloyd's original vulnerability factors – the homeless, those looked after by local authorities or in foster care, prostitutes, truants, those excluded from school, young offenders, children from families with substance-abusing parents or siblings and young people with conduct or depressive disorders – Becker and Roe (2005) found higher rates of drug use among those belonging to some or all of these vulnerable groups:

Only 5% of those who were not vulnerable used drugs frequently in the last year, while 24% of those in vulnerable groups had done so; those in vulnerable groups accounted for 28% of the total sample, but for 61% of the Class A drug users.

For those in more than one vulnerable group figures were worse – with 39% of those in more than one reporting frequent drug use compared to 18% of those in only one.

Dillon et al (2007) used a logistic regression model with the OCJS data to identify factors associated with taking drugs, shown in Table 12.17.

Table 12.17: Risk factors associated with taking drugs

10-16 age group	17-24 age group
• Serious anti-social behaviour	• Anti-social behaviour
• Weak parental attitude towards bad behaviour	• Early smoking
• Being in trouble at school (including truanting and exclusion)	• Being in trouble at school
	• Being impulsive
• Friends in trouble	• Being un-sensitive
• Being unhelpful	• Belonging to few or no groups
• Early smoking	
• Not getting free school meals	
• Minor anti-social behaviour	

Source: Dillon et al (2007)

From these findings it is clear that there is a distinct overlap between risk factors for offending and for drug use, adding weight to the argument that both behaviours may stem from a young person's various experiences of disadvantage. In particular, factors associated with a young person's relationship with his/her parents (parents in trouble with the police, a poor relationship with a parent, spending little or no time with a parent, and a weak parental attitude to bad behaviour) and with school (truanting, suspension and expulsion) appear to be highly associated with both offending and drug use. In addition, factors such as associating with a delinquent peer group and being involved with anti-social behaviour (some of it serious) suggests a lifestyle that exposes these young people to a range of deviant activities – including drug use and offending. In contrast, these findings also suggest that if young people are sufficiently attached to both their families and their schools, they are at far less risk of being involved in these behaviours.

Conclusion

The increasing availability of crime-related data has meant that much of this chapter has been concerned with providing a picture of offending behaviour among young people across the main national sources. In concluding, we review the main strengths and limitations of those data sources in relation to key variables associated with understanding the well-being of children and young people.

In relation to social class, the data is very limited. Only the British Crime Survey regularly collects information about household types that might give insights into the social background of young offenders, and given that this survey has only recently begun to consider the inclusion of those under 16, it will be some time before any details emerge. Furthermore, as a survey of victimisation, the British Crime Survey will be unable to provide data about offenders.

Data regarding ethnicity is also fairly limited. In administrative data the categories used are not helpful in providing anything more than very general findings, and self-report studies also remain limited in the extent to which they rely on broad categories of ethnicity. Given the potential for discrimination and disproportionality within the criminal justice system, this omission should be of concern.

Gender-related data is more consistently provided and across all the types of studies examined two findings are worthy of further consideration: first, that female offending patterns are changing and second, the apparent rise in female offending, particularly in categories of assault and physical violence, demands further investigation.

A final limitation of the data sources used here relates to age groups. While we would generally support the starting age of 10 for the regular collection of data about crime, the upper age ranges of many data sources means that it is difficult to separate those under 18.

It is clear from the data reviewed in this chapter that a high proportion of young people commit crime – but the majority of crime is still committed by adults. The findings also suggest that much of this crime is relatively minor, but there are some indications that girls may be committing more serious offences. Boys continue to commit more crime than girls, although the indications are that they may be desisting from crime at an earlier age than young women, whose offending behaviour continues into older age groups. Of particular concern are those findings that have begun to explore the relationship between offending and victimisation – the data reveals that far from being mutually exclusive groups, the victimised and the offenders are often the same children. It is possible that a greater focus on children as victims, rather than as offenders, may begin to address some of the underlying factors associated with crime and criminality among young people. Furthermore, policy and practice must continually recognise and respond to the way in which young people's experiences of disadvantage (particularly in terms of family life and school experience) expose them to participating in risky behaviour, such as offending and drug use.

Notes

[1] Those offences deemed serious enough to be recorded by the police. Includes all indictable offences.

[2] Those arrestees subsequently prosecuted by the Crown Prosecution Service.

[3] Offences committed by young people as reported by Youth Offending Teams that resulted in a disposal.

[4] The DMD includes anabolic steroids and a generic 'tranquilliser' category.

[5] Class A drugs included in this study were cocaine, crack, heroin, LSD, magic mushrooms, methadone, ecstasy and amphetamines if injected.

[6] These are expressed as odds ratios relative to a reference category given a value of 1 – so odds greater than one demonstrate an increased risk; those lower than 1 a decreased risk (Sanchez and Fuller, 2010).

THIRTEEN

Conclusion

Jonathan Bradshaw

This new edition of *The well-being of children in the UK* provides a more up-to-date picture of children's lives. The previous edition (published in 2005) contained data only up to 2003 and some of that related to the period either before the election of the Labour government in 1997, or before the government had released itself from the shackles of its election commitment to maintain the previous Conservative government's spending plans.

Now in 2011, we are able to present a more modern picture and perhaps a picture that provides a preliminary evaluation at least of the impact of the Labour government during 1997–2010.

In 2007, in an introduction to *The Children's Plan* and soon after the publication of UNICEF's Innocenti Report Card no 7 that had UK children at the bottom of the international league of rich nations, Ed Balls, former Secretary of State for Children, Schools and Families, claimed:

> ... for most children things are good. Despite recent reports to the contrary, virtually all children say that they are happy, healthy and cared for by their families. They are enjoying their childhood and are increasingly well-educated. Most are engaged, motivated and making a positive contribution. There is much to be proud of about the experiences and opportunities for children and young people in England today. (Ed Balls, quoted in DCSF, 2007a)

Ed Balls drew on a review (DCSF, 2007b) that covered only some of the ground of this book. In this concluding chapter we attempt an answer to the question, was Ed Balls right?

What is the comparative evidence?

Are things good for UK children? One important piece of evidence is how they are doing in comparison with children elsewhere – unless we know how we stand comparatively we cannot know how good we could be, even if we are better than we were. The comparative evidence has been drawn on throughout this book, and we present a summary here. The UNICEF (2007) Innocenti Report Card no 7 had the UK bottom of 21 countries, and:

- 18th on material well-being

- 12th on health and safety
- 17th on education
- 21st on family and peer relations
- 21st on behaviour and risks
- 20th on subjective well-being.

The Bradshaw and Richardson (2009) comparisons of the 29 European Union (EU) countries had the UK 24th out of 29 countries, and:

- 24th on health
- 21st out of 28 on subjective well-being
- 15th out of 28 on relationships
- 24th out of 26 on material well-being
- 18th out of 28 on risk behaviour
- 22nd out of 27 on education
- 17th out of 26 on housing.

Although the OECD (2009b) did not produce such a league table, it is easy to estimate one. The UK would have come 20th out of 30 OECD countries, and:

- 12th on material well-being
- 15th out of 27 on housing and the environment
- 22nd on education
- 20th on health and safety
- 28th on risk behaviour
- 4th out of 25 on quality of school life.

Innocenti Report Card no 9 (UNICEF, 2010a) is the first to attempt an index of the *dispersion* of child well-being, exploring inequalities in three domains. Out of 24 countries, the UK was:

- 19th on material well-being inequality
- 13th on educational inequality
- 11th on health inequality.

Overall the UK came in the fourth from lowest group of countries out of five.

So the UK does not do well in the international league tables of child well-being. For a country with its level of GDP it is under-performing, and it is under-performing on most domains of well-being. Compared with other rich countries, the UK does consistently badly on:

- *Material well-being:* the UK relative child poverty rates are comparatively high, and although we do better using deprivation measures, we are still not very good and we do very badly indeed in the proportion of children in workless households.

- *Health:* we are not good on infant mortality and low birth weight. Our immunisation rates are low. Breastfeeding is low. Self-assessed health is middling. We do comparatively badly on most health behaviours – obesity, diet, smoking, drinking, misuse of drugs. We do very badly on early sexual activity and teenage pregnancy. We are not bad on exercise. The one health indicator that we do really well on is our low childhood accidental deaths rates, which in Europe are most commonly caused by road traffic accidents. This is probably an achievement of policy – traffic calming and road safety education. But the nagging worry is that it is also the result of locking our children at home, not letting them roam, with knock-on effects on loneliness and obesity.

- *Subjective well-being:* we are middling on life satisfaction. It appears that relationships with parents are comparatively good and there is comparative evidence that relationships with friends have improved. Our children seem to like school.

- *Education:* we are middling on achievement. In the 2009 PISA (Programme for International Student Assessment) the UK did better at Science than Literacy and Maths. But our participation rates in post-statutory education and our not in education, employment or training (NEET) rates are comparatively very bad.

- *Housing:* we are quite good on overall housing satisfaction and living space but do much less well on inequalities in living space and environmental problems, especially crime, violence and vandalism.

These results are summarised in Table 13.1. Not all the domains have comparative indicators – in particular we are lacking comparative data on children and crime, children in care and the data on child maltreatment is not very satisfactory. A judgement has been made about whether the UK/Great Britain is comparatively good, middling or bad, depending on where it comes in an international league table of rich countries, using mainly OECD Family database, PISA, HBSC (Health Behaviour of School-aged Children) and EU-SILC (European Union Statistics on Income and Living Conditions) data. The comparator countries are not all the same. 'Good' means that the UK is in the top third of the distribution, 'middling' in the middle third and 'bad' in the bottom third. There are more 'bads' in this list (19) than there are 'goods' (8) or 'middlings' (15). This tends to confirm the judgements of the comparative indices that children in the UK are not doing well comparatively and not as well as they could be doing. Ed Balls might have been advised to acknowledge this in the quotation above.

Table 13.1: Comparative performance on child outcomes

	Comparative performance	Source
Material well-being		
Relative poverty before housing costs (BHC)	Bad	EU-SILC 2008
'Absolute' child poverty BHC	Bad	EU-SILC 2008
Material deprivation	Middling	EU-SILC 2008
Persistent poverty BHC	–	
Inequality	Bad	UNICEF (2010a)
Health		
Still births	–	
Infant mortality	Bad	OECD Health database (2010)
Child deaths	Good	WHO Mortality database
Low birth weight	Bad	OECD Health database (2010)
Breastfeeding	Bad	OECD Family database (2010)
Immunisation rates	Bad	OECD Family database (2010)
Self-assessed health	Bad	HBSC 2006
Obesity	Bad	HBSC 2006
Sex	Bad	HBSC 2006
Diet	Middling	HBSC 2006
Alcohol	Bad	HBSC 2006
Smoking	Bad	HBSC 2006
Drugs	Bad	HBSC 2006
Exercise	Middling	HBSC 2006
Inequality	Middling	UNICEF (2010b)
Subjective well-being and mental health		
Life satisfaction	Middling	HBSC 2006
Mental health	Middling	HBSC 2006
Suicide	Good	EAAD 2000-05
Talking to mothers	Middling	HBSC 2006
Talking to fathers	Middling	HBSC 2006
School friends kind and helpful	Middling	HBSC 2006
Education		
Literacy achievement	Middling	PISA 2009
Maths achievement	Middling	PISA 2009
Science achievement	Good	PISA 2009
Inequalities in achievement	Middling	UNICEF (2010b)
Staying on rates	Bad	OECD *Education at a Glance* (2010)
NEET	Bad	OECD Family database (2010)
Housing		
Housing satisfaction	Good	EU-SILC 2008
Living space	Good	EU-SILC 2008
Inequality in living space	Bad	EU-SILC 2008
Environment	Bad	EU-SILC 2008

(continued)

Table 13.1: Comparative performance on child outcomes (continued)

	Comparative performance	Source
Child maltreatment		
Fighting	Middling	HBSC 2006
Been bullied	Middling	HBSC 2006
Bullying others	Good	HBSC 2006
Children in care	–	
Crime	–	
Childcare		
Spending	Middling	OECD Family database (2010)
Enrolment 0-3	Good	OECD Family database (2010)
Enrolment 3-5	Good	OECD Family database (2010)
Costs to parents	Bad	OECD Family database (2010)
Staff/child ratios	Bad	OECD Family database (2010)
Time and space	–	

What are the national trends?

While it is important to know how we are doing compared to other countries, not least to have a vision of how much better we could be, we also need to know whether we are moving in the right direction in terms of child well-being. Comparative data can be used for this purpose but in practice it is more reliable to use national data. So what are the trends in child well-being? These have been reviewed in more detail in previous chapters and here the analysis is extracted and summarised.

What we attempt to do is to establish a set of indicators across the domains of well-being which can be used to produce a composite summary. This was what was attempted in the *Opportunity for all* reports, now abandoned, and less formally in the Annex to the Department for Children, Schools and Families (DCSF) report (2007b). The period of interest is broadly from 1997 or the mid-1990s to the latest available date – the Labour government period in office. Table 13.2 summarises the general trend over that period and then splits it down where possible into the first half and the second half.

The general conclusion of this analysis is that in the majority of domains of their lives, children are doing better.

- There are 36 ticks for the whole period – 23 for the first half and 34 for the second half.
- In contrast there are only 4 Xs – 8 for the first half and 2 for the second half.
- There are only 8 where there is no clear trend – 11 for the first half and 13 for the second.

Table 13.2: Trends in child well-being

	Labour period 1997-2010	Early Labour 1997-2004	Late Labour 2004-latest	Source
Material well-being				
Relative poverty BHC	✓	✓	◆	HBAI
'Absolute' child poverty BHC	✓	✓	◆	HBAI
Material deprivation	–	–	◆	HBAI
Persistent poverty BHC	✓	✓	✓	HBAI
Health				
Stillbirths	◆	X	✓	ONS
Infant mortality	✓	✓	✓	ONS
Child deaths	✓	✓	✓	ONS
Low birth weight	◆	X	✓	ONS
Breastfeeding	✓	✓	✓	ONS
Immunisation rates	X	X	✓	DoH
General health	✓	✓	✓	HSE
Longstanding illness	✓	✓	◆	HSE
Limiting longstanding illness	✓	✓	◆	HSE
Diabetes	X	X	X	HSE
Asthma	◆	◆	◆	HSE
Injuries and accidents	✓	✓	✓	DoT
Obesity	X	X	✓	HSE
Diet (fruit and vegetables)	✓	✓	✓	HSE
Alcohol	✓	◆	✓	HSE
Smoking	✓	✓	✓	HSE
Physical activity	–	–	✓	HSE
Sexually Transmitted Infections	X	X	X	HPA
Teenage conceptions	✓	✓	◆	ONS
Subjective well-being and mental health				
Happiness overall	✓	◆	✓	BHPS
Mental health	✓	◆	✓	ONS
Suicide	✓	✓	◆	ONS
Happiness with friends	✓	✓	✓	BHPS
Happiness with family	◆	◆	◆	BHPS
Happiness with school work	✓	◆	✓	BHPS
Happiness with appearance	◆	◆	◆	BHPS
Happiness with life	✓	◆	✓	BHPS
Happiness with school	–	–	✓	BHPS
Education				
Key Stage 2 attainment	✓	✓	✓	DfE
Five GCEs A*-C	✓	✓	✓	DfE
Level 2 qualifications	✓	–	✓	DfE
Staying on rates	✓	◆	✓	DfE
Exclusions	◆	–	◆	DfE
NEET	◆	◆	◆	

(continued)

Table 13.2: Trends in child well-being (continued)

	Labour period 1997-2010	Early Labour 1997-2004	Late Labour 2004-latest	Source
Housing				
Homelessness	✓	X	✓	CLG
Temporary accommodation	✓	X	✓	CLG
House conditions	✓	✓	✓	EHS/EHCS
Child maltreatment				
Fatal abuse	✓	–	–	Home Office
Physical abuse	✓	–	–	NSPCC
Neglect	◆	–	–	NSPCC
Children in care				
Length of spells in care	–	✓	✓	DfE
Placement stability	✓	–	✓	DfE
Education	✓	✓	✓	DfE
Childcare				
Formal participation	✓	✓	◆	Smith/Bryson
Crime and drugs				
Proven offences	✓	–	✓	YJB
Arrests	✓	◆	✓	YJB
Drug taking	✓	✓	✓	DMD
Worry about crime	✓	✓	✓	MORI

Notes: ✓ = getting better, X = getting worse, ◆ = no clear trend, – = missing data.

So the overall conclusion is that most elements of well-being have been getting better. It is important to remember that in many cases we may be getting better from a low base and still could and should be doing much better than we are.

Nevertheless here there is some support for the Ed Balls claim. While he never actually claimed that things were getting better for children (or at least not in this quotation), his claim was that 'for most children things are good ... virtually all children say that they are happy...' and so on. The only available test of whether things are good for British children is whether they are doing as well as children in other similar countries and the answer is that in too many domains they are not. The claim that virtually all children say they are happy etc is contestable. Certainly the majority are, but not all, and perhaps not virtually all. But in the end the statement is far too sanguine. New Labour had much to be proud of in respect of child well-being. They inherited a situation that was pretty dire and had begun to turn it round. But it is far from being good enough for Ed Balls to have been so confident.

Now and the future

Now we are faced with different economic circumstances and a different government. The evidence on child outcomes for the full period of the Labour government is still not available, and at the time of writing there is very little evidence at all on the impact on children of the recession, the change of government and its responses to the deficit.

The financial crisis in the UK began with the housing market in the US, where it was found that British banks had invested heavily in sub-prime housing loans. As a result, two banks were nationalised and two others were bailed out and forced to merge. The problems of the banks led to a collapse in lending, which had knock-on effects in the manufacturing industry, housing demand, house building and general levels of investment. The Labour government's response to the developing recession was radically anti-cyclical. It spent huge amounts of money propping up the banks – the Bank of England made repeated cuts in interest rates and then, with the encouragement of the Treasury, began 'quantitative easing' – increasing the money supply. This was supported by a host of fiscal and labour market measures.

The main transparent social impact of the recession was an increase in unemployment. By June–August 2009 the unemployment rate was 7.9%, up 2.1 percentage points on a year earlier. The number of unemployed people was 2.47 million. Unemployment then levelled off and was reasonably steady until it increased again in the quarter ending October 2010. There is an anxiety that this may be the first evidence that we could be entering a double-dip recession.

Under the Labour government there were no substantial cuts in benefits and services – in fact expenditure had been sustained, while revenue had fallen. Together with revenue going to support the banks, this resulted in a major increase in public sector borrowing. The country had to wait a long time to see measures announced to deal with this deficit. All parties were coy about the deficit in the May 2010 General Election but after the election the new Coalition government announced some immediate cuts, and then some further tax and benefit measures in an Emergency Budget in June 2010. However, the bulk of the government's proposals were left until the Comprehensive Spending Review was concluded, and the results were announced in October 2010. At the time of writing the country is still absorbing their impact and waiting for the outcomes of the Review to be implemented.

The Coalition government has decided to reduce the deficit by £81 billion by 2014/15. It chose to achieve this by taking 80% from spending and 20% from tax increases – although it now looks as if that balance is going to be 73%/27%.

There were three announcements that may help (poor) children:

- The child element of Child Tax Credit will be uprated by £180 per year above indexation in 2011/12 and £110 above indexation in 2012/13.

- The income tax personal allowance threshold will increase by £1,000 in 20011/12 and will benefit earners with incomes above the tax threshold, not just those with children.
- The 1% increase in National Insurance contributions announced by the previous government has been scrapped. This helps all earners above the threshold. But the losses in revenue will be offset by an increase in VAT.

However, there is a much longer list of measures that are likely to harm children and increase child poverty. They are, in no particular order:

- The maximum limit of childcare costs met under Working Tax Credit will be reduced from 80% to 70% – this could cost families up to £30 more per week.
- Abolishing educational maintenance allowances before the school leaving age is increased.
- Abolishing the Health in Pregnancy Grant.
- Abolishing Child Trust Funds.
- Reneging on the previous Labour government's commitment to extend free school meals to poor families in employment.
- Withdrawing Child Benefit from higher rate taxpayers (which will not hurt poor children in the short term but Child Benefit may suffer in the long term).
- Freezing Child Benefit for three years from 2011.
- Freezing Working Tax Credit for three years.
- Removing the baby element and proposed toddler element in Child Tax Credit.
- Lone parents to be expected to look for work once their youngest child reaches school age, from October 2011.
- Sure Start Maternity Grant restricted to the first child only.
- A £2,500 disregard of in-year falls in tax credits after 2012 and a reduction in the disregard from £25,000 to £10,000 on in-year increases.
- Cutting spending on Council Tax Benefit and making it a local function.
- Introducing a benefit cap will reduce the incomes of large families with children – the government estimates 50,000 families will be affected.
- Increasing VAT from 17.5% to 20%.
- Introducing a Housing Benefit cap and reduction in local housing allowances.
- Withdrawing entitlement to Working Tax Credit of couples with children working 16-24 hours per week.
- Uprating all benefits in line with the consumer price index (CPI) instead of the retail price index (RPI) or Rossi index.

Meanwhile, the government announced that it was reviewing the need for the Child Poverty Commission that is required under the Child Poverty Act, as part of a public consultation about the child poverty strategy. A review by Frank Field MP was published, calling for greater investment in a foundation stage, but also suggesting that it might be paid for by cutting back on Child Tax Credit upratings.[1]

It will take some time to assess fully the overall impact of this package. There are also the impacts on children of cuts in capital spending, general central and local government services (such as Sure Start) and the loss of 500,000 public sector jobs. The Institute for Fiscal Studies has concluded that the distributional consequences of the measures are regressive (Browne and Levell, 2010) (although the government seeks to deny this). The government has claimed that the Spending Review will have no 'measurable' impact on child poverty in the next two years. However, the Institute concludes (Brewer and Joyce, 2010) that between 2010-11 and 2013-14, average incomes are forecast to stagnate, and both absolute and relative poverty among children and working-age adults are expected to rise. Poverty beyond 2013-14 is likely to be affected by the Universal Credit that will need to be assessed when the government publishes its Welfare Reform Bill in 2011.

The Coalition government has made a big issue of fairness, and repeated the mantra that 'we are all in this together'. Only time will tell whether they have been fair to children. They should be judged on the answer to that question.

How will the judgement be made? Who will accumulate the evidence? Of course there are many government departments and other agencies contributing the evidence, but at the moment no one is reviewing the evidence across the board and caring about the results. There is still no *State of UK children* report produced in this country. The Office for National Statistics are not doing the job and, reeling from budget cuts, are not going to want to take this new task on. The Child Poverty Unit and the Child Poverty Commission, if it survives the Review, have rather narrower briefs. The same is true of the Child and Maternal Health Observatory. Perhaps the best hope lies in the newly established Child Wellbeing Research Centre, although it is responsible only for English children and has a time-limited contract.

Note

[1] http://povertyreview.independent.gov.uk/media/20254/poverty-report.pdf

References

A National Voice (2007) 'Please sir! Can I have some more?', Manchester: A National Voice.

Adamson, P. (2010) *The children left behind: A league table of inequality in child well-being in the world's rich countries*, Innocenti Report Card no 9, Florence: UNICEF Innocenti Research Centre.

Adelman, L., Middleton, S. and Ashworth, K. (2003) *Britain's poorest children: Severe and persistent poverty and social exclusion*, London: Save the Children.

Advisory Council on the Misuse of Drugs (2003) *Hidden harm: Responding to the needs of children of problem drug users*, London: Home Office.

Allen, M. (2003) *Into the mainstream: Care leavers entering work, education and training*, York: Joseph Rowntree Foundation.

Anderson, H.R. (2005) 'Prevalence of asthma', *British Medical Journal*, vol 330, p 1037.

Asher M.I., Montefort S,. Björkstén B., Lai C.K., Strachan D.P., Weiland S.K. and Williams H. (2006) 'Worldwide time trends in the prevalence of symptoms of asthma, allergic rhinoconjunctivitis, and eczema in childhood: ISAAC phases one and three repeat multicountry cross-sectional surveys', *Lancet* 2006; 368:733–43.

Ayres, M. et al (2001) *Arrests for recorded crime (notifiable offences) and the operation of certain police powers under PACE, England and Wales 2000/01*, Home Office Report 19/01, London: Home Office.

Ayres, M. and Murray, L. (2005) *Arrests for recorded crime (notifiable offences) and the operation of certain police powers under PACE, England and Wales 2004/5*, Home Office Report 21/05, London: Home Office.

Ayres, M., Murray, L. and Fiti, R. (2003) *Arrests for recorded crime (notifiable offences) and the operation of certain police powers under PACE, England and Wales 2002/3*, Home Office Report 17/03, London: Home Office.

Ayres, M., Perry, D. and Haywood, P. (2002) *Arrests for recorded crime (notifiable offences) and the operation of certain police powers under PACE, England and Wales 2001/2*, Home Office Report 12/02, London: Home Office.

Baker, C. (2007) 'Disabled children's experiences of permanency in the looked after system', *British Journal of Social Work*, vol 3, no 7, pp 1173-88.

Barn, R., Andrew, L. and Mantovani, N. (2005) *Life after care: The experiences of young people from different ethnic groups*, York: Joseph Rowntree Foundation.

Barnes, M., Butt, S. and Tomaszewski, W. (2008) *The dynamics of bad housing: The impact of bad housing on the living standards of children*, London: NatCen.

Barter, C. et al (2009) *Partner exploitation and violence in teenage intimate relationships*, Bristol/London: University of Bristol/NSPCC (www.nspcc.org.uk).

Beatbullying (2010) 'Bullying accounts for up to 44% of child suicides', Press release, 13 June.

Becker, J. and Roe, S. (2005) *Drug use among vulnerable groups of young people: Findings from the 2003 Offending Crime and Justice Survey*, Home Office Report 254, London: Home Office.

Belsky, J. (2006) 'Early childcare and early child development; major findings of the NICHD study of early child care', *European Journal of Developmental Psychology*, vol 3, no 1, pp 95-110.

Belsky, J., Barnes, J. and Melhuish, E. (2007) *The National Evaluation of Sure Start: Does area-based early intervention work?*, Bristol: The Policy Press.

Ben-Arieh, A. (2010) 'Developing indicators for child well-being in a changing context', in C. McAuley and W. Rose (eds) *Child well-being: Understanding children's lives*, London: Jessica Kingsley Publishers.

Berridge, D. (1997) *Foster care: A research review*, London: The Stationery Office.

Berridge, D., Dance, C., Beecham, J. and Field, S. (2008) *Educating difficult adolescents: Effective education for children in public care or with emotional and behavioural difficulties*, London: Jessica Kingsley Publishers.

Berthoud, R. (2001) 'Teenage births to ethnic minority women', *Population Trends 104*, London: The Stationery Office.

Better Regulation Task Force (2004) *The regulation of child employment*, London: Better Regulation Task Force.

Biehal, N., Clayden, J., Stein, M. and Wade, J. (1995) *Moving on: Young people and leaving care schemes*, London: HMSO.

Biehal, N., Ellison, S., Baker, C. and Sinclair, I. (2010) *Belonging and permanence: Outcomes in long-term foster care and adoption*, London: BAAF.

Blanden, J. and Machin, S. (2007) *Recent changes in intergenerational mobility in Britain*. Sutton Trust, London.

Blanden, J., Hansen, K. and Machin, S. (2010) The Economic Cost of Growing Up Poor: Estimating the GDP Loss Associated with Child Poverty, *Fiscal Studies*, 31, 3, 289-312.

Blum, R. W. and Nelson-Mmari, K. (2004) The health of young people in a global context. *Journal of Adolescent Health*, vol. 35:402-418.

Bolling, K., Grant, C., Hamlyn, B. and Thornton, A. (2007) *Infant Feeding Survey 2005*, NHS Information Centre (www.ic.nhs.uk/pubs/ifs2005).

Bradshaw, J. (1990) *Child poverty and deprivation in the UK*, London: National Children's Bureau.

Bradshaw, J. (ed) (2001) *Poverty: The outcomes for children*, London: Family Policy Studies Centre.

Bradshaw, J. (ed) (2002) *The well-being of children in the UK*, London: Save the Children.

Bradshaw, J. and Chzhen, Y. (2009) 'Lone parent families in comparative perspective', Paper for the 'One parent families in the family diversity context' Conference, University of Barcelona.

Bradshaw, J. and Finch, N. (2003) Overlaps in Dimensions of Poverty, *Jnl. Soc. Pol.*, 32, 4, 513-525.

Bradshaw, J. and Holmes, J. (2010) Child Poverty in the first five years of life in Hansen, K., Joshi, H. and Dex, S. (eds) *Children in the 21st Century: The first five years*, The UK Millennium Cohort Series 2, Bristol: The Policy Press 13-32.

Bradshaw, J. and Keung, A. (2011) 'Trends in child well-being in the United Kingdom', *Journal of Children's Services*, vol 6, no 1, pp 4-17.

Bradshaw, J. and Mayhew, E. (eds) (2005) *The well-being of children in the United Kingdom* (2nd edn), London: Save the Children.

Bradshaw, J. and Richardson, D. (2008) Does Child Income Poverty Measure Child Well-Being Internationally? *Social Policy and Society, Volume* 7, Issue 04, October 2008, pp 521-536.

Bradshaw, J. and Richardson, D. (2009) 'An index of child well-being in Europe', *Child Indicators Research*, vol 2, no 3, p 319 (www.springerlink.com/content/r5kq13v750q53782/?p=76a9631290a7476b9802650b9750b54d&pi=0%20).

Bradshaw, J., Finch, N. and Miles, J.N.V. (2005) 'Deprivation and variations in teenage conceptions and abortions in England', *Journal of Family Planning and Reproductive Healthcare*, vol 31, no 1, pp 15-19.

Bradshaw, J., Hoelscher, P. and Richardson, D. (2007a) 'An index of child well-being in the European Union 25', *Journal of Social Indicators Research*, vol 80, pp 133-77.

Bradshaw, J., Hoelscher, P. and Richardson, D. (2007b) *Comparing child well-being in OECD countries: Concepts and methods*, IWP 2006-03, Florence: UNICEF.

Bradshaw, J., Rees, G., Keung, A. and Goswami, H. (2010) 'The subjective well-being of children', in C. McAuley and W. Rose (eds) *Child well-being – Towards a better understanding of children's lives*, London: Jessica Kingsley Publishers, pp 181-204.

Bradshaw, J., Mayhew, E., Dex, S., Joshi, H. and Ward, K. (2005) 'Socioeconomic origins of parents and child poverty', in S. Dex and H. Joshi (eds) *Children of the 21st Century: from birth to nine months*, Bristol: The Policy Press, pp 71-108.

Bradshaw, J., Sturman, L., Vappula, H., Ager, R. and Wheater, R. (2007c) *Achievement of 15-year-olds in England: PISA 2006 National Report (OECD Programme for International Student Assessment)*, Slough: National Foundation for Educational Research.

Bradshaw, J., Sturman, L., Vappula, H., Ager, R. and Wheater, R. (2007e) *Student achievement in Northern Ireland: Results in Science, Mathematics and Reading among 15-year-olds from the OECD PISA 2006 Study (OECD Programme for International Student Assessment)*, Slough: National Foundation for Educational Research.

Bradshaw, J., Noble, M., Bloor, K., Huby, M., McLennan, D., Rhodes, D., Sinclair, I., and Wilkinson, K. (2009) A Child Well-Being Index at Small Area Level in England, *J. Child Indicators Research*, 2, 2, 201-219.

Brandon, M., Bailey, S. and Belderson, P. (2010) *Building on the learning from serious case reviews: A two-year analysis of child protection database notifications 2007-09*, DfE Research Brief RB040, London: Department for Education.

Brewer, M. and Joyce, R. (2010) *Child and working-age poverty 2010-2013*, IFS Briefing Note 115, London: Institute for Fiscal Studies.

Brewer, M., Goodman, A., Shaw, J. and Sibieta, L. (2009) *Poverty and inequality in the UK*, Commentary 109, London: IFS.

Briere, J. (1992) *Child abuse trauma*, Newbury Park, CA: Sage Publications.

British Household Panel Survey (www.iser.essex.ac.uk/survey/bhps).

Brooks, F., van der Sluijs, W., Klemera, E., Morgan, A., Magnusson, J., Gabhainn, S.N., Roberts, C., Smith, R. and Currie, C. (2009) *Young people's health in Great Britain and Ireland: Findings from the Health Behaviour in School-aged Children (HBSC) Survey, 2006* (www.hbsc.org/downloads/YoungPeoplesHealth_GB&Ireland.pdf).

Browne, J. and Levell, P. (2010) *The distributional effect of tax and benefit reforms to be introduced between June 2010 and April 2014: A revised assessment*, Briefing Note 108, London: Institute for Fiscal Studies (updates at www.ifs.org.uk/projects/346).

Bruegel, I. and Smith, J. (1999) *Taking risks: An analysis of the risks of homelessness for young people in London*, London: Safe in the City.

Bryson, C., Kazimirski, A. and Southwood, H. (2006) *Childcare and early years provision: A study of parents' use, views and experience*, DfES Research Report 723, Nottingham: DfES Publications.

Buchanan, A. (1999) 'Are care leavers significantly dissatisfied and depressed in adult life?', *Adoption & Fostering*, vol 23, no 4, pp 35-40.

Budd, T., Sharp, C. and Mayhew, P. (2005) *Offending in England and Wales: First results from the 2003 Crime and Justice Survey*, Home Office Research Study 275, London: Home Office.

Bunting, L., Webb, M.A. and Healy, J. (2010) 'In two minds? Parental attitudes toward physical punishment in the UK', *Children & Society*, vol 24, pp 359-70.

Burdette, H.L. and Whitaker, R.C. (2005) 'Resurrecting free play in young children: looking beyond fitness and fatness to attention, affiliation, and affect', *Archives of Pediatrics & Adolescent Medicine*, vol 159, pp 46-50 (www.childrenandnature.org/research/volumes/C16/16).

Burghes, L. (1994) *Lone parenthood and family disruption: The outcomes for children*, FPSC Occasional Paper no 18, London: Family Policy Studies Centre.

C4EO (Centre for Excellence and Outcomes in Children and Young People's Services) (2008) *Scoping review: Narrowing the gap in outcomes for children from the most excluded families through inclusive practice in early years settings*, London: C4EO.

Cameron, C. (2000) *Resolving childhood trauma. A long-term study of abuse survivors*, Thousand Oaks, CA: Sage Publications.

Cameron, C., Bennert, K., Simon, A. and Wigfall, V. (2007) *Using health, education, housing and other services: A study of care leavers and young people in difficulty*, Research brief, London: University of London, Institute of Education, Thomas Coram Research Unit.

Cashmore, J., Paxman, M. and Townsend, M. (2007) 'The educational outcomes of young people 4–5 years after leaving care: an Australian perspective', *Adoption & Fostering*, vol 31, no 1, pp 50-61.

Cawson, P. (2002) *Child maltreatment in the family*, London: NSPCC.

Cawson, P., Wattam, C., Brooker, S. and Kelly, G. (2000) *Child maltreatment in the UK: A study of the prevalence of child abuse and neglect*, London: NSPCC.

Caya, M.L. and Liem, J.H. (1998) 'The role of sibling support in high-conflict families', *American Journal of Orthopsychiatry*, vol 68, pp 327-33.

CEOP (Child Exploitation and Online Protection Centre) (2010) 'Key children's sites adopt ClickCEOP button as UK's Centre for Child Protection receives over 6,000 reports in a year', Press release, 5 November.

Cheung, S.Y. and Buchanan, A. (1997) 'Malaise scores in adulthood of children and young people who have been in care', *Journal of Child Psychology and Psychiatry*, vol 38, no 5, pp 575-80.

Children's Commissioner (2010) *Family perspectives on safeguarding and on relationships with children's services* (www.childrenscommissioner.gov.uk).

Children's Society, The (2006) *A good childhood? A question for our times*, London: The Children's Society.

Children's Society, The (2010) *Public attitudes to safeguarding children* (www. childrenssociety.org.uk).

Clarke, L., Bradshaw, J. and Williams, J. (2000) 'Family diversity and poverty and the mental wellbeing of young people', in H. Ryan and J. Bull (eds) *Changing families, changing communities: Researching health and well-being among children and young people*, London: Health Development Agency.

Clements, A., Fletcher, D., Parry-Langdon, N. (2008) *Three Years On: Survey of the Emotional Development and Well-being of Children and Young People*. Available at the ONS website at http://www.statistics.gov.uk/cci/article.asp?id=2063 (accessed on 06.01.2010).

CLG (Department for Communities and Local Government) (2006) *A decent home: Definition and guidance for implementation*, London: CLG.

CLG (2010a) *Local decisions: A fairer future for social housing*, London: CLG.

CLG (2010b) *English Housing Survey: Housing stock report, 2008*, London: CLG.

CLG (2010c) *English Housing Survey: Household report 2008-9*, London: CLG.

Coles, B., Godfrey, C., Keung, A., Parrott, S. and Bradshaw, J. (2010) *Estimating the lifetime cost of NEET: 16-18 year-olds not in education, employment or training*, York: University of York (www.york.ac.uk/depts/spsw/research/neet/).

Collishaw, S., Maughan, B., Goodman, R. and Pickles, A. (2004) 'Time trends in adolescent mental health'. *Journal of Child Psychological and Psychiatry*, vol. 45, 8:1350-62.

Conway, L. and Morgan, D. (2001) *Injury prevention*, London: BMJ Books.

Cornia, G. and Danziger, S. (1997) *Child poverty and deprivation in the industrialised countries 1994-1995*, Oxford: Clarendon Press.

Covell, K. and Howe, R.B. (2009) *Children, violence and families: Challenges for children's rights*, London: Jessica Kingsley Publishers.

Craig, T.K.J., Hodson, S., Woodward, S. and Richardson, S. (1996) *Off to a bad start: A longitudinial study of homeless young people in London*, London: Mental Health Foundation.

Craig, W. et al (2009) 'A cross-national profile of bullying and victimization among adolescents in 40 countries', *International Journal of Public Health*, vol 54, pp 216-24.

Creighton, S. (2004) *Prevalence and incidence of child abuse: International comparisons*, NSPCC Briefings, London: NSPCC.

Cross, E.J., Richardson, B., Douglas, T. and Vonkaenel-Flatt, J. (2009) *Virtual violence: Protecting children from cyberbullying*, London: Beatbullying.

Cullis, A. and Hansen, K. (2008) *Child development in the first three sweeps of the Millennium Cohort Study*, Research Report No DCSF-RW077, London: Institute of Education, University of London (http://publications.dcsf.gov.uk/eOrderingDownload/DCSF-RW077.pdf).

Cummins, R.A. (2009) 'Subjective wellbeing, homeostatically protected mood and depression: a synthesis', *Journal of Happiness Studies*, vol 10, no 6, pp 1-21.

Currie, C., Gabhainn, S.N., Godeau, E., Roberts, C., Smith, R., Currie, D., Picket, W., Richter, M., Morgan, A. and Barnekow, V. (2008a) *Inequalities in young people's health: Health Behaviour in School-aged Children (HBSC) study: International report from the 2005/2006 Survey*, Health Policy for Children and Adolescents, No 5, Copenhagen: World Health Organization, Regional Office for Europe (www.euro.who.int/en/what-we-do/health-topics/Life-stages/child-and-adolescent-health/publications2/2011/inequalities-in-young-peoples-health).

CYPU (Children and Young People's Unit) (2001) *Tomorrow's future: Building a strategy for children and young people*, London: CYPU.

Davies, P. (1999) *Learning and earning: The impact of paid employment on young people in full-time education*, London: Further Education Development Agency (www.eric.ed.gov/PDFS/ED439223.pdf).

Daycare Trust (2010) *The impact of the Comprehensive Spending Review on childcare*, Special edition, Daycare Trust policy e-bulletin (www.daycaretrust.org.uk/data/files/Policy/the_impact_of_the_spending_review_on_childcare.pdf).

DCMS (Department for Culture, Media and Sport) (2007) *Taking part: The National Survey of Culture, Leisure and Sport: Child Survey 2007*, London: DCMS.

DCSF (Department for Children, Schools and Families) (2007a) *The Children's Plan* (www.dcsf.gov.uk/childrensplan/).

DCSF (2007b) *Children and young people today: Evidence to support the development of the Children's Plan*, London: DfE (www.education.gov.uk/rsgateway/DB/RRP/u015312/index.shtml).

DCSF (2007/08/09) *Referrals, assessments and children and young people who are the subject of a child protection plan, England – Year ending 31 March 2007/2008/2009* (www.education.gov.uk).

DCSF (2008a) *Education and Skills Act 2008* (www.dcsf.gov.uk/educationandskills/).

DCSF (2008b) *The composition of schools in England*, Statistical Bulletin (www.education.gov.uk/rsgateway/DB/SBU/b000796/b02-2008.pdf).

DCSF (2009a) *The Children's Plan two years on: A progress report* (http://publications.education.gov.uk/default.aspx?PageFunction=productdetails&PageMode=publications&ProductId=DCSF-01162-2009&).

DCSF (2009b) *Participation in education, training and employment by 16-18 year-olds in England*, Statistical First Release, 16 June.

DCSF (2009c) *Special educational needs in England*, Statistical First Release (www.education.gov.uk/rsgateway/DB/SFR/s000852/sfr14-2009.pdf).

DCSF (2009d) *Pupil absence in schools in England, Autumn Term 2008 and Spring Term 2009*, Statistical First Release, 20 October.

DCSF (2009e) *Next steps for early learning and childcare: Building on the 10-year strategy*, Nottingham, DCSF Publications.

DCSF (2010a) *Level 2 and 3 attainment by young people in England measured using matched administrative data: Attainment by age 19 in 2009 (Provisional)* (www.education.gov.uk/rsgateway/DB/SFR/s000917/index.shtml).

DCSF (2010b) *Outcome indicators for children looked after: Twelve months to 30 September 2009, England*, Statistical First Release, London: DCSF/Office for National Statistics.

Dearden, C. and Becker, S. (2004) *Young carers in the UK: The 2004 report*, London: Carers UK (https://dspace.lboro.ac.uk/dspacejspui/bitstream/2134/627/3/YCReport2004%25255B1%25255D.pdf).

Defries, M. (2010) 'Pledge to extend free entitlement for nursery education to 15 hours is upheld', *Nursery World*, 7 June.

DENI (Department of Education Northern Ireland) and NISRA (Northern Ireland Statistics and Research Agency) (2009) *Attendance at grant-aided primary, post-primary and special schools 2008/09 – Summary statistics*, Statistical First Release (www.deni.gov.uk/statistical_first_release_school_attendance_2008_09.pdf).

Department of Education (2010) *Enrolments at Schools and in Funded Pre-school education in Northern Ireland* (http://www.equality.nisra.gov.uk/Percentage%20of%20child%20with%20special%20needs%20education%20schools%20and%20funded%20preschool%20edu%20centres.xls).

DfE (Department for Education) (2010a) *National curriculum tests and teacher assessments at Key Stage 2 and 3 in England, 2010 (Provisional)*, Statistical First Release (www.dcsf.gov.uk/rsgateway/DB/SFR/s000949/index.shtml).

DfE (2010b) *Permanent and fixed period exclusions from schools and exclusion appeals in England, 2008/09*, Statistical First Release (www.education.gov.uk/rsgateway/index.shtml)

DfE (2010c) *Participation in education, training and employment by 16-18 year olds in England* (www.education.gov.uk/rsgateway/DB/SFR/s000938/index.shtml).

DfE (2010d) *GCSE and equivalent results in England 2009/10 (Provisional)*, Statistical First Release (www.education.gov.uk/rsgateway/DB/SFR/s000963/sfr30-2010.pdf).

DfE (2010e) *Children with special educational needs 2010: An analysis* (www.education.gov.uk/rsgateway/DB/STA/t000965/osr25-2010.pdf).

DfE (2010f) *Referrals, assessments and children who were the subject of a child protection plan (2009-10 Children in need census, Provisional)* (www.education.gov.uk).

DfES (Department for Education and Skills) (2005) *Youth matters*, Cm 6629 (http://publications.education.gov.uk/eOrderingDownload/Cm6629.pdf).

DfES (2006) *Youth matters: Next steps* (www.connexions-gmerseyside.co.uk/media/loader.cfm?csModule=security/getfile&pageid=12371).

DfT (2010b) *Child casualties in reported road accidents*, Fact Sheet no 5 (www.dft.gov.uk/pgr/statistics/datatablespublications/accidents/casualtiesgbar/suppletablesfactsheets/childcasualties2008.pdf).

DH (Department of Health) (2003) Health Survey of England 2002 http://www.archive2.official-documents.co.uk/document/deps/doh/survey02/hcyp/hcyp01.htm)

DH (2006) Health Survey of England 2004 (http://www.ic.nhs.uk/webfiles/publications/healthsurvey2004ethnicfull/HealthSurveyforEngland Vol1_210406_PDF.pdf)

DH (2007) Infant feeding survey 2005: Early results (http://www.ic.nhs.uk/webfiles/publications/breastfeed2005/InfantFeedingSurvey190506_PDF.pdf)

DH (2010) *Breastfeeding initiation and prevalence at 6-8 weeks*, Statistical Release (www.dh.gov.uk/en/Publicationsandstatistics/Publications/PublicationsStatistics/DH_116060).

DH and DCSF (2009) *Healthy lives, brighter futures: The strategy for children and young people's health* (www.dh.gov.uk/prod_consum_dh/groups/dh_digitalassets/documents/digitalasset/dh_094397.pdf).

Diener, E. and Lucas, R.E. (1998) 'Personality and subjective well-being', in D. Kahneman, E. Diener and N. Schwarz (eds) *Hedonic psychology: Scientific perspectives on enjoyment, suffering, and well-being*, New York: Russell Sage.

Diener, E., Suh, E.M., Lucas, R.E. and Smith, H.L. (1999) 'Subjective wellbeing: three decades of progress', *Psychology Bulletin*, vol 125, no 2, pp 276-302.

Dillon, L., Chivite-Matthews, N., Grewal, I., Brown, R., Webster, S., Weddell, E., Brown, G. and Smith, N. (2007) *Risk, protective factors and resilience to drug use: Identifying resilient young people and learning from their experiences*, London: Home Office.

Directgov (2010a) *Click Clever, Click Safe* (http://clickcleverclicksafe.direct.gov.uk/index.html).

Directgov (2010b) *Child employment* (www.direct.gov.uk/en/Parents/ParentsRights/DG_4002945).

Dixon, J. (2008) 'Young people leaving care: health, well-being and outcomes', *Child & Family Social Work*, vol 13, no 2, pp 207-17.

Dixon, J. and Stein, M. (2002) *A study of throughcare and aftercare services in Scotland, Scotland's children: Children (Scotland) Act 1995*, Research Findings No 3, Edinburgh: Scottish Executive.

Dixon, J. and Stein, M. (2005) *Leaving care, throughcare and aftercare in Scotland*, London: Jessica Kingsley Publishers.

Dixon, J., Wade, J., Byford, S., Weatherly, H. and Lee, J. (2006) *Young people leaving care: A study of costs and outcomes*, York: Social Work Research and Development Unit, University of York.

Dobash, R.P. and Dobash, R.E. (2004) 'Women's violence to men in intimate relationships', *British Journal of Criminology*, vol 44, pp 324-49.

Dorling, D. (2010) *Injustice: Why social inequality persists*, Bristol: The Policy Press.

Downes, D. and Rock, P. (2003) *Understanding deviance* (4th edn), Oxford: Oxford University Press.

Drake, B. and Pandey, S. (1996) 'Understanding the relationship between neighbourhood poverty and specific types of child maltreatment', *Child Abuse and Neglect*, vol 20, no 11, pp 1103-18.

Duncan, S. (2007) 'What's the problem with teenage parents? And what's the problem with policy?', *Critical Social Policy*, vol 27, no 3, pp 307-34.

Dunn, J. and Deater-Deckard, K. (2001) *Children's views of their changing families*, York: York Publishing Services for the Joseph Rowntree Foundation.

Dunn, J., Slomkowski, C. and Beardsall, L. (1994) 'Sibling relationships from the preschool period through middle childhood and early adolescence', *Developmental Psychology*, vol 30, pp 315-24.

DWP (Department for Work and Pensions) (2007) *Opportunity for all: Indicators update 2007*, October, London: DWP (www.dwp.gov.uk/docs/ opportunityforall2007.pdf).

DWP (Department for Work and Pensions)(2008) *UK National Report on Strategies for Social Protection and Social Inclusion 2008-2010* (http://www.dwp.gov.uk/ docs/uknationalstrategyreport12-9-08.pdf)

DWP (2010) Households Below Average Income: An analysis of the income distribution, London: DWP (http://campaigns.dwp.gov.uk/asd/hbai/ hbai_2009/pdf_files/full_hbai10.pdf)

EC (European Commission) (2010) *The social situation in the EU 2009*, Brussels: EC.

Edgar, B. (2009) *European review of statistics on homelessness*, Brussels: FEANTSA.

Ehtisham, S., Barrett, T.G. and Shaw, N.J. (2000) 'Type 2 diabetes mellitus in UK children – an emerging problem', *Diabetic Medicine*, vol 17, no 2, pp 867-71.

Equality and Human Rights Commission (2010) *How fair is Britain?* (www. equalityhumanrights.com).

Equalities Review, The (2007) *Fairness and freedom: The final report of The Equalities Review*, London: The Stationery Office.

Ermisch, J., Francesconi, M. and Pevalin, D.J. (2001) *The outcomes for children of poverty*, DWP Research Report Number 158, Leeds: Corporate Document Services (http://campaigns.dwp.gov.uk/asd/asd5/158summ.asp).

Esping-Andersen, G. and Sarasa, S. (2003) 'The generational conflict reconsidered', *Journal of European Social Policy*, vol 12, pp 5-21.

ESRC (Economic and Social Research Council) (2010) *Britain in 2011: The state of the nation*, Swindon: ESRC.

EU-SILC (European Union Statistics on Income and Living Conditions) (http:// epp.eurostat.ec.europa.eu/portal/page/portal/microdata/eu_silc).

Evangelou, M., Brooks, G., Smith, S. and Jennings, D. (2005) *Birth to school study: A longitudinal evaluation of the Peers Early Education Partnership (PEEP) 1998-2005*, London: Department for Education and Skills (www.dfes.gov.uk/research/data/ uploadfiles/SSU2005SF017.pdf).

Evangelou, M., Sylva, K., Kyriacou, M., Wild, M. and Glenny, G. (2009) *Early years learning and development literature review*, DCSF Research Report 176, London: Department for Children, Schools and Families.

Farmer, C. (2005) *2003 Home Office Citizenship Survey: Top-level findings from the Children's and Young People's Survey*, London: Home Office.

Farrington, D. and Ttofi, M.M. (2009) *School-based programs to reduce bullying and victimization*, The Campbell Collaboration (www.ncjrs.gov/pdffiles1/nij/grants/229377.pdf).

FEANTSA (2007) *Child homelessness in Europe: An overview of emerging trends*, Brussels: FEANTSA.

Featherstone, B. and Evans, H. (2004) *Children experiencing maltreatment: Who do they turn to?*, London: NSPCC.

Finkelhor, D. and Jones, L. (2006) 'Why have child maltreatment and child victimization declined?', *Journal of Social Issues*, vol 62, no 4, pp 685-716.

Finkelhor, D., Ormrod, R.K. and Turner, H.A. (2007a) 'Poly-victimisation: a neglected component in child victimisation', *Child Abuse and Neglect*, vol 31, no 1, pp 7-26.

Finkelhor, D., Ormrod, R.K. and Turner, H.A. (2007b) 'Revictimisation patterns in a national longitudinal sample of children and youth', *Child Abuse and Neglect*, vol 31, pp 479-502.

Fitzpatrick, S., Pleace, N., Stephens, M. and Quilgars, D. (2009) 'Introduction: An overview of homelessness in the UK', in S. Fitzpatrick, D. Quilgars and N. Pleace, *Homelessness in the UK: Problems and solutions*, Coventry: Chartered Institute of Housing, pp 1-20.

Flatley, J., Kershaw, C., Smith, K., Chaplin, R. and Moon, D. (2010) *Crime in England and Wales, 2009/10. Findings from the British Crime Survey and police recorded crime* (2nd edn), Home Office Report 12/10, London: Home Office.

Ford, T., Vostanis, P., Meltzer, H. and Goodman, R. (2007) 'Psychiatric disorder among British children looked after by local authorities: comparison with children living in private households', *The British Journal of Psychiatry*, vol 190, pp 319-25.

Fuller, E. and Sanchez, M. (2010) *Smoking, drinking and drug use among young people in England 2009*, NHS Information Centre for Health and Social Care.

Furedi, F. (2001) *Paranoid parenting: Abandon your anxieties and be a good parent*, London: Allen Lane.

General Lifestyle Survey 2008 (www.statistics.gov.uk/downloads/theme_compendia/GLF08/GeneraLifestyleSurvey2008.pdf).

Gill, T. (2007) *No fear: Growing up in a risk averse society*, London: Calouste Gulbenkian Foundation.

Gillham, B., Tanner, G., Cheyne, B., Freeman, I., Rooney, M. and Lambie, A. (1998) 'Unemployment rates, single parent density and indices of child poverty: their relationship to different categories of child abuse and neglect', *Child Abuse and Neglect*, vol 22, pp 79-90.

GLA (Greater London Authority) (2001a) *Homelessness in London, 30*, GLA Housing and Homelessness Team (www.london.gov.uk).

GLA (2001b) *Homelessness in London, 28*, GLA Housing and Homelessness Team (www.london.gov.uk).

Gleave, J. (2009) *Children's time to play: A literature review*, London: National Children's Bureau (www.playday.org.uk).

Green, H., McGinnity, A., Meltzer, H., Ford, T. and Goodman, R. (2005) *Mental health of children and young people in Great Britain, 2004* (www.ic.nhs.uk/webfiles/publications/mentalhealth04/MentalHealthChildrenYoungPeopleSummary310805_PDF.pdf).

Greydanus, D.E. and Calles, J. (2007) Suicide in children and adolescents, *Primary Care*, vol. 34: 259-273.

GRO (General Register Office) for Scotland (2010) *Vital events reference tables 2008* (http://www.gro-scotland.gov.uk/statistics/theme/vital-events/general/ref-tables/2009/index.html).

Hansen, K. (2010) 'Teacher assessment of the first year at school', in K. Hansen, H. Joshi and S. Dex, *Children of the 21st century: The first five years*, Bristol: The Policy Press, pp 201-15.

Hansen, K. and Hawkes, D. (2009) 'Early childcare and child development', *Journal of Social Policy*, vol 38, no 2, pp 211-39.

Hansen, K. and Jones, M. (2010) 'Age 5 cognitive development in England', *Child Indicators Research*, vol 3, pp 105-26.

Hawthorne, J., Jessop, J., Pryor, J. and Richards, M. (2003) *Supporting children through family change: A review of interventions and services for children of divorcing and separating parents*, York: York Publishing Services for the Joseph Rowntree Foundation.

HM Government (2010) *Working together to safeguard children: A guide to inter-agency working to safeguard and promote the welfare of children*, London: Department for Education.

HM Treasury (2004) *Choice for parents, the best start for children: A ten-year strategy for childcare*, London: The Stationery Office (www.everychildmatters.gov.uk/_files/C7A546CB4579620B7381308E1C161A9D.pdf).

HM Treasury (2010a) *Public expenditure statistical analysis 2010*, Cm 7890, London: The Stationery Office.

HM Treasury (2010b) *Comprehensive Spending Review 2010*, London: The Stationery Office.

HM Treasury and DCSF (2007) *Aiming high for young people: A ten-year strategy for positive activities*, London: The Stationery Office (http://publications.education.gov.uk/default.aspx?PageFunction=productdetails&PageMode=publications&ProductId=PU214).

Hoare, J. and Moon, D. (2010) *Drug misuse declared: Findings from the 2009/10 British Crime Survey England and Wales*, Home Office Statistical Bulletin 13/10, London: Home Office.

Hobbs, S. and McKechnie, J. (1997) *Child employment in Britain: A social and psychological analysis*, Edinburgh: The Stationery Office.

Hobbs, S., McKechnie, J. and Anderson, S. (2007) 'Making child employment in Britain more visible', *Critical Social Policy*, vol 27, no 3, pp 415-25.

Hobcraft, J.N. and Kiernan, K.E. (2010) 'Predictive factors from age 3 and infancy for poor child outcomes at age 5 relating to children's development, behaviour and health: evidence from the Millenium Cohort Study', *Social Science and Medicine*, vol 69, no 10, pp 1476-83.

Hojer, I., Johansson, H., Hill, M., Cameron, C. and Jackson, S. (2008) *The educational pathways of young people from a public care background in five EU countries*, London: University of London, Institute of Education, Thomas Coram Research Unit.

Home Office (2003) *Recorded crime statistics 1898-2001/02* (http://rds.homeoffice. gov.uk/rds).

Home Office (2010) *Recorded crime statistics 2002/03-2008/09* (http://rds. homeoffice.gov.uk/rds).

Hooper, C.-A. (2002) 'The maltreatment of children', in J. Bradshaw (ed) *The well-being of children in the UK*, London/York: Save the Children/University of York, pp 103-21.

Hooper, C.-A. (2005) 'Child maltreatment', in J. Bradshaw and E. Mayhew (eds) *The well-being of children in the UK 2005 (volume 2)*, London/York: Save the Children/University of York, pp 182-201.

Hooper, C.-A. (2010) 'Gender, maltreatment and young people's offending', in B. Featherstone, C.-A. Hooper, J. Scourfield and J. Taylor (eds) *Gender and child welfare*, Chichester: Wiley-Blackwell, pp 61-93.

Hooper, C.-A., Gorin, S., Cabral, C. and Dyson, C. (2007) *Living with hardship 24/7: The diverse experiences of families in poverty in England*, London: The Frank Buttle Trust.

Howard, D. (2010) 'Cameron warns on child carer cuts', BBC News, 16 November (www.bbc.co.uk/news/education-11757907).

HPA (Health Protection Agency) (2010a) NOIDs reports (www.hpa.org.uk/ Topics/InfectiousDiseases/InfectionsAZ/NotificationsOfInfectiousDiseases/ NOIDSReportsAndTables/).

HPA (2010b) *STI annual data tables* (www.hpa.org.uk/stiannualdatatables).

Hunnicutt, G. and LaFree, G. (2008) 'Reassessing the structural covariates of cross-national infant homicide victimization', *Homicide Studies*, vol 12, pp 46-66.

IDF (International Diabetes Federation) (2006) *Diabetes atlas* (3rd edn), Brussels: IDF.

Institute of Education (2010) *Class has much bigger effect on white pupils' results*, 3 September, London: Institute of Education (www.ioe.ac.uk/newsEvents/43530. html).

Ip, S., Chung, M., Raman, G., Chew, P., Magula, N., DeVine, D. et al (2007) *Breastfeeding and maternal and infant health outcomes in developed countries*, Evidence Report/Technology Assessment No 153, Boston, MA: Agency for Healthcare Research and Quality, US Dept of Health and Human Services.

ISC (Independent Schools Council) (2010) *Pupil numbers* (www.isc.co.uk/ FactsFigures_PupilNumbers.htm).

Jackson, S., Ajayi, S. and Quigley, M. (2003) *By degrees: The first year: From care to university*, London: National Children's Bureau.

Jackson, S., Ajayi, S. and Quigley, M. (2005) *Going to university from care: Report by the By Degrees Action Research Project*, London: Institute of Education.

James, A. (2010) *School bullying*, NSPCC Research Briefing (www.nspcc.org.uk).

Jenny, C. and Isaac, R. (2006) 'The relation between child death and child maltreatment', *Archives of Disease in Childhood*, vol 91, pp 265-9.

Joyce, R., Muriel, A., Phillips, D. and Sibieta, L. (2010) *Poverty and inequality in UK: 2010*, IFS Commentary C116, London: Institute for Fiscal Studies.

Kazimirski, A., Smith, R., Butt, S., Ireland, E. and Lloyd, E. (2008) *Childcare and Early Years Survey 2007: Parents' use, views and experiences*, DCSF Research Report RR025, Nottingham: DfES Publications (http://publications.education.gov.uk/eOrderingDownload/DCSF-RR025.pdf).

Kendall, S., Rodger, J. and Palmer, H. (2010) *The use of whole family assessment to identify the needs of families with multiple problems*, Research Report DfE-RR045, London: Department for Education.

Kiernan, K. and Smith, K. (2003) 'Unmarried parenthood: new insights from the Millennium Cohort Study', *Population Trends 114*, pp 26-33.

Kramer, M.S. et al (2008) 'Breastfeeding and child cognitive development: new evidence from a large randomized trial', *Archives of General Psychiatry*, vol 65, no 5, p 578-84 (http://archpsyc.ama-assn.org/cgi/content/short/65/5/578).

Kumar, V. (1995) *Poverty and inequality in the UK: The effects on children*, London: National Children's Bureau.

Lai, C.K.W., Beasley, R., Crane, J., Foliaki, S., Shah, J., Weiland, S. and ISAAC Phase Three Study Group (2009) 'Global variation in the prevalence and severity of asthma symptoms: Phase Three of the International Study of Asthma and Allergies in Childhood (ISAAC)', *Thorax*, vol 64, pp 476-83.

Layard, R. (2005) *Happiness: Lessons from a new science*, London: Penguin.

Layard, R. and Dunn, J. (2009) *A good childhood: Searching for values in a competitive age*, London: Penguin and The Children's Society.

Lee, E. et al (2004) *A matter of choice? Explaining national variations in teenage abortion and motherhood*, York: Joseph Rowntree Foundation.

Lenhart, A. and Madden, M. (2007) *Social networking websites and teens: An overview* (www.pewinternet.org/~/media//Files/Reports/2007/PIP_SNS_Data_Memo_Jan_2007.pdf.pdf).

Lester, S. and Russell, W. (2008) *Play for a change: Play, policy and practice: A review of contemporary perspectives* (www.playengland.org.uk/resources/play-for-a-change--play,-policy-and-practice-a-review-of-contemporary-perspectives).

Levin, K.A., Currie, C. and Muldoon, J. (2009) 'Mental well-being and subjective health of 11- to 15 year-old boys and girls in Scotland, 1994-2006', *European Journal of Public Health*, vol 19, no 6, pp 605-10 (www.eurpub.oxfordjounals.org).

Licence, K. (2004) 'Promoting and protecting the health of children and young people', *Child: Care, Health and Development*, vol 30, no 6, pp 623-35, November.

Livingstone, S. (2007) 'From family television to bedroom culture: young people's media at home', in E. Devereux (ed) *Media studies: Key issues and debates*, London: Sage Publications (http://eprints.lse.ac.uk/2772).

Livingstone, S. and Bober, M. (2005) *UK children go online: Final report of key project findings*, London: LSE Research Online (http://eprints.lse.ac.uk/399/1/UKCGO_Final_report.pdf).

Livingstone, S. and Brake, D.R. (2010) 'On the rapid rise of social networking sites: new findings and policy implications', *Children & Society*, vol 24, pp 75-83.

Lloyd, C. (1998) 'Risk factors for problem drug use: identifying vulnerable groups', *Drugs: Education, Prevention and Policy*, vol 5, no 3, pp 217-32.

Lonne, B., Parton, N., Thompson, J. and Harries, M. (2008) *Reforming child protection*, London: Routledge.

Macdonald, G. and Macdonald, K. (2010) 'Safeguarding: a case for intelligent risk management', *British Journal of Social Work*, vol 40, pp 1174-91.

Macfarlane, A., Stafford, M. and Moser, K. (2004) 'Social inequalities', in *The health of children and young people*, London: Office for National Statistics.

Mackett, R., Banister, D., Batty, M., Einon, D., Brown, B., Gong, Y., Kitazawa, K., Marshall, S. and Paskins, J. (2007a) *Final report on 'Children's Activities, Perceptions and Behaviour in the Local Environment (CAPABLE)'*, London: University College London (www.casa.ucl.ac.uk/capableproject/download/CAPABLE_finalReport.pdf).

Mackett, R., Brown, B., Gong, Y., Kitazawa, K. and Paskinis, J. (2007b) *Setting children free: Children's independent movement in the local environment*, London: Centre for Advanced Spatial Analysis, University College London (http://eprints.ucl.ac.uk/3474/).

Macmillan, H.L., Wathen, C.N., Barlow, J., Fergusson, D.M., Leventhal, J.M. and Taussig, H.M. (2009) 'Interventions to prevent child maltreatment and associated impairment', *The Lancet*, 17 January, vol 373, no 9659, pp 250-66.

Mallon, J. (2005) 'Academic underachievement and exclusion of people who have been looked-after in local authority care', *Research in Post-compulsory Education*, vol 10, no 1, pp 83-103.

Marmot Review (2010) *Fairer society, healthy lives: Strategic review of health inequalities in England post 2010* (www.marmotreview.org/).

Marsh, A., Gordon, D., Pantazis, C. and Heslop, P. (1999) *Home sweet home? The impact of poor housing on health*, Bristol: The Policy Press.

Matthews, H. (2001) *Children and community regeneration: Creating better neighbourhoods*, London: Save the Children.

Maughan, B., Collishaw, S., Meltzer, H. and Goodman, R. (2008) 'Recent trends in UK child and adolescent mental health', *Social Psychiatry and Psychiatric Epidemiology*, vol 43, pp 305-10.

Mayhew, E. and Bradshaw, J. (2005) 'Mothers, babies and the risks of poverty', *Poverty*, vol 121, pp 13-16.

Mayhew, E., Finch, N., Beresford, B. and Keung, A. (2005) 'Children's time and space', in J. Bradshaw and E. Mayhew (eds) *The well-being of children in the UK* (2nd edn), London: Save the Children, pp 161-81.

Mayor of London (2007) *The state of London's children report*, London: Greater London Authority (http://legacy.london.gov.uk/mayor/children/docs/solc-main-2007.pdf).

McAuley, C. and Rose, W. (eds) (2010) *Child well-being: Understanding children's lives*, London: Jessica Kingsley Publishers.

McKechnie, J. and Hobbs, S. (2001) 'Work and education: are they compatible for children and adolescents?', in P. Mizen, C. Pole and A. Bolton (eds) *Hidden hands: International perspectives on children's work and labour*, London: RoutledgeFalmer, pp 9-23.

Meltzer H., Gatward R., Goodman R. & Ford T. (2000) *Mental Health of Children and Adolescents in Great Britain*. London: The Stationery Office.

Meltzer, H., Gatward, R., Corbin, T., Goodman, R. and Ford, T. (2003) *The mental health of young people looked after by local authorities in England*, London: Office for National Statistics.

Meltzer, H., Gatward, R., Corbin, T., Goodman, R. and Ford, T. (2004a) *The mental health of young people looked after by local authorities in Wales*, London: Office for National Statistics.

Meltzer, H., Gatward, R., Corbin, T., Goodman, R. and Ford, T. (2004b) *The mental health of young people looked after by local authorities in Scotland*, London: Office for National Statistics.

Merdinger, J.M. and Hines, A.M. (2005) 'Pathways to college for former foster youth: understanding factors that contribute to educational success', *Child Welfare League of America*, vol 84, no 6, pp 867-96.

Mhonda, J. (2007) *Reflections on Childhood*, London: GfK Social Research.

Ministry of Justice (2007) *Arrests for recorded crime (notifiable offences) and the operation of certain police powers under PACE, England and Wales 2005/6*, London: Ministry of Justice.

Ministry of Justice (2008) *Arrests for recorded crime (notifiable offences) and the operation of certain police powers under PACE, England and Wales 2006/7*, London: Ministry of Justice.

Ministry of Justice (2009) *Criminal statistics, England and Wales, Statistical bulletin 2008*, London: Ministry of Justice.

Mixmag (2010) *The Mixmag Drug Survey*, February, pp 44-53.

Monteith, M. and McLaughlin, E. (2004) *Children and severe poverty in Northern Ireland*, Belfast: Save the Children.

Mooney, A., Oliver, C. and Smith, M. (2009) *Impact of family breakdown on children's well-being: Evidence review*, DCSF Research Report RR113, London: Department for Children, Schools and Families.

MORI (2009) *Youth Survey 2008: Young people in mainstream education*, London: Youth Justice Board.

Munro, E. (2010a) 'Learning to reduce risk in child protection', *British Journal of Social Work*, vol 40, pp 1135-51.

Munro, E. (2010b) *Munro Review of child protection, Part One: A systems analysis*, London: Department for Education (www.education.gov.uk/munroreview/).

Murray, L. and Fiti, R. (2004) *Arrests for recorded crime (notifiable offences) and the operation of certain police powers under PACE, England and Wales 2003/4*, Home Office Report 18/04, London: Home Office.

NACRO (2005) *A handbook on reducing offending by looked-after children*, London: NACRO.

Neale, J. (2006) 'Children, crime and drug use', in J. Bradshaw (ed) *The wellbeing of children in the UK* (2nd edn), London: Save the Children.

NFER (National Foundation for Educational Research) (2010) *Children's online risks and safety: A review of the available evidence*, Prepared for the UK Council for Child Internet Safety (www.education.gov.uk/ukccis/).

NHS Information Centre (2009) *Statistics on smoking, England 2009* (www.ic.nhs.uk/pubs/smoking09).

NHS Information Centre (2010a) *National diabetes paediatric report 2008-09* (www.ic.nhs.uk/services/national-clinical-audit-support-programme-ncasp/audit-reports/diabetes).

NHS Information Centre (2010b) *Hospital activity: Hospital Episode Statistics 2009/10* (www.ic.nhs.uk/statistics-and-data-collections/hospital-care/hospital-activity-hospital-episode-statistics--hes).

NHS Information Centre (2010c) *NHS immunisation statistics, England, 2009/10* (www.ic.nhs.uk/statistics-and-data-collections/health-and-lifestyles/immunisation/nhs-immunisation-statistics-england-2009-10).

NHS Information Centre (2010d) *Health Survey for England* (www.ic.nhs.uk/statistics-and-data-collections/health-and-lifestyles-related-surveys/health-survey-for-england).

Nicoll, A., Ellimna, D. and Begg, N.T. (1989) 'Immunisation: causes of failure and strategies and tactics for success', *British Medical Journal*, vol 299, pp 808-12.

NNI (Neighbourhood Nurseries Initiative) Research Team (2007) *National Evaluation of the Neighbourhood Nursery Initiative: Integrated report*, London: Department for Education and Skills (www.ifs.org.uk/docs/nni_integrated.pdf).

O'Brien, M., Jones, D., Sloan, D. and Rustin, M. (2000) 'Children's independent spatial mobility in the urban public realm', *Childhood*, vol 7, no 3, pp 253-77.

ODPM (Office of the Deputy Prime Minister) (2002) *Homelessness code of guidance for local authorities*, London: ODPM.

ODPM (2003) *Sustainable communities: Building for the future*, London: ODPM.

OECD (2001) *Knowledge and skills for life: First results from the OECD programme for international student assessment (PISA) 2000*, Paris: OECD (http://www.oecd.org/dataoecd/44/53/33691596.pdf)

OECD (Organisation for Economic Co-operation and Development) (2007) *PISA 2006: Science competencies for tomorrow's world*, Paris: OECD.

OECD (2008) *Growing unequal? Income distribution and poverty in OECD countries*, Paris: OECD.

OECD (2009b) *Doing better for children* (www.oecd.org/els/social/childwellbeing).

OECD (2004) *Learning for tomorrow's world: First results from PISA 2003*. Paris: OECD. http://www.oecd.org/dataoecd/1/60/34002216.pdf

OECD (2010) *Education at a glance 2009: OECD indicators* (www.oecd.org/edu/eag2009).

OECD (2010) *OECD family database* (www.oecd.org/els/social/family/database).

OECD (2010a) *Health data 2010: Statistics and indicators* (www.oecd.org/health/healthdata).

OECD (2010b) IRTAD (International Road Traffic and Accident Database) (http://internationaltransportforum.org/irtad/pdf/risk.pdf).

Ofsted (2008) *TellUs3 national report* (www.ofsted.gov.uk/Ofsted-home/Publications-and-research/Browse-all-by/Documents-by-type/Statistics/Other-statistics/TellUs3-National-Report/(language)/eng-GB).

One Parent Families Scotland (2009) *Briefing for Welfare Reform Bill* (www.opfs.org.uk/policy/briefings/welfare-reform).

ONS (Office for National Statistics) (1998) *Key health statistics from general practice 1996*, Series MB6 No 1, London: ONS.

ONS (2003) *Census 2001: National report for England and Wales*, London: The Stationery Office.

ONS (2008) *Non-resident parental contact, 2007/08*, Omnibus Survey Report No 38 (www.statistics.gov.uk/downloads/theme_social/parentalcontact2007-08.pdf).

ONS (2009a) *Contraception and Sexual Health Surveys, 2000 to 2008/09* (www.statistics.gov.uk/downloads/theme_health/contra2008-9.pdf).

ONS (2009b) *Focus on children and young people* (www.statistics.gov.uk/StatBase/Product.asp?vlnk=15232).

ONS (2010a) *Child mortality statistics* (www.statistics.gov.uk/downloads/ theme health/child-mortality/Table1.xls and www.statistics.gov.uk/downloads/theme_health/child-mortality/Table2.xls).

ONS (2010b) 'Infant and perinatal mortality in England and Wales by social and biological factors 2009', *Statistical Bulletin* (www.statistics.gov.uk/pdfdir/ipm1110.pdf).

ONS (2010c) *Regional Trends: Online tables*, Table 10.12 (www.statistics.gov.uk/StatBase/Product.asp?vlnk=14161).

ONS (2010d) *Social Trends 40*, London: Palgrave Macmillan.

ONS (2010e) *Population estimates for UK, England and Wales, Scotland and Northern Ireland* (www.statistics.gov.uk/statbase/Product.asp?vlnk=15106)

Oroyemi, P., Damioli, G., Barnes, M. and Crosier, T. (2009) *Understanding the risks of social exclusion across the life course: Families with Children* Social Exclusion Task Force, Cabinet Office (http://www.lawcentres.org.uk/uploads/SEU_Risks_Families_and_Children.pdf)

O'Sullivan, A. and Westerman, R. (2007) 'Closing the gap: investigating the barriers to educational achievement for looked-after children', *Adoption & Fostering*, vol 31, no 1, pp 13–20.

Parke, R.D. and Buriel, R. (1998) 'Socialisation in the family: ethnic and ecological perspectives', in W. Damon (series ed) and N. Eisenberg (vol ed) *Handbook of child psychology: Vol 3: Social, emotional and personality development* (5th edn), New York: John Wiley & Sons.

Patterson, C.C., Dahlquist, G.G., Gyürüs, E., Green, A., Soltész, G. and EURODIAB Study Group (2009) 'Incidence trends for childhood type 1 diabetes in Europe during 1989-2003 and predicted new cases 2005-20: a multicentre prospective registration study', *The Lancet*, vol 373, no 9680, pp 2027-33.

Patterson, G.R. (1986) 'The contribution of siblings to training for fighting: a microsocial analysis', in D. Olweus, J. Block and M. Radke-Yarrow (eds) *Development of anti-social and pro-social behaviour*, New York: Academic Press.

Percy, A., McAlister, S., Higgins, K., McCrystal, P. and Thornton, M. (2005) 'Response consistency in young adolescents' drug use self-reports: a recanting rate analysis', *Addiction*, vol 100, pp 189-96.

Pickles, E. (2010) Speech to the Local Government Association Annual Conference, 7 July.

Platt, S.D., Martin, C.I., Hunt, S.M. and Lewis, C.W. (1989) 'Damp housing, mould growth and symptomatic health state', *British Medical Journal*, vol 298, pp 1673-8.

Play England (2009) *Playday 2009 opinion poll summary* (www.playday.org.uk/pdf/Playday-2009-opinion-poll-summary.pdf).

Pleace, N., Fitzpatrick, S., Johnsen, S., Quilgars, D. and Sanderson, D. (2008) *Statutory homelessness in England: The experiences of families and 16-17 year olds*, London: Department for Communities and Local Government.

Povey, D. (ed) and Hand, T., Singh, A. and Mulchandani, R. (2010) *Police powers and procedures, England and Wales 2008/9*, Home Office Report 06/10, London: Home Office.

Povey, D. and Smith K. (eds) and Hand, T. and Dodd, L. (2009) *Police powers and procedures, England and Wales 2007/8*, Home Office Report 07/09, London: Home Office.

Pritchard, C. and Williams, R. (2009) 'Does social work make a difference? A controlled study of former "looked-after children" and "excluded-from-school" adolescents now men aged 16-24 subsequent offences, being victims of crime and suicide', *Journal of Social Work*, vol 9, no 3, pp 285-307.

Pritchard, C. and Williams, R. (2010) 'Comparing possible "child-abuse-related-deaths" in England and Wales with the major developed countries 1974-2006: signs of progress?', *British Journal of Social Work*, vol 40, no 6, pp 1700-18.

Public Bill Committee House of Commons, Edinburgh: One Parent Families Scotland.

Quigley, M.A., Kelly, Y.J. and Sacker, A. (2007) 'Breastfeeding and hospitalization for diarrheal and respiratory infection in the United Kingdom Millennium Cohort Study', *Pediatrics*, vol 119, no 4, e837.

Quilgars, D. (2011) 'Youth homelessness', in V. Busch-Geertsema, E. O'Sullivan, N. Pleace and D. Quilgars (eds) *Review of homelessness research in Europe*, Brussels: FEANTSA, pp 187-210.

Quilgars, D., Johnsen, S. and Pleace, N. (2008) *Youth homelessness in the UK: A decade of progress?*, York: Joseph Rowntree Foundation.

Quilgars, D., Searle, B. and Keung, A. (2005) 'Mental health and well-being', in J. Bradshaw and E. Mayhew (eds) *The well-being of children in the UK* (2nd edn), London: Save the Children, pp 134-61.

Radford, L., Corral, S., Bradley, C., Fisher, H., Bassett, C., Howat, N. and Collishaw, S. (2011) *The maltreatment and victimisation of children and young people in the UK: NSPCC research findings*, London: NSPCC.

Reading, R., Bissell, S., Goldhagen, J., Harwin, J., Masson, J., Moynihan, S., Parton, N., Santos Pais, M., Thoburn, J. and Webb, E. (2009) 'Promotion of children's rights and prevention of child maltreatment', *The Lancet*, 24 January, vol 373, no 9660, pp 332-43.

Rees, G. and Lee, J. (2005) *Still running 2: Findings from the Second National Survey of Young Runaways*, London: The Children's Society.

Rees, G. and Stein, M. (1999) *The abuse of adolescents within the family*, London: NSPCC.

Rees, G., Bradshaw, J., Goswami, H. and Keung, A. (2010a) *Understanding children's well-being: A national survey of young people's well-being*, London: The Children's Society.

Rees, G., Haridhan, G. and Bradshaw, J. (2010b) *Developing an index of children's subjective well-being in England*, London: The Children's Society.

Ridge, T. (2002) *Childhood poverty and social exclusion*, Bristol: The Policy Press.

Ridge, T. (2005) 'The challenge of child poverty: developing a child-centred approach' in H. Hendrick (ed), *Child welfare and social policy*, Bristol: The Policy Press.

Ridge, T. (2009) *Living with poverty*, London: DWP.

Rendall, M. (2003) 'How important are intergenerational cycles of teenage motherhood in England and Wales? A comparison with France', *Population Trends 111*, Spring.

Richardus, J.H., Graafmans, W.C., Verloove-Vanhorick, S.P., Mackenbach, J.P., Euronatal International Audit Panel and Euronatal Working Group (2003) 'Differences in perinatal mortality and suboptimal care between 10 European regions results of an international audit', *BJOG: An International Journal of Obstetrics and Gynaecology*, vol 110, pp 97-105.

Riggio, H.R. (1999) 'Personality and social skill differences between adults with and without siblings', *Journal of Psychology*, vol 133, pp 514-22.

Roberts, F., Mathers, S., Joshi, H., Sylva, K. and Jones, E. (2010) 'Childcare in the pre-school years', in K. Hansen, H. Joshi and S. Dex (eds), *Children of the 21st century: The first five years*, Bristol: The Policy Press.

Roberts, I., Li, L. and Barker, M. (1998) 'Trends in intentional injury deaths in children and teenagers (1980-1995)', *Journal of Public Health Medicine*, vol 20, no 4, pp 463-6.

Robson, K. (2009) 'Changes in family structure and the well-being of British children: evidence from a fifteen-year panel study', *Child Indicator Research*, 3 (1) (www.springerlink.com/content/3837303h43mq7n4k/).

Rodgers, B. and Pryor, J. (1998) *Divorce and separation: The outcomes for children*, York: York Publishing Services for the Joseph Rowntree Foundation.

Roe, S. and Ashe, J. (2008) *Young people and crime: Findings from the 2006 Offending Crime and Justice Survey*, Home Office Report 09/08, London: Home Office.

Rowlands, J. and Statham, J. (2009) 'Numbers of children looked after in England: a historical analysis', *Child & Family Social Work*, vol 14, no 1, pp 79-89.

Royal College of Physicians (1994) *Homelessness and ill health*, London: Royal College of Physicians.

Runyan, D.K. et al (2010) 'International variations in harsh child discipline', *Pediatrics*, vol 126, no 3, pp 701-11.

Safe on the Streets Research Team (1999) *Still running – Children on the streets in the UK*, London: The Children's Society.

Sammons, P., Sylva, K. and Melhuish, E.C. (2003) *Measuring the impact of pre-school on children's social/behavioural development over the pre-school period*, Technical Paper 8b, London: University of London, Institute of Education.

Sammons, P., Sylva, K., Melhuish, E., Siraj-Blatchford, I., Taggart, B., Barreau, S. and Grabbe, Y. (2007a) *Effective Pre-School And Primary Education 3-11 Project (Eppe 3-11) influences on children's development and progress in key stage 2: Social/behavioural outcomes in year 5*, DCSF Research Report, 007 (www.dfes.gov.uk/research/data/uploadfiles/DCSF-RR007.pdf).

Sammons, P., Sylva, K., Melhuish, E.C., Siraj-Blatchford, I., Taggart, B., Grabbe, Y. and Barreau, S. (2007b) *Effective Pre-school and Primary Education 3-11 Project (EPPE 3-11) Summary report: Influences on children's attainment and progress in Key Stage 2: Cognitive outcomes in Year 5*, DfES Research Report RR8, Nottingham: DfES Publications.

Sammons, P., Sylva, K., Melhuish, E.C., Siraj-Blatchford, I., Taggart, B., Barreau, S. and Grabbe, Y. (2008) *The influence of school and teaching quality on children's progress in primary school*, DCSF Research Report 028, London: Department for Education and Skills (www.dfes.gov.uk/research/data/uploadfiles/DCSF-RR028.pdf).

Savage, T. (ed) (2009) *Profiling London's rough sleepers: A longitudinal analysis of CHAIN data*, London: Broadway Homeless and Support.

Save the Children UK (2007) *Living below the radar: Severe child poverty in the UK* (www.savethechildren.org.uk/en/docs/sevchildpov-summary.pdf).

Sawtell, M. (2002) *Lives on hold: Homeless families in temporary accommodation*, London: The Maternity Alliance.

SCIE (Social Care Institute for Excellence) (2005) *The health and well-being of young carers*, Research Briefing 11 (www.scie.org.uk/publications/briefings/briefing11/index.asp).

Scottish Executive (2009) *Domestic abuse recorded by the police in Scotland, 2008-09* (www.scotland.gov.uk).

Scottish Government (2009) *Pupils in Scotland 2009*, Part 9 (www.scotland.gov.uk/Publications/2009/11/05112711/9).

Scottish Government Social Research (2007) *Programme for International Student Assessment (PISA) 2006: Highlights from Scotland's results* (www.scotland.gov.uk/socialresearch).

Scottish Homes (2001) *Young people at risk of homelessness*, Edinburgh: Scottish Homes.

Sefton, T. (2004) *A fair share of the wealth: Public spending on children in England*, CASEreport 25, London: STICERD, London School of Economics and Political Science.

Sempik, J., Ward, H. and Darker, I. (2008) 'Emotional and behavioural difficulties of children and young people at entry into care', *Clinical Child Psychology and Psychiatry*, vol 13, no 2, pp 221-33.

Sharp, C. and Budd, T. (2005) *Minority ethnic groups and crime: Findings from the 2003 Offending Crime and Justice Survey*, London: Home Office.

Shatwell, S. (2003) 'We're just like other kids', Unpublished report by the Homeless Project, Leeds.

Shi, N., Cheung, C., Lee, M. and Chen, H. (2009) 'Gender differences in the continuance of online social networks', *Communications in Computer and Information Science*, vol 49, Part 2, pp 216-25.

Sibert, J.R., Payne, E.H., Kemp, A.M., Barber, M., Rolfe, K., Morgan, R.J., Lysons, R. and Butler, I. (2002) 'The incidence of severe physical child abuse in Wales', *Child Abuse & Neglect*, vol 26, pp 267-76.

Sidebotham, P. and Heron, J. (2006) 'Child maltreatment in the "Children of the Nineties": a cohort study of risk factors', *Child Abuse & Neglect*, vol 30, no 5, pp 497-522.

Sidebotham, P. and the ALSPAC Study Team (2000) 'Patterns of child abuse in early childhood, a cohort study of the "Children of the Nineties"', *Child Abuse Review*, vol 9, pp 311-20.

Sidebotham, P. et al (2002) 'Child maltreatment in the "Children of the Nineties": deprivation, class and social networks in a UK sample', *Child Abuse & Neglect*, vol 26, pp 1243-59.

Sigfusdottir, I. D., Asgeirsdottier, B.B., Sigurdsson, J.F. and Gudjonsson, G.H. (2008) Trends in depressive symptoms, anxiety symptoms and visits to healthcare specialists: A national study among Icelandic adolescents. *Scandinavian Journal of Public Health*, vol. 36, pp 361-368.

Simon, A. (2008) 'Early access and use of housing: care leavers and other young people in difficulty', *Child & Family Social Work*, vol 13, no 1, pp 91-100.

Sinclair, I., Baker, C., Lee, J. and Gibbs, I. (2007) *The pursuit of permanence: A study of the English care system*, London: Jessica Kingsley Publishers.

Sinclair, I., Baker, C., Wilson, K. and Gibbs, I. (2005) *Foster children, where they go and how they get on*, London: Jessica Kingsley Publishers.

Sivarajasingam, V., Wells, J.P., Moore, S. and Shepherd, J.P. (2009) *Violence in England and Wales 2008: An Accident and Emergency perspective*, Cardiff: Violence and Society Research Group, Cardiff University.

Sivarajasingam, V., Wells, J.P., Moore, S. and Shepherd, J.P. (2010) *Violence in England and Wales 2009: An Accident and Emergency perspective*, Cardiff: Violence and Society Research Group, Cardiff University.

Skinner, C. (2005) 'Childcare', in J. Bradshaw and E. Mayhew (eds) *The well-being of children in the UK* (2nd edn), London: Save The Children.

Smart, C., Neale, B. and Wade, A. (2001) *The changing experience of childhood: Families and divorce*, Cambridge: Polity Press.

Smith, J. (2003) *Who is at risk of homelessness in North Staffordshire? A study of young homeless people and their pasts*, Stoke-on-Trent: Centre for Housing and Community Research, Staffordshire University.

Smith, K. and Flatley, J. (eds) and Coleman, K., Osborne, S., Kaiza, P. and Roe, S. (2010) *Homicides, firearm offences and intimate violence 2008/09*, Home Office Statistical Bulletin 01/10, London: Home Office.

Smith, R., Poole, E., Perry, J., Wollny, I. and Alice Reeves, with Cathy Coshall and John d'Souza (2010) *Childcare and early years survey of parents 2009*, Research Report DFE-RR054 (www.education.gov.uk/publications/eOrderingDownload/DFE-RR054.pdf).

Social Exclusion Unit (1999) *Teenage pregnancy*, Cm 4342, London: The Stationery Office.

Social Exclusion Unit (2003) *A better education for children in care*, London: Office of the Deputy Prime Minister/Social Exclusion Unit.

Sourander, A., Santalahti, P., Haavisto, A., Piha, J., Ikaheimo, K., Helenius, H. (2004) Have there been changes in children's psychiatric symptoms and mental health service use? *Journal of the American Academy of Child and Adolescent Psychiatry*. vol. 43, pp 1134-1145.

Stack, N. and McKechnie, J. (2002) 'Working children' in B. Goldson, M. Lavalette, and J. McKechnie (eds) *Children, welfare and the state*, London: Sage.

Statham, J. and Chase, E. (2010) *Childhood wellbeing: A brief overview*, Briefing Paper 1, Southampton: Childhood Wellbeing Research Centre, University of Southampton.

Stein, M. (2005) 'Young people leaving care: poverty across the life course', in G. Preston (ed) *At greatest risk: The children most likely to be poor*, London: Child Poverty Action Group, pp 166-79.

Stein, M. (2008) 'Resilience and young people leaving care', *Child Care in Practice*, vol 14, no 1, pp 35-44.

Stein, M. (2009) *Quality matters in children's services: Messages from research*, London: Jessica Kingsley Publishers.

Stein, M. (2010) *Increasing the numbers of care leavers in 'settled, safe accommodation'*, Vulnerable Children Knowledge Review 3, London: C4EO.

Stocker, C. and Dunn, J. (1990) 'Sibling relationships in childhood: links with friendships and peer relationships', *British Journal of Developmental Psychology*, vol 8, pp 227-44.

Stonewall (2007) *The school report: The experiences of young gay people in Britain's schools*, London: Stonewall.

Strachan, D.P. (1988) 'Damp housing and childhood asthma: validation of reporting of symptoms', *British Medical Journal*, vol 297, pp 1223-6.

Sutton, L. (2008) 'The state of play: disadvantage, play and children's well-being', *Social Policy & Society*, vol 7, no 4, pp 537-49.

Sutton Trust, The (2010) *Education mobility in England: The link between the education levels of parents and the educational outcomes of teenagers* (www.suttontrust.com/news/news/social-mobility-in-england/).

Sweeting, H., Young, R. and West, P. (2009) GHQ increases among Scottish 15 year olds 1987-2006, *Social Psychiatry Psychiatric Epidemiology*, vol 44:579-586.

Sylva, K., Melhuish, E.C., Sammons, P., Siraj-Blatchford, I. and Taggart, B. (2004) *The Effective Provision of Pre-school Education (EPPE) Project: Final report. A longitudinal study funded by the DfES 1997–2004*, London: DfES (http://publications.education.gov.uk/eOrderingDownload/SSU-FR-2004-01.pdf).

Sylva, K., Melhuish, E.C., Sammons, P., Siraj-Blatchford, I. and Taggart, B. (2008) *Effective Pre-school and Primary Education 3-11 Project (EPPE 3-11): A longitudinal study funded by the DfES (2003-2008), Promoting equality in the early years, Report to The Equalities Review*, Wetherby: Communities and Local Government publications.

Sylva, K., Taggart, B., Siraj-Blatchford, I., Totsika, V., Ereky, S., Gilden, R. and Bell, D. (2007) 'Curricular quality and day-to-day learning activities in pre-school', *International Journal of Early Years Education*, vol 15, no 1, pp 49–65.

Tabberer, S. (2002) 'Teenage pregnancy and teenage motherhood', in J. Bradshaw (ed) *The wellbeing of children in the UK*, London/York: Save the Children/University of York.

Thomas, J. (2009) *Current measures and the challenges of measuring children's well-being*, Working Paper (www.statistics.gov.uk/downloads/theme_social/Measuring-childrens-wellbeing.pdf).

Tick, N.T., van der Ende, J., and Verhulst, F.C. (2007) Twenty-year trends in emotional and behavioural problems in Dutch children in a changing society, *Acta Psychiatrica Scandinavica*, vol. 116, pp 473-482.

Tomlinson, S. (2005) *Education in a post-welfare society*, 2nd Edn, Maidenhead: Open University Press.

Towner, E. (2002) '"The prevention of childhood injury", Background paper prepared for the Accidental Injury Task Force', in Department of Health, *Preventing accidental injury: Priorities for action, Report to the Chief Medical Officer of the Accidental Injury Taskforce*, London: Department of Health.

Tromans, N., Natamba, E. and Jefferies, J. (2009) 'Have women born outside the UK driven the rise in UK births since 2001?', *Population Trends 136*, pp 28-42.

Twenge, J. M. (2000) The age of anxiety? Birth Cohort change in anxiety and neuroticism, 1952-1993. *Journal of Personality and Social Psychology*, vol 79, pp 1007-1021.

UN (United Nations) (1989) The convention on the rights of the child, New York: United Nations.

UN (2006) *Violence against children: United Nations Secretary-General's Study* (www.unviolencestudy.org/).

UNICEF (2001b) *A league table of teenage births in rich nations*, Innocenti Report Card no 3, Florence: UNICEF Innocenti Research Centre.

UNICEF (2003) *A league table of child maltreatment deaths in rich nations*, Innocenti Report Card no 5, Florence: UNICEF Innocenti Research Centre.

UNICEF (2007) *Child poverty in perspective: An overview of child well-being in high income countries*, Innocenti Report Card no 7, Florence: UNICEF Innocenti Research Centre.

UNICEF (2010a) *The children left behind: A league table of inequality in child well-being in the world's richest countries*, Innocenti Report Card no 9, Florence: UNICEF Innocenti Research Centre.

UNICEF (2010b) *The state of the world's children 2010* (www.unicef.org/rightsite/sowc/).

Valois, R. F., Zullig, K. J., Huebner, E. S. and Drane, J. W. (2004) Life satisfaction and suicide among high school adolescents. *Social Indicators Research*, vol 66:81-105.

Värnik, A., Kõlves, K., Allik, J., Arensman, E., Aromaa, E. et al (2009) Gender issues in suicide rates, trends and methods among youths aged 15-24 in 15 European countries. *Journal of Affective Disorders*, vol 113: 216-226.

Viner, R.M. and Taylor, B. (2005) 'Adult health and social outcomes of children who have been in care: population-based study', *Pediatrics*, vol 115, no 4, pp 894-99.

Wade, J. and Dixon, J. (2006) 'Making a home, finding a job: investigating early housing and employment outcomes for young people leaving care', *Child & Family Social Work*, vol 11, no 3, pp 199-208.

Wade, A. and Smart, C. (2002) *Facing family change: Children's circumstances, strategies and resources*, York: York Publishing Services for the Joseph Rowntree Foundation.

Wade, J. and Biehal, N. with Clayden, J. and Stein, M. (1998) *Going missing: Young people absent from care*, Chichester: John Wiley & Sons.

Wade, J., Biehal, N., Farrelly, N. and Sinclair, I. (2010) *Maltreated children in the looked after system: A comparison of outcomes for those who go home and those who do not*, Research Brief DFE-RBX-10-06, London: Department for Education.

WAGC (Welsh Assembly Guidance Documents) (2008) *Guidance to local authorities – Childcare Act 2006*, March.

Ward, K., Sullivan, A. and Bradshaw, J. (2007) Income and Poverty, in K. Hansen, and H. Joshi (eds) *Millennium Cohort Study Second Survey: A user's guide to initial findings*, Centre for Longitudinal Studies, Institute of Education, University of London.

Welsh Assembly Government (2009b) *Schools in Wales: General statistics 2009*, Chapter 8: Special education (http://wales.gov.uk/docs/statistics/2009/0910 29schoolsgen09ency.pdf).

Welsh Assembly Government (2010a) *A survey into the prevalence and incidence of school bullying in Wales*, Cardiff: Welsh Assembly Government Social Research.

Welsh Assembly Government (2010b) *Exclusions from schools in Wales, 2008/09*, First Release (www.wales.gov.uk/statistics).

WHO (World Health Organization) (2004) *Young people's health in context: Health Behaviour in School-aged Children (HBSC) study: International report from the 2001/2002 Survey*, Copenhagen: WHO.

WHO (2005) *Multi-country study on women's health and domestic violence* (www.who.int/gender/violence/who_multicountry_study).

WHO (2007) *Mortality database 2007: Tables* (www.who.int/healthinfo/morttables/en/index.html).

WHO and UNICEF (2008) *World report on child injury prevention*, Geneva: WHO.

WHO Europe (2006) *Young people's health in GB and Ireland: Findings from the Health Behaviour in School-aged Children (HBSC) study 2006*, Edinburgh: HBSC Coordinating Centre, University of Edinburgh.

Wilcox, S. (2010) *The UK Housing Review, 2009/10*, York, Coventry and London: Joseph Rowntree Foundation, Chartered Institute of Housing and Council of Mortgage Lenders.

Wilkinson, R. and Pickett, K. (2009) *The spirit level: Why more equal societies almost always do better*, London: Allen Lane.

Wilson, B. (2010) 'Children with a non-resident parent', *Population Trends 140*, pp 53-81.

Wilson, B. and Stuchbury, R. (2010) 'Do partnerships last? Comparing marriage and cohabitation using longitudinal census data', *Population Trends 139*, pp 37-63.

Wilson, D., Sharp, C. and Patterson, A. (2006) *Young people and crime: Findings from the 2005 Offending Crime and Justice Survey*, Home Office Report 17/06, London: Home Office.

Wilson, V., Malcolm, H., Edward, S. and Davidson, J. (2008) '"Bunking off": the impact of truancy on pupils and teachers', *British Educational Research Journal*, vol 34, no 1, pp 1-17.

Wood, M., Barter, C. and Berridge, D. (2011: forthcoming) *'It's just me, standing on my own two feet': Disadvantaged teenagers, intimate partner violence and coercive control*, London: NSPCC.

World Bank (2006) *World development indicators 2006* (http://data.worldbank.org/data-catalog).

YJB (Youth Justice Board) (2004) *Youth Justice Board annual statistics 2002/3, England and Wales (B118)*, London: YJB (supplementary disposal data tables available from www.yjb.gov.uk/).

YJB (2005) *Youth Justice Board annual statistics 2003/4, England and Wales (B193)*, London: YJB (supplementary disposal data tables available from www.yjb.gov.uk/).

YJB (2006) *Youth Justice Board annual statistics 2004/5, England and Wales (B253)*, London: YJB (supplementary disposal data tables available from www.yjb.gov.uk/).

YJB (2007) *Youth Justice Board annual statistics 2005/6, England and Wales (B316)*, London: YJB (supplementary disposal data tables available from www.yjb.gov.uk/).

YJB (2008) *Youth Justice Board annual workload data 2006/7, England and Wales (B351)*, London: YJB (supplementary disposal data tables available from www.yjb.gov.uk/).

YJB (2009) *Youth Justice Board annual workload data 2007/8, England and Wales (B380)*, London: YJB (supplementary disposal data tables available from www.yjb.gov.uk/).

YJB (2010) *Youth Justice Board annual workload data 2008/9, England and Wales*, London: Youth Justice Board and Ministry of Justice (supplementary disposal data tables available from www.yjb.gov.uk/).

Youngblade, L.M. and Dunn, J. (1995) 'Individual differences in children's pretend play with mother and sibling: links to relationships and understanding of other people's feelings and beliefs', *Child Development*, vol 66, pp 1472-92.

Young-Hyman, D., Tanofsky-Kraff, M., Yanovski, S.Z., Keil, M., Cohen, M.L., Peyrot, M. and Yanovski, J.A. (2006) 'Psychological status and weight-related distress in overweight or at-risk-for-overweight children', *Obesity*, vol 14, no 12, pp 2249-58.

Index

Page references for figures and tables are in *italics*; those for notes are followed by n

E

early education *see* childcare and early
  education
ecological perspective 4
education 1, 5, 111–12, 133–4, 263, *264, 266*
  attainment at end of KS2 111, 113–15, *114*
  attainments at 15+ 111, 115–17, *115, 116,*
    117, 118
  and child employment 171
  and child poverty 34, *34*, 50
  competences at age 15 118–19, *120*, 121,
    122, 123
  looked after children 30, 175, 185–6, 188,
    267
  NEETs 128–30, *129, 131*
  and parents' income 40, *40*
  school exclusions 126–8, *127, 128*
  school types 112–13
  school well-being 124, *124, 125*
  and social background 132–3
  special educational needs 130, 132, *132*
  spending 8, *8*
  truancy 125–6, *126*
  young carers 173
  see also childcare and early education
Effective Provision of Pre-School Education
  (EPPE) Project 222, 224–5
Ehtisham, S. 69
elderly people, spending 9, *9*
emotional abuse 191, 202–3
emotional disorders 89, 101, *101*, 103, 105
emotional neglect 199
employment
  and child poverty 35, *36*, 38, *39*
  see also child employment
England 10
  absence from school 126, *126*
  alcohol 79, *80*
  attainments at 15+ 115, *115, 116, 117*
  breastfeeding 61
  bullying 205
  care leavers 187, 188, 189–90
  childcare and early education 214
  child employment legislation 169–71
  child population 14, *14*
  child poverty 31, *31*, 32–4, *32, 33, 34*
  domestic violence 202–3
  education competences at age 15 119, *120,*
    121, *122, 123*, 133
  exclusions 134
  fertility rate 16, *16*
  homelessness 143, 144, *145*, 146, *147*, 148,
    153, 155n
  house conditions 136, 137, *137*

immunisations 61, *62*
looked after children 175, 176, 177, *177,*
  178, *178*, 179, 180, 181, 182–3, 184, 185
mental health 101–2
NEETs 128–9, *129*
obesity 75, *75*
physical activity 77
school absence rates 111
school exclusions 126–8, *127*
school types 112–13
self-assessed health 63, *64*
smoking 78, *78*
special educational needs 130, 132, *132*
stillbirth, infant and child mortality *56*
subjective well-being 92, *93*
suicide 105–6, *106*, 107, *107, 108*
teenage pregnancy 86
English Housing Survey 137–8, *267*
  neighbourhoods 150–1, *151*
environment, and child poverty 34, *34*
Epping Forest 86
Ermisch, J. 133
Estonia
  alcohol *80*
  asthma *71*
  broken families *23*
  childcare and early education *223*
  child poverty *43, 45*, 46, *47, 48, 49*
  diabetes *70*
  education competences at age 15 *120,*
    122, 123
  house conditions *140*
  infant and child mortality *56, 57, 58*
  lone parenthood *21*
  NEETs *131*
  neighbourhoods *153*
  obesity *76*
  self-assessed health *67*
  sexual intercourse *81*
  smoking *79*
  spending on children *6, 7*
  subjective well-being *94, 100*
  suicide 107, *108*
  teenage fertility rate *85*
  workless households *44*
ethnicity 13, 17–18, *18*
  and alcohol 79
  and asthma 72
  and bullying 205
  and child maltreatment 209
  and child poverty 35, *36*, 38, *39*
  and drug use 251–2
  and health 68–9, *68*
  and house conditions 137–8
  looked after children 179